C000224535

DESPITE THE ODDS

Despite the Odds

ESSAYS ON CANADIAN WOMEN AND SCIENCE

❦

Edited by Marianne Gosztonyi Ainley

MONTREAL

Véhicule Press

1990

The publisher gratefully acknowledges the assistance of The Canada Council.

Some of the essays have previously appeared in the following publications: "Adolescent Females and Computers: Real and Perceived Barriers" by B. Collis in *Women and Education: A Canadian Perspective* (Detselig, 1987); "The Public Record" by C. Chu and B. MacDonald, in *Scientia Canadensis* (No. 12, 1988); "The Ontario Medical College for Women" by L. de la Cour and R. Sheinin in *Canadian Women Studies/les cahiers de la femme* (Vol. 7, no. 3, 1986); "Feminist Research into Genetic Hazards in the Workplace" by K. Messing in *Alternatives* (Dec. 1987–Jan. 1988); "The Career Goals of Female Science Students" by N. Nevitte et al in *The Canadian Journal of Higher Education* (No. 18, 1988); "Women and Photography in Ontario" by D. Pedersen and M. Phemister in *Scientia Canadensis* (No. 9, 1985); "Harriet Brooks" by M.F. Rayner-Canham and G.W. Rayner-Canham will appear in a modified form in *American Journal of Physics*; "Women in Ontario Pharmacy" by E.W. Stieb, G.Coulas and J. Ferguson in *Pharmacy in History* (Vol. 28, No. 3, 1986), American Institute of Pharmacy.

*For my mother, Sári, who showed me that
a woman can have non-traditional interests,
and for my father, Martin Gosztonyi (1896–1987)
who encouraged my early interest in science.*

List of Illustrations

Contents

II. BIOGRAPHICAL STUDIES

III. CONTEMPORARY CONCERNS

Preface

The idea for a collection of essays on Canadian women and the sciences was conceived in June, 1988, while I was discussing with my friend, Mary Baldwin, the lack of reading material on Canadian women and science. During the previous year, while teaching "Women, Science, and Technology — Historical and Contemporary Perspectives" at the Simone de Beauvoir Institute, I spent much time searching for a set of easily-accessible readings on Canadian women and science and technology. I requested reprints and work-in-progress papers from the few colleagues who were working on Canadian women and the sciences, and thus, my students had access to new scholarship that was not yet available to others.

Following our initial discussion, I began to work on an outline. I approached Nancy Marrelli and Simon Dardick of Véhicule Press, and with their enthusiastic endorsment began to cast around for prospective contributors.

Despite the Odds is the outcome of this search, and it is a collaborative venture. It has many visible contributors, the authors, and I am grateful for their willingness and cheerfulness in going along with my suggestions. It has been a pleasure working with them, and I hope that we will have the opportunity to do so again.

Every book also has its invisible contributors. *Despite the Odds* came into being because of the vision of Mary Baldwin, whose support and friendship has been invaluable to me since the late 1960s, when we both worked as "invisible chemists." Mary has long been interested in women and science, and in 1976–77, together with Allannah Furlong, taught the topic as part of an advanced interdisciplinary seminar at Concordia University.

This book could not have been done without the constant support of my husband. The history of science, like other all consuming vocations, intrudes upon one's family life. David Ainley has encouraged my return to graduate school, and for the last dozen years supported my interest in various aspects of the social history of Canadian science. I can never thank him enough for the help, companionship, and down-to-earth advice he provided as I waded my way through the complexities of, to me, new areas of scholarship. In many ways, the book also owes its existence to the encouragement of other members of my family, particularly my children, Vicky and Mark.

I shall always be grateful to Michael Hogben, who introduced me to the history of science, and to Pnina Abir-Am, Margaret Gillett, Isabelle Lasvergnas-Grémy, Andrée Lévesque, Karen Messing, Margaret Rossiter, and Rose Sheinin, who have encouraged my research on women and science. Most important to me for the last three years has been the stimulating atmosphere created by Principal Arpi Hamalian and my colleagues at the Simone de Beauvoir Institute, particularly Monique Genuist, Dana Hearne, Elizabeth Henrik, Susan Hoecker-Drysdale, Homa Hoodfar, Joan Kohner, Heather-Jon Maroney, Barbara Meadowcroft, Joan Sherwood, and Peta Tancred-Scheriff; Belinda Bowles and Laila Dhanani have also helped in innumerable ways. My students in 1987–88 and 88–89 provided me with stimulation, new ideas, and an environment that allowed me to explore the ways women, science and technology have been connected. Our discussions helped me more than they could have imagined.

Others whose friendship and assistance is gratefully acknowledged include Jane Atkinson, Barbara Bain, Michael Brodhead, Kyra Emo, Mary Gilliland, Anne Habbick, Daryl Hafter, Stewart Holohan, Mary and Stuart Houston, Louise Lafortune, Louise de Kiriline Lawrence, Lesley Lee, Gertrude McLaren, Roberta Mura, James M. Neelin, Iola Price, Prudence Rains, Nellie Reiss, Nancy Schumann, Margaret and Fred Silk, Doris and J. Murray Speirs, Marion and Jack Steeves and the late Brenda Carter.

And to Nancy Marrelli, archivist, editor, historian, and new friend — thank you!

Despite the Odds

Introduction

Despite the Odds is about women in science, and their accomplishments and difficulties in nineteenth and twentieth century Canada. It reflects a broad view of science that includes medicine, mathematics, social and applied science, technology, and innovation, and presents science as a social activity practiced in a variety of settings on many different levels. The articles describe issues and experiences that were representative of what happened to Canadian women in science in the past, and shed light on the problems faced by contemporary women scientists.

The historical essays in the first section deal mostly with the larger issues concerning women's entry into, and participation in, science, their publication record, and their experiences as volunteer or paid scientists in an increasingly complex Canadian scientific community. The essays also address issues concerning women as the users, and the public of, specific technologies, such as photography and electrical household technology.

The second section provides detailed studies of Canadian women in a variety of sciences. The selection of biographies depended on the availability of documentation, and on the willingness of scholars to provide essays for this volume. While the documentation is far from uniform, it is clear that the biographical essays add a rich new dimension to existing works on Canadian women in other walks of life.

The third section deals with universal contemporary concerns in a Canadian context, such as girls and computers, career expectations and opportunities, scientific collaboration, the status of women scientists in the 1980s, genetic hazards in the workplace, and the changing faces of science.

Women have long participated in science as members of the various scientific disciplines in Europe and in North America. They have been active in a multiplicity of roles: as discoverers of plants, animals, and astronomical objects, as creators of scientific theories, and as teachers, researchers, and authors of important works on science. Many women received prestigious awards for their scientific work. Others contributed to technology and industry, and invented a variety of machines and processes. So, why do we know so little about them?

One reason is that women have been under-represented in positions of power within an increasingly complex scientific community. This is the result of complicated historical processes, which first obstructed women's higher education and career advancement, and then, because of rampant stereotyping, obscured and minimized their actual participation in science. Women's consequent lack of visibility was further compounded by the minimal representation of their achievements in textbooks and reference books.

There are two major reasons why *Canadian* women scientists have been excluded even from histories of women and of science: 1) Women's historians in Canada have been overwhelmed with the tasks of discovering the experiences of literary figures, immigrant women, school teachers, missionaries, prostitutes, and others in their attempt to create a social history of Canada almost entirely ignored by traditional historians. 2) The history of science is a new discipline in our country (although not in Europe and the United States). There are few historians of Canadian science, and they are overwhelmed with the task of creating a comprehensive history of Canadian science and technology.

Women scientists, as always, have gotten short shrift from both groups of scholars; their experiences have been for the most part excluded from the new scholarship. So it is not surprising that publications on Canadian women in science and technology have been scarce, widely dispersed, and often published in obscure, hard-to-obtain, specialist journals. A particularly serious problem is the lack of primary documentation. Until recently, most Canadian universities and research institutes have not had an archival policy, and documentation that could illuminate the experiences of many Canadian scientists, male and female, has been lost forever. Moreover, the diaries and letters of women scientists have largely disappeared, because no one, not even the women scientists who wrote them, thought them important enough to save! These factors continue to hinder research on the history of Canadian women and science.

In the western world, the practice of science has changed over the years. During the *pre-professional* period (up to the mid-to-late nineteenth century), science was an avocation, an intellectual pursuit carried out alone or with a few congenial friends in the field, in private natural history "museums," or in studies and laboratories at home. During the last one hundred years, science has become a complicated set of activities, carried out mainly by *professional* scientists, in a hierarchical social and institutional structure. The process of institutionalization and professionalization of science did not occur in all countries and all sciences at the same time. In Canada, for instance, this occurred later than in the United States. The way science is practiced and institutionalized always has important implications in all countries for the careers of men and women scientists.

In the *pre-professional* period, for instance, there were few paid positions in science anywhere, and most scientific knowledge was acquired by apprenticeship. Women in Canada, as elsewhere, had access to education, and therefore science, only through their male relatives, or friends, sponsors, or patrons, who encouraged their scientific activities. But scientific work is time-consuming and most women, because of their family and social obligations, had less time to devote to science than did the men.

During the *professionalization process* (1850–1890), science changed in Canada, as it did elsewhere. Educational opportunities expanded, science was taught in a growing number of academic institutions, and the large new group of trained scientists formed specialized disciplinary associations. Canadian science also became increasingly independent of its European origins and connections and, after 1850, exchange of ideas and specimens, collaboration, and publication happened more and more in a North American context.

Women's educational opportunities improved after 1870, at about the same time as when science in Canada became increasingly professionalized. While there were still not many women who were professional scientists, science became one of several new options which provided intellectual challenge and work opportunities to women.

The *professional period* in Canadian science began in the late nineteenth century, and by the 1920s, many disciplines were professionalized. Although the teaching loads were still onerous, funds and equipment for research scarce, and the pay low, science provided career options for both men and women — at least in theory — and women were soon regarded by men as competitors for scientific posts.

Men, socialized to see women's role as wife/mother/homemaker, rationalized that women would "only" marry and leave their jobs and thus there was no point in encouraging them to obtain higher degrees, or employing them in challenging scientific positions. Women scientists, who had been socialized to be non-competitive, went into science because they enjoyed doing science; or they chose it, as others selected literature, or any number of other fields, because it offered them independence from restrictive family obligations, and an alternative to marriage and motherhood.

The practice of science has become increasingly complicated and hierarchical, and we can envisage the twentieth-century scientific community as a pyramid. There is little room at the top, and there are few highly-visible, well-paid, powerful scientists. In fact, the realities of day-to-day scientific work are carried out by those lower down in the imaginary pyramid, by graduate students, assistants, technicians, support personnel, high school science teachers, and popularizers of science. Many of these invisible scientists were and are women, and their hidden contributions to science and society as researchers, teachers, and editors of scientific journals have so far been minimized or neglected.

The essays in this book redress this neglect, illustrate the wide range of activities engaged in by Canadian women scientists, and underline the difficulties encountered by female science graduates. Some provide new insights about our pioneer women scientists; others introduce eminent women whose accomplishments and difficulties have until now been known only to a few of their contemporaries.

From *Despite the Odds* it is evident that only a handful of Canadian women scientists became "successful." These women advanced, albeit slowly, on the academic or government ladder, to become full professors, or relatively high-level government researchers.

A second group of women fared less well. They had more difficulty in the workplace, less recognition, and lower positions and pay than their successful sisters. Some, even with doctorates, had to teach in secondary schools. Others found no positions because of the Depression, anti-nepotism rules at universities, or a variety of other reasons.

Many of them could contribute to science only through their husbands' institutional positions, in a "two-person single career."

A third group of women pursued science as volunteer investigators (or independent scholars), while a fourth group, perhaps the largest of all, gave up all hope of scientific work and became homemakers.

From *Despite the Odds* we can learn that there were certain trends in the experiences of Canadian women in science. Marriage, in most cases, was detrimental to a woman's career advancement, although there were some notable exceptions (e.g. Blossom Wigdor). Women rarely advanced as fast, or earned as much, as their male colleagues with comparable education and experience, and often had to make choices male scientists were not called upon to make. Like the men, women practiced science on a variety of levels, and *despite the odds* entered many non-traditional fields.

It is apparent that a volume of this size and scope cannot possibly include all aspects, all experiences, all institutions. Much remains to be discovered about Canadian women and the sciences. Funds will have to be obtained by many researchers to study the experiences of women scientists in individual institutions that employed them, such as universities, research laboratories (particularly in the biomedical sciences), and industry. I hope that this book will serve as an inducement for further research, that it will persuade granting agencies to fund other investigations on this important but neglected topic, and that it will whet the appetites of other writers and researchers to help increase our knowledge of Canadian women and science.

I. HISTORICAL STUDIES

MARIANNE GOSZTONYI AINLEY

Last in the Field? Canadian Women Natural Scientists, 1815–1965

Introduction

Natural history has been studied in Canada since Jacques Cartier's first voyage in 1534, but until recently, the contributions of women to the study of nature have remained invisible. Natural history, like mathematics, can be studied without institutional affiliation, at will, any place, any time; therefore, it was accessible to women even during the early period in the history of science. Women have contributed to Canadian natural history in a number of ways; their contributions range from observations and collections made by ladies and western settlers, to the more narrowly-defined research work of laboratory scientists. Women studied plants, animals, rocks, and fossils; they investigated wood-destroying fungi and the biology of marine organisms. They worked as volunteer investigators or helpmates to their husbands, as university teachers and government researchers. As natural history became more specialized, the research methodology more sophisticated, and the sciences more institutionalized, women went along with these developments. When the professionalization of a science meant that advanced degrees were required, some women sought higher education and upgraded their qualifications.[1] Others remained content to work outside the institutional framework of science, as part of a team, or as independent scholars. Some faced an uphill struggle to obtain recognition, while others achieved prominence in their chosen area of science.

In "Canadian Women Natural Scientists — Why Not?" (1976), Lorraine C. Smith asked: "But what of *women* in the natural sciences?" and gave short biographical accounts of 19 women "working in natural sciences in Canada [who] did not fear to enter a man's world." She wrote: "Although they were few in number, they were able to elucidate problems and advance our knowledge, but, perhaps most important of all, they opened the door for other women to follow."[2] They were *visible* because they published books and articles (both scientific and popular) and achieved "firsts" in the workplace and in scientific associations.

Since the time of Smith's article, much more research has been done on women and science in general, and some, including my own work, on Canadian women and science in particular. New evidence shows that the well-known and honoured women natural scientists were only the tip of the iceberg; they were the elite members of a much larger group of women scientists who have contributed to knowledge about natural history in Canada.[3] Who were the women in this large group, and how and what did they contribute to science?

It is important to remember that in Canada, as in Australia and New Zealand, natural history was first studied by men, who were part of a European scientific tradition that sought to master nature. In fact, most of the early scientific activities in Canada occurred as by-products of the exploring and/or colonizing activities of western European nations.[4] During the seventeenth and eighteenth centuries, the study of Canadian natural history was a cooperative venture between the actual observers and collectors, and European naturalists who, without actual experience with Canadian natural history, incorporated specimens into their collections and utilized the information they received in their popular and scientific works.

From New France, descriptions and specimens of plants and animals were sent to France for identification, evaluation, classification, and incorporation into existing frameworks of science.[5] Upper-class French women were among the private individuals who included Canadian specimens in their collections. Prominent among them was Madame de Bandeville, whose large collection provided information on Canadian birds for Mathurin-Jacques Brisson's *Ornithologie* (1760).[6]

British scientists found useful natural history information in the notebooks and reports of seventeenth-century navigators and explorers in the north. By the late seventeenth century, the Royal Society of London enlisted the support of intelligent, practical men, the Hudson's Bay Company factors, upon whose observations scientists could rely.[7] Many of the factors married native women. As these women were familiar with local plants and animals, it is quite likely that some of them were instrumental in providing much sought-after specimens to European scientists.[8] The extent of their contributions to science awaits further study.

During the early nineteenth century, the establishment of garrisons and numerous settlements provided conditions in which an indigenous scientific culture could slowly develop. Increasing wealth and leisure time, improved networks of roads and better communications within Canada and with Europe, and the United States led to the exchange of information with others who shared similar interests. While the earliest naturalists in Canada were men, by the second decade of the nineteenth century, women had also begun to contribute to the study of nature.

The Pre-Professional Period

The first known women natural scientists in Canada came from the British upper and middle classes. Lady Dalhousie (née Christian Broun, 1786–1839) collected plants in Nova Scotia in 1816. With her friends, Harriet Sheppard (née Campbell, d. 1837) and Anne Mary Perceval (née Flower, 1790–1876), she was among the founders of Canada's first learned society, the Quebec Literary and Historical Society (1824).

Because of their education, social position, and circle of friends, these women had access to up-to-date natural history studies, and exchanged information and specimens with British naturalists. But, like other Canadian botanists at the time, Lady Dalhousie and her friends also corresponded with members of the emerging American botanical community. And while they all sent plants to Kew Gardens in England, Anne Mary Perceval also gave collections to American botanists William Darlington and L.D. Von Schweinitz, and corresponded with John Torrey. She was cited in Torrey and Grey, *Flora of North America* (1838–43), and (with Dalhousie, Sheppard and a Miss Brenton from Newfoundland) in W.J. Hooker, *Flora Boreali Americana* (1829–40).[9]

Harriet Sheppard did not restrict her scientific interest to plants. She is the author of the "earliest publication on the shells of Quebec, indicating considerable knowledge of the vocabulary and literature of conchology." She also gave talks and published papers on archaeology and ornithology.[10]

Women of the leisure class continued to study plants throughout the nineteenth century. Ann Grubble Haviland (b. 1818 in the United Kingdom) collected in Prince Edward Island for Kew Gardens in 1849–54.[11] Lucy Lawson, "an accomplished botanist," the wife of Scottish-born Queen's University professor George Lawson, was among the founding members of the Botanical Society of Canada (1860). There were other "lady members," who were accorded "equal privilege." Like other members of learned societies, these women could participate in, and profit from, the formal and informal meetings of like-minded naturalists.[12]

Catharine Parr Traill (1802–1899), a "backwoods" settler, was in a less favourable position. Like many English ladies, she was educated at home, and she made collections of plants and other natural history objects. After emigrating to Canada in 1832, Traill became interested in Canadian plants, but as she could not draw, her encounters with the unknown Canadian flora resulted in "verbal descriptions and dried specimens, all duly sorted and tagged."[13] Although frightened of the Canadian wilderness, Traill brought to her environment a knowledge of Latin and "true scientific curiosity." She studied Frederic Pursh's, *A Systematic Arrangement and Description of the Plants of North America* (1814), named the flowers in English, and sent a collection of plants to Edinburgh University. Later, with the help of her niece, Agnes Fitzgibbon, Traill published *Canadian Wildflowers* (1868) and *Studies of Plant Life in Canada* (1885). Traill's unrecognized forte was her interest in the *process* of science. She was curious about events leading to observable geological formations, and she can be considered one of the first Canadian ecologists, because she observed and described plant succession after forest fires.[14]

Other women botanists and collectors were active well into the twentieth century. Among them were Martha Black (1866–1954) in the Yukon, and Edith Farr (b. 1864), Mary Shaefer (1861–1939) and Julia Henshaw (1869–1937) in Alberta and British Columbia. Henshaw provided scientific advice to the Canadian government botanist, John Macoun. Marion Moodie, a Calgary area naturalist (and nurse) also corresponded with Macoun, and sold plant collections to various North American museums. Sister Sainte-Amélie (née Marie-Anna Dugas, 1851–1922) established a herbarium at the Convent of Sainte Croix, Montreal, some time around 1889. By 1918, the herbarium consisted of 5,000 specimens, collected by her in the Montreal area.[15]

The women botanists mentioned above were active in the field; their long gowns did not impede them from searching for specimens in wet bogs, meadows, or dense forests. And they were not prevented by men from engaging in outdoor scientific activities. Like other women in Victorian England and the British colonies, women in Canada indulged in the widespread mania for collecting natural history specimens that formed an integral part of nineteenth-century scientific culture.[16]

Like botany, zoology was an important part of nineteenth-century natural history studies. Charlotte Flett King (b. ca. 1860), the native wife of Hudson's Bay Company trader William King, sent zoological collections to American naturalists, and to museums, such as the Smithsonian Institution. In 1892, her husband informed a correspondent: "my wife has made a small collection of skins of Skunk, Ermine, Musk Rat, Mink and Foxes, etc. for Mr. Frank Rupen of the Ohio University."[17] Moira O'Neill (1864–1955), a rancher and author from southern Alberta, described plants and animals in her popular articles. Margaret and Esther Wemyss, homesteaders in Manitoba and Saskatchewan, participated in a continent-wide bird migration study from 1892 to the 1940s. Elsie Cassels (1865–1938) of Red Deer, Alberta, published several papers on birds, and during the early 1920s was vice-president of the Alberta Natural History Society.[18]

Science as a Career?

Although by the 1890s, much of Canada's flora, fauna, and geology had been surveyed, collected, and described, new roads and better means of transportation permitted naturalists to explore new areas. During that same period, improved economic conditions made advanced education available to more people than ever before. Science now became a career for many men, and even for some women, and trained scientists conducted detailed investigations of nature in the laboratories attached to universities and government research institutions.

Experiment, the investigation of a particular topic by controlled manipulation, became an important part of science, and biology emerged as the science of life processes, replacing both natural history *and* physiology.[19] Nevertheless, some natural scientists retained a broad approach and continued with their field studies, while others integrated field and laboratory investigations.

The institutionalization and increased professionalization of the sciences resulted in a number of other changes. At universities, general natural history was replaced by more specialized courses in botany and zoology. At the same time, geology became an "earth" science, often taught as part of the engineering course.[20] The emergence of new scientific disciplines also led to the establishment of new scientific associations. These provided forums for the growing number of experts in the new fields to exchange ideas, meet colleagues at conferences, and publish research results in the societies' journals.

By the 1890s, it became possible to approach science as a career, rather than just as an avocation. Although the availability of professional positions for women lagged behind the growing educational opportunities, some women found employment as teachers at private and public schools, and even at universities.[21]

During the first half of the twentieth century, women pursued science in a variety of ways. In theory, women could aspire to scientific careers, but in practice, only a handful obtained appropriate positions and due recognition. The highly visible careers of a few women natural scientists have long obscured the fact that others, even those holding doctorates, could work only as high school teachers, demonstrators, instructors, or research assistants. Some women who obtained scientific degrees never even sought positions; others had to retire from their positions after marriage and/or childbirth. Obliged by convention to give up their professional status, many women continued to contribute to science — as volunteers.

Although certain male-dominated sciences (for example, geology) were difficult for women to enter, women had a comparatively easy time in newer areas that had great economic potential (for example, mycology). The rate at which a science grows can influence "the career of an individual scientist," and this can have serious implications for "recruitment policies and the attitude of scientists towards women or minority groups trying to enter their field."[22] The relationship between a science's rate of growth and women's career opportunities is not always clear-cut, however. As we shall see, Canadian women's experiences have differed from discipline to discipline, as well as from one institution to another. Some male scientists in expanding fields (for example, H.S. Jackson in mycology) encouraged women's entry into graduate departments. A lack of male experts in economically-important scientific areas (such as petroleum geology) also ensured improved professional opportunities for women.

One can analyze the career paths and experiences of twentieth-century Canadian women natural scientists in several ways: according to their disciplines, their institutional affiliations, or their "careers." Within each scientific field, two major categories can be established: 1) the *successful stream*, women whose careers advanced relatively well within academic and government institutions, and 2) the *obstructed stream*, women with professional training whose careers hardly advanced at all or who, for a variety of reasons, could not find appropriate or any paid employment in Canada. In some fields, there has also been a *volunteer stream*, researchers who worked through their husbands' positions, conducted independent studies attached to some scientific institution, or worked on their own.

Although the available documentation is far from complete, I will attempt here to provide some insight into the variety of experiences Canadian women have had as natural scientists.

Geology

By the beginning of the twentieth century, geology, with its practical implications for mining and metallurgy, was taught at a number of Canadian universities (for example, Acadia, New Brunswick, McGill, Toronto and Alberta). Although there is no record of women having studied geology at the old, established eastern universities, in 1918, the ten-year-old University of Alberta granted a B.A., Honours, to Canada's first woman geology graduate Grace Anna Stewart (1893–1970).

Stewart, a petite, energetic girl, went on to study for her M.A. (1919–20) while she worked as an assistant to Professor John Andrew Allen, in the department of geology. While completing her Ph.D. in paleontology at the University of Chicago, under Stuart Weller (1922), she also worked during the summer for the Research Council of Alberta (1919–20) and the Geological Survey of Canada in Ottawa

(1921–22). At that time, there were no career opportunities for a woman geologist at Canadian universities, and Stewart knew that "prejudice against women as geologists was strong in the Canadian Survey."[23]

Stewart soon found a good position with Ohio State University. Although Professor Allen hoped "that at some near future date" Stewart would "obtain a satisfactory position on this side of the international boundary line,"[24] she did not, and the talented Grace Anna Stewart was lost to Canadian science.

The *only* woman geologist in the first half of this century to have a "successful" academic career in Canada was Madeleine A. Fritz (b. 1896). A Maritimer with a childhood interest in "how the mountains were made," Fritz took a general arts course at McGill University, with no clear idea of pursuing a career in geology. At McGill, she became fascinated by the fossil collection in the Peter Redpath Museum, and was influenced by several good geology professors. Her friendship with Alice Wilson (see "Alice Wilson (1881–1964): Explorer of the Earth Beneath Our Feet"), and the field trip the two women made to Manitoba, further convinced Fritz that fossils were exciting, and that studying them could lead to a career.[25]

Fritz decided to do a Ph.D. in geology, and enrolled at the University of Toronto in order to study under the eminent paleontologist, W.A. Parks. Her research on the fossil organisms found in rocks under Toronto was carried out at the Royal Ontario Museum of Paleontology (ROM), and before obtaining her Ph.D. in 1926 she published several papers on the stratigraphy and paleontology of the Toronto area.[26]

Fritz began her career as paleontology assistant in the Royal Ontario Museum. In 1935, she became assistant director of Paleontology and, concurrently, obtained a teaching appointment (part-time) as associate professor at the University of Toronto. Unfortunately, her salary for either of these positions could not be determined.

Although Fritz could not recall feeling discriminated against, it took her 20 years to achieve full professorship. In spite of her slow advancement, Fritz, a small, determined woman, considered herself a successful scientist (she was elected fellow of the Royal Society of Canada in 1942), teacher, and administrator. Perhaps she contrasted her experiences with those of Wilson, who had trouble obtaining leave to study for a degree and getting funds for field work. But Fritz had a powerful mentor in Dr. Parks, and the University of Toronto, although not always kind to women, was more flexible than was the Geological

Survey. As a result, Fritz had no difficulty in obtaining her doctorate or going out into the field. Later, as curator of the Royal Ontario Museum of Paleontology, she was in charge of the fund for research trips.[27] By all accounts, her career was unique for the times.

At the Geological Survey (established in 1842), career opportunities and advancement for women were far from satisfactory. Originally, members of the Survey were employed to map the natural history resources of this vast land. They also collected geological, botanical, and zoological specimens for the Survey museum.[28] As the exploration parties laboured under difficult conditions, women were not even considered for scientific positions.

Although women began working for the Survey in the early 1880s, few of them rose to positions of importance. In fact, among the survey's many scientific and technical employees, women always remained in the minority, working instead as librarians (for example, M.C. Barry, 1882– , J. Alexander, 1889– , F.B. Forsey, 1913–), clerks (Alice Wilson, 1909–11), assistants (paleobotany M.C. Stopes, and stratigraphic paleontology J.D. Dart, 1923–), or photographers (L.A. Salt, 1913– ; M.C. Brown, 1914–). Of the many women employed by the Survey before the Second World War, only Alice Wilson rose to a permanent *scientific* position. In the post-war period, Helen Belyea became the best-known woman geologist of the Survey.

Belyea (1913–86), like Fritz, had an early interest in geology, and she studied it, together with languages, at Dalhousie University (B.A. 1934, M.A. 1936) and Northwestern University (Ph.D. 1939). Upon graduation, Belyea could find no position as a geologist. She taught school until 1943, served in the Canadian navy, and eventually joined the Geological Survey as a "technologist" in 1945. Within a year, she was made technical officer and, in 1947, was advanced to the position of geologist. "The discovery of oil in Devonian rocks at Leduc, Alberta, in 1947 sparked a decision by the Geological Survey to establish an office in western Canada."[29] Belyea was one of two geologists to move to the new Calgary office in 1950.

"Helen Belyea began to work in Alberta when the petroleum industry was a man's world. But this small determined woman, with a daunting intellect, who never suffered fools gladly, was quickly accepted as a valued colleague . . . ."[30] Although in the post-war period, petroleum geology and the oil industry were rapidly expanding, and the scarcity of male experts meant better career opportunities for women, strictures against field work still existed. In fact, Belyea was the only woman at the Geological Survey's Calgary office who went out into the field. Others were barred from field work until 1970 for a variety of "reasons." A reflection of the attitudes of the time was the fact that the wives of geologists objected to other women being in the field with their husbands. But Belyea could not be stopped.

Belyea never took on administrative responsibilities. It is not clear whether her volatile personality prevented her from being offered administrative positions, or whether she simply chose to do what she liked best, investigating the geology of the Devonian system (the rocks in which oil was discovered). She was a successful scientist, paid as much as any male scientist of the same rank.[31]

Belyea was often honoured for her accomplishments: in 1956 she received the Barlow Memorial Medal from the Canadian Institute of Mining and Metallurgy; in 1964 she was elected fellow of the Royal Society of Canada. She also received two honorary doctorates (from Windsor and Dalhousie Universities), and in 1976 was named Officer of the Order of Canada.

Belyea, like Stewart, Wilson, and Fritz, remained single. Quite likely, this contributed to her successful career. Even as late as the mid-century, many women geologists found that once they married, they found it hard to continue their professional careers. In the absence of detailed life histories, we cannot say whether giving up work was sometimes a personal choice, or was always something foisted upon women geologists by official policy and/or prevailing attitudes. We do know that in the early 1950s, most male geology graduates of the University of Alberta were "actively engaged in the Geology profession . . ." By contrast, "women graduates have almost all married."[32] Presumably, they exchanged active engagement in the profession for family life. The geology department's records from that time also indicate that of the 287 geology graduates of the University of Alberta (before 1953), 13 (4.5%) were women. Of these, only Grace Anna Stewart had obtained an academic post, and that, in the United States. Of the six women who had graduated in geology before the Second World War, three were married and not employed; one, Vera Lee Stoner (B.Sc. 1919, M.Sc. 1921) worked as secretary at the University of Alberta geology department, and another, Mary Turner (M.Sc. 1936), became a school teacher after she married. During the period 1945–53, seven women graduated in geology. In 1953, five of them were married and

34

were not employed; the remaining two, Evelyn Linke (B.Sc. 1950) and Helen (Kay) Leskiw (B.Sc. 1953), worked in the oil industry.[33]

The oil companies did not require that their employees have doctorates; in fact, they preferred scientists without this advanced degree. While this fact enabled more women to work as geologists, most women geologists graduating in the 1950s still faced obstacles in their careers. The experiences of two McGill University graduates illustrate this fact. During the early 1950s, Kyra Defries (B.Sc. 1953), like most geology students at that time, worked in micropaleontology, studying thin core sections to identify microscopic organisms. She also edited technical reports for the Quebec Department of Mines. Defries received no encouragement to go to graduate school. In 1955, she married Wally Emo, a fellow geologist. After that, like many women before her, Kyra had access to scientific work only through her husband. Eventually, she gave up all thought of a career in geology. Instead, she used her knowledge of geology to teach in a private school, and gave up science entirely when she became a university administrator.[34]

Another McGill graduate, Dorothy Eadie (M.Sc. 1954), found employment with Gulf Oil in Calgary, doing stratigraphic research, mostly in the laboratory. In the late 1950s, she was one of four women scientists (three geologists and one geophysicist) at Gulf. During the same period, five women geologists were employed by Shell Oil. Like her colleagues, Eadie was considered an engineer, and became a member of the Alberta Society of Petroleum Geologists. But in 1960, when she married an accountant working for Shell Oil, Eadie had to retire because of a "possible conflict of interest." Although Dorothy Eadie Wyer never held another paid position in geology, after her return to Montreal in 1964 she served as a docent at the Redpath Museum, using her considerable knowledge of geology to teach visiting school children.[35]

By the 1960s, the study of geology could lead to a career in petroleum geology, magnetic methods, marine geology, or mineralogy. A few women geologists now had visible careers: at the Geological Survey, Frances Wagner was a stratigraphic paleontologist in environmental marine geology, M.A. Gilbert, a geochemist, and M.E. Bower, a geophysicist. But most women in geology continued to serve as assistants (studying core samples), or worked as librarians, data compilers, or laboratory technicians. And while women geologists worked for the Survey, ran exploratory parties, and served as consultants, except for

Madeleine Fritz, they did not teach at universities. In fact, even at the beginning of the 1980s, women geologists in academic institutions were "still a tiny minority in Canada."[36]

Botany

Botany has been taught at Canadian universities since the mid-nineteenth century. At first, botanical studies focused on morphology and taxonomy, but by the early twentieth century, botany had become a diversified discipline. Plant pathology, mycology, cytology, and later, genetics, emerged as areas of specialization. In contrast to general botanical studies, plant pathology and mycology, areas of great economic importance, were offered only at certain institutions, such as the University of Manitoba, Macdonald College, and the University of Toronto.

Career opportunities for women in botany were different from those in geology and zoology. Canadian women were able to teach botany at secondary schools and universities. A few of them fared well in academe, while others were not so successful. By contrast, women working in various branches of the federal Department of Agriculture appeared to have more satisfying experiences.

The story of Carrie Derick, the first Canadian woman university teacher in botany, is explored elsewhere in this volume (see "Carrie Derick (1862–1941) and the Chair of Botany at McGill"). An examination of the careers of other university-trained women botanists shows a variety of career experiences, from successful to obstructed.

Muriel V. Roscoe (1897–1990) was born and educated in Nova Scotia, graduating with a B.A. in biology (Acadia, 1918). After teaching school for some time, she went to study botany at Radcliffe College (the women's college affiliated with Harvard University) in Massachusetts, obtaining an A.M. in 1925, and a Ph.D. in 1926. In 1926, Roscoe was offered the post of instructor in botany at Acadia University. She was promoted to assistant professor in 1927, and full professor in 1929. In addition to teaching, Roscoe did work in cytology, including chromosomal studies of cultivated apple varieties. Despite the obvious usefulness of this research, during the early 1930s, she was refused a grant by the National Research Council of Canada, for reasons that are still not clear.

In 1940, Roscoe was offered the prestigious position of warden of Royal Victoria College (RVC), at McGill University, with an appointment as assistant professor in the botany department. Why Roscoe agreed to a demotion is not known, and no information is available concerning her salary at either university. We do know that during the late 1930s, Acadia, a small university, did not pay any faculty member more than $3,000. By contrast, at McGill, in 1939, Dr. George Scarth, head of the botany department, earned $5,000, and a male assistant professor's salary was $2,650. But the working conditions at McGill were much worse than those at Acadia. Roscoe found, for instance, that the "ample research facilities" promised her were not available, and the two available microscopes fell "short of requirement for cytological work."[37] In fact, a microscope had to be borrowed for her.

At McGill, Roscoe was promoted to associate professor (1943), then to full professor (1948); she also served as acting chairman and, later, chair of the department (1945–62). Eventually, she was appointed Macdonald Professor of Botany (1955–65). Roscoe "enjoyed the competition with men — and believed it a challenge to do" her best. She never had to apply for any position that she held, and was unaware of any discrimination. She did feel, however, that her administrative positions, combined with her duties as warden of RVC, left her little time to pursue research in plant anatomy and embryology, and that she "had no personal life."[38]

Lulu Odell Gaiser (1896–1965) studied in Canada (A.B., University of Western Ontario, 1916) and the United States (A.M. Columbia University, 1921; Ph.D. 1927), and worked at Columbia and for the United States Department of Agriculture before being hired, in 1925, as lecturer at McMaster University. The progress of Gaiser's career and the salaries she was paid are well documented (while those of most of the other women discussed in this paper are not). We know that her initial salary was $2,000, and that she received annual increments until 1930, when she became associate professor, with a salary of $2,800. During the 1930s, at McMaster, like elsewhere in Canada, there were salary cuts. However, Gaiser's career continued to advance. Gaiser became professor of botany (1936), acting head of the department (1937), head of the department (1942), and senior professor of botany (1946–49). Her field was cytotaxonomy in higher plants, and she published more than 20 scientific papers on the subject (three of them as co-author). She was also interested in the social welfare of people, especially women. Apparently, "her outside interest caused much unpleasantness in the department," and in 1949 she left for an appointment as research fellow at Harvard University.[39] Returning to Canada in 1954, Gaiser carried out a floristic survey of Lambton County, Ontario, with support from the Ontario Agricultural College and the American Philosophical Society. While doing the survey, she worked on several Indian reservations and involved native women in her collecting activities.[40]

Dorothy Forward (b. 1903) intended to study chemistry, but in her first year at the University of Toronto switched to botany, because it "seemed to deal with more fundamental questions . . ." She was encouraged by botany professor Dr. J.H. Faull, who acted as her mentor, and, after her B.Sc., offered her the position of graduate assistant (with a stipend of $1,000). At the same time, the head of the zoology department offered her a position as secretary to the department; this, to him, "seemed entirely appropriate" for a woman biology graduate. By the time Forward finished her M.A. (1928), she had decided to specialize in plant physiology (Ph.D. 1931). Although she could have had a job with the civil service paying $1,800 a year (it took her almost 20 years to achieve that salary at the university), she decided to remain in an academic environment. But as during the Depression jobs were scarce the only position she could find was lecturing twice a week at McMaster University in Hamilton. She did not obtain a permanent position at the University of Toronto until 1935 — as assistant in plant physiology, for which she was paid $1,500 per year. In a later interview, Forward recalled that her advancement was slow because she was a woman. One of her male colleagues was promoted ahead of her because "he had a wife to support" a typical justification of the time. Forward went into science knowing that it was a man's world, but she was not happy with the treatment she received. Like many other women of her day, she thought that the best way to deal with the situation was to do a good job. Although her career progressed more smoothly after the war, Forward stated that she did not do science for the sake of remuneration or fast advancement, but because it was what she wanted to do.[41]

From the available evidence, it is clear that many other women scientists, particularly those whose careers were obstructed, had a similar attitude to their work. These were the women who, even holding doctorates, worked at universities in low level and/or adjunct positions, part-time, or even without pay, taught in private and public schools, had interrupted careers, or ended up pursuing science as an avocation. Women scientists with partially or entirely obstructed careers may well have formed the largest group of Canadian women in science.

Lillian May Hunter (1892–1970) taught in rural schools before studying science at the University of Toronto (B.A. 1921, M.A. 1924), and Radcliffe (Ph.D., biology, 1935). Because of the Depression, she could not find an academic position; from 1936 to 1961 she taught in a variety of public and private schools. Although Hunter had "engaged in exacting research" on algae and rust in Canada, the United States, and Britain, published a number of important papers, received fellowships and awards (including the $1,250 Canadian Federation of University Women [CFUW] Travelling Fellowship in 1931), and was elected "Frater" of the American Association for the Advancement of Science (1943), she never had the career she hoped for. Like many other Canadian women scientists, she "made do," taught where she could, and remained interested in science.[42]

The career of Eleanor Silver Keeping (née Dowding, 1901) followed a circuitous path. Silver studied botany at the University of Alberta (B.Sc. 1922, M.Sc. 1923) and worked as instructor and lecturer in botany until 1928. A $1,000 CFUW Travelling Fellowship enabled her to spend a year in England. At the same time, she also obtained grants from the National Research Council and the Royal Society of England. Later, she received a Hudson's Bay Company Research Fellowship (1930), a Banting Research Foundation Award (1931), and a National Research Council Grant (1944). Competition for these awards was extremely fierce, and Silver was not only deserving, but was able to find the requisite supporters for her grant applications. After she completed her Ph.D. (University of Manitoba, 1931), her career seemed assured. Dr. Reginald Buller, her advisor, who had employed her as a student assistant, was anxious to further Silver's career, and wrote letters of recommendation on her behalf.[43] Silver returned to the University of Alberta, but after she married mathematician Fred S. Keeping, who "encouraged her lively interest in continuing her research," she found that "as wife of a faculty member she couldn't expect to receive a salary."[44] So she worked as research assistant at the Dominion Experimental Farm, Edmonton (1934–49), while also being "on staff" (without pay) at the University of Alberta. In 1949, she was hired as lecturer in mycology. Later, she conducted research in medical mycology for the National Research Council and the Alberta Provincial Laboratory of Public Health.

Between 1924 and 1966, Eleanor Keeping published nearly 40 research papers, served as associate editor of the *Canadian Journal of Microbiology* (1958), and was instrumental in interesting physicians and public health officials in medical mycology. She never received a decent salary or held a permanent position. Nevertheless, she contributed to science, and lived a life "rich in the discovery of facts."[45]

Someone who fared less well was Dr. Jane Spier. An instructor in botany at McGill University from 1928, she resigned her position, such as it was, in 1938, because of "her projected 'plunge into matrimony'."[46] And Marcelle Gauvreau (1907–68), a graduate in botany of the Université de Montréal (1933), could find no teaching or research position at any francophone university. Instead, she worked at the Montreal Botanical Gardens, as a popularizer of natural history along with the renowned Brother Marie-Victorin.[47]

Constance MacFarlane (b. 1907) was at least able to obtain teaching positions — at various high schools. She even became principal of Mount Allison School for Girls, before securing a post (1946–48) as a sessional lecturer in botany at the University of Alberta. After that, her career improved. From 1949 to 1970, she was director, Division of Applied Biology, of the Nova Scotia Research Foundation, and concurrently held the position of part-time associate professor of biology at Acadia University.[48]

It is evident that, while many women obtained graduate degrees in botany, only a few achieved success in the scientific community. Among the 121 Master's degrees conferred by the University of Toronto's botany department from 1916 to 1960, 35 (29.7%) were earned by women. Of the 98 Ph.D. degrees granted by the same department during the same period, 16 (16.3%) were given to women. Of those women, only two, J. Gertrude Wright (1923) and Dorothy Forward (1931), obtained jobs at the University of Toronto. Wright worked for 30 years as an assistant professor. Five other women Clara W. Fritz (1924), Irene Mounce (1929), Mildred K. Nobles (1935), Ruth Macrae (1941), and Luella K. Weresub (1957) found employment in mycology with the government and/or in industry.

Because of the obvious economic usefulness of the study of food plants, in the early years of this century, government positions became available for the investigation of certain plants and their diseases (as well as of the insects that were useful or harmful to Canada's agriculture.) The various divisions of the Department of Agriculture and Horticulture employed many women, including Faith Fyles and Isabella Preston (see "Isabella Preston (1881–1964): Explorer of the Horticultural Frontier"). In 1911, Fyles (1875–1961), a McGill graduate in botany (B.A. 1900) and an excellent artist, became the sole assistant to the new dominion botanist, Hans Gussow. Fyles studied wheat stem-rust, as well as wild rice and poisonous plants, and published articles and a book for the science service of the Department of Agriculture.[49]

By the 1920s, mycology and plant pathology emerged as important branches of botany, requiring expertise with the microscope as well as in the field. The Department of Agriculture employed several women to conduct research on fungi and to investigate plant pathology (see "Margaret Newton: Distinguished Canadian Scientist"). The women mycologists employed by the government studied at the University of Toronto, under H.S. Jackson and J.H. Faull. Clara W. Fritz (1889–1974), the elder sister of geologist Madeleine A. Fritz, worked as instructor of botany at the University of Toronto (1923–25) while completing her doctorate (1924). In 1925, she became the first Canadian woman timber pathologist, and was employed at the Forest Products Laboratory, an organization sponsored by government, industry, and McGill University. She worked as timber pathologist for 29 years, and after her retirement taught part-time at the University of Western Ontario (1954–58).[50]

Mildred K. Nobles (b. 1903) studied at Queen's University (B.A. 1929, M.A. 1931) and at the University of Toronto (Ph.D. 1935). In an interview, she recalled that working days were long, but there was great enthusiasm among the graduate students in plant pathology-mycology at the University of Toronto. Nobles joined the Division of Mycology of the Department of Agriculture in 1935, and worked with forest pathologists across Canada, "isolating pure fungus cultures" for purposes of identification.[51] She developed a flexible key system for the identification of wood-rotting fungi, "distinguishing the species on the basis of evolutionary developments." The system has since been adopted by scientists all over the world. In 1963, Dr. Nobles was elected fellow of the Royal Society of Canada. Perhaps because there were other women working in the mycology division, Nobles was not aware of any sexual discrimination, and she dislikes the designation "woman scientist."[52]

Irene Mounce (1894–1987) began working in the mycology division's laboratory in Ottawa in 1924, as assistant plant pathologist, at a salary of $1,920 per year. She did field work in British Columbia, and conducted pioneering investigations on the sexuality of fungi. She appeared to have a "successful career," attaining the positions of plant pathologist (1931), senior assistant agricultural scientist (1938, salary $2,820) and agricultural scientist, grade three (1940), a high position at the time. But "Dr. Mounce's career in mycology-plant pathology ended when she married Gordon M. Stewart in 1945, and was required to resign because of her marital status."[53]

Ruth Macrae (b. 1903), a brilliant student at McGill University (B.A. 1924, M.Sc. 1926), worked as research assistant to Buller at the University of Manitoba, and joined the mycology laboratory in Ottawa as a research officer in 1931. She studied the genetics and sexuality of some of the higher fungi, and identified the fungus that causes Dutch Elm disease. Her career in the civil service progressed well. She never married.[54]

After the Second World War, the government mycology laboratory in Ottawa continued to offer career opportunities to women. The laboratory employed at least 10 women, among them Dr. Louella K. Weresub (1918–1979), Mary Elliott (d. 1976), and Ruth Horner Arnold (d. 1978). During the period 1945–55, there were so many women working in that laboratory, that mycology came to be considered "women's work."[55] Although detailed records of the women's salaries are not available, it seems that they were paid regular civil service wages, but because of their job descriptions, they did not earn as much as men with similar expertise.[56]

Zoology

From the late nineteenth century, zoology has been a widely-taught subject at Canadian universities. At first, most courses and research in zoology were concerned with invertebrate and vertebrate anatomy, and embryology. Simple marine organisms increasingly offered suitable specimens for laboratory investigation, but until the mid-twentieth century, the study of birds and mammals was pursued at only a few Canadian institutions. Entomology was often taught in a separate department. This was because the study of useful and harmful insects had economic implications for agriculture and forestry, and thus, federal and provincial grants were usually available for establishing entomology departments.

Job opportunities in zoology certainly existed. In 1917, for instance, J.P. McMurrich found that

> the greatest weakness in Zoology in Canada was the lack of trained men to use the facilities of the universities . . . . due . . . to the absence of sufficient incentive to induce young men to dedicate their lives to research science when other professions held greater reward.[57]

Women who in any case went into science not for monetary or other rewards, but for the love of it, studied zoology and conducted research on a variety of organisms from the early years of the twentieth century. While studying zoology was relatively easy, career opportunities for women in this broad field were far from uniform.

By the 1920s, women zoologists were employed on the teaching staffs of several Canadian universities. However, detailed investigation of the careers of some Canadian women zoologists shows that in many cases things did not proceed as smoothly as entries in *American Men and Women in Science* or the various *Who's Who* would lead us to believe.

Helen Battle (b.1903), the first woman to obtain a Ph.D. in marine zoology (University of Toronto, 1928), had a successful career at the University of Western Ontario; she was appointed assistant professor in 1929, associate professor in 1933, and full professor in 1947. In a later interview, Battle maintained that she had had strong supporters for her research, and had never faced discrimination. Although her career path was relatively smooth, perhaps because she never married, Battle recognized that some other women were less fortunate than herself. She "campaigned to improve the place of women in universities and encouraged many to take up careers in science."[58] Battle's investigations into the embryological effects of carcinogens and work in other areas of experimental biology were honoured by both the Canadian and the larger scientific communities. She was elected fellow of the American Association for the Advancement of Science, and second president of the new Canadian Society of Zoologists (1962–63), and was awarded several prestigious medals.

Dixie Pelluet (b. 1896) had a more checkered career. She studied botany at the University of Alberta (B.A. 1919) and the University of

Toronto (M.A. 1920), and spent 1922–23 at University College, London supported by a $1,000 CFUW Fellowship. She was interested in ecology and biology, and changed her field from botany to zoology (Ph.D., Bryn Mawr, 1927). Although eager to work in Canada, Pelluet was obliged to teach at various American colleges; in 1931, she was offered a post at Dalhousie University teaching elementary zoology, with a starting salary of $2,200. Pelluet, who had first-class credentials and excellent recommendations from her previous employer, responded by asking for $2,600. She obtained both the appointment and the higher pay. She remained assistant professor for a decade, and when finally promoted to associate professor she discovered that the new appointment carried no pay increase. Her salary, like those of other Canadian academics of the time, remained frozen until after the Second World War. Only in 1947 did she receive a pay increase, to $3,000. Although Pelluet cared more about recognition and official advancement than about pay increases, she was prepared to fight for her rights. Official correspondence in the Dalhousie University Archives provides a clear testament to her spirit, determination, and self confidence.

In 1934, Pelluet asked the Dalhousie president, Carleton Stanley, to give his word that she could continue teaching after her marriage. She did not tell him, however, that her future husband was a colleague, knowing that after the wedding, "Stanley would not go back on his word as a gentleman."[59] The secrecy was necessary, because in the 1930s, women at some universities in Canada (as in the United States) were still expected to resign their positions when they married. Actually, the rules and expectations of any given institution often depended on the discretion of individual department heads and university presidents. Although Pelluet was allowed to retain her position after marriage, 20 years after her initial appointment she still wrote: "I have been unjustly penalized for a) my sex, which I cannot help, b) my marital status which is my private concern and does not interfere with the fulfilling of my academic duties."[60] Indeed, it was only after much fighting that Pelluet, a well-known researcher in fish embryology, was appointed full professor with a salary of $10,000. This was in 1964, three months before her retirement at the age of 68. The university then hired three men to replace her!

As an undergraduate at McGill, Joan Anderson Marsden found that some of her professors, like V.C. Wynne-Edwards and N.J. Berrill were "non-sexist," while others, such as John Stanley, believed that "men

Dorothy Mitchell "in the field," Saskatchewan, 1921.
Courtesy of the Royal Ontario Museum Archives.

Science in the family. Prince Edward Island ca. 1932. Edith Berkeley
(*standing*), her mother Martha Treglohan (*seated*), and daughter
Alfreda B. Needler holding the fourth generation, Mary Needler (Arai).
Courtesy of A. W.H. Needler.

Doris Huestis Speirs studying nesting Evening
Grosbeaks near Lake Nipigon, Ontario, ca. 1946.
Ontario Archives, s–*18298.*

Louise de Kiriline Lawrence in her outdoor
"laboratory," Pimisi Bay, Ontario, ca. 1940.
Courtesy of Georgina Rawn.

Women in the field. Madeleine Fritz and Elvira
Hammel with guide, Abitibi River region, 1947.
Courtesy of Joan Burke, Royal Ontario Museum.

should be looked after by women."[61] As she had no grants, she could not continue her studies; she taught at the University of British Columbia until she could enter the graduate program at the University of California (Ph.D. 1951). Dr. Marsden recalls that after her doctorate, she was offered a contract job at McGill, "at a salary I could not live on," and she had to teach at night at Sir George Williams College to make ends meet. Eventually, "poverty, insecurity, and lack of status overcame timidity," and she plucked up enough courage to demand a promotion to assistant professor. Much to her surprise, she received the promotion (in 1958), and wondered why it had not occurred to her to ask for it earlier. Belatedly, she "was learning to live in the jungle."[62] During the 1960s, with changes in university personnel and politics, Marsden received further promotions, to associate professor in 1962, and full professor in 1967.

If the cases discussed above constituted "successful" careers for women zoologists, what of the women who never made it to the rank of professor? Before 1960, the careers of most women zoologists were obstructed; women worked as demonstrators, lecturers, and assistant professors. These appointments usually carried heavy teaching loads, minimal salaries, and little opportunity for research. It followed that those holding them had few or no scientific publications, and this fact, in turn, hampered their career advancement. By 1961, women constituted 16 percent of the 1,666 Canadians identified by the census as "biological scientists"[63] but academic jobs for women remained scarce.

Among the women zoologists with obstructed careers was Kathleen (Kay) Terroux (1900–1984), who worked at McGill. A lecturer before obtaining her Ph.D. in 1930 Terroux, who was married to a physicist also working at McGill, had to be content with the poorly-paid positions of demonstrator (1931–32), assistant, and lecturer until 1944. Her lack of advancement was due partly to the Depression, partly to her marital status, and partly to her lack of research output.[64] Eventually, she left the zoology department to become assistant professor of physiology!

With an M.Sc. from the University of Saskatchewan, obtained in 1924, Winnifred Hughes (b. 1900?), became lecturer in zoology at the University of Alberta. Her initial salary was $1,500. Hughes had a heavy teaching load (as did others at the university); she also helped William Rowan, the head of the department, develop teaching aids (for example, charts and specimens). After she completed her doctorate at the University of Chicago, in 1929, Hughes became assistant professor of zoology at the University of Alberta at a salary of $2,500. She remained in that position, without a pay raise, for over 12 years.[65] In 1941, her pay was finally adjusted to $2,600, and she later received minor annual increments. In 1946, she was named associate professor, but it took considerable struggle by Rowan to achieve this. He had recommended Hughes for full professorship, but the administration refused to give it to a woman who "is not actively productive in research."[66] That Hughes was overworked and underpaid, and had practically no time to conduct research or even write up earlier research results, did not change the attitude of the administration.

One could expect that there would have been career opportunities for women in Canada in marine biology, a new area of great economic and theoretical importance in which there was an insufficient number of male experts. In fact, most university zoology departments in Canada had at least one person conducting research on marine organisms, and a few professors even encouraged their female undergraduates to conduct investigations and specialize in this field.

Marine biology was important to the Canadian government. The Fisheries Research Board was created in 1898, and within a decade three biological stations were established, a floating marine biological station in 1899, and two permanent ones (on the Atlantic and Pacific coasts) in 1908. However, the Board had no full-time employees in marine research until the mid–1920s. The stations provided "research facilities for academic scientists and their students." The investigators who received room and board, and perhaps travelling expenses, spent their summers at the biological stations, studying various aspects of marine life, such as invertebrate and vertebrate animals, their food and diseases.[67]

Although there were few Canadian women natural scientists who had academic positions, the research opportunities offered by these stations attracted women scientists and science students from various universities to come for one or more summers. In fact, during the years 1908–58, women constituted 17 percent (37 women) of the investigators at the Atlantic Biological Station. Many of the students came from the University of Toronto, supported by their mentor, zoology professor Archibald G. Huntsman, who was also the station's curator and director. Others were encouraged to study marine zoology by Philip Cox at the University of New Brunswick, and C. MacLean Fraser and

W.A. Clemens at the University of British Columbia, who were affiliated with the Pacific Biological Station.

During the 1920s and early 1930s, women graduate students, volunteer investigators, and the few women scientists employed by Canadian universities, published their research results in *Contributions to Canadian Biology*. In 1930, for example, 20 percent of the authors published in that journal were women. In 1933 that proportion was 31 percent. However, in 1938, towards the end of the Depression, no woman published in the journal.[68] The publication record reflects, to some extent, the status of women marine biologists. Evidently, by the time women specializing in marine biology finished graduate school, jobs had become scarce at university zoology departments because of the Depression. Thus, Viola M. Davidson (Ph.D. 1933), a Toronto school teacher who did her research at various biological stations, had to continue teaching at the Central High School of Commerce after obtaining her doctorate. Women who already had employment, particularly if they were single, kept their positions (Battle), while married women were glad to be able to retain even low-level positions (for example, Terroux). Many women when married, lost their jobs, accepted unsuitable posts, worked as volunteer investigators, or even gave up science entirely.

Dr. Gertrude Smith Watney (b. 1901, B.A. 1923, M.A. 1926), for example, a University of British Columbia instructor in biology and zoology (1926-28), was promoted to assistant professor in 1930. Her interest in the ecology of clams led her to further graduate study at the University of California, Berkeley (Ph. D. 1934). Watney recalled that after her marriage to a colleague, she retained her position "until there was a change in the head of the Department of Zoology in 1940 . . . . when I left the University in 1940 I no longer had access to a laboratory or equipment.[69] Between 1927 and 1940, Watney published eight papers, enjoyed her studies and professional life, and was not aware "of any difference in the treatment" she received because she was a woman. She did wonder, however, if her married status "influenced the decision of the *new* head of the Zoology department not to renew my appointment in 1940."[70]

After she married a colleague in 1940, Virginia Safford Black, M.A. (b. 1914), worked as secretary and technician in the Ontario Fisheries Research Laboratory, as well as zoology demonstrator at the University of Toronto (1941–44). She could find positions only as demonstrator in the zoology laboratories at Dalhousie University (1944–47) and the University of British Columbia (1947–50). Although she had a good publication record, after 1950, for reasons that are not clear, Black continued her research as a volunteer investigator. She remained unaware of any discrimination, and remembers her years in the laboratory as "happy stimulating" times.[71]

In spite of the promise of marine biology as an expanding field of science with career opportunities for women, during the Depression, academic jobs remained scarce. The few available government jobs went to men. These were as directors of the marine biological and fisheries experimental stations, and of smaller laboratories, such as the one on Prince Edward Island. When, in 1936, funds were made available by "Parliament to enable the Biological Board of Canada to undertake a thorough investigation of the eastern Canadian lobster fisheries" (including lobster biology), a new job was created. A.H. Leim, director of the St. Andrews station, personally wrote to various universities seeking a likely candidate. The "man" had to have previous research experience and would be required to travel "a good deal." Because of this, Leim wrote "it [is] most unlikely that women would prove satisfactory as investigators."[72]

As opportunities and attitudes changed, women eventually did get paid positions at the Fisheries Research Board. One of them was Delphine Maclellan, a Dalhousie science graduate (B.Sc. 1936). In the mid-1940s, as a young widow supporting two children, Maclellan was offered a position at the Atlantic Biological Station to work, part-time, with the Atlantic Herring Investigation Committee. But the pay was minimal, and the work routine and lacking in intellectual challenge. When she began receiving a widow's pension in 1946, Maclellan gave up her job. It was another decade before she returned to marine biology, to work on plankton with the International Passamaquody Commission on a four-year project; her starting salary was $2,610. Maclellan's new investigations involved microscopic work, and she enjoyed the intellectual challenge of working out the interrelationships of various plankton species.

In 1961, Maclellan enrolled in the graduate program in oceanography at McGill (M.Sc. 1964), studying copepods, while teaching part-time in the laboratory. Although she "suffered from resentment on the part of new [male] staff in the department, who were wary (or jealous) of [her] non-traditional qualifications," she remained at McGill, earning

$5,000 per year. In 1967, she was promoted from senior staff demonstrator to lecturer, in 1973 to assistant professor, and in 1979, the year before her retirement, to associate professor, with a salary of $26,000. But she had had almost to crusade for a better salary, a decent pension, and appropriate status recognition.[73]

Before the Second World War, a few women worked as assistants in the entomology department of various universities. After the war, women entomologists found government employment, and their careers advanced reasonably well. Among them were Margaret MacKay (b. 1914), editor of *The Canadian Entomologist* (1963–65), who discovered the "first fossil evidence of Lepidoptera before the Cretaceous period."[74]; Helen Salkeld (b. 1926), head of the Comparative Morphology Section (1969–71), and the Experimental Taxonomy Section of the Entomology Branch of the Department of Agriculture (1972–73), and Liang-Yu Wu (b. China, 1910), an expert on the taxonomy and morphology of nematodes.[75]

In contrast to the study of organisms that had utilitarian implications for agriculture, or of minerals and fossils that had relevance to mining, metallurgy and the oil industry, studies of birds and mammal were less important branches of government research. And although knowledge about insect- and grain-eating birds was important for agriculture, and fur-bearing and game animals had implications for the Canadian economy, few people were employed by the government or by universities to study bird or mammal biology.[76]

Very few women were employed before 1960 by the Dominion Parks Branch (which protected migratory birds and studied game birds), the National Museum's Vertebrate Zoology Division (which studied bird and mammal distribution and taxonomy), and the various provincial museums. Not one woman in these institutions rose to the position of research scientist or curator.

Dorothy Mitchell, daughter of Saskatchewan Natural History Museum naturalist-taxidermist H.H. Mitchell, was, in 1921, the first Canadian woman zoology field assistant (serving as camp cook and collector of bird and mammal specimens).[77] But as at that time women were not allowed into the field, at least not by government authorities, the Museum's *Annual Report* for 1922–25 does not even mention her name; she is simply referred to as "an assistant."[78]

Kathleen E. Ball, an honours graduate in zoology from the University of Western Ontario (B.Sc. 1944), worked during the mid–1940s for

Harrison F. Lewis, chief of the Dominion Parks Branch. Unhappy with government restrictions, which prevented women from doing field research, she went to Cornell University to pursue graduate studies in ornithology (M.S. 1946, Ph.D. 1949), doing field work, alone, on Pelee Island. At that time, ornithology was only partially professionalized. Jobs were scarce even for men, and Ball, a married woman, could find only part-time positions, as a lecturer in ornithology and ecology at the University of Alberta.[79]

After the Second World War, the Zoology Division of the National Museum, a long underfunded branch of the government, finally received appropriations for hiring additional zoologists. The requirements for these positions were one year of post-graduate study and research experience. Finding male zoologists proved to be difficult, however, because of low enrolments of men during the war, and although there were many capable women zoology graduates, the outmoded attitude that "girls are handicapped in field work" worked against them.[80] Eventually, in 1952, Violet Humphreys (1919–1984) was hired as assistant to government ornithologist W. Earl Godfrey. For the next three decades, her work was "typical of the vital but too often under-recognized contribution made by support staff at all museums."[81] Humphreys' investigations were confined, however, to the museum proper; despite the fact that she was an energetic, capable field naturalist, she was never sent on any government field expedition, because she was a woman.

Volunteer Investigators

Although in the period up to 1965 many women gave up scientific work when they married, some chose to continue working, as part of a team, through their husband's institutional affiliation. This situation was, in fact, a throwback to earlier times, when women generally had access to science only through their male relatives.[82] Women scientists trained in the twentieth century had more options than their foremothers, but because of built-in discrimination, institutional constraints, or high unemployment, they were still sometimes obliged to participate in a "two-person single career."[83] Although the documentation is uneven, we know that the practice was widespread in Canada, as it was in the United States and Britain.

Zoologist Dr. Annie Porter Fantham was able to do research only in her husband's laboratory at McGill University. A graduate of University College, London, Dr. Porter had taught at London and Cambridge, and was the head in South Africa of both the department of parasitology, at the University of Witwatersrand, and the Institute of Medical Research. When her husband obtained a post at the zoology department at McGill, in 1932, Sir Arthur Currie, Principal of McGill, would not give her a teaching post, "and only would give her Research Associateship." Currie felt that "if she wanted to teach she should teach elsewhere, but did not like husband-and-wife business" at the university.[84] Thus, Porter "helped" her husband with his courses and carried out her own research in *his* laboratory until his death in 1937. She soon found that "the Research Associate appointment was for the session" and she would be given only until the spring convocation to "complete any work on which she is engaged."[85]

Porter had hoped to be "retained as a member of the Department of Zoology either . . . [as] Research Associate or in some other capacity."[86] But Professor T.W.M. Cameron did not want her in the zoology department, because he and Porter had long been "scientifically jealous enemies," and the principal was advised by the dean that "Mrs. Fantham should be left in no doubt that she does not fit into the University plans . . . ."[87] The university was wary of granting space and equipment to a woman scientist who was neither employed nor connected to it through any male relative.

Although other situations as unpleasant as that encountered by Annie Porter cannot be documented, her case was far from unique; other women also found access to work through their husbands' positions. Some institutions proved kinder to women who, working in a "two-person single career," contributed to science without remuneration. This was particularly the case in marine biology. Thus, during the 1920s and 30s, Elsie O'Donoghue and Dr. Lucy Smith Clemens had access to research because of their husbands' positions at, respectively, the University of Manitoba and of British Columbia. Their publications reflect this cooperation.

Although the extent and variety of the cooperation is not yet fully known, husbands helped their wives in a variety of ways. In some cases, it was just by providing financial stability to support the wife's scientific interests; in others, by providing institutional affiliation for her independent research.

Edith Berkeley (nee Dunington, 1875–1963) was unique, because in 1918 she *chose* to give up a paid position as zoology assistant at the University of British Columbia to study the taxonomy of *polychaetes* at the Pacific Biological Station. Edith had studied medicine, and later zoology, at University College, London, but had had no chance to pursue research, because from 1902 to 1914 she lived in India with her husband, Cyril Berkeley, an agricultural chemist. They moved to the Okanagan Valley of western Canada in 1914, and three years later, Edith was hired to teach zoology at the University of British Columbia, at $30 per month, while her husband earned $100 per month in the department of bacteriology. During the summer of 1917, Edith collected teaching materials at the Pacific Biological Station, Nanaimo. The beauty of the place and the rich research opportunities offered by the complex world of the sea awakened her original interest in *polychaetes*, a class of marine organisms, and in 1918 she gave up her paid position and became a volunteer investigator. It is not known just what prompted her decision. Money was not a cause for concern, as the Berkeleys had saved much of their income in India. Did she fear losing her job? At other Canadian universities, the return of war veterans meant considerable expansion of various departments, and western universities were actually seeking qualified personnel. While the Master's degree was desirable for good university positions in zoology, and Edith had never pursued graduate studies, the available evidence suggests that it was the opportunity to do research at the biological station, rather than the lack of career opportunities at the University of British Columbia that prompted her to make the move.

So Edith Berkeley, at the age of 43, embarked on her major research, the complex relationships in *polychaete* taxonomy. Eventually, her husband gave up his own work on the biochemistry of marine organisms to help her with her research. From 1923, Edith published a series of papers on her own (12) and with her husband (34) in *Contributions to Canadian Biology, Nature, The Canadian Field Naturalist, Proceedings of the Zoological Society*, and other prestigious journals. Her publications are a testimony to her hard work, determination, and scientific acumen. Within a few years, she became the recognized expert in her field, and several organisms were named after her. In recognition of her excellence as a scientist, in 1969 the University of British Columbia inaugurated the Edith Berkeley Memorial Lectures.[88]

Dr. Alfreda Berkeley Needler (1903–51), the daughter of Edith and

Cyril Berkeley, studied zoology at the University of British Columbia and the University of Toronto (Ph.D. 1930). After she married A.W.H. Needler, she had no paid employment. But when her husband became the head of a small Fisheries Research Board station on Prince Edward Island, she had an opportunity to do research in marine biology. Using an old-fashioned dentist's drill to make holes in the shell of oysters to sample the gonads, she conducted investigations for seven years on the sex reversal phenomenon in these animals. Her work resulted in several prestigious publications. In 1941, the family moved to the St. Andrews station, and Alfreda, by this time the mother of three children, investigated the so-called "red-tide," marine organisms which cause paralytic shellfish poisoning. She continued as a volunteer researcher until her untimely death in 1951.[89]

The contribution of women volunteers to ornithology has been varied. The Wemyss sisters were part of a large-scale migration investigation that was begun in the nineteenth century, and Elsie Cassels became an expert in bird distribution. In 1917, women were instrumental in establishing the Province of Quebec Society for the Protection of Birds, one of Canada's oldest conservation associations.

The three best-known Canadian women ornithologists were volunteer investigators. Margaret Howell Mitchell (1901–1988) was interested in both ornithology and geology, and had hoped to become a geologist. At the University of Toronto, she studied biology, geology and paleontology. The other students regarded her as somewhat of a puzzle: "Fraternizes with flowers and communes with birds . . . Analyst of minerals . . . Future: — a nest-domestic or avian (latter preferred at present)," said the caption under her 1924 graduation photo in the student yearbook, *Torontoniensis*.[90] The only employment she was able to find was as secretary in the paleontology department of the Royal Ontario Museum. When, after her marriage in 1927, Peggy Mitchell gave up her position and offered her services as a volunteer to the ROM's department of ornithology, the offer was accepted with alacrity, and Mitchell spent the next eight years working on the Museum's passenger pigeon inquiry. Although she had no official title and, of course, no pay, she was the first woman research affiliate of any natural history museum in Canada. In 1929, she published a small pamphlet on the extinct passenger pigeon, and in 1935, a monograph, *The Passenger Pigeon in Ontario*. The monograph was the first comprehensive study of this once-abundant bird species, and it was praised by members of the ornithological community. In addition to its inherent scientific interest, the book is important as the first major contribution by a Canadian woman ornithologist. Mitchell also published several papers on bird behaviour, and, in 1957, a monograph on Brazilian birds. In 1958, the American Ornithologists Union (AOU) recognized her accomplishments by electing her member of that organization.[91]

In "Suggestions for Ornithological Work in Canada" (1915), P.A. Taverner recommended life-history studies as a field with much scope for original research.[92] But in Canada, as in the United States, most early life-history studies were short-term investigations. In the late 1930s, Doris Mills (née Huestis, 1894–1989) became the first Canadian woman ornithologist to do extensive field work. She focused on the evening grosbeak, and for more than a decade, travelled all over Ontario, studying all aspects of the life history of this species. Her letters, notes, and daily journals of observations, filled with detailed descriptions, are illustrated with her own drawings. Doris also conducted specimen studies at the Royal Ontario Museum and, in the 1940s, pursued comparative life history studies between captive bred and wild birds, becoming the acknowledged expert of the evening grosbeak. Now married to ornithologist J. Murray Speirs, she also worked, alone and with him, on the life history of other birds. Ironically, although she spent much time in northern Ontario doing her field research, in 1946, she was prevented by the Ontario Ministry of Natural Resources from accompanying her husband, who was studying the detrimental effects of DDT, because "camp life was too rough for women."[93] Doris Speirs became a friend and mentor to other Canadian women ornithologists (including Louise de Kiriline Lawrence) and, during the early 1950s, established the Margaret Nice Ornithological Club in Toronto. Named after a noted American ornithologist, the club was formed because, even in the 1950s, the all-male Toronto Ornithological Club, would not admit women.[94]

Louise de Kiriline Lawrence (née Flach, 1894, in Sweden) began observing and banding birds in her "outdoor laboratory" around her property near North Bay, Ontario, during the Second World War. By 1945, she was concentrating on regional studies of birds, observing territoriality, nesting, and feeding behaviour. She published papers in *The Canadian Field Naturalist* (1947, 1949), *The Auk* (1948), and *The Wilson Bulletin* (1949), and in 1954, became the first Canadian woman to be elected member of the American Ornithologists Union. Her major work, *A Comparative Life History Study of Four Species of Woodpeckers*, was published in 1967 as one of the prestigious Ornithological Monograph Series of the AOU. In addition to her many scientific contributions, Lawrence's books and nature stories, published in *Audubon*, did a great deal to popularize ornithology and promote conservation. In 1969, she received the John Burroughs Medal, one of the most distinguished awards for nature writing.[95]

Conclusion

From the foregoing, it is evident that during the period 1815–1965 Canadian women contributed to the study of nature in a variety of ways. During the colonial period, they pursued natural history studies which provided information and specimens to members of a still-small international scientific community. The second half of the nineteenth century saw the development of an indigenous Canadian scientific community. It was a period of rapid growth in western science, during which the increased institutionalization and professionalization of the various sciences led to higher educational requirements and a growing number of paid positions. When educational opportunities for women improved, women pursued higher studies, and some aspired to scientific professions.

In spite of government interest in areas of science with economic importance, in Canada, as in the United States, opportunities for good careers were mostly limited to men. Clearly, improved educational opportunities did not lead to equally good professional opportunities for women. With competition for employment, women found it difficult to find positions commensurate with their abilities and qualifications. Traditional attitudes towards women prevailed during this period. The consequences were institutional constraints, lower pay, slower advancement, and much waste of women's talents and scientific productivity.

Despite the difficulties most women had to face in pursuing their interest in the natural sciences, many persevered and made contributions to geology, botany, and zoology in academe, government research laboratories, industry, or as independent researchers. Some were successful as professionals, while others had obstructed careers.

Most remained single because, particularly during the Depression, marriage and scientific work were considered incompatible. This was the view of department heads, division chiefs and others who were in a position to hire and fire personnel, but often, even women themselves internalized this norm and maintained that a woman could not have two careers. Women who chose marriage over paid employment used various strategies to be able to continue their scientific work. Some became part of a "two-person single career," in order to obtain access to funds, facilities and exchanges of ideas. Others continued their scientific work as volunteer investigators.

The analytical categories used in this essay (for example, "successful" careers) do not necessarily reflect how the women themselves viewed their status within the scientific community. From the foregoing examples, it is evident that Canadian women scientists perceived their own situations in a variety of ways. Roscoe, Nobles, and Battle, who had unusually good careers, maintained that they encountered no discrimination. Even some women who had what we could term obstructed careers, like Watney and Black, failed to notice any open or hidden biases against women scientists. But others, like Pelluet, fought every inch of the way to obtain recognition commensurate with their abilities and experience. It is clear that in spite of similarities in socialization, the expectations of Canadian women natural scientists varied considerably, as did their tolerance, or even awareness, of inequality. Some fought for advancement and recognition; others, to this day, would deny the existence of any discrimination. Some enjoyed competition with male colleagues; others accepted the fact that a woman could not advance in a man's world. The wide divergence in women's own perception of their situations at the workplace was partly due to their socialization, and partly to individual differences of personality and experiences.

In spite of the prevailing bias that prevented the advancement of many Canadian women natural scientists, the women with the most visible careers were honoured by the male scientific establishment. However, these were the exceptions, the pioneers, the visible tip of the large group of Canadian women natural scientists. Only a minority of the women employed as scientists were elected to fellowship in the highly-professionalized Royal Society of Canada (Wilson, Fritz, Newton, Belyea, Nobles). Scientific associations, on the other hand, admitted women (both professionals and volunteer investigators) to high categories of membership and offices (Louise de Kiriline Lawrence, elective member AOU, Helen Battle, president, Canadian Society of Zoologists).

The experiences of Canadian women natural scientists who received the much-sought-after travelling fellowship given annually by the Canadian Federation of University Women is perhaps more representative of what happened to women of great scientific potential. Of the 16 scholarships conferred between 1921 and 1937, six went to women showing research potential in the natural sciences: Dixie Pelluet (1922), Alice Wilson (1926), Silver Dowding Keeping (1928), Lillian Hunter (1932), Constance MacFarlane (1933), and Marie Hearne (1935), a McGill genetics graduate and the first Ph.D. to receive the fellowship. As is well documented, Pelluet and Wilson had to fight for advancement and increases in pay. Keeping, Hunter and MacFarlane had careers that were more or less obstructed. Hearne, who showed great promise in her original research on carcinogenic substances in tissue culture, and spent time in England with J.B.S. Haldane and others, became a research assistant in the Banting Institute in Toronto.[96]

It is evident that the career paths of Canadian women natural scientists were far from smooth. It is also clear that, in spite of all these difficulties, many women pursued science. While their careers did not follow the patterns of those of most male scientists, their experiences show that, in spite of the prevailing view of the scientist as a white male working in a laboratory, science has been done in a variety of ways and in many different settings. The womens' experiences also show that in spite of the institutionalization and professionalization of science, alternative ways of studying nature have been possible. Despite the odds, women natural scientists formed an integral part of the developing Canadian scientific community. They most certainly were *not* last in the field!

CLARA M. CHU and BERTRUM H. MACDONALD

The Public Record: An Analysis of Women's Contributions to Canadian Science and Technology Before the First World War

The place of women in the development of science and technology in Canada has in recent years begun to receive the attention of scholars, but so far, most of the research has concentrated on the contribution of women after the First World War.[1] In this paper, we focus on women who were involved in Canadian science and technology prior to the Great War, and who published either the results of their research, or reports of scientific and technical activity. Our interest in pursuing this study was spurred by the availability of *Science and Technology in Canadian History: A Bibliography of Primary Sources to 1914*.[2] The recent publication of this research tool (hereafter referred to as the *Bibliography*) has made a variety of studies possible, including the investigation of the communication of scientific and technological information by women.

In the absence of other records, primary literature provides a type of evidence, which leads to a particular profile of past activities and people. Our investigation pays attention to the published record, and no attempt is made to shed light on the role of women who did not publish.[3]

The data for this study were obtained from the database of the *Bibliography*, which brought together a wealth of information not readily available elsewhere, and provided an unparalleled opportunity for analyzing women's contributions to Canadian science and technology.

The parameters of the data are as follows: (1) only primary works, that is, monographs and journal articles of the pre–1914 period, were examined; (2) Canadian science and technology were defined to include any scientific or technological work published in Canada or abroad by a Canadian, and those works which had sufficient Canadian content published in Canada or abroad by a non-Canadian; (3) Canada was taken to mean the territory circumscribed by current national boundaries; (4) science and technology were given a broad interpretation, so that topics which might now be considered on the fringe or outside the field were included. Hence, geographical works (such as, settlers' guides, or descriptions of voyages and explorations) were included because of their natural history descriptions and/or their topographic or cartographic data. Except for those publications treating physiology or anatomy, medical works were excluded[4]; and (5) primary works published during the more than three centuries before 1914 were considered.

The process of identifying women authors[5] was a task fraught with problems, as some first names, such as Leslie and Shirley, are not sex specific. Information on first names used by either sex was sought from name dictionaries, author annotations in the bibliographic entries, or biographic sources.[6] Women who published under pseudonyms, or who provided only initials rather than full first names, perhaps because they did not want to be identified, have their work questioned, or face publishing problems, were difficult to pin down, unless the individuals were prominent and had already been identified as women either in biographies or by name authority agencies.[7] We made no attempt to ascertain the sex of authors of works published anonymously.

After we finalized the list of women authors, we extracted from the *Bibliography* for examination bibliographic records for all the works entirely authored or co-authored by each woman. To determine the subject of each work, we used the following method of analysis: (1) for monographs, we took the broad subject category which predominates in a work to be the subject, and (2) for journal articles, we took the broad subject category of coverage of the serial or journal where the article was published to be the subject (for example, the subject of an article in the *Canadian Horticulturist* is HORTICULTURE). It should be remembered, as was noted earlier, that the subject range of science and technology is broad, following that of the *Bibliography*.

To obtain further data on the women in our list, biographical sources and guides to manuscripts were checked. For example, a search of the *Union List of Manuscripts in Canadian Repositories*, using all the women's names, was conducted, but as Ainley[8] also discovered, this strategy was not very fruitful. Our search for publicly available personal documents of the women authors in our study has yielded records for only 10, and published biographical data is available for only 36 women. Since any thorough study of early women scientists and technologists has to include the primary literature, we will now look closely at what may be the only available public record of the contributions made by women to Canadian science and technology prior to the First World War.

The manual search through the *Bibliography*, followed by verification of uncertain authors, revealed 145 women authors with 26 variant names (a total of 171) out of 10,086 possible authors with 824 variant names (a total of 10,910). Women publishing on Canadian scientific and technical topics prior to 1914, therefore, constituted 1.4 percent of all authors in the *Bibliography*. By comparison, Enros' *Biobibliography*[9] shows that in a subsequent period (1914–1939), in Ontario alone, the percentage of women authors had increased to 8.8 percent (or 107 out of 1213 authors).

The women authors wrote 248 works: of these, 57 (or 23%) are monographs, and 191 (or 77%) are journal articles. This publishing pattern is different from the total of the authors identified by the *Bibliography*, where 9.8 percent of all works are monographs (5,690 of 58,109), and 90.2 percent are journal articles (52,419 of 58,109). Women published an average of two works, in comparison to approximately three works per author for the total *Bibliography* (approximately 24,000 of the 58,109 works in the *Bibliography* were brought out anonymously and were not included in the analysis). While we have no other studies with which to compare our findings about the publishing patterns of men and women scientists and technologists, for a later period, Cole and Zuckerman found that "more than 50 studies of scientists in various fields show that women publish less [about 50 percent less] than men. Moreover, correlations between gender and productivity have been roughly constant since the 1920s."[10] The same publishing trend seems to be evident in our data.

We turn now from an examination of general patterns, to a closer inspection of the data. The earliest two monographs authored by women deal with scientific topics: the first, by Lady of the Principality, 1833, considered anthropological topics,[11] and the second, by Anna Brownell Jameson, 1839, discussed anthropological and natural history subjects.[12] The earliest two monographs on applied science authored by a woman were published by Eliza Maria Jones in 1892 and 1893, and deal with dairying and animal husbandry.[13] The earliest two journal articles by Canadian women were both published in 1829, and deal with scientific subjects: one, by Countess Dalhousie, is on botany, and the other, by Mrs. Harriet Sheppard, on invertebrates.[14] The first woman to publish on a technological subject was a Mrs. Loudon, who wrote a journal article on "Formation of Hot-Beds" in 1849. Women's work on technological topics started later than those on scientific topics, particularly in monograph format (1849 for a journal article on a technological topic, as compared to 1829 for a scientific journal article, and 1892 for a monograph on a technological topic, in contrast to 1833 for one on a scientific topic). Since many historical analyses of science and technology have overlooked women, explanations that would account for the publishing pattern just outlined are not immediately evident.[15] Cummins, McDaniel, and Beauchamp have suggested that, at least with regard to invention, there is a public/private element which delegates some of women's work, such as home-based or domestic inventions, to the privacy of the home.[16] The work of many women, therefore, remained hidden, and only as activities such as domestic science became more established in their own right did technological work by women get into the public domain. While not conclusive, this view may explain the later appearance of technological works by women in our study.

By the mid–1870s, Canadian women were publishing annually, but up to 1914, no more than 13 works (journal articles and monographs combined) were ever published by women in any one year.

As Tables I and II show, women wrote on a variety of topics. We see that women's monographs dealt mainly with the sciences, while journal articles treated primarily applied sciences. Only five of the 57 monographs (8.8%) addressed a technological topic, in comparison to 126 out of the 191 journal articles (66%). The most popular scientific areas were natural history, anthropology (including archaeology and ethnology), travel, general science, and entomology. In applied science and technology, agriculture (including animal husbandry, apiculture, and horticulture), architecture and building, and mining received the most attention. Agriculture is the dominant topic of all the publications (118 out of 248, or 47.6%). All applied science monographs deal with agriculture.

Most of the works by women were published in Canada (see Table III). Forty-four percent of the monographs (25 out of 57) were published in Canada, mainly in Ontario (16 works), and 85.4 percent of the journals (41 out of 48) were published in Canada. Canadian journals account for 94.2 percent of the journal articles (180 out of 191). Three works were published in languages other than English:[17] two monographs (one in German, published in 1839 in Germany, and one in French, published in 1894 in Canada), and one journal article on field and fodder crops, which was published in 1860 in the only French-language Canadian journal that figured in our study, *Agriculteur*.[18]

Of the women authors whose place of birth or residence could be determined, 65.5 percent (or 95 out of 145) were born or resided in Canada. Many of them (55.2% or 53 out of 96) were from the province of Ontario. Of the 35 foreign women authors, 26 were American, eight British and one Mexican. The place of origin of 15 women authors could not be determined with certainty.

While most of the women did not receive higher education, 17 (or 11.6%) had some university education, which may or may not have led to degrees. Eight of them were American.[19] The following nine were Canadian: Emma Sophia Baker, B.A. (Victoria University, 1899), Ph.D. (Toronto, 1903, psychology); Clara Cynthia Benson, B.A. (University College, 1899, honours in physics and chemistry), Ph.D. (Toronto, 1903, chemistry);[20] Harriet Brooks, B.A. (McGill, 1898, gold medal in mathematics and physics), M.A. (McGill, 1901); Susannah Amelia Chown, B.A. (Toronto, 1907?), Carrie Matilda Derick, B.A. (McGill, 1890, gold medal in natural science), M.A. (McGill, 1896); Faith Fyles, B.A. (McGill, 1900, botany); Annie Louise Macleod, B.A. (McGill, 1904, first-class honours in chemistry), M.Sc. (McGill, 1905), Ph.D. (McGill, 1910, chemistry); Maud Lenora Menten, B.A. (Toronto, 1904), M.B. (Toronto, 1907), M.D. (Toronto, 1911), Ph.D. (Chicago, 1916, biochemistry);[21] Rosalind Watson Young, B.A. (McGill, 1895, gold medal in natural science), M.A. (McGill, 1901).

Of the 145 women authors considered in our study, three (Annie L. Jack, Catharine Parr Traill, and Henrietta F. Buller) were the most prolific. Annie L. Jack published 29 journal articles between 1877 and 1911, all on horticulture. Catharine Parr Traill contributed seven monographs and four journal articles on botany between 1855 and 1906. Henrietta F. Buller published nine journal articles between 1886 and 1893 on apiculture. Not all women were as prolific as these; a few published three or four works, but most published only one.

Although most women published as sole authors (81.4% or 118 out of 145), 27 of the 145 women authors (18.6%) published jointly with others. Eight women co-authored with other women, and 19 women published with men. Thirteen of the women who collaborated with men were the principal authors, and in only six cases were they secondary authors.

Authorship considered in a broad sense does not necessarily imply active work in science and technology *per se*. In our list of women, four were translators, one an illustrator, and one wrote the biographical introduction to a work by James Cook. Others more closely allied to science and technology included 16 educators, four museum or lab assistants, six literary authors, three journalists, four members of the editorial board of journals, and one secretary of an horticultural association.[22] Nine of the educators taught in post-secondary institutions.

A number of studies have found that one of the variables which influenced women's involvement in science was their association with men who were scientists.[23] These men not only increased some women's interest in scientific pursuits, they also gave women entry into the field. Six women on our list were related to men involved in science and technology, and had access to science through them.[24]

Another characteristic of the publishing record worth noting is that some women brought their own perspective to their writing, or wrote specifically for a female audience. For example, five works described travel, geography, natural history, and ethnology from a woman's outlook. A Mrs. Townsend wrote about a woman's experience raising poultry.[25] In 1902, Elsie A. Dent published "Women's Work in Astronomy."[26] Moreover, there were six periodical articles which introduced possible occupations for women; for example, three dealt with apiculture, and another three with horticulture. In all cases, the occupations were indicated in the titles. Rossiter's study of American women's work in science between 1880 and 1910 found that many middle-class magazine articles (often written by women) also hailed new opportunities for women.[27] However, the newest areas of women's work in science were in low-ranking and low-paying scientific or low-paying social service positions, which usually did not enable those working in them to publish on science and technology. Our data highlight some women's experiences outside the home, and give accounts of their contributions to science and successes in agricultural pursuits.

Several scholars writing on women in other countries have developed models to illustrate women's participation in science. For example, in her analysis of American women in science between 1830 and 1880, Sally Kohlstedt used three categories: the first generation, or "independents," are those women who worked autonomously, and whose efforts did not receive much attention; the second generation was made up of mid-nineteenth-century American women who popularized and disseminated science, such as educators and illustrators; and the third generation consisted of American women who had to choose between amateur activities and professional careers.[28] Other historical analyses of American women in science have found that their acceptance into the scientific world took the form of occupational sex segregation.[29] While the above American categories are not entirely congruent with the Canadian situation, they can serve as a guide for the analysis of women's contributions to Canadian science and technology prior to the First World War.

From our Canadian data, we can say that the "first generation" of women contributed to science through their writings on the natural history, ethnology, and geography of different areas of Canada, resulting from travels, which were usually done with men. These women, who were mostly from the British leisure class, were usually better educated than the general population.

The "second generation" of women who contributed to both science and technology consisted of educators, journalists, translators, illustrators, assistants in museums, and literary authors who wrote popular science works and textbooks.

The "third generation" of women who make up the majority of the women in our study, fall into two categories[30]: (1) "amateurs" or "volunteers" who wrote on applied science, especially agricultural topics for example, Annie L. Jack (horticulture), and Henrietta F. Buller and Ethel Robson (apiculture). Most of these women belonged to horticultural or apicultural associations; (2) "professionals" teaching at universities and colleges, or working as assistants in museums or laboratories.

In late Victorian Canada, women who held professional positions were required to resign when they married. Some became popularizers of science and technology (for example, Rosalind Watson Young, a teacher before marriage, published mining and geographical works as an "amateur"). By contrast, Annie L. Jack, who was a teacher until she married a fruitgrower, probably would not have contributed so extensively to horticulture if she had not married.

Most of the women of the "third generation" participated in local natural history associations, and those who worked professionally also belonged to specialized scientific societies. Women's membership in applied science and/or technological associations was limited to horticultural and apicultural societies, and such affiliation seems to have influenced women to publish.

From the publishing record, we can characterize the contribution of women to the communication of Canadian scientific and technical information. For the period prior to the Great War, women made up 1.4 percent of all currently-known authors of works on Canadian science and technology. Topics such as geography, natural history, anthropology, botany, and agriculture predominated. Through their publications, women had an important role in popularizing science and technology. In an expanding field of study, many women may have been on the periphery, yet their work was important in making science and technology available to the public at large and specifically, to women.

A bibliographic analysis of the primary literature, such as the one we have provided, furnishes one window on the activity of women in Canadian science and technology prior to 1914. This analysis, while revealing in its own right (whether or not other primary literature, such as personal documents, is available), calls for further research that will include a study of the work of other women whose chief contribution was not through publication.

TABLE I

Characterization of Monographs Published by Women

A. *Subject Content*

SCIENTIFIC TOPICS

Anthropology – General	3
Anthropology – Archaeology	2
Anthropology – Ethnology	7
Botany	15
Mathematics	1
Natural History	2
Physics	1
Science – General	2
Travel*	16
Zoology	2

TECHNOLOGICAL TOPICS

Agriculture	5

GENERAL TOPICS

Societies/Associations	1

TOTAL 57

B. *Format*

TEXTBOOKS**

- Mathematics	1
- Natural history	2
- Pathology	1

TOTAL 4

C. *Language*

French	1
German	1

* *Monographs on "Travel" include descriptions of journeys or explorations, and settlers' guides, which include the natural history, geology, anthropology, or geography of an area.*
** *Refers to the number of textbooks out of the total 57 monographs.*

TABLE II

Characterization of Journals in which Women Published Articles

A. *Subject Content*

	NO. OF JOURNALS	NO. OF ARTICLES
SCIENTIFIC TOPICS		
Anthropology – General	1	1
– Archaeology	1	2
Astronomy	3	3
Biology -General	2	2
Botany	7	7
Chemistry	2	2
Geology	1	3
Natural History*	4	21
Physiology	1	1
Psychology	1	3
Science	5	14
Zoology – Entomology	2	6
TECHNOLOGICAL TOPICS		
Agriculture – General	4	14
– Animal Husbandry	1	1
– Apiculture	2	26
– Horticulture	3	72
Architecture and Building	3	4
Engineering	1	1
Mining	2	4
Patents	1	1
Technology – General	1	3
TOTAL	48	191

B. *Journals Not Published in Canada*

Foreign Journals (from the total) 7   11

C. *Language*

French (Canadian Publication) 1   1

* *Includes literary and historical journals which published articles on natural history, among other topics.*

TABLE III

Place of Publication

A. *Monographs*

NO. OF MONOGRAPHS

Canada	25
– Ontario/Canada West (16)	
– Quebec/Canada East (9)	
United Kingdom	16
United States	11
Unknown	4
Germany	1
TOTAL	57

B. *Journals*

NO. OF JOURNALS

Canada	41
United States	5
United Kingdom	2
TOTAL	48

MARGARET GILLETT

Carrie Derick (1862–1941) and the Chair of Botany at McGill

In the mid-1980s, the government of Quebec sponsored a series of inquiries into the status of women — academic and non-academic — at all of the universities in the province. One of the last of Quebec's institutions of higher learning to set up an equity study under this program was McGill University. This seems consistent with McGill's reputation as a conservative institution. However, we should recall that McGill was the first Canadian university to appoint a woman to a full professorship. Her name, Carrie Derick, professor of morphological botany, commonly appears in chronologies listing landmark events in the history of Canadian women. The appointment was made in 1912, an early date in the history of Canadian women's higher education, and it was quite remarkable for an institution that had admitted women as undergraduates only in 1884. The fact that Derick was in the sciences, rather than the humanities, may also seem strange, and raise speculation about the circumstances of her promotion and the nature of McGill in 1912. What would an equity study have found if it had been conducted in that year?

We can reconstruct the findings of such a hypothetical study with a fair degree of accuracy by examining the McGill University calendar for 1912–13. In that year, there were five faculties at the University: medicine, arts, applied science (engineering), law and agriculture plus the School of Household Science and the School for Teachers. The total enrolment was about 2,000 students, of whom 470 were women.[1] The total number of people listed as "Officers of Instruction" was 321, of whom 22 were women. The women included classroom teachers at the practice school, who should probably not be considered to have true academic appointments. However, they are in the calendar and, with them, women constituted just 6.5 percent of the teaching staff; without them, the figure is 5.6 percent. If the two schools are omitted, and only the Faculties considered, the proportion of women is three percent. Any way you look at these figures, women hardly formed a critical mass — which is said to be necessary before promotions can be contemplated.

If we looked closely at the women "Officers of Instruction" in 1912, we would find that all but one were unmarried, and that four held administrative positions (warden of Royal Victoria College, curator of the Medical Museum, director of women's physical education, and head of the School of Household Science — but not principal of the School for Teachers, although teaching was by that time a "women's profession"). There were seven women teaching in arts, two in agriculture, one in medicine,[2] none in law or applied science, four in household science and seven in the School for Teachers. Those who taught were distributed by rank across a wide range:

Women Officers of Instruction, 1912

Professor	1
Associate Professor	0
Assistant Professor	1
Lecturer	4
Sessional Lecturer	1
Tutor	2
Instructor	4
Teacher	4
Assistant	2
TOTAL :	19*

* *Because three of the 22 women are listed in their administrative capacities only.*

If the 1912 McGill figures were compared to those of today, it would be found that today's numbers are higher, and that there is now a greater percentage of full-time women academics (17.6%). But there would be something familiar about the pattern of distribution — a decided clustering in the lower ranks, with the figures pretty thin on top. In 1912, there was one assistant professor, no associate professor, one full professor. We might well wonder how that one professor got there, with no associate cohort and only one assistant. Here, surely, was a statistical aberration.

This statistical deviant was Carrie Derick. The board of governors had just appointed her professor of morphological botany. Why? The obvious answer is, "because she was very good." It is generally acknowledged that being very good is a necessary, but not sufficient, condition for a woman to be promoted. It might be asked why "morphological botany," why not "botany"? Could this have been a second chair, back in the days when there was usually only one professor in a department, and he was next to God ? Was Derick's precedent-setting professorship second-class? If so, did she get it just because she was a woman? Who got the real chair? Who was Carrie Derick anyway? Was she a genius? A renowned researcher? An aggressive feminist? Did she have special mentors? A highly supportive network? Carrie Derick was certainly a special person.

Carrie Matilda Derick[3]

Carrie Matilda Derick was born on January 14, 1862, in Clarenceville, in the Eastern Townships, Quebec. Her mother, Edna Colton Derick, was an American, and her father, Frederick Derick, was of Loyalist ancestry. She obtained her early education at the Clarenceville Academy, and began to teach there at the age of 15. She later took teacher training at the McGill Normal School in Montreal, from where she carried off the J.C. Weston Prize and the Prince of Wales Medal. In 1881, she returned to Clarenceville as principal of her old school. But the pull of Montreal was too strong, and in 1883 she went back there to teach at a private school for girls. Four years later, she enrolled in the McGill faculty of arts. She was then 25 years old. What a delight she must have been to teach — a mature, brilliant, intellectually-engaged student. In 1890, she earned her B.A. with first class honours, achieving a cumulative average of 94 percent, the highest in the university for that year.[4] She took prizes in classics and zoology as well as botany, and won the Logan Gold Medal in natural science.

It is no wonder that the following year, David Penhallow, professor of botany, asked this outstanding student to return to his department as his part-time assistant for "a sum not exceeding $200."[5] In 1892, while Derick was teaching math and science to the girls at the Trafalgar Institute, Penhallow arranged for her to be appointed part-time demonstrator in botany. Thus, she became the first woman on McGill's instructional staff, receiving a salary of $250 per year.[6]

If our study were to look at the rates of promotion of women at McGill, we would see that Carrie Derick continued as a part-time demonstrator for four years. In that period, she earned her M.A. (1896), after which Professor Penhallow recommended that she be promoted to the rank of lecturer and given a full-time appointment. The board of governors proved unwilling to take such a leap; instead,

it was remitted to the Principal to secure the whole services of Miss Carrie Derick as Demonstrator in the Department of Botany at a salary of not more than $750 per annum.[7]

The principal, Sir William Peterson, found that this was not so easy to arrange. While Miss Derick might well have been pleased at the prospect of a full-time appointment at McGill, she was not so thrilled that she was prepared to take a cut in earnings with no improvement in rank — especially if she either knew or suspected that a young man with only a B.A. was getting $750 to start as a demonstrator.[8] Principal Peterson was thus constrained to report that, because Miss Derick was at present "in receipt of considerable emoluments from the Trafalgar Institute," she "could not undertake to [give] her whole time to the University for the remuneration offered . . . ."[9] Into the breach stepped the champion of women's education at McGill, Sir Donald A. Smith (later Lord Strathcona). It was he who had provided the money that had made it possible for women students to be accepted in 1884, and on this occasion, he came to the rescue by authorizing payment of an additional $250. This enabled the governors "to appoint Miss Derick as Lecturer in Botany and Demonstrator in the Botanical Laboratory" at a salary of $1,000 per year.[10] Carrie Derick was on her way.

Penhallow and his protégée worked well together. This was noted by McGill's unofficial poet laureate, Stephen Leacock, who wrote:

Dr. Penhallow, it would need a Herrick
To sing your work and that of Carrie Derick,
Nor shall my halting Muse in vain essay
Such sweet cooperation to portray.[11]

Derick held the positions of lecturer and demonstrator for eight years without increase in salary. In those days, there was no union or professional organization to help fight for benefits, but this pioneering academic woman had the courage to speak up for herself. In 1904, after she had written to the principal complaining of "unfulfilled promises of advancement," she was finally promoted to assistant professor. This involved a further increase of salary of $250, but on the understanding that she teach an additional summer course in botany.[12]

Meanwhile, Carrie Derick had continued her studies. She spent three summers at Harvard, and seven doing research at the Wood's Hole Biological Station in Massachusetts, where Penhallow had secured at least one table for "such [McGill] students as are qualified for the work."[13] Another summer (1898) she attended the Royal College of Science in London, and, with a fairly generous grant of $400 from McGill and a leave of absence (1901–02), she spent 18 months in Germany. There, she visited laboratories and botanical gardens at the Universities of Munich and Berlin, and studied for two semesters at Bonn. Although she did the research required for a higher degree, she did not receive it, because the University of Bonn did not at that time award the Ph.D. to women.

Long before genetics was a recognized field, Derick laid the foundations of the study of this discipline at McGill. She introduced a seminal course on "Evolution and Genetics," and her research on heredity earned her a national and international reputation. In particular, her paper on "The Early Development of the Florideae," published in *The Botanical Gazette* (Chicago), attracted a good deal of attention on both sides of the Atlantic. It was abstracted in *The Journal of the Royal Microscopical Society*. Other scientific papers on topics such as "Nuclear Changes in Growing Seeds," "Heredity and Environment," "Anabiosis," "Nuclear Differences Between Resting and Active Cells," and "Holdfasts of the Rhodophyceae" appeared in journals such as *Science, The Canadian Record of Science,* and *Transactions of the Royal Society of Canada.* Carrie Derick was one of the relatively few women whose work was acknowledged through a listing in *American Men of Science* (1910).

She also gave many public lectures and wrote learnedly, but comprehensibly, for the scientifically uninitiated. For example, she wrote articles like "On the Border," an imaginative account of life in the Eastern Townships, which appeared in the now-defunct *McGill University Magazine*,[14] and "The Trees of McGill University," which appeared in the still-flourishing *McGill News*.[15] In 1900, she wrote a series of 28 illustrated articles on Canadian plants for *The Star Weekly*, a newspaper with wide circulation. Some of these essays were reprinted as "Flowers of the Field and Forest."

Carrie Derick became a fellow of the American Association for the Advancement of Science, and member of appropriate professional groups, such as the Botanical Society of America, the American Genetics Association, and the Canadian Public Health Association. This list may appear rather dull, for memberships like these may be considered routine. But at the turn of the century they were *not*. Professional organizations were only just opening up to women, and by joining them and writing for their publications, Derick was helping break and hold new ground.

As well as being a respected scholar, Carrie Derick was a concerned citizen. Her contributions to society as a whole went well beyond botany, and she had a truly impressive curriculum vitae. She was very active in the early days of the McGill Alumnae Society, playing a major role in the development of one of its first important projects, the Girls' Club and Lunch Room. This was a project financed and administered by the earliest women graduates of McGill, in order to provide nourishing food, pleasant rooms, evening classes, and a variety of social amenities for working-class women. Derick was the first corresponding secretary of the Club. She also served for five years (1892–1897) as the third president of the Alumnae. Her interest in women's causes in general ranged from public support for individuals like Annie Langstaff, McGill's first woman law graduate (1914), who (unsuccessfully) sued the Quebec bar for the right to practice law in this province, to active participation in the suffragist movement, to involvement and holding office in the Montreal Local Council of Women, as well as the National and the International Council of Women. She also presented a brief on Montreal women wage-earners to the Royal Commission on Industrial and Technical Training (1910–13).

Carrie Derick, 1890.
Notman Photographic Archives, McCord Museum.

It is not surprising that such an outgoing, energetic, altruistic woman as Derick should have won recognition, or that her expertise should frequently have been called upon. She gave scientific testimony to a number of commissions, government departments, and professional organizations on topics such as fungus diseases, juvenile delinquency, and mental deficiency. She was a member of the Executive Committee of the National Council of Education, and the first woman on the Protestant Committee of the Council of Public Instruction of the Province of Quebec, an appointment she held for 17 years (1920–1937). She was a great believer in the power of education and environment, but, as a geneticist and contemporary of Marie Stopes, she was something of a crusader for eugenics. She was even bold enough to lecture Sir Jean-Lomer Gouin, prime minister of the very Catholic province of Quebec in the era of very large families, on — of all subjects — birth control. After that interview, the Prime Minister is said to have exclaimed: "Elle m'a tellement fait rougir, cette vieille fille de McGill!" ("How she made me blush, that old maid from McGill!")

Derick was the very model of the professional academic woman, and her multi-faceted competence was appreciated at McGill. Thus, when in 1909 Professor Penhallow became ill, Miss Derick was asked to take charge of the department on a temporary basis until he recovered. Penhallow's illness lingered month after month. Derick continued to act as chair. After Penhallow's death in 1910, she was formally asked to be responsible for the botany department. She received a salary increase, and was now earning $2,000 per year, a quite respectable sum at the time.[17]

By February, 1912, a new professor of botany had still not been appointed, and Derick, having done the job for about three years, assumed that she would get the position. Therefore, she cannot have been happy when she learned from Principal Peterson that the board of governors had decided unanimously "to throw the appointment to the Chair of Botany open and let it be known on both sides of the Atlantic that we are in search of a professor."[18] The principal told her, "In these altered circumstances, it will be natural for you to make application in the usual way." However, it was not until the end of April that she did formally apply for the chair of botany.[19] By then, an advisory committee had been struck, references were being checked and interviews were taking place. What was to be "a long and . . . extremely interesting contest"[20] was already well under way.

The Chair of Botany

There were several candidates for the chair of botany from Canada and Britain, and at least eight from the United States. The principal made it clear that McGill wanted "nothing but the best,"[21] and that "a great deal in the selection will turn upon personality."[22] As well as a person of high scientific standing, he was looking for someone "who is known to be a good teacher and an effective lecturer who can make an interesting presentation of his subject even outside the walls of his classroom; someone who has good personal qualities that would enable him to get on well with others, both students and colleagues ... who was capable of representing, with forcefulness and acceptability, an important department in a large university which has to do its work in a great centre of population."

To consider all the applications was obviously a time-consuming affair and, even in those days, which we like to think of as more leisurely, the selection committee had difficulty finding convenient times to meet to handle the number of candidates. The principal, who was directly involved, and who was getting ready to sail to Britain on the "Empress of Ireland" on June 14 to attend several important conferences, can be forgiven if he felt overwhelmed by the 150 letters and 300 publications related to the chair of botany that were cluttering his office.[24]

High on Peterson's short list was a man from Alabama, Francis E. Lloyd. He was professor of botany in the Alabama Polytechnic Institute and plant physiologist at the Agricultural Experimental Station, a man with a strong list of publications and well-known referees. He was six years younger than Carrie Derick and a graduate of Princeton (A.B. 1891, A.M. 1895). He had been professor of biology at Columbia University for the first five years of the twentieth century, and was closely associated with the New York Botanical Garden, exploring, directing research studies, and lecturing under its auspices, as well as contributing to its journal.[25] He had been on scientific expeditions to Mexico (1890), Alaska (1896), and Dominica (1903).[26] He was an expert on carnivorous plants (and was later to write a comprehensive text on the subject), and was one of the earliest American scientists to experiment with guayule as a source of rubber. On this, too, he wrote a book, *Guayule* (1911).

The principal of McGill considered Francis Lloyd to be "in the front rank of botanists,"[27] and his career, which included some business experience as head of the botanical and experimental department in a commercial enterprise, to be "quite striking." This opinion was supported by the advisory committee and the more than a dozen referees whose views were solicited. In general, the referees regarded Lloyd as exceptional in both teaching and research, said he was a vivid lecturer and thought he was a "splendid character" — although two referees mentioned that he was "unconventional in his habits and not perhaps the staid type of which professors are usually made."[28] This possibly non-McGillian quality gave Peterson some concern, because he deemed it essential to "have a man who is beyond criticism on the score of personality."[29] All the same, Professor Lloyd was the Principal's preferred candidate. He was formidable competition for Carrie Derick.

By the beginning of June, it looked very much as if this glamorous man from Alabama was all set for the appointment. However, at the eleventh hour, one of the most prominent members of the Board of Governors began a strenuous campaign in favour of "the local candidate." Sir William Van Horne, the railroad baron, in a series of letters to the Principal, urged "the fitness and the claims of Miss Derick."[30]

He began with a little anecdote:

"Many years ago I heard a remark from a distinguished and most successful railway manager which made a deep impression on my mind and which has governed me ever since and to which I attribute so much of success as I have had. He was urged by his Directors to appoint to an important vacancy a man of considerable reputation from a distant railway and he replied that he would rather have his own damned fools than other people's smart fellows."

"I don't mean to imply by any means," said Sir William Van Horne, "that Miss Derick is any kind of a fool — far from it — but . . . . distant men like distant terrors are the greatest. When we look at men from a distance we cannot see the dust on them nor discover their weak spots . . . ."[31]

He recommended Carrie Derick because of her attainments in science, her qualifications as a teacher, and her whole-hearted devotion and service to McGill.

Sir William Peterson responded carefully to Sir William Van Horne, acknowledging that others involved, especially the deans of arts

(Moyse) and of law (Walton) had also favoured "the local candidate." Nevertheless, he insisted that the vote of the advisory committee had been unanimous and that the process had been correct. He was clearly not in favour of affirmative action or, as he put it, "where it is admitted that our candidate could not possibly prevail elsewhere against the outsider and where it is urged that he or she should be allowed to prevail here simply because of a McGill connection, I cannot so far extend my natural prejudice in favor of McGill people."[32] The principal also denied charges that he had "shown undue discrimination against Miss Derick by sending applicants round to see the Governors and not sending her." (The excuse that this procedure was not really necessary because the governors already knew Miss Derick would hardly be acceptable these days.)

Sir William Van Horne's support for Carrie Derick was strong, but why did he leave it so late? His four letters to the principal on this subject are all dated June, and Peterson, with his trip abroad looming closer, was anxious to get the matter settled. Perhaps Van Horne had earlier expected the advisory committee to choose Derick, but had just got an inkling that it would decide against her, so he approached the principal only then. In any event, even his request that Peterson delay taking a recommendation to the Board of Governors was denied. Thus, on June 12, 1912, the Board appointed as Macdonald Professor of Botany, at a salary of $3,000, Francis E. Lloyd.[33]

It was an unequivocal decision, but not one that was arrived at lightly. Carrie Derick had been a viable candidate, and even the possibility of appointing her without outside competition seems not to have been dismissed quite out of hand. There were several men — at least two deans and a member of the board — who had strongly supported her. But Peterson had considered that "a high position in a separate department of Morphological Botany ought . . . to meet the needs of the case."[34] Peterson had suggested that she be promoted to associate professor but "it did not surprise . . . [him] when the Board asked why we should not go out of our way to compliment her specially not to Associate Professor but Professor of Morphological Botany." Thus, the board came to its history-making decision:

"In recognition of Miss Carrie M. Derick's long and faithful service in the Department of Botany, she is appointed Professor of Morphological Botany, at a salary of $2,000 per annum."[36]

Crisis in the Botany Department

It did seem like a high appointment, the first of its kind at McGill, the first time a professorship had been conferred upon a woman in Canada. It certainly appeared to be a significant step forward for academic women. But it was an illusion. *It did not carry with it a seat on faculty, and it did not involve any increase in salary.*[37]

Miss Derick was not amused. She was not impressed. She was not satisfied. She wrote to the principal, who reported to the board her dissatisfaction and her request for further consideration.[38] But the board did not budge. It left it to the principal and the two professors to devise a *modus vivendi* for the strange new situation of two professors in one department, that of botany, and one of them a woman — a feisty Canadian woman who resented being passed over in favour of a younger American man.

To make matters worse, much worse, the principal explained to Carrie Derick that hers was a courtesy title, that although called "professor of morphological botany," she was not in fact a "professor," nor was it intended that she should teach only morphological botany."[39] The notion of a "courtesy title" must really have rankled. So must have her entry in the 1912–13 McGill *Calendar*. At that time, people were listed hierarchically: the principal first, then the dean, professors in order of seniority and the warden of Royal Victoria College followed by a statement, "These constitute the Faculty of Arts," then a small gap followed by the heading "Other Officers of Instruction." Prominent at the head of the list of "Others" was Carrie Derick. She was, in effect, below the salt.

By the end of the first term, a crisis had developed in the botany department. Even in that time it was evident that Professors Lloyd and Derick "had entirely different conceptions of . . . [their] mutual relations."[40] He assigned her work that she considered more appropriate for an ordinary demonstrator. She complained that, even as an assistant professor, she had had a greater degree of autonomy and did not now "think it right and fitting for . . . [her] to conduct laboratory work, demonstrations or other junior work, subsidiary to lectures given by another professor."[41] Professor Lloyd, who acknowledged that he had been told both before and after his appointment that "the University set a very high valuation on Miss Derick's services, and . . . the incumbent of the Chair of Botany would be expected, naturally, to treat her with the highest degree of consideration and chivalry,"[42] nevertheless wondered whether he should force the issue. He recognized that if he did, he "might be doing both Miss Derick and the University a grave injustice by making it impossible for Miss Derick to do otherwise than resign."[43]

It was a standoff. Francis Lloyd wanted to assert his authority; Carrie Derick was not willing to do work that she considered beneath her dignity and unworthy of her status. By Christmas, the matter had to be referred to the dean of arts, then up to the principal. Lloyd was advised not to force the issue, because McGill did not want to lose Carrie Derick. The only solution was for the University to appoint a demonstrator to do the demonstrator's work, thus permitting Professor Derick to maintain her self-respect and to engage in teaching, research, and other activities in accordance with her own interests, and for Lloyd to have the help he needed.

Professors Derick and Lloyd must ultimately have worked out their differences. Both stayed in the botany department for many years — Derick until her resignation because of poor health in 1929,[44] and Lloyd, until his retirement in 1934. Both had fruitful careers, leaving behind them a rich intellectual legacy of publications and successful graduate students (for example, Faith Fyles, artist-naturalist and Assistant Dominion Botanist, was a student of Derick's; McGill Vice-Principal Gordon Maclachlan was a student of a student of Lloyd's). The university closed out Derick's career by making her McGill's first woman emeritus professor, and her former students presented her with a purse of gold.

Retrospect and Prospect

In having to choose between Derick and Lloyd, the university had almost an embarrassment of riches. Without doubt, the principal and the board had a difficult decision to make, and they reached what they probably thought was an imaginative compromise. They were less patriarchal than they might have been, but less enlightened than they might have seemed and less progressive than they have been given credit for. It really should have been a great honour and a pleasure for Carrie Derick to have been appointed the first woman professor, but she was not deluded. She was, as Sir William Van Horne recognized, no fool. She knew hers was an empty title. Also, she was never happy about the "morphological" part of it since morphology was not her primary interest.[45] And she knew full well that she had been passed over.

There is a lesson to be learned from this — that the appearance of equity must not be taken at face value. These days, although we would dearly like to think that the battles have been won, we can still expect to find discrepancies between men and women in rank, salary, and rate of promotion — indeed, that is the basic assumption of the Quebec series of equity investigations. Discrimination these days may be more subtle, but it still exists.

DIANA PEDERSEN and MARTHA PHEMISTER

Women and Photography in Ontario, 1839–1929: A Case Study of the Interaction of Gender and Technology

The course of technological change, historians have recognized, is frequently influenced by traditional values and prevailing attitudes which may, in their turn, be modified in response to the introduction of new technologies. A new technology, however, can also be manipulated to reinforce, rather than challenge, traditional values. The process by which this happens has not been well studied or understood by historians. In recent years, feminist historians have turned their attention to the interaction of new technologies with the social construct "gender," examining both the ways in which women have responded to, and been affected by, new technologies, and the effect of new technologies on prevailing ideas about women.[1] This paper will argue that despite the enthusiastic response of nineteenth-century women to the new and potentially gender-neutral technology of photography, this technology was initially used in accordance with preexisting gender roles and, consequently, came to reinforce those gender roles. An examination of women's relationship to photography in Ontario between 1839 and 1929 demonstrates that in the early decades of photography, contemporary sex-role stereotypes combined with the nature of the technology to limit women's active participation as photographers, and encouraged a more passive, "feminine" role as consumers of the products of photography. Later in the century, when simplified, more accessible photographic technology and changing standards of appropriate behaviour for women appeared to offer new opportunities for women as photographers, the advertising and marketing strategies of the new consumer-oriented photographic industry acted to reinforce the notion that women's relationship to photography was appropriately that of rank amateur and passive consumer. Women photographers remained marginal in the profession, and the successful achievements of a few did not in any way challenge the widely-held view that women were technological incompetents.

The case of women and photography in Ontario allows us to examine simultaneously several aspects of women's relationship to technology that have been largely ignored in the burgeoning scholarship in the field. In her pioneering article, which asked the question "Was the female experience of technological change significantly different from the male experience?", Ruth Schwartz Cowan outlined "four significant senses in which the relation between women and technology has diverged from that of men": women as bearers and rearers of children, women as workers, women as homemakers and women as anti-technocrats.[2] In a review essay surveying the literature which has appeared in the United States since Cowan first wrote, Judith McGaw notes that the bulk of scholarship on women has concerned itself with the technology of homemaking and the technology of the non-domestic workplace. Less attention has been devoted to areas falling outside Cowan's four fields, such as, for example, "technology as a tool for enhancing sex differences and reinforcing sex-role stereotypes through clothing, cosmetics and hairdressing; the technological preconditions for and consequences of women's increasing importance as consumers; and the differential impact on women of technologies generally examined only from a masculine perspective."[3] This study will address itself to some of these neglected areas.

As a technology used by both women and men in the nineteenth and early twentieth centuries, photography suggests the complex relationship of technology to social conventions and attitudes in a way that studies of domestic, or "female," technologies do not. This preliminary examination of women and photography in Ontario[4] suggests that in the early years, women's responses to photographic technology clearly differed from those of men, and that they did so in a manner which reflected social convictions about women's scientific and artistic abilities, women's role in the family, women's relationship to other women, and women's economic importance as consumers. Later, promoters of photography simply elaborated on these themes in their marketing of new forms of photographic technology. Not only did they use different promotional strategies to reach female camera buyers, but they also employed women in advertisements as an effective strategy for conveying the impression that cameras were easy to use. Thus, even where women and men used the identical technology in a similar fashion, their activities were frequently perceived differently, and the products of their efforts valued unequally. Not only did gender influence or limit access to the new technology of photography, but women and men were assigned distinct roles in its development, production, and dissemination, indicating the pervasiveness of contemporary assumptions about sex roles. It is hoped that these tentative findings about women's relationship to photography will demonstrate the importance of relating technology to gender and sex-role stereotypes.

For the first three decades following the invention of photography, in 1839, few women became photographers in their own right. Photography in its early period was not the popular recreational pastime that it would later become. It was dominated by professionals, and a small group of dedicated amateurs, who practiced it as a scientific pursuit. Societal conventions and attitudes dictated that the membership of these groups would be predominantly male, and that women's enthusiastic response to the new process would be channelled into less-active forms of involvement with photography. Women's place in the photographer's studio during the early years of photography was, for the most part, in front of the camera rather than behind it.

News of the invention of the daguerreotype, named for its originator, Louis Jacques Mande Daguerre, reached Toronto May 3, 1839, when *The Patriot* reprinted a letter written by Samuel Morse from Paris.[5] Vastly superior to earlier processes, such as photogenic drawing, the daguerreotype captured the public imagination, and had profound social consequences, particularly in North America, where it remained the dominant process for the next 15 years.[6] It is not known when the first daguerreotypes were taken in Ontario, but the first extant Toronto advertisement for "photographic likenesses" appeared on July 27, 1841.[7] Price wars in Toronto sometimes resulted in the advertising of daguerreotype portraits for as little as one dollar. The editors of *The Independent* observed, on the opening of a new daguerrean portrait studio in 1850, "Our citizens should not lose so good an opportunity of having their likenesses taken 'to the life' both for their own and their friends satisfaction, particularly when they can do so at so trifling a cost."[8] Despite the fact that the brilliance and clarity of the well-made daguerreotype has not, in some respects, been surpassed by modern processes, the "mirror image" had some significant defects, notably the inability of the daguerreotype process to produce duplicate images, which led ultimately to its demise. By 1860, it was almost obsolete.

In the mid-1850s, photography was revolutionized by the introduction of the collodion process, which was as fast as daguerreotypy and produced superb negatives on glass, thus allowing the duplication of images. The new process involved cleaning a glass plate, coating it with iodized collodion guncotton dissolved in ether and alcohol — sensitizing it in a silver nitrate bath, and then exposing and developing the plate before it had a chance to dry out. Hence, it became known as the "wet-plate" process. Collodion positives on glass, actually negatives laid on a black backing, were known as ambrotypes, and replaced the daguerreotype as the most popular form of photography in Canada in the late 1850s.[9] The wet-collodion process dominated photography in Ontario until the mid-1880s. Requiring less skill, and a modest investment in apparatus and materials in comparison with the daguerreotype process, it was practiced by butchers, hairdressers, tobacconists, dentists, and itinerant photographers, who set up operations at the beach and fairground, making the photographic portrait accessible to most sectors of the population, including those who would never enter a studio.

During the early years of photography, social conventions were not particularly conducive to its adoption by the upper and middle-class women who had the necessary leisure and financial resources to pursue it as a hobby. In particular, the close association of photography with science mitigated against serious involvement by women. In an age which was fascinated by the wonders of science and technology, photography was described by a British observer in 1855 as "par excellence THE scientific amusement of the higher classes."[10] Nineteenth-century women of the upper and middle classes were not totally ignorant of new developments in science, but their knowledge of the physical sciences was not generally sufficient to encourage or permit an interest in photography. It is true that the new girls' academies, seminaries, and colleges increasingly featured science, especially natural history, as part of the curriculum, that a growing number of books and magazine articles about science were directed at women, and that women made up a substantial proportion of audiences at public scientific lectures. Nevertheless, this instruction was rudimentary compared with that received by boys of the same class, and it was frequently rationalized on the grounds that it would make women more stimulating companions to men and would fit them to instruct their children in scientific matters. Women were encouraged to become " 'cultivators' of science, not necessarily 'practitioners.' "[11] In addition, it was felt that women's interest in science was most appropriately expressed through the healthful pursuit of natural history — perhaps an expedition to the seaside to collect shells or fossils, or a romp through the fields with a butterfly net.

Photography, in contrast to the more ladylike study of natural history, demanded a considerable chemical expertise during the daguerreotype and wet-plate eras. Early photographers were, of course, responsible for developing and printing their own images, requiring the possession of a home darkroom stocked with the many chemicals necessary for every stage of the operation. The wet-collodion process, which demanded that the plate be developed immediately following exposure, made photography in the field a formidable undertaking for women who were hampered not only by extremely restrictive clothing, but also by notions of female frailty and delicacy. Outdoor photography required, in addition to a portable darkroom — a tent-like structure which collapsed into a large box — chemicals for coating, sensitizing, developing, and fixing glass plates, dishes and tanks, a container for water, and, of course, the camera, plateholders, and tripod.[12] As a later article on photography for "lady amateurs" observed in 1884:

> For many years photography was a sealed book to any but those of wealth and leisure, or making it their profession. A donkey-load of apparatus and some most fearfully poisonous ingredients were required. The baths left ineffaceable stains on the fingers; the whole apparatus was cumbersome, heavy and costly.[13]

Photography during its early years was complicated, awkward, expensive, and intimidating; it was also dangerous. As one student of the phenomenon of "death in the darkroom" has observed about the nineteenth century: "For good reason, this can be called the Heroic Age of photography."[14] Photographers routinely worked with volatile chemicals, such as ether, in poorly-ventilated darkrooms heated with gas or an open fire, frequently producing lethal explosions. Attempts to retrieve valuable silver from used silver nitrate baths often resulted in the accidental production of nitro-glycerine, with fatal consequences. Collodion, made from explosive gun-cotton, was frequently ignited by inflammable ether vapours. The most vulnerable photographers were "those who knew just enough chemistry to prepare standard solutions from well-tried formulae but not enough to safely experiment with new processes."[15] Many other photographers were killed or incapacitated by their frequent contacts with poisonous mercury compounds and ether fumes; still others, as well as unsuspecting members of their families, died as a result of accidentally ingesting such compounds as potassium iodide, silver nitrate, or potassium cyanide. Photography was, and was widely known to be, a highly-dangerous pursuit. Upper and middle-class women who wished to engage in it risked being regarded as eccentric, if not lunatic, by families and friends, who regarded photography as an activity which was totally inappropriate for a refined and respectable woman.

The constraints imposed by the technology of early photography thus combined with social conventions about femininity to channel women's enormous enthusiasm into a passive rather than active participation in the new process of making photographs. Women flocked in droves to the photographer's studio, where they were promised by one Toronto photographer that they might "have an opportunity of seeing their beautiful selves transformed by living light into pictures of Silver, set in *Caskets of Gold.*"[16] Like their male contemporaries, women were impressed with the low price of the photographic likeness in comparison with the painted miniature. They marvelled at the realism of the photographic portrait, although they also expressed a certain ambivalence about its unfailing truthfulness, sometimes less flattering than the painted likeness. Acknowledging the importance of their feminine clientele, photographers offered specific instructions to their female subjects as to how they might obtain the most satisfactory product:

> . . . a lady, inclined to stoutness and of extra height, should select a color for the principal robe which disguises these deviations from the "juste milieu." Black, which *absorbs* all luminous rays, has the effect to *diminish* the apparent bulk, and black, therefore, is her

appropriate color . . . . A *pale* complexion is improved, by a *pale-green* head-dress into a delicate pink hue, through the operation of the principle of *harmonious contrast in colors* . . .; while one of *lemon-yellow* would heighten this paleness to very ghastliness.[17]

To attain the desirable small "bee-stung" mouth, considered essential to the beautiful face, women were asked by nineteenth-century photographers not to smile or say "cheese," but to repeat such words as "peas," "prunes," or "prisms."[18]

The thousands of surviving studio portraits attest to the enthusiastic interest of Ontario women in the new technology of photography, and their desire to use it for purposes of their own by participating in the making of images which had a particular significance to them.[19] Women appear in hundreds of portraits of proud families presenting themselves at their best for the photographer, and historians are now searching these images for patterns which will shed light on the dynamics of relationships within the family.[20] Equally common are portraits of women with their husbands, most frequently standing slightly in profile with one hand on the shoulder of their seated husband — a pose that may have indicated deference, or perhaps the desire to show a best dress to full advantage. Many women made regular visits to the photographer's studio for a portrait with their children, something which it appears that nineteenth-century fathers rarely did. Groups of women visited the studio as an affirmation of their participation in the group, and in celebration of their accomplishments — clubs, sports teams, co-workers, classes of schoolgirls, participants in theatrical productions, members of voluntary organizations. The evidence of the photographs, confirming literary documentation of the strength of nineteenth-century women's friendships, suggests that ties between women were extremely strong.[21] It was very common for female friends to visit the studio together, and sisters, or mothers and daughters, often regrouped as a unit at the photographer's studio, even after marriage had separated them. Women frequently visited the studio alone to obtain a likeness for their own satisfaction or perhaps to present as a gift to friends and relatives, choosing a costume which particularly pleased them, or which had some special significance, such as a uniform, a theatrical costume, or even a new hat they had trimmed themselves. Finally, they used photography to observe important rituals

94

and rites of passage — most frequently, marriage, but also christenings, confirmation, "coming out" in society, graduation, wedding anniversaries, and widowhood.

Another instance of women's indirect, but significant, support for the new process of photography was their enthusiastic participation in several photographic crazes which swept Europe and North America in the 1850s and 1860s. In the same way that most women had been encouraged to express their interest in natural history only by collecting and labelling fossils, plants, and butterflies, rather than by pursuing more detailed studies of their subjects, so, too, did they learn that it was more appropriate for them to collect photographs than to make them. The invention of stereo photography led to the acquisition of a stereoscope by virtually every upper-and middle-class family. Looking at stereo views, which give an impression of three-dimensionality considered quite novel at the time, became a popular form of parlour amusement.[22] A stereoscope with one dozen views could be purchased for as little as 25 cents in Toronto in 1860, and one dealer advertised a wide range of views of the United States, Europe, Asia, Canadian cities, portraits of the Royal Family and other celebrities, mythical and scriptural subjects, ghost pictures, and stereoscopic valentines.[23] After 1861, which saw the spectacular launching of "cartomania," women avidly collected, following the example of Queen Victoria herself, *carte de visite* portraits — small photographs mounted on a card measuring approximately two-and-one-half by four inches — of friends, relatives, and celebrities. When the obvious need for some means of storing and organizing all these portraits led to the marketing of the photograph album, women, as the traditional record-keepers of the family, generally assumed responsibility for maintaining it.[24] Looking at photographs and albums, and perhaps sharing and exchanging images with their friends, came to be seen as activities that were particularly appropriate for leisured women, ranking with novel-reading, letter-writing, and fancy needlework. In fact, it was common for photographers, in selecting props appropriate to their subject, to pose female subjects much more frequently than males with a photograph album, a stereoscope, or holding photographs in their hands.

Despite the constraints and conventions which limited active female participation in photography during the daguerreotype and wet-plate eras, some women did manage to achieve success as serious amateur and professional photographers. Upper-and middle-class women were sometimes able to engage in amateur photography, despite its close association with science, because of the "double aspect" of early-nineteenth-century photography, which was reflected in the two kinds of photographers who produced the earliest images. While one group consisted of "chemists, optics engineers and all those who liked to dabble in science," photography was also practised by a significant number of former painters and art students.[25] In fact, a debate raged throughout the nineteenth century over whether photography consti-tuted a science or a fine art.[26] Early female amateur photographers, almost without exception, perceived photography as demanding sensi-tivity, an appreciation of beauty, and a highly developed artistic ability. In the *London Quarterly Review* in 1857, Lady Elizabeth Eastlake, wife of Sir Charles Eastlake, the first president of the Photographic Society, defended the practice of taking a picture slightly out of focus to enhance its artistic beauty, dismissing the objections of the devotees of scientific photography:

> As soon could an accountant admit the morality of a false balance, or a sempstress the neatness of a puckered seam, as your merely scientific photographer be made to comprehend the possible beauty of "a slight *burr* [sic]." His mind proud science never taught to doubt the closest connexion between cause and effect, and the suggestion that the worse photography could be the better art was not only strange to him, but discordant.[27]

It was but a short step from here to the argument that women's sensitivity and artistic talents made them particularly suitable for certain kinds of photography, notably portraiture. Such reasoning helps to explain the success of a few isolated individuals, outstanding among whom was Julia Margaret Cameron, in England, who became internationally famous for her portraits of royalty, literary figures, and other celebrities.[28]

The rather more significant numbers of women who succeeded as commercial, rather than amateur, photographers in the early decades belonged to a third group of practitioners, whose members dominated the field after the 1850s. The tradesmen-photographers brought a "mercantilist attitude" to the practice of photography; for them, the problem of whether photography constituted an art or a science "caused no anguish."[29] In the face of the necessity of earning a living, early women photographers of the "tradesmen" class were presumably less troubled than their more affluent sisters by notions of female scientific and technical ineptitude. It is increasingly being recognized by historians of photography that women, although a minority, were more active in the early years of the profession than has been acknowledged to date. Several thousand women operated as successful commercial photographers in the United States during the nineteenth century.[30] Probably the first female daguerreotypist in Canada was a Mrs. Fletcher, who described herself in a Montreal newspaper in 1841 as "Professor and Teacher of the Photogenic Art," and modestly announced that she was "prepared to execute Daguerreotype miniatures in a style unsurpassed by an American or European artist."[31] The identity of the first woman photographer in Ontario is not as yet known to us, but it appears that there were at least 20 of them operating throughout the province by the 1860s.[32] One of the earliest must have been Mrs. William H. Coombs, of Kingston, who advertised herself as a "daguerrian artist" in the *Daily British Whig* in 1854.[33] Another pioneer was a Miss Kelly, daughter of a prominent local merchant, who set herself up in business in Kemptville in 1855.[34] In most cases, none of the images produced by these early women professionals have survived. We know of their existence mainly through their listings in local business directories, a source which is not always reliable, as some directories listed male, but not female, photographers, perhaps because of a prejudice against women in business.[35]

William C. Darrah, a noted American historian of photography, has observed that the careers of these early women photographers sort themselves into several patterns — patterns which appear to hold true for women photographers in Ontario as well.

(1) Widows who continued to operate the studio after the death of the husband, or established their own, sometimes for many years . . .

(2) husband and wife teams, with the imprint indicating both were operators;

(3) sisters or daughters who learned photography in the family business and struck out on their own;

(4) assistants and colorists who acquired skills and found employment as camera operators, often in branch galleries; and

(5) women who paid for instruction in photography in order to find employment in the field or establish their own business.[36]

Mrs. Charles Lamb, professional photographer,
Athens, Ontario. Self-portrait, ca. 1905-1910.
Ontario Archives, 13484-30.

Jessie Dixon, active member of the Hamilton Camera Club, and friends,
ca. 1905. (Note that Dixon, top right, is activating the shutter release).
Hamilton Public Library, Special Collections.

Unidentified Ottawa "snapshooter," ca. 1910.
Ottawa City Archives.

Kodak promotional photograph, ca. 1924.
Eastman Kodak Archives, Rochester, New York, 924-10.

The little that we do know with any degree of certainty about early women photographers in Ontario tends to confirm Darrah's observations and suggests that, for the most part, women acquired their expertise and equipment through close male relatives, usually fathers or husbands.[37] Elvira Lockwood, for example, was the daughter of pioneer photographer Joseph Lockwood, and, while still in her teens, took over his Ottawa studio upon his death in 1859. She combined a successful business in photography with the teaching of oil and china painting, her photographs bearing the imprint "Artist" or "Photographic Artist."[38] She never married, but operated the studio until sometime in the early 1890s. A few women operated as part of a husband and wife team, like the Mr. and Mrs. Miller who ran a studio in St. Catharines in 1865.[39] Some of the single women were the daughters of druggists, suggesting that their familiarity with the handling of chemicals had prepared them for a career in photography. Lilly Koltun has uncovered the activities of several Toronto women photographers in the pre-Confederation era. A Miss Elizabeth Crewe and a Mrs. Fitzgibbon were both active in Toronto in 1865 and 1866. A Mrs. Meyer, who ran a Ladies' School, and may have been the wife of photographer Hoppner Meyer, entered and won in the professional artists' categories at the exhibitions in Toronto, and in 1859, at the Union Exhibition, received first prize for "Best Collection of Photographs."[40] The *Semi-Weekly Leader* in March, 1855, reprinted the outline of a speech by American feminist Lucy Stone, who held up the example of a woman who became a "daguerrean artist," and "ere long was earning thousands of dollars by her profession."[41] As Koltun has observed, however, women who were hired as photographer's assistants were not so lucky; advertisements for assistants or operators in the 1860s offered wages of between $400 and $500 per annum.[42]

Despite this activity on the part of a few women photographers, women during the daguerreotype and wet-plate eras remained marginal in the profession. We know of none who were landscape photographers. Most female commercial photographers specialized in portraiture, and it was widely believed that as women, being more tactful and patient, they were more adept at photographing uncooperative children. At any rate, their activities did little to counter the public image of the serious photographer as male. As late as 1880, the imprints of a Miss Dukelow of Iroquois, Ontario, described her as the "only Lady Photographer in Canada," a claim that was patently false.[43] This brazen falsehood, however, tells us clearly that women photographers in Ontario were indeed perceived as a rarity if one could make such a claim and expect it to be believed. In the public mind, women were consumers, not producers, of photographs, and photography remained an activity for which most women were considered neither suited nor qualified.

During the 1880s and 1890s, a number of important changes occurred both in the technology of photography, and in the prevailing beliefs about what constituted appropriate behaviour for women. Photography became less complex, less expensive, and much more accessible to the non-professional. Women, at the same time, were entering the labour force and institutions of higher learning in greater numbers than ever before, challenging many of the traditional constraints on their activities, and generally becoming much more visible in the world outside the home.[44] As a result, significant numbers of women began to participate more actively in photography as photographers, rather than as mere consumers of photographs. Their activities, however, did not lead to a new respect for the woman photographer, nor to a rejection of traditional ideas about women's inability to cope with complex technology. On the contrary, the promotion of the new, simplified photographic technology helped to reinforce both the widespread perception of women as technically incompetent, and the association of serious photography with men.

The first major technological breakthrough occurred in the early 1880s, when the invention of the gelatin dry plate opened up photography to the amateur. These commercially-manufactured glass plates were delivered from the factory ready to use, already coated with a durable sensitized emulsion. This meant that the photographer no longer had to prepare the plates in the darkroom, and could develop them at leisure, eliminating the need for a cumbersome portable darkroom. Lower cost, too, made photography increasingly accessible with the dry-plate process. A complete outfit, consisting of a bellows camera with lens, plate holder, tripod, and carrying case could be had for $10, and a set for printing, toning, fixing, and mounting prints was available for less than five dollars.[45] The lighter-weight cameras and greater convenience of the new process resulted in an enormous increase in the number of amateur photographers. In the early 1880s, a flood of new equipment and photographic manuals aimed at these amateurs, many of whom were women, appeared on the market.[46]

Dry-plate photography was more easily reconciled to prevailing standards of appropriate female behaviour; it did not challenge them, however, as evidenced by the author of *How to Make Pictures: Easy Lessons for the Amateur Photographer*, who enquired in 1882: "Can the gentler sex resist an accomplishment which henceforth may combine the maximum of grace and fascination?"[47] He did not consider the grace of male amateurs engaging in their newfound passion worthy of remark.

The popular perception of the woman photographer, from 1890 on, was that of a rank amateur who carried a Kodak. The marketing of the first Kodak camera, in 1888, completed the process of opening up photography to the amateur, and to the chemical ignoramus in particular. These lightweight and uncomplicated box cameras, which sold for about $25, did not use heavy glass plates, but, instead, used the first commercially-produced transparent roll film, made possible by improvements in the manufacture of celluloid.[48] The revolutionary Kodak system, developed by George Eastman, provided the first complete developing and printing service. For a fee of $10, the camera was returned to the factory, unloaded and reloaded with film sufficient for an additional 100 exposures, and returned with the processed prints to the consumer.[49] The philosophy of the Kodak system was explained by Eastman himself in *The Kodak Primer*:

> ... We furnish anybody, man, woman or child, who has sufficient intelligence to point a box straight and press a button ... with an instrument which altogether removes from the practice of photography the necessity for exceptional facilities, or, in fact, any special knowledge of the art. It can be employed without preliminary study, without a darkroom and without chemicals.[50]

As the famous slogan proclaimed, "You press the button, we do the rest."

Eastman pioneered many modern mass marketing techniques, and what we refer to today as lifestyle advertising. Potential consumers were urged to remember the Kodak at Christmas time, at weddings, and most especially, at vacation time. Eastman was the first to develop and market a camera specifically for children. Less than a year after the launching of the Brownie, which sold for a mere dollar, a 1901 Kodak trade circular reported that "the Brownie cameras already sold have made more than 100,000 film consumers," confirming Eastman's shrewd judgment that the Kodak fortune was to be made not on the sale of cameras, but on the sale of film.[51] In keeping with these marketing techniques, Kodak ads made frequent use of female models, a common practice of the day. As American historian Judith Papachristou has observed about the late nineteenth century:

> Representations of women dominated the abundant printing — advertising products, decorating calendars, and gracing postcards. Like flowers, birds, cherubs, and flaming sunsets, female faces and figures were commonly used by artists and photographers. As decorative elements, they were attracted to products as diverse as jewellry, tobacco, soap powder, sailboats, and books, used to catch attention, please, and sell.[52]

Female models, unlike the rare males who were occasionally used in advertisements for cameras, attempted to charm the potential consumer, but for Eastman, they served an additional useful purpose. His objective was to demystify photography, and female models, especially little girls who were perceived as lacking any technical abilities, simply reinforced the message of the simplicity of the Kodak system. If they could use a Kodak camera or operate a home developing machine, then surely anybody could.[53]

In keeping with modern advertising techniques, Eastman also targeted women as a distinct market for photographic equipment and supplies, which he set out to capture by identifying photography with an image or lifestyle that would appeal to women, especially young women. In 1901, he launched the Kodak Girl Campaign, in a successful attempt to create a symbol which identified photography with leisure, glamour, and femininity.[54] The Kodak Girl image was intimately linked to the popular conception of the New Woman, a product of major social changes affecting women, particularly young unmarried women, large numbers of whom were seeking higher education, taking employment, and thus gaining financial independence from their parents, and becoming much more physically active than nineteenth-century conventions had permitted. The Kodak Girl followed in the tradition of another New Woman symbol — the Gibson Girl, an enormously successful cartoon character created in the 1890s by the American Charles Dana Gibson.[55] Both the Gibson Girl and the Kodak Girl functioned as symbols which captured the idealized essence of contemporary young womanhood — modern, active, elegant, sophisticated, independent, but not so bold as to be thought unrespectable. Although Eastman was certainly not the only camera manufacturer to make use of women in advertising, no other campaign rivalled the enormous popular appeal of the Kodak Girl.

In targeting women as a distinct market for Kodak cameras, Eastman also catered to what were perceived as feminine tastes and concerns. Ads directed at women tended to describe the cameras as simple to operate, lightweight, stylish, and elegant. In 1926, Kodak introduced the Petite — according to the ads, a diminutive camera, gay and joyous to the eye, and available in five charming hues. This was followed in 1928 by the Vanity Kodak, a camera and matching case embossed with gold and lined with silk, available in shades of Bluebird, Cockatoo, Jenny Wren, Redbreast, and Seagull. Later that year, both Kodak and Ansco marketed, for the height of fashionable elegance, a coloured camera and vanity case with matching lipstick holder, compact, mirror, and change pocket. The "feminine" camera, however, turned out to be less than successful as a marketing ploy, as some colours proved more popular than others, and women would frequently leave at home a camera whose colour didn't match their ensemble of the day. By 1934, popular cameras had reverted to basic black.[56] It should be noted that the only serious attempt by Kodak to link its cameras with the prevailing image of masculinity occurred during the First World War. Soldiers were encouraged to buy the Vest Pocket Kodak camera, advertised as "The Soldier's Kodak camera," and to "Make your own picture record of the War."[57] There never was, however, anything resembling a Kodak Boy.

Whether or not women were responding to Kodak's appeals to their femininity, they took up photography with a vengeance. After the turn of the century, cameras gradually became accessible to a much wider range of women, including many working women, than had been true in the past.[58] The evidence of the photographs suggests that young women responded most readily to the new popularity of photography, and that they were most likely to use their cameras in the types of situations suggested by the ads. Young working women recorded their expeditions to the park or the beach with their friends. Schoolgirls took a camera to summer camp, and it is rare to find a group portrait at camp that doesn't contain several cameras somewhere in the picture.

One summer camp in Algonquin Park, in 1911, featured its own adolescent camp counsellor on photography, who produced high-quality images of life at camp in her own darkroom.[59] The Toronto Girl Guides introduced a photographer's badge in 1916, for which a Guide required "a knowledge of the theory and use of [the] lens and the construction of cameras and the action of developers" and, in addition, had to "take, develop and print 12 separate subjects; 3 interior, 3 landscape, 3 instantaneous action photos, and 3 portraits."[60] College students used their cameras to record the more pleasant aspects of student life, such as making ice cream or playing hockey.[61] Women who worked as "farmerettes" during the First World War often compiled albums which recorded their experiences, again with the emphasis on fun and friendship.[62] It was only rarely that women used their cameras to record the more mundane aspects of their daily life and work. To a certain extent, this phenomenon resulted from the technical limitations of these simple cameras, which made indoor photography difficult. More probably, however, it resulted from the concerted effort by the industry, especially by Kodak, to associate photography with leisure, glamour, and youth. Photography was not only intimately associated with leisure activities; it had become a recreational pastime in itself.

This flurry of activity on the part of women with Kodak and other popular cameras did not necessarily mean that they were being taken seriously as amateur photographers. The launching of popular photography by Kodak had resulted in a backlash reaction on the part of those who called themselves "serious" or "true" amateurs. These photographers continued to use the dry-plate process and work in the darkroom, regarding with contempt the hordes of "bicycling Kodakists" and "hand-camera fiends," and suffering under the "reproach brought upon them by the obtrusive and impertinent conduct of thousands who think that the whole art of photography chiefly consists in pressing a button."[63] As a defensive measure, they organized themselves into clubs in cities across the country, although activities were concentrated in Ontario. The clubs were dedicated to the promotion of amateur photography, and its recognition as an art, and recent research has revealed the wide scope of their activities:

These organizations provided forums where both amateurs and professionals could meet to exchange experiences, and to hear lectures on photography. They could consult photographic manuals and periodicals, use club darkrooms and workrooms, and participate in photo excursions and a variety of social events. Moreover, by organizing annual public exhibitions and by fostering contacts in the United States and the United Kingdom, clubs introduced Canadian amateur photography to a wider audience.[64]

Women participated in these clubs, sometimes serving on the executive, and frequently taking prizes at competitions and exhibitions. They were often relatives, frequently daughters, of male club members. May Ballantyne belonged to a family of photographers, and was the daughter of James Ballantyne, one of the original members of the Ottawa Camera Club, which was founded in 1894. She herself served as vice-president of the club in 1898–1899.[65] Jessie Dixon was an active member of the Hamilton Camera Club, and frequently took prizes at club competitions. Her high-quality images reveal her familiarity with the pictorialist technique favoured by serious photographers of the day.[66] Nevertheless, women remained a minority of club members. Their initial admission to the clubs frequently aroused considerable controversy, and they were not necessarily accorded the same status as the male members. The Toronto Camera Club, for example, denied lady members the use of its rooms during the evenings, except on the first and third Mondays of each month.[67] It also appears to have been the general rule that women members served on club executives only in the capacity of vice-president, perhaps indicating that this post was more decorative than responsible.

The dry-plate process, which had encouraged more women to participate in photography as serious amateurs, also resulted in increasing numbers of female professionals. As more young women entered the labour force in the decades around the turn of the century, photography won increasing acceptance as an appropriate alternative to more traditional occupations. An 1894 British publication entitled *What Our Daughters Can Do For Themselves: A Handbook of Women's Employments* listed photography, between pharmaceutical chemistry and poultry-keeping, in its lengthy catalogue, offering advice on how to acquire training and the amount of capital required to set up operations.[68] This did not necessarily imply, however, an increased awareness of women's technical abilities, as those who advocated photography as a profession for women did so on the grounds of women's supposed artistic sensibilities. In 1895, one writer in the

Canadian Photographic Journal observed "that women have a great deal of natural artistic talent, and if they once conclude to start out and become photographers, there is no doubt that they will succeed in it. The business pays well and by its very nature seems to invite women, as there are no unpleasant features about it."[69] Similarly, the American author of a 1910 manual of advice for female job-hunters noted that women "are successfully managing photograph galleries in all our cities, towns and other places. Owing to their skill in grouping and their instinct for effects, they are producing more acceptable work than the men."[70]

By the turn of the century, there were over one hundred women photographers in business in Ontario, but they remained, nevertheless, a minority within the profession.[71] Access remained difficult, owing to the need for capital to set up a studio, and the high fees required for a period of apprenticeship to a professional photographer. A 1919 vocational guidance manual prepared for use in Ontario school libraries warned prospective female photographers of the need for training, special gifts, and a good business sense.[72] In the same year, an article in *Saturday Night* on "Photography as a Profession for Women" advised on how to overcome some of these difficulties, promising in the end "not only a pleasure, but also a remunerative profession — one which places you high in the ranks of the world's workers, and which gives you an honorable standing among artists the world over."[73]

For most women who sought employment in photography, however, the opportunities were considerably less glamorous. Throughout the nineteenth century, women with artistic training were often hired or operated independently as photographic colourists, who painted over photographs with watercolours, oils, or Indian ink. A Mrs. W.K. Sargent advertised in *The Globe* in 1858 that "Photographs sent from a distance if accompanied by a correct description of hair, eyes, complexion, etc., can be coloured, and the likeness accurately preserved."[74] In factories, women performed the bulk of the operations involved in the retouching of negatives, and the finishing, colouring, and mounting of photographs; they covered and gilded daguerreotype cases in the first New England factories, and assembled and boxed cameras in the Kodak factory in Toronto in the early 1920s.[75] A 1919 Canadian advice manual for girls listed the following opportunities for women who wished to pursue a career in photography:

Requirements: Average intelligence and education.
Terms: Gallery Assistant, $7.00 per week. Spotter, $8 to $10 per week.
Producer in spotting, $10.00 Retouching negatives, $12.00 to $20.00.
Artists, $26.00. Studio work — in Reception room, $16.00 to $18.00. (Good knowledge of human nature required.) Operators, $20 to $25.00. (As high as $40.00 has been given.)[76]

We know little about the conditions under which these women worked. The employment of women in the photographic industry, and the fact that they were assigned certain operations in particular, has not generally been considered worthy of analysis by historians of photography.[77] Much of this work, however, must have involved prolonged exposure to dangerous chemicals in a poorly ventilated setting. One young Ottawa woman, Elizabeth Archibald, took up photography as a trade when in her early twenties, going to work in the studio of the renowned society photographer, William Topley, in the late 1880s. She remained in the studio for 10 years, during which time she also began to take her own photographs and develop them at home. While we cannot know for certain what caused the gradual deterioration of her health during those years, and her untimely death in 1897, at the age of 31, the members of her family have always believed that she was poisoned by the chemicals with which she worked.[78] If so, she was probably not the only female casualty of the photographic industry.

The employment of women workers in the photographic industry, and the achievements of some women as serious amateur and professional photographers, did not lead to any revision of the widely-held ideas about women's scientific ineptitude and inability to cope with complex technology. It was the Kodak Girl, not the serious amateur with her dry-plates and tripod, who came to symbolize the woman photographer. The popular image of the female photographer was shaped not by the activities of individual women, but by the photographic industry, which reinforced traditional views of femininity in order to sell cameras. Ads for cameras and supplies consistently implied that women were vain and preoccupied with fashion, that they were lacking in technical expertise, and that they used their cameras for peculiarly feminine purposes. While women were increasingly welcomed as consumers of film and camera equipment, their status within the profession remained marginal. An illuminating example of the societal attitudes which mitigated against women achieving commercial success in photography is an article on the work of Minna Keene, "How a Woman Found Fame With a Camera," which appeared in *MacLean's Magazine* in 1926.[79] Keene, a "home-loving wife and mother, of Oakville, Ontario" had won international recognition for her pictorialist studies, and was a fellow of the Royal Photographic Society, the only woman in Canada and one of only six women to have earned this honour. The author of the article, Alan Maurice Irwin, waxes rhapsodic over Keene's talents as an artist — one would never realize from the article that she must have worked with chemicals and fairly sophisticated camera equipment — and simply cannot restrain his frequent expressions of admiration for this "charming hostess" and "home lover." He concludes: "Artistically, she is a success. Commercially? There is too much of the artist in this woman, who is first of all a successful wife and mother, to worry about commercial recognition." He neglects to point out that a male photographer with similar talents would not have had to feel himself demeaned by achieving commercial, in addition to artistic, success.

This study of women and photography in Ontario, it is hoped, helps to illuminate somewhat the complex nature of the relationship between gender and technology, and shows that the introduction of a new and potentially gender-neutral technology does not necessarily lead to the revision of traditional attitudes and beliefs about sex roles. Indeed, the technology can help to reinforce the existing belief structures. Women responded enthusiastically to photography, but their active participation as photographers was constrained by conventional ideas about femininity, and their work was not accorded the same respect as that of male photographers. Indeed, most photographic images produced by women during these years remained invisible, for women were excluded from the control of the industries which determined how photographs were used. Photographic images of women abounded, in advertising, in the press, in periodical literature, in pornographic publications, in books; yet most of those who produced these images were men, as were almost all of those who exercised the power of selection. Images made by women and images reflecting women's perceptions of themselves and their experiences remained private images, so long as women lacked access to the technologies of dissemination. Photography provided some women with a new career alternative and many others, both serious amateurs and female "snap-shooters," with pleasure, enhanced self-esteem, and an opportunity to create visual records of their own experiences. Yet, ironically, both those photographic images which achieved widespread public visibility and the advertising of photographic equipment and supplies contributed to the perpetuation of traditional negative stereotypes about women's natures and capabilities.

LYKKE DE LA COUR and ROSE SHEININ

The Ontario Medical College for Women, 1883 to 1906: Lessons from Gender-separatism in Medical Education

Women pursuing a career in medicine in Canada during the late nineteenth century faced numerous obstacles. Foremost was gaining access to appropriate education. Most existing medical schools refused to admit female students. At the Toronto School of Medicine and the Medical Faculty of Queen's University, where limited enrolment was finally granted to women in the 1870s and early 1880s respectively, the attitude to women students was one of hostility. Obnoxious behaviour and derogatory comments regarding female physicians put unpleasant and unwarranted stress on female students. Pressure from male students and faculty ultimately resulted in the re-imposition of bans on women at both medical schools by 1883.[1]

Demands for education in medicine for women finally resulted, in the fall of 1883, in the establishment of the Kingston Women's Medical College and the Women's Medical College, Toronto. These schools were designed to provide female students with "equal but separate" medical education. The former was linked to Queen's University, the latter to the University of Trinity College.[2] In this article, the history of the Woman's Medical College, Toronto, and its role in advancing the cause of women in medicine, is examined in the light of an operative strategy of educational separatism. The Toronto college, which in 1894 became the Ontario Medical College for Women, had significant implications for female medical students, women in the profession, as well as women in the community, and must be evaluated accordingly.

On October 1, 1883, the Woman's Medical College, Toronto, opened in a small building at 227 Sumach Street. While annual reports issued by the college boasted of lecture rooms, anatomical and physiological museums, a chemical laboratory, and a dissecting room "well supplied with subjects," in reality, facilities were quite meagre at first.[3] Faculty repeatedly had to assure guests to the school that the word "college" indeed was not a misprint for "cottage." The chemistry department was "portable." The museum doubled as a janitor's bedroom, and heating left much to be desired during the winter months. But as one visitor to the college noted: "All this was nothing in comparison with the fact that here at last girls had an opportunity to study medicine."[4]

Initially, responses to the opportunity afforded by a women's medical school were few. Only three women enrolled for the first session of classes; two were reportedly daughters of friends of one of the founding professors.[5] The next five years saw an average of four new students per year.[6] In the late 1880s, attendance increased substantially, with 20 women registering for first-year studies by the fall of 1888 and 11 registering in the following year. By December, 1889, plans were under way to erect new premises for the college. A professor at the school was confidently writing to a supporter: "Evidently the College has taken root, and I have very little doubt but its success will be greater year by year."[7] In the fall of 1890, the college moved to a large, new building at 291 Sumach Street, where facilities were greatly expanded. The school now housed a lecture hall capable of seating over 50 students, microscopical and chemical laboratories, and reading rooms. The old college building became a dissecting room.

The Woman's Medical College, Toronto, was never empowered to grant degrees, but it qualified female students to sit the medical examinations at Trinity College, Victoria, and Toronto universities. Lectures and demonstrations were given at the college. Clinical instruction was provided through arrangements established with the major Toronto hospitals — Toronto General, the Hospital for Sick Children, and St. Michael's. "Special Hours" in the public wards were designated specifically for female students. Separate post-mortem classes were

The Ontario Medical College for Women,
291 Sumach Street, Toronto, Ontario.
Women's College Hospital Archives.

conducted, and segregated seating was provided in the operating theatres.[8]

Although special attention was given to ensuring that the curriculum provided was identical to that offered in medical schools for men, several features of instruction at the Woman's Medical College were unique to the institution and the medical education of women. Emphasis was placed on courses deemed "of the utmost importance to women practitioners" — gynaecology, obstetrics, and the diseases of children.[9] In an attempt to provide students with added practical experience in obstetrics, a midwifery service was established by the college in 1891. Under the supervision of the lecturer in obstetrics and an assistant accoucheur, students provided women in the community with pre- and post-natal care, and attended home births.[10] A Dispensary for Women was created in 1898 by Drs. Ida Lynd, Jennie Gray, and Susanna Boyle, graduates of the Woman's Medical College. As instructors of the college, they offered students essential clinical experience, while providing for the needs of women in the community. In the dispensary, women in their primary years of medical studies received instruction in dispensing and pharmacy, while female students in their final years assisted in clinic activities.[11]

Thus, in the process of educating women physicians, the Woman's Medical College, Toronto, initiated health care services novel for the times — medical treatment for women by members of their own sex. Furthermore, as indicated in the college's reports and references in medical journals, the midwifery and dispensary clinics were utilized most by poor and working-class women. Maternity care was provided by the school for a fee of 50 cents,[12] considerably less than the usual rate charged by most male physicians. C. Lesley Biggs noted that, in the 1870s, doctors were billing $5 to attend home births.[13] Although poor women in Toronto could use the Burnside Lying-in Hospital in the late nineteenth century, few did so, according to studies on childbirth in Ontario. Social conditions, and the fear of puerperal fever which was associated with hospitals, often kept women away.[14] It is difficult to ascertain how many expectant mothers actually took advantage of the college's maternity program. Only one annual report listed utilization rates: it showed that over a one-year period in 1898–1899, 60 women used this service.[15]

The Women's Dispensary, on the other hand, appears to have had a high volume of patients, especially considering the facilities and staffing available. In the first year of operation, 1898–99, clinics were held three days per week, and approximately 1,200 treatments were handled. Increased attendance necessitated the expansion of clinics to six days per week by 1900. By 1903–1904, annual reports recorded over 7,500 dispensary treatments.[16] As with the maternity service, special financial accommodations were made for women unable to pay. Medical advice was given free of charge, and medicaments dispensed for only a "nominal" fee.[17]

Funding for the Woman's Medical College, Toronto, came primarily from donations and students' fees. Finances, even in the best of times, were a constant source of difficulty. Faculty were not paid for most of the 23 years of the college's existence.[18] Apparently, any surplus funds were used to expand and improve facilities. In 1894, the school experienced a financial crisis. While enrolment had continued to average 11 new students per year, several of the donations promised for the upcoming session did not materialize.[19] In a bid to save the college, a major reorganization was undertaken: the school became a joint stock company, with 17 faculty members each subscribing $1000 which they held in stock. The name of the college, now incorporated, was changed to the Ontario Medical College for Women (Limited).[20] These actions coincided with the closing of the Kingston Women's Medical School. Faltering enrolments, as well as financial difficulties, had made it impossible for the Kingston college to continue. With only one women's medical school in Canada, and a new financial basis, the Toronto College was optimistic about the future. In its report for 1896, the school announced that:

> . . . a new interest has been awakened in the College, and many applications for information have been addressed to the Board giving conclusive evidence that the hopes upon which the Directors based the reorganization were on a solid foundation.[21]

Unfortunately, optimism at the college was short-lived. Despite the measures taken in 1894, economic problems persisted. The financial report for the year ending 1901 showed the school operating at a loss.[22] In addition, enrolment was beginning to decline. After peaking in 1895, with 18 new first-year students, numbers steadily dropped. From 1901 to 1905, first-year enrolment averaged only six new students per year. The reason for the decline was simple — yet ominous for the future of the women's college. At long last, medical faculties of American and

Canadian universities were beginning to admit women to co-educational programmes. In 1895, the Johns Hopkins University in Baltimore opened its doors to female medical students, as did Cornell in 1899. By the early 1900s, Canadian universities such as Western, Dalhousie, and the University of Manitoba were graduating women in medicine.

The demise of the Ontario Medical College for Women was, in a sense, inherent in its origins as a facility for equal but separate medical education for women. Although the college was affiliated with the Trinity College University from 1884 to 1906, there is not one single reference to the women's school in a comprehensive history of the Trinity Medical College written by G. Spragge.[23] In theory and practice, the future women physicians were nurtured and mentored separately and distinctly from their male colleagues. By the early 1900s, students at the Ontario Medical College for Women were increasingly questioning the logic of a university system which would permit women to sit their medical examinations under university auspices, yet ban them from the classrooms.[24] Although official regulations still barred women from studying medicine at the university, several had begun to attend medical classes in 1904 and 1905. Academic concerns were also being raised by the female students. Dr. R.B. Nevitt, dean of the Ontario Medical College for Women, reported in 1905:

> The women feel that as present situated they have not an equal opportunity with the men of becoming acquainted with the idiosyncracies of examiners, and that this loss influences their competitive standing.[25]

In 1905, as a result of the economic and enrolment problems, directors and faculty at the Ontario Medical College for Women proposed the creation of a faculty of medicine for women at the University of Toronto. They suggested that female students use all university facilities, but that their classes should continue to be segregated and taught by a separate faculty. According to the proposal, 11 instructors from the Ontario Medical College for Women (six women and five men) would form the new faculty. Dr. Augusta Stowe-Gullen was recommended for the position of dean of women.[26] The university rejected this suggestion completely and instead announced: "the Faculty of Medicine . . . is now prepared to register female students."[27]

In the spring of 1906, the Ontario Medical College for Women closed, and female students transferred to the University of Toronto. With the closing of the college, Dr. Stowe-Gullen prepared a brief history of the school wherein she concluded:

> ... let us feel no sorrow at the order of procedure ... The spirit of the age is monopolistic. Small medical, or preparatory colleges, are not consonant with prevailing thought, and their death knell has been sounded. It is conceded that the interests of the student, the profession, and the public, are best attained by university life, and university training. The greater facilities afforded, concentration of work, combined with a reduction of expenditure in time and energy, constitutes an alluring academic picture; and compensates for the loss of personal interest.[28]

But were the interests of female students, women in the profession, and women in the community, best served with the closing of the school? For women students and those in the profession, the closing of the women's medical school had particular and important ramifications. As Veronica Strong-Boag noted, the decline in the number of female physicians in the early twentieth century "was not unrelated to the closing of the Ontario Medical College for Women."[29] Quotas on female enrolment, discrimination in admission criteria, lack of adequate financial support, lack of positive reinforcement in career plans, as well as unpleasant and prejudicial attitudes in university classrooms, resulted not only in decreased numbers of female medical students, but also in deteriorated conditions of study.

Dr. Elizabeth Stewart, who graduated from the Faculty of Medicine in 1907, remembered women students as being "cordially hated" at the University of Toronto. Out of 10 women with whom she began medical studies, only four reached graduation.[30] At the Ontario Medical College for Women, six out of every 10 students graduated. Women students also lost exposure to female role models when they transferred to the university. Women physicians had instructed students at the college and dispensary. Although the Women's Dispensary continued to operate after the closing of the school, student involvement declined. Thus, emerging women doctors were faced exclusively with male teachers and mentors — many of whom were actively opposed to women in the medical profession.

For women physicians, the closing of the college represented a loss of opportunities for practical experience. Female doctors formed nearly 30 percent of the total teaching staff at the Ontario Medical

College for Women, whereas there were no female professors of medicine at the University of Toronto. Although staff on the faculty of the Ontario Medical College for Women never received salaries, and women were given lesser positions as lecturers, demonstrators, and department assistants (few ever reached the professional level), the psychological and practical benefits in terms of the teaching and clinical experience provided by the college, nevertheless was of significance when no other medical schools would hire female physicians.

Women in the community also experienced losses as a result of the closing of the Ontario Medical College for Women. The midwifery service of the obstetrics department was lost when the school closed. Fortunately, the Women's Dispensary continued to operate as an independent institution, and was eventually transformed into the Women's College Hospital in 1911.

From 1883 to 1906, the Women's Medical College, Toronto, and the Ontario Medical College for Women served the professional and educational needs of women in medicine through the only strategy available to them at the time, that of "equal but separate" medical education. During this period, they graduated 111 female physicians. The impact of these women's medical schools on female members of the profession and on women's health was of significance. But what of their effect on medical education and the practice of medicine?

The Ontario Medical College for Women appeared at the time to have little impact on the medical profession. Restrictive policies on female enrolment in medical programs at the university were removed through pressure exerted by women students themselves. Women entering medical training after 1906, as students in the Faculty of Medicine of the University of Toronto, were faced once again by male faculty and students, who expressed hostile attitudes towards them. Hospitals and medical faculties persistently refused to appoint women to staff positions, despite the growth in the number of female doctors.

Notwithstanding, the Toronto and Kingston women's medical colleges were key events in the evolution of the medical profession in Canada. Together with the women's suffrage movement, the movement for higher education, the earliest women physicians, the graduates of the women's medical schools, and the few men who fought for co-education, the colleges stimulated the development of full and equal education for women in all disciplines including medical science. Moreover, the women's medical colleges helped lay the foundation in a number of important branches of public health and preventive medicine by providing the early medical training of women who would pioneer in these fields. While gender-separatism in medical education did not erode all the obstacles confronting women in medicine, it nevertheless marked the permanent entry and presence of women in the medical professions.

ERNST W. STIEB, GAIL C. COULAS and JOYCE A. FERGUSON,
assisted by ROBERT J. CLARK and ROY W. HORNOSTY

Women in Ontario Pharmacy, 1867–1927

Women wishing to enter pharmacy in nineteenth-century Ontario apparently did not encounter the obstacles faced by their counterparts in the other traditionally male-dominated health professions.[1] At the Ontario College of Pharmacy (OCP), in Toronto, the first woman attended the school during the spring of 1883, after the teaching institution had been established on a permanent basis for only a year. The number of women in the school remained small until after the First World War, with only some 40 identified for the period, 1883 to 1918. The contrast with today's situation is startling. For the past decade, women have constituted approximately two-thirds of the student body in the Faculty of Pharmacy at the University of Toronto, with more than 100 graduating each year. That is, all the female graduates combined of the first 35 years of the school would constitute only about 40 percent of the number of women in a single class today.

Although the first woman attended the teaching school of OCP in 1883, women had previously practiced pharmacy in Ontario. Between 1871, the founding of the OCP, and 1882, the establishment of the first formal school, some women had taken the OCP licensing examinations, and a few practiced prior to 1871. Because the earliest organizational records begin in the year of Canadian confederation, 1867, documentation about women in pharmacy is sketchy before confederation.[2]

There is a curious reference to a woman pharmacist in Niagara, in 1832, in a letter from Mrs. William Radcliff writing from Upper Canada (Ontario) to her husband in Dublin:

> Physicians are very much wanting here, and apothecaries still more. Ignorant persons act in that capacity, who scarcely know the name of the drugs they sell. At Niagara that most necessary branch is solely conducted by a female, who compounds medicines and puddings with equal confidence, but not equal skill.[3]

Certainly in 1832, there was no legislation that effectively controlled either medicine or pharmacy in what is now Ontario, although there were at least three pharmacies in Niagara. One, established by a doctor, had been taken over by his wife, possibly the woman mentioned by Mrs. Radcliff.

The emergence of women in a profession is a multi-faceted process, which needs to be studied in the context of social, economic, and historical developments. In Ontario (and Canada as a whole), the change relative to pharmacy is currently proceeding more rapidly than in any other health profession. This dramatic reversal of sex composition has come largely during the past decade,[4] but the beginnings of this trend reside in the late nineteenth century. One can merely speculate about some of the developments, and the available sources often permit us to do little more than that.

For a wide variety of reasons, involving class and economics, the working woman was not socially accepted during the Victorian decades; the roles of wife and mother were the principal ones assigned to women in a male-dominated society. Even at the beginning of the twentieth century, "women suffered from a host of fears and built-in [social constraints] that curbed [personal] initiative."[5] In the 1890s, women began to be accepted as cashiers, bookkeepers, clerks, and sales persons; they worked mostly in the garment industry, domestic service, teaching, office work, and food industries. One of the most striking characteristics of the female labour force was its fragmentation: of the nearly 90 occupations employing more than one woman in 1891 in Toronto, approximately one-quarter employed fewer than five women.[6] While women of the poorer and middle classes increasingly took their places in various occupations during the nineteenth century, and while the depletion of the male labour force during the First World War opened new opportunities for them in the 1920s, they still suffered owing to various forms of patriarchal authority in the workforce, if not in the family.[7]

In view of the historical context, the entry of women into Ontario pharmacy appeared to be relatively easy, although that may be attributed to a number of factors. Our records suggest certain explanations for the contrast with the medical profession in particular: a comparatively enlightened attitude within pharmacy; the absence of specific prohibitions, which existed in other countries and in other health professions; the economic advantages, especially in rural settings, of husband-wife, father-daughter teams, sometimes involving a physician as one of the partners; the manpower situation; and the participation of women in organizational affairs of pharmacy at an early stage. Even some of the rather chauvinistic comments found in the contemporary literature can be judged progressive by the general standards of the time.

Five women were on the first register for the OCP in 1871: E. Adamson of Oil Springs, Martha M. Gordon of Port Colborne, Mary Anne Kane of Amherstburg, Isa(bella) Parker of Owen Sound, and Mary Ann Wade of Port Stanley.[8] In the cases of Mary Anne Kane, Isa(bella) Parker, and Mary Ann Wade, there was a male of the same family name in the same town on the register of the OCP and/or on the membership list of the Canadian Pharmaceutical Society (C.Ph.S.).[9] It is difficult to determine from extant manuscript and printed records how long these women may have been in practice before they joined the OCP in 1871. It would appear that Kane and Parker joined the C.Ph.S. as early as 1868.[10] The only clue we have is a note in the November, 1896, issue of the *Canadian Pharmaceutical Journal*, indicating that Mrs. Kane had moved her premises and, tangentially, that she had been in business for 30 years (i.e. from about 1866). The note also refers to her as "one of the lady pharmacists of the province," which seems to imply that there were so few of the species particularly owning and managing their own practices, that the fact deserved mention with such a descriptive phrase.[11] Ironically and inexplicably, however, the OCP register of the period shows Mrs. Kane going out of business earlier the same year.[12]

Mrs. Kane, as well as Mrs. Adamson, were also among the first women to run for the OCP Council; Mrs. Kane twice, in 1879 and 1881, and Mrs. Adamson in 1881. (There had been a third woman nominated in 1881, who had declined the nomination.) The 13 candidates with the

Architectural drawing of the first permanent home of the Ontario
College of Pharmacy, 44 Gerrard Street East, Toronto, Ontario, 1887.
Courtesy of E. Stieb.

most votes were considered elected. In 1879, Mrs. Kane, with 51 votes, stood twenty-first in a field of 32. In 1881, Mrs. Kane, with 54 votes, stood twenty-seventh in a field of 43 candidates, while Mrs. Adamson trailed her by two places and two votes, standing twenty-ninth with 52 votes. None of the announcements or discussion about the elections paid any special attention to the distinction of male versus female. What is more remarkable is that the women were able to garner as many votes as they did. According to our estimates, there was a maximum of seven women in practice at this time, which suggests considerable confidence on the part of their male peers for them to elicit this kind of support.[13]

Although the sample is admittedly very small, it is clear that all five women were from small towns rather than cities, and that, in every case but one, they were married. In all but one case, they were married to pharmacists who can also be identified among the registers or membership lists of the period. In the case of Mrs. Kane, it appears that she operated the pharmacy alone for all except the first few years. It was not uncommon for women to take over a pharmacy when a husband or father died. Indeed, the practice suggests there may have been economic advantage or necessity behind such arrangements.[14] Also, there may have been greater social acceptability in rural communities for working women, including those who were married. The small town aspect appears to predominate throughout the nineteenth century, and indeed, right up to the First World War. In addition to the five women identified as practicing pharmacy in 1871, there were four who attended the OCP and another seven who qualified for licensure without attending the school in the period from 1871 until 1900. In the latter group, only three were married women, and only one of the group was from other than a small town, and she was married to, or was the daughter of, a physician who had served as her preceptor. Apprenticeship with a member of the family was also a common practice at this time, and it continued into the early part of the twentieth century. When the family member was also a physician, this practice undoubtedly offered even greater economic and social advantages. One of the women who registered without attending the OCP school, Helen E. Reynolds-Ryan, was herself a physician — a rarity at this time. However, she maintained her pharmacy registration for only a few years.[15]

During the sixty-year period covered by our study (1867–1927), slightly more than 10 percent of the women identified appear to have been in practice with a relative, and a like proportion apprenticed with a relative. Furthermore, approximately the same size group appeared to be related to, apprenticed with, or working with physicians. Equally interesting is the fact that the family names begin to repeat themselves (there were six sets of sisters), as do the names of individuals and pharmacies linked with these female pharmacists. What we lack for the moment is an indication of how the female picture compared with the male as far as some of these dynasties of pharmacists are concerned.

The first woman to attend the OCP school (established in 1882) was Jessie G. McCallum of New Hamburg, Ontario. The extant information about her is scant. The records show that she was apprenticed to an F.H. McCallum, and that she applied to take the licensing examinations of OCP in December of 1883. Unfortunately, her name does not appear among the 32 successful candidates in a field of 57. Moreover, there is nothing further about her in surviving OCP records. There is a little information about her preceptor, presumably her father, F.H. McCallum. He joined the Canadian Pharmaceutical Society (C.Ph.S.), the lineal predecessor to the OCP, in August 1868 as an assistant. He was then identified as being from Toronto. At the time he joined the OCP in June, 1871, just after it had been created by the first Ontario Pharmacy Act, he was shown as being from New Hamburg.[16]

The standard academic program that Jessie McCallum took in the spring of 1883 consumed the brief period from March 13 to June 15. Classes were held mostly in the mornings, to permit those with appropriate arrangements to continue working and/or apprenticing in pharmacy. For a fee of $36, she received instruction in pharmaceutical and practical chemistry (lectures and laboratory), materia medica (lectures), botany (lectures), dispensing (practical), and elementary chemistry (lectures).[17]

Of the three women who followed Jessie McCallum at the OCP school before 1900, one, Mary Hattie Alexandria Johnson, has the distinction of being the first woman identified as an honorary class officer — she was honorary vice-president for the graduating class of 1897.[18] She also has the questionable honour of being the first woman to benefit from expenditures for a "lady student," reported at the February 1896 meeting of OCP Council, namely a brush and comb, wash stand, glass, toilet set, table cover, and carpeting, all for a grand total of $16.73.[19] Of those four women who attended the teaching college, the first three evidently did not pass the OCP licensing examinations; the last, Hattie Johnson, passed the examinations, but there is no record that she became registered, at least under her maiden name. The change in name is one of the problems associated with interpreting data relative to this subject. The failure to become registered after completing the educational requirements is puzzling, unless this step was not considered essential in those instances where women were associated with a family practice operated by a relative.

Although there was very little delay from the time when the educational program was established, in 1882, at the OCP, until the first woman enrolled in 1883, fully a decade passed after the Phm.B. degree became available on an optional basis, in 1892, before a woman earned that degree, in 1902. The honour belongs to Miss Kate H. Mac-Crimmon, of Ripley, whose preceptor appears to have been her physician father. Miss MacCrimmon, like Hattie Johnson before her, was also elected honourary vice-president of her class. Miss MacCrimmon also had the distinction of having had classmates of her own gender, Miss Alice S. Curry (also elected an honorary vice-president), of Minden, and Miss Alpha J. Yeomans, of Mount Forest, both of whom also appear to have apprenticed under their fathers.

During the period from 1900 to the beginning of the First World War, in 1914, 23 women enrolled at the OCP (compared to four between 1882 and 1900); 13, or slightly more than one-half of the women enrolled, earned the Phm.B. During the considerably shorter period of the war itself, 1914–1918, 14 women (including the first two nuns) attended, and 10 of them earned the Phm.B. During this latter period, at least half the women in pharmacy seemed to be from larger cities rather than small towns, which had been the general rule previously. This phenomenon was undoubtedly encouraged by the temporary loss from pharmacy of those pharmacists who enlisted in the armed forces and went overseas. It also paralleled the increasing participation of women during the twentieth century in all areas of public life.[20] From the end of the First World War to 1927, the last year of the one-year program, approximately 94 women attended the OCP school, and of these, 65, or approximately 70 percent, earned their Phm.B. degrees. Thus, for the period 1882–1927 approximately 135 women attended the OCP school, mostly after 1900, and about 88 or two-thirds, earned the Phm.B. Remarkably, there were more than twice as many women (94 versus 41) attending during the period 1918–1927 than during the entire period from 1882 to that time — a span of time four times as long (nine years versus 36).

In the United States, as in Canada, there were certainly some women practicing pharmacy before the first schools of pharmacy opened, or accepted female students. Elizabeth Greenleaf established a pharmacy in Boston as early as 1726 or 1727, and Elizabeth Marshall owned and operated her family's well-known pharmacy in Philadelphia from about 1804 onward. The first woman to graduate from an American school of pharmacy was Mary C. Putnam (Jacoby), from the New York College of Pharmacy, in 1863. Other individuals are identifiable in the 1870s, but before the 1880s, they appear to have been the exception rather than the rule. The first explicit notices welcoming women appeared in calendars of pharmacy schools in the 1880s, probably as an aftermath of the conclusion of the 1879 meeting of the American Conference of Pharmaceutical Faculties (predecessor to the present AACP), indicating that schools of pharmacy no longer saw any reason why women should not be admitted. Although there were regional variations, the number of women enrolled increased steadily as the century progressed, with an estimated 1,000 to 1,500 women attending American schools of pharmacy during the century. Still, women constituted fewer than five percent of American pharmacy students at the end of the century.[21] That percentage doubled between 1927 and 1936.[22]

Indeed, by the time of the First World War, the number of women in schools of pharmacy in the United States had apparently become large enough to encourage the formation of the first sororities for women in pharmacy. Thus, Lambda Kappa Sigma was founded about 1917–18, and Kappa Epsilon shortly afterward, in 1921.[23] While the sororities survived, some other manifestations of the increasing role of women in American pharmacy disappeared when women really came into their own, and no longer represented a curious anomaly. The Women's section of the American Pharmaceutical Association (A.Ph.A.) is a case in point. Established in 1913, it was disbanded in 1922 for fear of appearing to discriminate. The A.Ph.A.'s record had been exemplary. The first woman joined in 1882, and a woman was first elected to office (third vice-president) in 1895.[24]

With minor exceptions, women gained admission to schools of pharmacy on the European continent mainly in the 1890s.[25] In Britain, the doors to the school of the Pharmaceutical Society opened officially to women in 1872, having been closed tight during the previous decade, after the unofficial attendance by one woman in 1862. Registration with the society was another matter, with the first female registrant being recognized in 1879, four years after she completed the requirements.[26]

Seen within the context of developments in the United States and Britain, that is, open acceptance by the 1880s, it is perhaps not so surprising that women seem to have been accepted into the teaching school of OCP as early as 1883. However, their registration to practice in Ontario by 1871, and perhaps their actual practice as early as the 1830s, suggests that their position in the profession was established in Ontario before it was in Britain. Indeed, we may recall that while the Pharmaceutical Society of Great Britain admitted the first woman to membership only in 1879, a woman member of OCP was that same year already running for a council seat, with significant support.

Considering how few women did attend pharmacy school in Ontario during the early years, it is surprising that there were not more references to that fact — that is, the novelty or rarity of the situation — either in the journals, or in the reports of the deans, or in the notes of student activities. One student, however, does appear to have made an impression on her classmates, and that was Mary D. Vail, of Toronto, who was in the junior term in the fall of 1900. She did not return to do the senior term in the spring of 1901, because she had yet to complete her apprenticeship. "The absence of Miss Vail," wrote a student correspondent, "is a source of regret. However, her bright and sunny face haunts us still, though we are denied the honour of singing 'Just one girl at the OCP' "[27] Not only was she chosen honorary vice-president of the class, but she was also elected vice-president of the football team![28] An earlier entry in "College Notes," ventured only that one of "the gentler sex" was among those in attendance during the fall term of 1887.[29] It is true that there was usually a toast proposed to the ladies at some of the early banquets, but we suspect this was of a generic type, like that offered in February, 1883, which simply exhorted: "God bless them! The longer we live, the better we like them."[30]

Edward B. Shuttleworth editorialized on the subject of women in pharmacy in the *Canadian Pharmaceutical Journal* in December, 1872. He did so by way of response to the official admission of women to the school of the Pharmaceutical Society of Great Britain after a ten-year ban. The sentiments expressed in the editorial are so unusual for the time, that we may be forgiven for quoting at some length:

If we are to have lady doctors, we do not see how anyone can offer any consistent opposition to lady pharmacists. If their qualifications to practice either of these callings or professions be guaranteed by their submitting to the same educational tests as men, we may consent to leave the consideration of sex out of the question. It is, however, necessary that these conditions be rigidly carried out in one case as the other, and to this end it is only right that equal educational facilities should be allowed.

Unfortunately, Shuttleworth went on for a paragraph too long and revealed himself to be still a Victorian gentleman, if a somewhat enlightened one:

We do not think that lady pharmacists will ever be a very numerous class. Our churlish bachelors may rest perfectly easy on that score. No department of labor, or sphere in life, seems so adapted to females as the domestic, and generally speaking, ladies, themselves, are not slow in finding this out. It has almost invariably been found, by those who have experience in these matters, that however proficient a female may become in any avocation, she seldom becomes attached to it to such a degree that she will not desert if for the charms of the domestic hearth . . . But . . . the mothers of our children, will, at least, be none the worse for their knowledge of the virtues of the *elixir paregoricum*, or the regulating qualities of *pulvis Gregorii*.[31]

A few years later, in 1879, as the British Pharmaceutical Society debated whether to admit women as members, and thus, practitioners, Shuttleworth was again moved to comment in a similar vein:

The practice of the profession of pharmacy, requires, above all, a mind stored with hard-edged facts; a judgement sober and matured; a manner free from all impetuosity; and habits accurate and precise. These, as well all must know, are very strongly marked characteristics of the daughters of Eve.

But again, he goes on a bit too long and a bit too patronizingly in linking these admirable qualities with innate characteristics inherited from Eve![32]

How much Shuttleworth's views may have mellowed, or how much they depended upon circumstances, is difficult to determine. In 1870, in a brief review of a new woman's journal, he categorically stated that he "didn't believe in Women's Rights."[33] Yet, a few years later, he was writing as already noted, and commenting on the "gallantry" of one American school (1881–82) and of the Pharmaceutical Society of Ireland (1875–76) which opened their doors to women, while pointing to the lack of it on the part of the British Society, which refused to do so (1875–76).[34]

Also somewhat chauvinistic in tone, is a report on a survey conducted during the summer of 1883 by the Toronto *Evening News*, concerning women in pharmacy. The conclusion reached after talking to some Toronto pharmacists was that there was indeed a place for women, because women customers would usually prefer to deal with another woman, and "in ordinary cases, men would rather be served by a nice-looking woman." The editorial writer in the *Canadian Pharmaceutical Journal*, responding to the story, agreed with the comments, but felt that there were some disadvantages to having women pharmacists: "We fear that pretty drug clerks would quickly be taken from behind the counter and placed before the altar, and no doubt very careful wives and capable mothers would they make."[35]

More than a quarter of a century later, at the dawn of the Edwardian age, the philosophy appears to have changed only slightly. W.J. Dyas mused in the *Canadian Druggist*:

The present age is one in which women are striving for and securing prominent positions in the various professions. It is doubtful if any professional pursuit of a business character is more congenial to a woman's temperament than that of pharmacy. The amount of study needed to fit her for its practice is quite within her capabilities; the labor involved in the pursuit of it is not arduous, and the tasty character of the work is such as to make it attractive for her. The long hours are the only drawback, and these are equally objectionable to men as to women. In fact women who are accustomed to household duties are apt to think less of this objection than men are.

While not desiring to advocate that our young women should seek to enter this field of duty, we are personally convinced that in many respects women are better adapted for work of this kind than men. It is well known that men have never shown comparative skill with women in the pursuit of nursing, where attention and strict observance of the physician's instructions are necessary. These qualities are equally needed behind the drug counter, and we feel sure that none of our male friends would attempt to deny that they could be equally exhibited there by the female sex.

This article also ends with what many supporters of women's rights today might consider to be a questionable compliment:

It must be said, to the credit of our college boys, that they are exceedingly chivalrous in their treatment of the lady undergraduates who take the course with them, and no one will be more willing to accord credit to a lady graduate who is successful in taking a high position than they.[36]

By the last year of the First World War however, the tone had changed considerably, at least as far as some men were concerned. "Women in pharmacy is now an accomplished fact," began one editorial, then continued, "and the keen desire of the close observer is that this condition become permanent . . . it is most desirable that women become permanently interested in the craft."[37] After going into some detail about the admirable qualities that suited women to the task, the writer concluded: "we have in woman the ideal pharmacist of the twentieth century, and one of the most desirable by-products of the war."[38]

However, another article written about the same time about the suitability in pharmacies of female clerks, also occasioned by the wartime shortage of male assistants, dwells more upon the superior ability of women to make sales of articles about which they might be expected to have a personal knowledge. Taken from the *Red Cross Messenger*, and entitled "Pharmacy in Skirts," the article (reprinted in the *Canadian Pharmaceutical Journal*) suggested that one benefit of the change would be "more artistically dressed windows, better arranged showcases and stores that will have a greater appeal to women."[39] To that writer, the ideals of female domesticity still appear to be a major reason for accepting women in pharmacy. A disturbingly similar philosophy is still being voiced by a writer in 1923, close to the end of the period under discussion here. The writer dismisses medicine, dentistry, surgery, engineering, and law as unsuitable for women for various reasons. From the suggestion that a woman's place is really in the home, he proceeds to argue that this makes them ideally suited for pharmacy . . . presumably because they would always be on the premises ready to serve. He then goes on to argue that the best possible combination was a woman pharmacist married to a physician, because she could not only best meet his needs in their professional dealings, but could also enhance "her husband's good standing in the community."[40] The concluding paragraph perhaps says it all: "Women, married or unmarried, should be in the house. Pharmacy requires you to be in, for the hours of the day. Why, ladies, should you not pursue this profession?"[41] While there were no letters to the editor responding to this philosophy, it is interesting to speculate what women then in practice or in the OCP school must have thought. Of the 10 women in the class of 1924, when this article appeared, two stood in the upper 20 percent of the class, and one of these earned the top prize for biology.[42] However women in pharmacy may have been perceived in Ontario in the late 1920s, it is clear that more and more of them decided that pharmacy was a suitable profession for them. That trend has continued to the present time.

DIANNE DODD

Women in Advertising: The Role of Canadian Women in the Promotion of Domestic Electrical Technology in the Interwar Period

The assumption that technology is now and has always been an exclusively male creation is at last being questioned,[1] particularly in the area of domestic technology, which has a direct impact on women's work in the home. This study of women's contribution to technological development impinging upon the private sphere is of necessity focused on advertising and promotion, as women have been largely excluded from the engineering side. Initial studies of industry and advertising in the 1920s and 1930s, when consumer capitalism was consolidated, have tended to portray the vulnerable woman consumer as the pawn of the capitalist[2] with advertising women abandoning the feminist aspirations of an earlier generation and serving as the handmaidens of capitalism.[3] The following analysis of the advertising message which advertising women helped formulate, and examination of their role in industry will, it is hoped, revise this initial impression of women's alliance with industry in the promotion of domestic electrical technology.

Women clearly made a significant, although unrecognized, contribution to the dissemination of a technology which they believed to be of value to women. But more than promoting the practical benefits of domestic technology for their male colleagues in industry as part of the general strategy of democratized consumption,[4] advertising women added a unique gender perspective to the advertising message, which amalgamated an acceptance of the sexual division of labour and the male monopoly on technology with demands for recognition of the value of domestic labour, improved status, and increased financial autonomy within marriage for the homemaker. Women's marginal position in the advertising industry and their genuine, though sometimes failed, attempts to represent women's interests to industry, are clearly revealed in advertising industry journals where women were critical of their own industry.

Advertisements in popular Canadian women's magazines with national circulation, such as *Chatelaine, Maclean's* women's pages, and the *Canadian Home Journal*, were examined. As the circulation of these magazines increased three- or even four-fold between 1920 and 1934,[5] advertisers began to appeal to larger segments of the Canadian population with their message of consumption. As well, advertising and electrical industry journals were used,[6] including one major American advertising journal, *Printers' Ink*. Owing in large part to the Americanization of the Canadian economy, the Canadian industry served largely to modify the American manufacturers' message for the Canadian audience[7] and failed to develop an independent approach.

Although electrical appliances are by no means the totality of domestic technology, they are important by virtue of their versatility and availability. Electricity was applied to almost all of the work processes in the home which were amenable to mechanization, including cooking, food preparation and preservation, cleaning, and laundry. As a technology crucial to the industrialized world in the interwar period,[8] which also provided increasingly inexpensive material comforts in the home, electricity was popular. And, as rates of electrification increased rapidly — by 1939 62 percent of Canadian homes (predominantly urban) were electrified[9] — the use of domestic electrical appliances also increased. In Ontario for example, the market saturation[10] of irons rose from 89.2 percent in 1924 to 99.8 percent in 1938, and washing machines rose from 15.8 percent to 51.2 percent in the same period.[11] As demand for appliances increased prices fell. Although Canadians enjoyed cheap and abundant power, the rate of electrification was not uniform. Urban industrialized areas enjoyed a sizable advantage, with Ontario and British Columbia leading the way.[12]

EMANCIPATION

THE first great step towards the lightening of household labour was the introduction of running water into the house. The second step was the installation of electricity. Countless comforts and conveniences are thus placed at the command of the women of our Dominion.

Merely the turn of a knob—and the modern electric washing machine pulsates with life and sets about its task. Merely the flick of a switch, and—. smoothly, quickly, quietly—The many "wheels" of housekeeping begin to turn; ironing, cooking, cleaning. Merely the touch of a button and the rooms are flooded with light.

One of the many services performed by the Northern Electric Company is the distribution of dependable electrical "servants" for the home.

In some of the Old World countries the women still kneel to scour their clothes in the streams.

Northern Electric
COMPANY LIMITED
A National Electrical Service

INFORMATION

The Northern Electric Company manufactures the telephone and its accessories, wires and cables for the transmission of power, fire alarm systems, public address systems, and talking motion picture apparatus.

FIGURE I

Advertisement. *Maclean's*, 15 March 1930.

VISION

Canadian Hydro Plants Captivate
the Imagination of the World

FEW people realize the speed with which Canada is leaping forward into the new electrical era.

Among the numerous hydro-electric developments under way in Canada, two, by their magnitude, have captivated the imagination of the world.

One is at Queenstown on the Niagara River, where the Ontario Hydro-Electric Power Commission is completing the installation of a plant totalling over 500,000 h.p. The other, at the head of the Saguenay River, will have an ultimate capacity of 1,280,000 h.p., of which a large amount will be used in a new industry to be established there—the manufacture of aluminum.

The mighty force of Niagara everybody knows, but few realize the force of the Saguenay. This river in northeastern Quebec is the single outlet of five large and many smaller rivers which run into Lake St. John. This mighty flood pours through the tumultuous Grand Discharge, rushing down over 300 feet to sea level—equal to the drop at Niagara—and flowing a thousand feet deep for sixty miles to the St. Lawrence, to be lifted bodily out of its bed by great engineering works that harness its powers.

This work means the establishment in Canada of another centre of hydro-electric energy comparable to that of Niagara!

For thirty-five years it has been the function of the Northern Electric Company to manufacture and make available the means of transmitting and distributing electrical energy in every form. In the Canada of the future we look forward to an opportunity for even greater service to the public.

Northern Electric
COMPANY LIMITED
Equipment for transmitting Sound and Power

Information

Hydro-electric development in Canada represents a total investment estimated at $767,000,000. At present rate of progress this total will reach $1,750,000,000 by 1940.

This is number 15 of a series of advertisements issued in the interest of Canada's electrical development.

FIGURE 2

Advertisement. *Maclean's*, 15 April 1926.

Although women did have some input into the design and manufacture of domestic electrical technology in an advisory capacity,[13] their input was channelled predominantly into the area of advertising, promotion, and marketing. In contrast to the engineers who designed appliances and were given full credit for their creation,[14] the women who merely promoted them were marginalized. Women were excluded from male advertising clubs, being forced to form separate women's clubs,[15] and were notably absent from such professions as electrical engineering. The *Canadian Home Journal* gave little encouragement to women contemplating an engineering career, noting that "at least two of our most famous Canadian colleges refuse to accept women in the Faculty of Applied Science and Engineering."[16] It was also reported that the only woman member of the Junior Branch of the Electric Institute was Hazel M. White, an employee of Northern Electric, who had taught school at the beginning of her career, "as the idea of a woman doing electrical engineering was considered preposterous."[17]

As few sources remain which give insight into the private thoughts and feelings of advertising women, relatively little is known about these educated middle-class women who came to their profession from a variety of fields,[18] many with training in domestic science or home economics. Some were former teachers, sales clerks, stenographers, or newspaper writers. In 1938, the *Canadian Home Journal* advised young women hoping to break into this "glamorous" profession that they would need a university degree, some business training, as well as good breeding, energy, and ambition. Many were single, however there appear to have been some who combined traditional homemaking with a career.[19]

As in all highly competitive fields, the successful were handsomely rewarded, but most women who worked at the lower levels of the advertising industry, merely earned a respectable living.[20] Women worked as copywriters, researchers, space buyers, and other consultants; some worked freelance, while others were employed directly by advertising agencies, or worked for the advertising departments of manufacturing firms, newspapers, or large retail stores.

Women's numerically-strong presence in the advertising industry was a by-product of the early twentieth-century realization that women did most of the family purchasing.[21] The need to win over "Mrs. Consumer," as she was dubbed, left an obvious role for educated professional women to play in advising industry and its advertisers on what women wanted and how best to appeal to them. Women's domestic expertise gave them their primary qualification, as "women can frequently give the feminine slant when writing of things pertaining to their own sphere that are outside of a man's personal experience."[22] Given the rigidity of the sexual division of labour in the early twentieth century, few men could claim such expertise while practically all women could.

Besides interpreting women's interests to industry, advertising women also promoted advertising among other women, using their links with women's clubs and associations. The Women's Advertising Club of Toronto, Canada's first such club, was formed in 1933. In 1936, it presented a playlet to various women's groups entitled "Mrs. Consumer Looks at Advertising." The play emphasized the "service rendered by advertising in cutting costs to the consumer, assuring quality, creating employment and a higher standard of living."[23]

Why did these women propagandize advertising to women? Did they, like many of their contemporaries, believe in the benefits of technology which industry, through advertising, promised to bring to an increasing number of Canadians, or did they deliberately mislead Canadian women? While historians now agree that domestic technology has eliminated drudgery[24] and has had a homogenizing effect on the class structure, it is also true that technology de-skilled the housewife, devalued her labour, and increased her dependency on large economic/technological systems.[25] Neither has technology fully delivered on its promise of leisure for women, owing to rising standards of health, cleanliness, childcare, and family privacy.[26] Can we assume that the promoters of domestic technology foresaw these mixed blessings, or even if they had, would not have judged them to be worth the price?

Advertising women's support for democratized consumption should not be seen as a repudiation of the pre-First World War women's movement, which had sought, among other reforms, professionalization of homemaking through the application of science and technology to household management.[27] Middle-class Canadian women's organizations promoted domestic reform, in part through the teaching of domestic science in Canadian schools, and became involved in consumer advocacy.[28] Advertising women shared with these maternal feminist predecessors the desire to apply science and technology to domestic labour, and to give women a voice in the way goods were packaged, marketed, advertised, and priced. By the 1920s, the domestic reform movement had become institutionalized in the home economics profession, and had allied with business in applying technological resources to the home. Advertising women did not abandon the goals of domestic reform; however, they did adopt the business strategy of democratized consumption as a means to that end.

For some of these professional women, who do appear to have been much more enthusiastic about domestic technology than traditional homemakers, it offered an opportunity to combine careers and home-making. While advertisers exaggerated the servant shortage with depictions of the "servantless home," it was clear to observers that the availability of full-time live-in helpers would continue to decline, as it had from the 1890s to the 1920s.[29] Domestic technology helped make domestic labour palatable for the middle-class housewife, and made more effective use of the limited domestic labour available. Domestic technology not only addressed the problems of middle-class profes-sional women, however; it also offered working-class women, whom industry increasingly tried to reach by the 1930s, true labour saving and an elevated standard of living.

Domestic technology offered enough benefits, both to its promoters and potential users, to ensure the support of advertising women. Although advertising women were much more critical of the advertis-ing fraternity in industry journals than in popular magazines, which received a large measure of their revenue from advertising, in neither medium did they question the beneficial impact of labour-saving domestic technology. One professional woman, writing for *Printers' Ink* told advertisers:

> We women take off our hats to all these wonderful household helps. We extol the minds that invented them, and bless the advertisers who bring them to our notice.[30]

Mabel Crews Ringland, a freelance advertiser, household advisor for T. Eaton Co., and prominent industry author, stated that women were also entitled to the benefits of progressive obsolescence. If men could scrap their battleships and cars before their use was exhausted, in favour of the latest technological developments, then women should be able to do the same with appliances,[31] she felt. While advertising women may have had reservations about individual gadgets, many of which were of marginal value, domestic technology as a whole appears to have been sacrosanct. It is not surprising, then, that the exaggerated claims and frivolous sales strategies some manufacturers used in promoting products angered women.

Advertising women also felt that the educational value of advertising had been amply demonstrated in the dissemination of information on the nutritive value of foods, the role of germs in the spread of disease, and so on.[32] This could hardly be denied. Ideally, women hoped that advertising would live up to its educational potential by providing women with enough product information to enable them to make buying decisions on the basis of product characteristics and their own needs and income — just as professional buyers did for their employers in industry and government.

Advertisers quickly learned to exploit the popularity of technology, particularly domestic technology. The strategy of democratized consumption, although it appealed to business interests as a measure of social control designed to placate worker unrest and expand markets,[33] also appealed on a more popular level to the faith in technology as a leveller of class distinctions, fueled by the tremendous technological breakthroughs of the late nineteenth and the early twentieth centuries.[34] In a series of ads in the 1920s, jointly sponsored by the Association of Canadian Advertisers and the Canadian Association of Advertising Agencies,[35] industry promised that advertising would stimulate demand, making possible mass production and ever falling prices for increasingly sophisticated goods. In its institutional ads, the electrical industry also linked itself to the promise of greater prosperity and equality,[36] but emphasized home enhancement. Canadian General Electric, for example, asserted that the luxuries of ancient kings faded into insignificance beside the comforts made possible in Canadian homes by the flip of a switch.[37] Of course, greater democratization of wealth would come, not through redistribution, but growth in overall prosperity; the lowly worker was offered a chance to aspire to standards set by former elites.

As well, the advertisers suggested that the worker's wife, as a result of his greater prosperity, could be liberated from domestic drudgery (*Figure 1*). Women were thus offered the opportunity to have a role outside the home on par with wealthier women.[38] In the general advertising message, however, women's liberation was never more than a sub-theme. Sexual equality was equated with relief from manual labour, and even this limited emancipation was clearly subordinate to

FIGURE 3

Advertisement. *Maclean's,* 15 May 1938.

First aid
to mothers in safeguarding baby's health

Frigidaire reduces risks that come with sultry days . . . .

The Frigidaire Cold Control
A development of Frigidaire and General Motors engineers.

"Watch baby's health in summer!" Down through the ages grandmothers passed this warning on to mothers. For with summer came the dangerous "critical period."

For years mothers faced warm weather with dread. The dangers that confronted their children in summer were *mysterious* dangers. They knew not *what* to guard against.

But how different it is today. There's nothing mysterious now about the risks that come with summer. It's simply that foods spoil more quickly and bacteria develop more rapidly. And to meet these risks, health authorities everywhere pre-scribe better refrigeration.

You can provide this better refrigeration with Frigidaire . . . the automatic refrigerator which is powerful enough to keep food at temperatures well below 50 degrees . . . always.

Power that gives a wide margin of safety

Frigidaire operates automatically. It has a wide range of *surplus power* . . . power that keeps foods fresh and wholesome . . . power that safeguards health day and night, summer and winter . . . unfailingly.

This surplus power means added safety . . . the difference between certainty and doubt . . . and as more than 750,000 Frigidaire users will tell you . . . a feeling of security beyond all price. Call at the nearest Frigidaire display room and see the exclusive features of Frigidaire, including the new Cold Control . . . find out about the low prices and the liberal G.M.A.C. terms.

Safe and unsafe refrigeration explained in free book . . . write for it

We have prepared a new book that explains the dangers of inadequate refrigeration and tells how they may be avoided. It is illustrated with photographs taken through a microscope. Mail the coupon for a copy of this book . . . today. Frigidaire Corporation, Subsidiary of General Motors Corporation, Toronto, Ontario.

Frigidaire Corporation,
Sterling Tower, Toronto, Ont.

Please send me your book on healthful refrigeration, also the Frigidaire Recipe Book.

Name.....................................

Address..................................

Town...................Prov.........

FRIGIDAIRE
The QUIET *Automatic Refrigerator*

FIGURE 4

Advertisement. *Maclean's*, 1 July 1929.

the more important goal of class equality.

The benefits of technology did not come without a price, of course. The advertising images of womens' and workers' former enslavement contrast sharply with the new vision of freedom and comfort, placing the male fraternity of scientists/engineers in the role of knights in shining armour. In the advertisement in *Figure 2*, the message of prosperity was accompanied by an illustration of "progress" personified in a young woman, seated at a crystal ball glowing with visions of a bright future, while four very scientific-technical looking experts (all male) stood behind her. As one Canadian General Electric advertisement which encouraged "electric-minded" young men to go into the electrical field[39] implied, electrical technology was a male preserve.

Despite these limitations, women ensured that gender issues were addressed in the advertising message. As authorship of advertisements is never revealed, it is impossible to tell which ads were written by women; however, their presence can be felt in the advertising messages' subordinate, but no less real, gender perspective. This sensitivity to gender issues within the family was clearly more prevalent in advertisements for specific appliances which were directed at women than in "lifestyle" advertisements directed at both sexes, or in ads for higher-priced items, such as ranges and refrigerators. Advertising women did promote domestic technology for all of the obvious material benefits of comfort, cleanliness, health, convenience, leisure, and the ability to cope with the "servantless home." However, they also contributed to the general advertising message of prosperity and class equality with their own unique philosophy of "equality of spheres." Accepting the sexual division of labour and the male monopoly on technology, advertising women nevertheless promoted an elevation of the private sphere to a position of equality with the public, by implying that women's labour had equal value with men's, and that housewives deserved improved status, better working conditions, and a degree of financial autonomy within marriage.

It is telling that advertisers found it necessary to stress economy and results, as well as the labour-saving capacity of appliances, because of the devalued and unpaid nature of housework.[40] The luxury stigma associated with labour saving was an impediment, especially when selling to the lower-income groups. The consequent exaggeration of higher standards for the family vis-à-vis women's convenience can be seen in advertising for electric refrigerators, which stressed appeals to health, nutritional standards,[41] and cleanliness. Jack Frost made this rare appeal to labour saving in 1920:

> Housewives the country over have wished for a refrigeration that would do away with the nuisance of leaky drip pans and clogged drain pipes — of dirt tracked floors and the damp, germ-laden, fluctuating temperature of melting ice. The wish mothered a wonderful invention, and an even, dry, chill cold of electric refrigeration was perfected.[42]

As well, many ads which did promise to improve the housewife's working conditions, simultaneously promised benefits for the whole household, such as replacing the expensive and troublesome labour of domestic servants and/or laundresses. Advertisers noted that machines never got cross or rebellious,[43] and one fictional housewife commented in an advertisement for the Apex cleaner, "It's more dependable than a servant and does much of the work far better."[44] The refrigerator industry used the economy appeal extensively in the mid-to-late 1930s, in an attempt to reach the lower income market. Westinghouse, for instance, claimed that the householder could save five to seven dollars per month on food bills, because of preservation of leftovers, saving on bulk purchases, etc.[45]

Advertisements also linked the saving of women's labour with the enhancement of a middle-class lifestyle in the home. Table-top appliances, such as grills, toasters, and coffee percolators, were promoted as entertainment aids for the "servantless home," allowing the cook to attend the table and prepare food at the same time.[46]

Another of the benefits of technology to be enjoyed by all in the family was improved health. Vacuum cleaner manufacturers promised quick and easy extraction of the "germ-laden dirt and dust" that was allegedly a constant danger to the family's health.[47] Refrigerator ads also exploited the health theme. One ad made this commonsense observation:

> Of what avail are healthy cows, sanitary creameries and pasteurization to protect the purity of baby's milk, if after delivery to the home it is placed in a refrigerator cooled by damp, germ-laden melting ice.[48]

Increased recognition of milk's capacity to promote bacterial growth, carry disease-causing germs, and contribute to an already high infant mortality rate[49] added an air of urgency and moral imperative to the argument for better refrigeration. However, the conclusion cannot be avoided that children's health was valued much more highly than women's welfare.

In the early 1930s, large electrical manufacturers began advertising a full range of electrical appliances, and promoted the modern electric home. Although the ads portrayed a male perspective on the home (*Figure 3*), it appears that the woman's role was shifting from household drudge to valued companion. She could now legitimately share in the joys as well as the labours of family life.

Positive appeals to modernity in ads were generally directed at men, who were allowed a more active role in science and technology. Moffat, Westinghouse, and Kelvinator, for example, all linked their company names with the achievements of modern science in ads[50] for the expensive appliances which involved both husband and wife in the buying decision. The conventional wisdom, largely supported by home economists, was that women disliked "technical talk" and advertisers were encouraged to avoid it.[51]

Women could benefit from the technology as passive recipients, however. One 1929 Frigidaire ad (*Figure 4*) offered mothers relief from the age-old fears associated with infant illness. The illustration of a man handing a young child a glass of milk from the refrigerator, while its mother looked on, visually demonstrated the contention that knowledge and control over disease was a product of male-dominated science, from which women were excluded.

Despite the stress on practical benefits for the family, and the exclusion of women from technical expertise, women's interests were not completely subordinated. Advertisers did attempt to educate both men and women to elevate the status of housework[52] and appeals to women's interest in saving labour, especially in ads for the less expensive appliances, were a perpetual theme. One 1923 advertisement featured an electric iron, which was "scientifically designed so that the handle is shaped to fit the hand and is tilted slightly so as to take all the strain from wrist and forearm, eliminating the fatigue in arm and back so commonly caused by ordinary irons."[53]

Advertisers also emphasized leisure for the housewife. The fictional housewife in one 1920 vacuum cleaner advertisement exclaimed, "Of course I have time to go! The Apex has done my cleaning."[54] Another advertisement informed the new bride that the Apex takes the monotony out of housework — "that sweeping and dusting, stooping and bending day after day which tires one out — giving you hours of time to keep up your girlhood friends and associations."[55]

The practice of using the language of science and/or business to raise the status of women's domestic labour was borrowed from the earlier domestic reform movement. National advertisers promised to end the drudgery of washday by applying "businessman-husband" rationale to the housewife's work. Ads reminded women that they needed and deserved practical convenience in the home, the same as men had in business, for "housekeeping is the most important business on earth."[56] A Blue Bird washing machine ad was typical in conveying an impatience with old-fashioned methods, the will to bring housework under the same kind of control as work performed in business and the professions, and the belief that if men got a taste of the indignity of unassisted domestic drudgery, "THEN there will be a Blue Bird Washer in every Canadian home."[57]

If the exercise of the wife's right to partake of the benefits of modern technology necessitated a realignment of the family's financial resources from husband to wife, advertisers happily condoned that. With the adherence to the Mrs. Consumer as professional homemaker model, and frequent appeals to bring the home up to workplace standards, national advertisers condoned women's right to control at least part of the family's finances.

Despite these demands for reform, however, the outer limits of the homemaker's job were still dictated by male needs, as was occasionally indicated in references to meals prepared to the "king's taste."[58] Westinghouse and CGE, in their "better home" ads, portrayed husbands as providers of conveniences, who might enjoy their benefits but who usually did not use them, with the exception of the radio (see *Figure 3*).

In addition to adding a gender perspective to the advertising message, some advertising women offered an internal critique of mainstream advertising practice. While not all women in advertising adhered to this critique and some were more critical than others, there were enough voices raised in protest to make the critique significant. By taking on the cause of the largely unorganized and sporadic consumer movement,[59] which originated with women's groups[60] — both middle-class and those affiliated with the left[61] — advertising women attempted to represent women's interests to industry. Mabel Crews Ringland, for example, wrote in both *Marketing* and *Printers' Ink*, criticizing her male colleagues for their treatment of women[62] and their failure to take women's protests against corporate and advertising abuses seriously.[63] Ringland used the demands of consumer advocates to encourage industry reform. She warned her colleagues that if they did not respond, Mrs. Consumer would demand of her leaders "a square deal through some modification of the present system, cooperative stores or an entirely new set up."[64]

Advertising women also criticized their male colleagues for failing to treat homemakers seriously. They demanded strict adherence to the "Mrs. Consumer as professional homemaker" model. One woman contended that women were much less impressed by fine rhetoric than by sound reasoning, and beseeched advertisers to recall the old suffrage slogan "women are people."[65] She contended that advertisers "too often build up in their minds a fancy picture labeled "Woman" which partakes too much of the good old conventional "angel-idiot" conception of women to be true to any wide class of modern women."[66] She asserted that a housewife's tasks in the matter of purchasing were enormously more varied than those of any manufacturer or buyer in any line of business, and that housewives were "as much interested in their business of running their households as any business man is in introducing improvements into his factory."[67]

Advertising women also condemned the use of sexual stereotypes to sell products.[68] The classic image of the pretty housewife dressed in an impractical frilly apron and high heel shoes, standing beside the electric washer, about to take on the Monday morning task, seemed to epitomize advertising women's frustration with male advertisers' all-too-frequent lapses into fantasy.

Part and parcel of the professional homemaker ideal, which advertising women tried to uphold, was the demand for more and better product information, and the use of rational, rather than emotional, appeals in advertising. As Ringland expressed it:

> There is no little resentment against the advertising "magician" who draws synthetic salvation, sex appeal and health bunkum out of the most unromantic products of everyday use. Even the "average" woman who obviously rates as a moron in advertising circles, doesn't want to be kidded quite that much.[69]

Another woman writing for *Printers' Ink* condemned advertisers for their appeal to fantasies of labour elimination:

Don't try to convince us that your article is an Aladdin's lamp, that all we have to do is to rub it and some genii [sic] will appear and do the work while we sit idly by, play the piano or read and improve our minds. Tell us how much time and how much labour it will save us, but don't tell us that a washing machine takes care of the washing, a mangle does the ironing, a vacuum cleaner keeps the house clean, a patent dishwasher clears the table, washes and wipes the dishes and puts them away — that all one has to do in the morning is to turn on a switch and breakfast is served while our lady, as well as friend husband, read the morning paper.[70]

Ida Bailey Allen, writing in *Printers' Ink*, suggested that manufacturers provide more information in the form of diagrams or illustrations showing women how to operate washing machines, booklets on laundering, and so on.[71] Another woman advised that the advertising and merchandising of washing machines and the like should include pertinent information on electric current and water usage.[72]

Although Ringland and several other advertising women accepted the importance of the homemaker, they resented the industry's exclusive focus on her, criticizing male colleagues for assuming that all women were full-time homemakers, and ignoring the businesswoman.[73]

Advertising women have been criticized for their adoption of the "Mrs. Consumer" model because it served the interests of capitalists and reinforced the sexual division of labour. It is true that these women did not question, at least not publicly, the assumption that homemaking was women's work and technology a male preserve, sadly denigrating their own considerable contribution to domestic technology in the process. Yet the "Mrs. Consumer" model, for all its imperfections, did give women the voice they sought in industry. The fact that that voice turned out to be terribly weak must be blamed as much on women's marginal position in industry and the discrimination they faced, as on their naïveté or insincerity.

Women were continually reminded by their industry colleagues who, in fact, controlled technology. They probably felt they could have made few inroads into this jealously-guarded territory. One male advertiser, who deeply resented women's criticism of advertising, unwittingly summarized the male approach to advertising and household technology. He ignored the contribution women themselves made, and portrayed domestic technology as a gift from men to women, of which they should be more appreciative. He told a women's group:

> None of you would be here to take a crack at advertising if it were
> not for advertising. It helped produce the saved time you took to
> come here today. You would be home bending over a hot stove or
> digging a winter vegetable out of its cold storage place in the
> cellar.[74]

Ringland and others of like mind did not enjoy universal support
even among women. In response to the criticism of manipulative
emotional appeals in advertising, one advertising woman suggested
that "woman is first a dreamer, visionary and deeply romantic." "If
you are selling vacuum cleaners, washing machines or any other utility,
then sell dreams of leisure hours, of rest, of happy, contented homes
and simplified housework."[75]

Ringland's appeal to industry to heed the consumer movement was
largely ignored, as were other aspects — although not all — of
advertising women's advice. One of Ringland's male colleague infuri-
ated her with this all-too-typical dismissal of women's organized
opposition to advertising:

> We advertising men do not know what the masses really think
> about advertising. Of course we know what women leaders think.
> They are quite vocal about it. They criticize. How far their ideas
> percolate down among the masses who read and buy from adver-
> tising is a question we would like to explore.[76]

Likewise, the Association of Canadian Advertisers and the Canadian
Association of Advertising Agencies pronounced in 1938 that the
consumer movement had been exaggerated and kept aflame by professional agitators and was no real threat to advertising.[77]

Women's demands for more information were often met with the
objection that specifications on composition, construction, and performance of a commodity could not be understood by consumers, and
that consumers didn't want to be bothered by such intricate details
anyway.[78] While it may be true that most consumers would or could
not master specifications on all of the many products in use in the
twentieth-century home, this is no reason to deny such information to
those who wanted it. It is an argument on par with the anti-suffrage
contention that because the majority of women do not want the vote,
no woman should have it.

As well, few advertisers recognized the existence of married women who were also employed, or paid any real attention to single business women,[79] as women critics advised. Market research conducted by advertisers and their medium, national magazines, continued throughout the period to legitimize the focus on the typical consumer — the urban, middle-income, young, married homemaker.[80]

Conclusion

While women's position in the advertising industry was subordinate, and their advice often ignored, advertising women did have some input into the manufacturing, marketing, and advertising of domestic technology, helping to "technologize" domestic labour. The "Mrs. Consumer" model did give women a limited voice in industry, and domestic technology offered enough real material benefits to ensure women's support. As well, advertising women were able to add a gender perspective to the advertising message, and formulate a critique of the male-dominated advertising industry.

By focussing exclusively on reforms to the private sphere, and keeping silent on women's role in the public sphere, however, advertising women provided a poor foundation from which to demand real equality. The more limited "equality of spheres" which advertising women ended up endorsing could too easily be transformed into a justification for the status quo, with "domestic reform" serving as compensation for exclusion from the public sphere.

Nevertheless, a full assessment of advertising women's unsuccessful attempts to reconcile the capitalist program of democratized consumption and the traditional family, with women's equality, remains a difficult task, in part because of the scarcity of private sources. Whatever the final word on advertising women's motivations, their efforts should be judged in light of the limitations they had to work with. The hostility of male colleagues toward women's incursions into the male preserve of science and technology, the pervasiveness of the sexual division of labour, women's subordinate position in industry, as well as the professional biases of many advertising women who were also home economists, produced an essentially conservative approach to domestic reform.

Women Sociologists in Canada: The Careers of Helen MacGill Hughes, Aileen Dansken Ross, and Jean Robertson Burnet

All disciplines reflect in their development and structures the society in which they exist, and therefore reflect its power relations and patterns of selection. When we assess an organized discipline, as distinct from a field of knowledge, we see the obstacles to, and unevenness of, the participation and recognition of women. Although they have contributed to knowledge throughout history, women have found themselves excluded or marginalized in the contexts of modern educational institutions and professional organizations.[1] The relation between the development of a discipline and the careers of its practitioners can be seen best in terms of the intersection of history and biography. This examination of the careers of three Canadian women sociologists is an attempt to understand that nexus.

Sociology, the science of society and one of the youngest sciences, was given its name by Auguste Comte, a French philosopher, in his *Cours de Philosophie Positive*, 1830–42,[2] however, it was not until the 1890s that sociology became an established academic discipline in Europe and North America. In the nineteenth and early twentieth centuries, when women were not present in great numbers in colleges and universities, many women took up sociological matters in connection with their efforts to ameliorate community problems and to advance the causes of the disadvantaged, often of women, in society.[3]

The careers of Flora Tristan (1903–1844), Harriet Martineau (1802–1876), Charlotte Perkins Gilman (1860–1935), Olive Schreiner (1855–1920), Annie Besant (1847–1933), and Beatrice Webb (1858–1943) serve as examples of women of different class origins who were actively engaged in sociological issues and social research. Women's active participation in social science associations in Britain and America in the nineteenth century reflected their concern with social problems, practical measures for social progress, and numerous women's issues, such as suffrage, property rights, and economic equity. Women's entry into the social science professions and academe was certainly aided by the activities and concerns of their sisters in earlier generations.

The Emergence of Sociology in Canada

Sociology, in addition to being a young science, was a late bloomer on the academic scene in Canada. In his portrait of the emergence of sociology in Canada, S.D. Clark tells us that after the First World War Chicago-trained H.A. Innis and others, sought to make the study of Canadian society a distinct enterprise.[5] (Innis's views on women in social science in Canada will be noted later.) Strong departments of history, economics, and political science emerged in the 1920s, but only one department of sociology was formed in this period, at McGill, in 1922. At the University of Toronto, sociologists were trained in the department of political economy, which sent its graduates to Saskatchewan, Manitoba, and New Brunswick.[6] Some universities, like Queen's and Alberta, resisted introducing sociology into their curricula. As late as 1938, there were fewer than 10 trained sociologists in Canada.[7] In Canada, as in the United States, it was actually anthropology which cut the path as an acceptable academic enterprise for its sister discipline.

Canadian Women in Sociology

In this essay we will take a look at women sociologists in Canada in the early decades of academic sociology. Women who entered the field of sociology early and made contributions have been ignored as founders and leaders in the establishment of the science. This lack of recognition reflects not only male dominance in the discipline, but also the career patterns of women which are affected by marriage and children, the exigencies of employment, discriminatory policies of academic administrators, anti-nepotism rules, and slow acceptance in the research field.[8]

I will examine the early participation of women in Canadian sociology through the lives and work of three women: Helen MacGill Hughes, Aileen Dansken Ross, and Jean Robertson Burnet. They are among the first generation of Canadian women sociologists and are a particularly interesting group. By birth they represent the geographical spectrum of Canadian society. Helen Hughes was born in Vancouver in 1903; Aileen Ross, in Montreal in 1902; and Jean Burnet, in Toronto, in 1920. Hughes and Burnet chose sociology as a career rather early; Ross came to it later, as a result of social service work. All three found themselves, on the recommendations of male mentors or colleagues, at the University of Chicago for their doctoral work, which they completed respectively in 1935, 1950, and 1948.

Hughes, Ross, and Burnet spent their lives in academe, teaching, conducting research, editing major publications and, perhaps most importantly, practicing sociology in the field, "Chicago-style."[9] The topics of their research included news and human interest stories, race and ethnic relations, crime and delinquency, nursing as a profession, the family in India, homeless women, language and ethnic studies.

Three questions will be explored in our consideration of the careers of these Canadian women sociologists: (1) What were their contributions to the development of discipline in this country? (2) What were their career patterns and general experiences as members of the first generation of Canadian sociologists? (3) How did they perceive their own lives and careers? Their experiences help us to understand the participation of women in a relatively young science as it emerged in North America.

Helen MacGill Hughes

Helen MacGill was born in Vancouver in 1903, the first daughter of Helen Gregory, a well-educated (B.A., M.A. and LL.D.) feminist lawyer, judge, and writer from a rather *avant garde* family of educated women, and James Henry MacGill, a lawyer. Helen Gregory had two sons from a previous marriage and, as a widow had supported her family as a journalist (her law studies came later). She and MacGill had two daughters. Helen's younger sister, Elsie Gregory MacGill, also reaped the benefits of having educated feminist parents and entered the field of engineering. She was the first woman to graduate in electrical engineering at the University of Toronto (1927), and in aeronautical engineering from the University of Michigan (1929) and she designed a special-duty trainer plane, "The Maple Leaf," for the Mexican air force.[10]

Of great significance for both Helen and Elsie were the role models of mother and grandmother. The maternal grandparents had encouraged their mother in her pursuit of several advanced degrees and in her active feminism. Helen Gregory was "the best educated and wittiest woman in any circle, uncommonly venturesome and in many respects unconventional."[11]

Helen MacGill received a Bachelor of Arts degree in German and economics from the University of British Columbia in 1925. For an undergraduate sociology course she had done an essay on anti-Oriental immigration legislation in British Columbia, for which she undoubtedly received support at home, and this work led her to a new understanding of discrimination as a *form* of social interaction.

She and several of her fellow economics students were encouraged by the department chairman to pursue graduate studies. Near the end of her final term at UBC Helen heard a lecture on Chinatown presented by Winifred Raushenbush[12] from the University of Chicago, which enlivened her interest in sociology, and another talk by Robert E. Park, perhaps the leading sociologist in America at that time, who visited UBC and gave a lecture on the form and structure of cities. Park persuaded Helen to apply to the University of Chicago for graduate study, although she had been offered a graduate fellowship already by the Carola Woerischofer School of Economics at Bryn Mawr.

Helen MacGill entered the graduate program at the University of Chicago in 1925 with a research fellowship. She was the only woman among six or seven research fellows. She completed work for the master's degree at the end of her second year of study (1927) with a thesis entitled "Land Values as an Ecological Factor in the Community of South Chicago." Using Park's theory of urban invasion and succession, she related land values to land use and relation to the urban centre. During the summer of 1927, she married Everett Cherrington

Hughes, a fellow student, and they moved to Montreal where Hughes had accepted his first academic appointment at McGill University. Hughes, a minister's son from Ohio, came to sociology after teaching YMCA night-school classes to immigrants in Chicago. Hughes and MacGill, "Park's favourite students," extended the influence of Robert Park through their work in sociology.

After one year at McGill, during which Everett Hughes finished his doctoral thesis, in addition to fulfilling teaching duties, Helen began her doctoral work at Chicago. She studied in Chicago for at least one quarter each year in order to satisfy residence requirements. During her stays in Chicago, Helen lived with the Parks. As a result of Park's strong encouragement and his own interests, her thesis focused on newspaper human interest stories as a form of popular literature. The significance of Robert Park as a mentor for Helen Hughes is clear from her autobiographical writing, and her published work.[13] For instance, Park encouraged her to present a paper at the 1935 American Sociological Society meeting on news as defined in 28 daily newspapers published in Berlin in 1932, a period during which she and Everett were on leave in Germany.[14] She submitted her doctoral thesis in 1935, was granted her Ph.D. in 1937, and published her thesis in 1940 under the title *News and the Human Interest Story*. This was one of the earliest studies in the sociology of journalism, specifically the human interest story as a cultural form.[15] In his Introduction to Hughes's book, Park emphasized that "this investigation was important because it seems to open up to empirical investigation the whole matter of the role and influence . . . of popular literature in contemporary life."

Upon returning to McGill University, Everett and Helen worked together in the field, gathering data in French on Cantonville (Drummondville) for a study published as *French Canada in Transition*. They "jointly did the field work for the study," as Everett notes in the preface to the book, although no other mention is made of Helen's collaboration.[16] Helen gives us a slightly different version:

We lived one summer in Cantonville, absorbed in the zestful enterprise of analyzing together the population of the market-town-turned-industrial-town . . . we walked on both sides of every street in the town, mapping every house and recording its occupants . . . [we enjoyed] the challenge and delight of doing it all in French . . . [17]

From 1927 to 1930, Helen Hughes was a teaching fellow at McGill, and from 1929 to 1937, she held the position of assistant in sociology, in which capacity she may have served as a teaching and/or research assistant. Everett's rank from 1927–37 was assistant professor of sociology. The policy of McGill principal Sir Arthur Currie was not to employ husbands and wives. It should be remembered that during the Depression, it was not considered justifiable to employ wives of employed men; limited jobs had to be "evenly distributed." Consequently, anti-nepotism rules were established in North American universities prohibiting employment of husbands and wives in the same institution. These regulations, which continued to exist until the 1970s, were part of the institutionalization of discrimination against women in higher education. Statistics demonstrate that women's presence in academe diminished proportionately at every academic rank over the decades following the Depression.

The Hugheses returned to Chicago in 1938, as Everett had been given a faculty post. They came with a six-week-old daughter, and had another daughter two years later. The move was very difficult for Helen, who was depressed about leaving friends (and perhaps Canada), but admitted little to others because she felt one should not complain. After approximately 14 years in Chicago, Helen, who had lost her Canadian citizenship upon marriage and had been a registered alien in the United States, decided to become an American citizen. It was a practical decision. She needed a passport to travel in Europe with her family, and she wanted to involve herself in the political campaign of Adlai Stevenson.[18]

She was to discover that marriage created marginality for her in her career as well as her citizenship. Helen stayed home for the next five years (1938–43) to raise her children. "I had an undiluted diet of housebound domesticity until the youngest entered nursery school." She then entered paid employment, beginning a rather long career as an editor. She took on the job of liaison between the University of Chicago department of sociology and *Encyclopedia Britannica*. In 1944, she was asked by editor Herbert Blumer, with one day's notice, to take over the editorial office of the *American Journal of Sociology*.[19] Over nearly two decades at the *Journal* Helen MacGill Hughes was rewarded for her effectiveness and skill with titles of rank rather than salary increases. Although she was offered other jobs at the University of Chicago Press, she preferred to work "as a sociologist in a sociology department," (the *Journal* was a publication of the department at that time). Hughes held the positions of editorial assistant (1944–46), assistant editor (1946–54), and managing editor (1954–61) of the most important and prestigious journal of the discipline. It was always a part-time and poorly-paid job, but love of the work and of the field kept her in the post. "Now I am reminded of those seventeen gratifying years once every month when my pension of $19.58 arrives,"[20] she later wrote. In "Maid of All Work or Departmental sister-in-Law? The Faculty Wife Employed on Campus," she adds that that experience "led to nothing further . . . not even to a place on any of the by-then numerous sociological periodicals."[21]

How much power she had as a managing editor of a leading scientific journal is difficult to assess, but the editor and the three associate editors, all male sociologists, most likely made the major decisions on articles and the general shape of the journal. Jean Burnet who, as a graduate assistant, worked on the journal with Helen Hughes, felt that Helen must have had a good deal of power, as she probably discussed with Blumer, the editor, the acceptance and rejection of articles, supervised the graduate students doing the day-to-day work, and was generally a much stronger, "more definite" person than the previous managing editor:

> I'm sure she had input. She was a vocal and persuasive woman, bright, well-trained and confident . . . She was a "force of nature," very vigorous and active as a sociologist and as a journalist.[22]

The fact that Hughes was neither editor nor associate editor but remained managing editor indicates however that there were limits to her power and status in matters related to the *Journal*.

Helen served as a science correspondent for *Scientific Monthly* and *Time Magazine* (1944–48), writing stories of interest emanating particularly from universities on education, social science, science, and medicine. She often had several part-time jobs simultaneously assisting on research projects, making local arrangements for visiting academics, even ghostwriting books on medical problems. She was also raising two children during this time.

Helen Hughes developed a passion for certain projects. Drug addiction was relatively new in those days especially among women. When Howard Becker was conducting his research on young drug addicts, and interviewed a female addict for over 27 hours, Helen realized that such a story should be published. She put it together and had it published by Houghton Mifflin in 1961 under the title *The Fantastic Lodge: The Autobiography of a Girl Drug Addict.* Helen made clear that the title was chosen by Everett, and the brief preface is signed by Helen MacGill Hughes and Everett C. Hughes, although why this is so is not clear.[23] Ten years after it was published, the book was reissued in paperback in England and America, as well as in French translation, and it continued to sell.

In 1961, Helen again followed her husband, this time to Cambridge, Massachusetts, where he had accepted a professorship at Brandeis University. It was difficult for Helen to leave the journal, partly because of the dread of no job ahead. But she quickly became involved in part-time research at the Joint Center for Urban Studies of Harvard and M.I.T. and the Florence Heller School for Advanced Studies in Social Welfare at Brandeis.[24] In spring, 1965, during Everett's half-year leave to lecture and do research at the Université de Montreal and McGill, Helen taught a sociology course on social change at Sir George Williams University.[25]

About 1967, Helen Hughes was invited to participate in a major project at the American Sociological Association, "Sociological Resources for the Secondary Schools," subsidized by the National Science Foundation and aimed at providing good sociological material for students in social studies. Helen became editor (1967–72), and eventually produced seven readers on the city, the family, race and ethnic relations, delinquents and criminals, social organizations, population growth and the complex society, and crowd and mass behaviour — all standard areas which required knowledge of a wide range of sociological research.[26]

Later, she was invited to write the article on Robert Ezra Park for the *International Encyclopedia of the Social Sciences* (vol. 11, 416–19, 1968). She edited two more books, one of which was on the sociology of the deformed face. About this time, Helen began editing the Rose Monograph Series of the American Sociological Association. And in the early 1970s she served on the publications committee, among others, of the ASA.

In 1973 the Eastern Sociological Society presented Helen MacGill Hughes with its Award of Merit. She was especially honoured, as she knew that that award generally went to someone with a "straight" career. Her joy over such an honour, however, did not alter her realism about her own career in sociology:

> The committee was moved by the conviction, new then, that there is more than one way of being a sociologist. This idea was, I suppose, in the minds of the Nominating Committee when in 1975 it put me on its slate for president-elect [of the American Sociological Society]. I lost the election, which might be evidence that there are, after all, few degrees of freedom in pursuing the science of society.[27]

Nevertheless, at the age of 76 Helen Hughes was elected President of the Eastern Sociological Society (1979–80).

She had an opportunity to reflect on the fortunes of women in society, when in 1969, members of the newly-formed Sociologists for Women in Society elected her vice-president. In 1974 she was asked to offer a graduate seminar on "Women, Men and Social Change" at Northeastern University, and later at Tufts, and at Boston University. She "tried hard to keep it from being like some of the new courses which are more activism than analysis." At Northeastern she also taught a graduate seminar on "Public Opinion and Mass Media," the subject of her original research. These experiences made Hughes particularly aware of the exploitation and marginality associated with part-time teaching.[28]

In an era when there were so few women in the discipline, women were sometimes given extra support and attention by established scholars; this seems to have been done by the Chicago sociology faculty. However, upon leaving graduate school and exploring the job market, women were left to their own resources. As a young Ph.D. faculty wife Helen Hughes felt fortunate to have paid work of any kind. But later, as she looked back, she felt differently about her situation:

> Why was I content, all those years, to let accidental connections and friendly interventions determine the course of my life as a sociologist? Had I been more realistic, I should have envied the small handful of women of my academic generation who began in lectureships in the departments and climbed up the ladder ... My many jobs, often overlapping, add up to a busy and gratifying life. But do they add up to a career?[29]

Missing was "that scholarly progression through a sequence of research." She had no doubt that her writing and editing were worthwhile, but

> when I take a hard look at my curriculum vitae, I admit that while I can claim to be continuously interested in mass media, popular culture, and academic women, my work has not been consistently cumulative.[30]

As Helen MacGill Hughes became increasingly aware of the many factors which shaped her own professional life, she wrote or edited several articles and booklets to further our understanding of women's status in sociology.[31] It was not only motherhood but, perhaps mainly, status as faculty wives which affected the participation in sociology of many women. In discussing the career of sociologist Caroline Rose, whose husband Arnold Rose was also a sociologist, Hughes says of married women academics:

> Women in academic life are less likely to begin with strong sponsorship. If they are married they follow their husbands' moves, often help him with his own work and, wherever they are, may then become available for any work within their reach, the institution, of course, defining the reach. They seek out their own niche, rather than being sought by the institution, as is the case of women on the regular faculties. They work part-time, sometimes at more than one place at one time — again as Caroline did. They are found on the margins . . . they start lower down and do not catch up. Only some of their problems are occasioned by domestic obligations. Many academic women are, in fact, unmarried. In any case, part-time employment, marginal and temporary employment, and an interrupted career are strikingly more in evidence in the female model than in the male.[32]

Aileen Dansken Ross

There are various routes by which one arrives at a career. Aileen Ross came to sociology after several years of social service and volunteer work, and an early interest in economics. Ross was born in 1902 into an established Montreal family. Her grandfather, an immigrant from

Aileen D. Ross and friends, India-Canada Asssociation, Montreal, 1956.
Photo by Richard Arless Associates.

Jean R. Burnet at work, early 1950s.
Courtesy J.R. Burnet.

Helen MacGill Hughes and Everett C. Hughes,
Tougaloo, Mississippi, 1956.
Courtesy Elizabeth Hughes Schneewind.

163

Scotland, had founded the first chartered accountancy firm in Montreal, and her father continued in the company. Gertrude Emma Holland and John Wardrope Ross had six children, of which Aileen was the fourth.

After some schooling at the Institut des Essarts in Switzerland, she attended Trafalgar Institute in Montreal, which at that time did not encourage advanced education for women. Like other girls of her class, she expected to grow up, marry, and have children. She was not particularly interested in science as a child. During the 1920s, as a member of the upper class, Aileen did volunteer work for the Junior League at the Griffintown Club with the Girl Guides.[33]

Ross's interest in sociology developed during the Depression, when she toured Russia and was favourably impressed with economic planning there. This led to her decision, at the age of 33, to pursue studies in economics at the London School of Economics, with sociology as a complementary field. Although she found English sociology rather uninspiring, Karl Mannheim's brilliance influenced her almost-immediate decision to pursue sociology.[34] Mannheim was particularly excited by the Chicago School, and advised Ross to go there for advanced studies.

Ross went on to Chicago and studied under Louis Wirth, Herbert Blumer, and Everett Hughes.[35] She completed her master's thesis in 1941, on "The French and English Social Elites of Montreal." After working briefly as an advisor in rural adult education at McGill's Macdonald College, Ross became a lecturer in sociology at the University of Toronto (1942–45). As the only one of a staff of three who was a Chicago School sociologist, she felt rather isolated. In 1945, she became a lecturer at McGill where all the faculty in sociology were Chicago-trained.[36] She was the only woman in the department. Between 1945 and 1951 she completed work for her doctorate with a thesis done under the supervision of Everett Hughes on French-English relations in the Eastern Townships of Quebec.[37] In 1951 she was given an appointment in the McGill department of sociology as assistant professor. Ten years later she was promoted to associate professor and in 1964, to full professor. She is now emeritus professor of sociology.

As Helen Hughes was Canadian and as the Hugheses had spent 11 years at McGill, in Chicago Aileen Ross developed a particularly close, lifelong friendship with them. Later they vacationed together in the Gaspé and maintained contact over many years.

Ross's research and career in sociology developed in a way commensurate with those of any male in the field. She taught courses generally related to her areas of interest and research. She held several positions in learned and professional societies and was active, true to her Chicago training, in non-academic councils and institutes, such as the University Settlement, the Canadian Institute of International Affairs, UNESCO, the Overseas Institute of Canada, the Royal Commission on Bilingualism and Biculturalism, the Shastri Indo-Canadian Institute, the Women's Shelter Foundation, and the Canadian Human Rights Foundation. She has published five monographs and approximately 30 articles, chapters, and papers on a diversity of social subjects and cultural contexts.

Ross experienced no difficulty in getting research funds, was never rejected and never perceived the granting process as one of great competition. Her projects were supported by the Social Science Research Council, as well as other sources. The breadth of Ross's research is indicative of the advantages and freedom she enjoyed as a single woman professional. When Ross was asked, "which research is closest to your heart?" her reply was "each one — you live it and each is a joy."[38] Her first major project after her doctoral thesis was based upon a year (1954) which she spent in India studying the family. This research, she indicated in an interview, was particularly exciting. She spent time in Bangalore and New Delhi, and had five or six research assistants (university students) who interviewed people in various languages. She also had some help from women in high positions in education in India. The research was funded by The Canada Council.[39] One of the offshoots of this research was her role in the founding of the Shastri Indo-Canadian Institute in Montreal, of which she was acting president (1965–68), president (1968) and director of the McGill Chapter (1969–1970).

As research methods, she preferred interviews and participant observation to questionnaires and elaborate statistical analyses. Participant observation was not difficult in India because of the pluralism of the society and the prevalence of English in the country. She spent a great deal of time on this project, reading the literature, developing hypotheses, training assistants, and gathering data. The study is a comprehensive and insightful examination of the effects of industrial and technological change on urban Hindu middle and upper class families in the 1950s. It was published in 1961, under the title *The Hindu Family in Its*

Urban Setting. That same year appeared another of her studies, *Becoming a Nurse.*[40]

In the volume on nursing, Ross acknowledges her indebtedness to the writings of Helen MacGill Hughes and Everett Hughes and her appreciation for the "many hours of stimulating conversation with them and their warm and sensitive insight [which] have deepened my understanding of human behavior in general and the nursing profession in particular."[41] Reflecting the Chicago tradition, the study was written "as far as possible, in the words of nurses," and was based on term papers written by nurses on various aspects of the profession, their own backgrounds and socialization into nursing during the years 1948 to 1958, interviews with nurses and an examination of the structure and dynamics of the nursing profession.

Ross returned to India in 1961 for a year, and in 1965 for the summer. She had shifted her focus to students in India. Using a sample of 250 students from 14 colleges, as well as interviews with lecturers and others, she developed an analysis of the student movements of the time in India, and related them to the effects of rapid social change in that country, and to student movements around the world in the 1960s. The research was funded by the Social Science Research Council of Canada and the Centre for Developing Area Studies at McGill. Her book, *Student Unrest in India: A Comparative Approach*, was published in 1969.[42] In 1970, while working on revisions for this book, Ross wrote a Christmas letter which very well expressed her attachment to India and her keen desire to understand the winds of change there. It began: "coming back to India is always like coming back home." On the matter of social change in the midst of unrest, she concluded:

> ... as I firmly believe that it is the middle classes who must handle the transition from a simple to a complex society, I think they deserve, and in fact need, every possible motivation and comfort to make the intense strain and stress bearable. I once wrote an article with the rather sentimental title "Heroes of the Middle Ranks." For I have watched many of these middle class Indians — doctors, professors, teachers, businessmen, social workers — struggling to keep the machinery going, year after year, with a minimum of "industrial" assistance. Many not even able to afford any relaxing recreation, and certainly no travel or holidays abroad. Best of all, many of these Indians now seem to implicitly realize

the improvement, and I sense a new hope, and a new confidence in themselves that is heartening.[43]

Ross's other research projects concerned various aspects of philanthropy, and French-English relations in Quebec. In 1976 she published *The People of Montreal: A Bibliography of Their Lives and Behaviour.* Several articles she wrote during this period dealt with women's work roles, particularly in business in India and Canada.

In the late 1970s, the plight of homeless women became a concern to Ross and, in 1977, with Sheila Baxter, a social worker, she organized Chez Doris, a shelter for homeless women in Montreal. Ross strongly opposed the term "bag lady" and wanted to promote a greater understanding of the situation of women without homes. She studied these women for five years, and published the results in 1982, in *The Lost and The Lonely: Homeless Women in Montreal.*[44]

Aileen Ross enjoyed a long, meaningful and productive career as a sociologist. Her career included research and professional activities in other countries, as well as years of productive and congenial work relationships with colleagues at McGill University. The profession of sociology was small enough during most of those years to make it possible to know everyone across Canada, and to correspond, and renew acquaintances at meetings. In terms of Ross's experience at McGill, nothing could have been more congenial. As she reminisces, "it was a time when . . . walls separating disciplines were not high and we mixed indiscriminately . . . with colleagues from . . . many disciplines." And it was a time of departmental consensus and congeniality.[45]

How did Ross fare as a woman in the department of sociology at McGill? She said she was paid equally to her male colleagues ('we knew our salaries') and was never denied a raise in salary or a promotion because of her sex. She never once felt the slightest discrimination at McGill.

Overall, Ross feels "incredibly fortunate" about her career which she describes as "one great joy."[46] She went about her work and was not conscious of herself as a role model for women students. She noted that, particularly in the early days of the department, when there were only a few graduate students, "naturally, the senior men got the graduate students." As indicated in her research, Ross was sensitive to the work of women as they pursued careers in sociology, nursing, business, and education and as they began to play more active roles in society. For example, in her work on the student movements in India, she was particularly interested in the increased activity of women in education and society at large. She had women assistants for her research and, later, women graduate students. Perhaps most significantly, she turned her concerns to those women who were down and out in her community, studied them, wrote about them, and contributed to the establishment of centers to help them.

Most recently, Dr. Ross has been involved in a study of men on low incomes, who live mostly in single rooms and have no families. The research represents her continuing interest in the lonely and the homeless.[47]

Aileen Dansken Ross, whose career in sociology has spanned more than four decades, pursued teaching and research with very little encumbrance due to her sex. She entered and worked in sociology during the period of the discipline's establishment and expansion. With so few people in the field, competition and discrimination seemed to be minimal. Ross had other advantages as well: she was part of an established Montreal family which had an interest in education; she was single and independent, able to travel and carry out her professional activities, and to take on numerous extra-academic commitments.

Jean Robertson Burnet

The third woman pioneer in Canadian sociology, almost a generation younger than Helen MacGill Hughes and Aileen Dansken Ross, is Jean Robertson Burnet. Born in Toronto in 1920, she was one of three children of Jemima Sheals and John Burnet, who had emigrated separately from Scotland. Jemima Sheals, whose parents in Edinburgh had died, was one of a group of domestic workers who emigrated to Canada. John Burnet had left Scotland with his family, and in Canada, became a printer like his father. As parents of two daughters and a son, Jemima and John reflected the Scottish attitude that everyone should get as much education as desired.[48]

Jean Burnet was educated at Strathcona Public School and Owen Sound College and Vocational Institute in Owen Sound, Ontario. She received her Bachelor of Arts degree from the University of Toronto in 1942, and her master's degree in 1943. Like Helen MacGill Hughes and

Aileen Ross, she pursued her doctoral studies in sociology at the University of Chicago, where she received her Ph.D. in 1948.

How did Burnet come to sociology? Her strong interest in race and ethnic relations began early when she had been disturbed by the way blacks were treated in Owen Sound. Friends who had studied sociology in college discussed the discipline with her. She decided to enroll in the University of Toronto's social and philosophical studies program which appealed because it was broad and unspecialized. At that time sociology was taught within the university's department of political economy. In her autobiographical article, "Minorities I Have Belonged To," Burnet comments that "when I began to study sociology, it was new, weak and regarded with suspicion and scorn in Canada." It was regarded by some as specious, and by others as lacking in rigour, heretical (both Victoria and St. Michael's college opposed sociology), or socialist. "It added insult to injury that sociology attracted women, and at a time when men were having to leave their studies for the armed services, too."[49]

Burnet's interest in the discipline motivated her towards graduate school. "I never thought of applying for a graduate fellowship and no one suggested that I do so," but she received a teaching assistantship of $250 at the University of Toronto while she completed her master's degree. Burnet then set off to do a doctorate at Chicago where she studied with several eminent men in sociology (Burgess, Ogburn, Warner, Wirth, Hughes, Blumer, and Redfield in anthropology).[50] She assisted Everett Hughes a little, and worked with Helen Hughes in the office of the *American Journal of Sociology*. "Like all Canadians, I benefitted greatly from the warm kindliness of Helen and Everett Hughes, and from the informal information service on Canada they provided."[51]

Burnet maintained her Canadian identity and made Canadian society her sociological laboratory during her graduate studies. "I almost always chose to do my papers on Canadian topics. When I did not, on at least one occasion Professor Hughes insisted that I do so."

In 1945, Burnet began teaching as an instructor at the University of Toronto while writing her dissertation, which was a community study of Hanna, Alberta, in the wheat-growing area hit by drought and the Depression of the 1930s. Published in 1951 under the title *Next-Year Country*,[52] the study was done in 1946 under the supervision of Everett Hughes and Del Clark, who served as director of the project.

This study was especially important as an analysis of a community that was fertile ground for the Social Credit movement in Alberta. In a larger sense the study had to do with the transformation of an agricultural economy into an industrialized one, the subsequent conflicts between town and country, and the responses, in this Canadian context, of various ethnic groups and social classes to one another. A measure of the importance of Burnet's study is the fact that it was reissued in 1978 in paperback.

After completing her doctorate, Burnet spent one year (1948–49) as visiting lecturer at the University of New Brunswick, then returned to a faculty position at the University of Toronto where she remained until 1967. She had advanced by that time to the rank of associate professor. Up to the time when she went to Ottawa, in 1963, to work for the Royal Commission on Bilingualism and Biculturalism, she had had no sabbatical leave, and had not received the promotions and salary increases which she felt she had a right to expect. In 1967 she was offered the chair of the department of sociology at Glendon College, York University, with the rank of professor. She served as chair from 1967–72, and again from 1974–76, and remained at York until 1985.[53]

In addition to her academic posts, Burnet served in numerous organizations concerned with ethnic history and multiculturalism, including the Multicultural History Society of Ontario, the Canadian Ethnic Studies Advisory Committee on Multiculturalism, Department of the Secretary of State, a UNESCO joint project on cultural development in countries with several cultural groups, and (as a research associate) the Royal Commission on Bilingualism and Biculturalism.

In 1972, Burnet published her second book, *Ethnic Groups in Upper Canada*,[54] based upon her masters thesis of 1943. It was the first of a series of publications by the Ontario Historical Society of completed graduate research projects of relevance to the Society.

This work is especially valuable for its explanation of the clash of British and American cultures in Ontario during the eighteenth and nineteenth centuries, and of the kinds of accommodations which had to be made in the context of Upper Canada. The study focuses on social institutions, using historical, sociological, academic, and personal documentation.

Recently, Burnet has compiled a collection of papers on immigrant women in Canada, which were given at a 1985 University of Toronto conference on immigration and ethnicity in Ontario. The collection is entitled *Looking into My Sister's Eyes: An Exploration of Women's History.*[55] The papers are portrayals of the "lived experience" of immigrant women in Canada, and they provide an alternative to the white, male, British perspectives which have predominated in the social histories of Canada.[56]

Burnet held several important professional positions which involved a kind of pioneering, especially for women. In the early decades of social science in Canada, most social scientists belonged to the Canadian Political Science Association (CPSA). In response to their minority status in 1955 approximately a dozen Canadian sociologists and anthropologists founded the Anthropology and Sociology Chapter of the CPSA. In 1966, the chapter left the CPSA and became the Canadian Sociology and Anthropology Association (CSAA) with a membership of 100.[57]

Burnet served as secretary of the CPSA Chapter (1960–65), and managing editor of the *Canadian Journal of Economics and Political Science* (1962–63). At that time, the editor did everything and had a great deal of power in making decisions about which articles would be published. She enjoyed the work very much. In 1963 she became the first editor-in-chief of the *Canadian Review of Sociology and Anthropology/La Revue Canadienne de Sociologie et d'Anthropologie*, a position she held for five years. She also served as secretary/treasurer of the Canadian Sociology and Anthropology Association. In fact, until the 1970s, Burnet was among the very few women in the higher ranks of the CSAA.[58]

As editor of the *Review*, Burnet had to endure some very difficult moments. Before the second issue had been published, charges of discrimination against westerners were made. An investigation by a committee of sociologists found no grounds for the charges, but Burnet was the victim of considerable harassment. She decided to offer her resignation, if necessary, although she did not want to do so. The bad feeling finally dissipated.[59]

Burnet, like Ross, was among the few women in sociology in the discipline's early days in Canada. She tells us that

There were a few other women in the Department of Political Economy, as instructors or lecturers; most women were, however, in Social Work, Household Science — clearly related to what was seen to be women's role — or in languages, where there was a good deal of drudgery to be done as cheaply as possible. Women who aspired to academic careers were told straightforwardly that they should not set their sights too high: that, for example, many years of service and high scholarly productivity might possibly lead as far as an associate professorship, but not a professorship. Nor should they hope for many women colleagues: Harold Innis, Chairman of the Department of Political Economy and the most influential social scientist in Canada, held that women could never be scholars. He also claimed that if women and Jews were hired, more and more women and Jews would enroll as students, and there were already too many in the social sciences. So much for role models.[60]

Women could not belong to the Faculty Club at the University of Toronto, so they formed their own organization. When visiting scholars were entertained at the Faculty Club, Burnet and her female colleagues could not attend.

On exceptional occasions a luncheon might be held elsewhere, to which women could go: one luncheon, in honor of a woman guest lecturer, was held at the York Club, into which the visitor and I had to find our way by a special back entrance marked "Ladies." It was around 1960 that the Faculty Club moved out of Hart House and began to admit women. The men made gallant speeches about ending a long deprivation of female company, but we women were aware that the rules of Hart House forbade not only women but also wine and wondered which lack our colleagues had felt more keenly.[61]

Asked to join an organization mainly of wives of senior faculty men for luncheons and bridge parties, the young professionals like Burnet found themselves stereotyped by other women:

Some pressure was put on the women lecturers, or at least on me, to join and undertake such chores as telephoning members, since single women toying with careers were thought to have more time for such things than wives and mothers.[62]

In describing her experiences at the University of Toronto, Burnet felt that her "comradely relations" with colleagues were very important:

... They helped me to distinguish what happened to me because I was a woman from what happened to me because I was a sociologist, or because I was junior in status. There were, of course, a good many hardships and grievances, real and imaginary, that we sociologists shared and others that all young members of the academic community shared. Nowadays when academic women associate more with other women, they may have fewer contacts with their male colleague-competitors, and thus be less able to make such distinctions.[63]

The question as to whether women have to be better than men to make it in the male world is an open one for Burnet, but she clearly feels that women had to be good to be accepted into academe in the 1940s and 1950s;

It is sometimes said that women have to be better than men to make it in whatever particular men's world is under discussion. I am not sure that this is so; in any event, quality is hard to gauge in our work. Probably women in academic life in the 1940s and 1950s had to be good to be taken seriously at all as intellectuals; in any event if they were not competent no one had much compunction about firing them.[64]

However there were serious obstacles to becoming "extraordinarily good": "restricted access to information" which resulted from such things as exclusion from faculty clubs and other network situations where professional contacts and collegial relations were strengthened; "being single," when domestic circumstances were taken into account, as occasionally happened in awarding grants, fellowships, or even degrees; and "being married," when it was assumed that a married woman did not need financial assistance "because she had a man to support her."[65]

But being a woman teaching in a university engendered the greatest obstacle, "the vulnerability of a woman lecturer" wary of the metaphorical "black book" which makes people new in any occupation vulnerable; overhearing disparaging student remarks about female professors, or colleagues" contempt for universities which were "staffed by Asians and women." Burnet tells us that "Once, in a bookstore, I heard one student telling another that I had been fired."[66]

Burnet explains that feelings of vulnerability underlie the fact that women could not or did not refuse to do the "dirty work" of the university such as

> looking after correspondence courses, evening and summer courses, all at egregiously low rates of pay — but salaries were generally so low that even a little extra helped — taking up collections for the United Appeal or for gifts for departing staff members, giving tutorials in other people's courses, serving on the most boring and least esteemed of committees. Of course, the "dirty work" interfered with scholarship, but there was always the dreadful menace, "If women want to insist on so-and-so, it'll be easy enough for us to get along without women."[67]

Recalling her own consideration of her vulnerability when asked to become the editor of the *Review*, Burnet said she had wondered whether the fact of her being a woman would damage the *Review*'s reputation or set a bad precedent (editor as woman's work). She also wondered whether the attacks on the *Review* (from the West) would have been "as venomous if they had been directed against a man."[68]

Burnet realizes that consciousness and concern about the status of women in sociology have been slow in developing, and that Canadian women still suffer discrimination both inside and outside the universities, but women are now better organized to protest and to exact rectifications: "My young colleagues find themselves alone less often than I did."[69]

Burnet's interest in race and ethnic relations generated her initial attraction to the field of sociology, and she found, by the 1960s, that the area was highly relevant to an understanding of Canadian society. Her work with ethnic groups and multiculturalism led to her appointment as a research associate for the Royal Commission on Bilingualism and Biculturalism in 1963, and she prepared Book 4 of the Commission's report.

> In these research activities I was able to return to the problems that had first attracted me to sociology, in which my experiences as a member of an emerging academic discipline, an ethnic group threatened by invasion and a sex subject to occupational discrimination could serve as a basis for understanding and in which, conversely, my research and reflection could throw light on my personal dilemmas and contradictions of status.[70]

Presently, she is chair of the board of directors and chief executive officer of the Multicultural History Society of Ontario. Her most recent book, *Coming Canadians* is an historical and institutional overview of research on immigration and ethnic history in Canada, which serves as an introductory volume to a series on the subject entitled "Generations."[71]

The Careers and Legacy of Three Pioneers

As Helen Hughes reminds us, we know relatively little about the earlier generations of women in sociology, how they chose the discipline, conducted their research and teaching activities and, in many cases, managed the dual set of responsibilities of family life and career.[72] Hughes's life shows rather strikingly the consequences, in that era at least, of being married to a professional man, particularly in one's own discipline, even though the partnership is strong.[73] She represents the pattern of women scientists who, as she put it, have had to "work any unoccupied portion of the vineyard."[74]

We also learn, perhaps particularly from the examples of married women, that there are "diverse ways of serving a discipline." If Hughes can be seen as playing a special role in sociology, it was as that of editor. Nevertheless, she had important publications of her own, about which she was so modest as to be self-effacing. In the absence of a regular full-time academic position, it seems that even Helen Hughes herself was unconvinced of their significance.[75]

The career patterns of Aileen Ross and Jean Burnet are quite different. As single women they were able to pursue graduate studies and subsequently research and teaching in a relatively unhampered way that resembled the typical male pattern. All three of these women entered sociology when the discipline was still small, insecure, and rather marginal, but growing at a steady pace. Given the small number of women sociologists at that time, these women seem to have been accepted as social scientists, although only Ross felt that she was not discriminated against in terms of rank and salary.

These women were asked to play significant roles in the activities of the profession in organizations within and outside of academe. But there was some "settling for" which they had to do. MacGill Hughes's career was defined by the exigencies of her husband's career moves.

Ross and Burnet served on the executives of the CPSA and CSAA but never reached the presidencies. Instead, Ross was made Honorary President of CSAA in 1979, and Burnet was given a life membership in 1969. Both Hughes and Burnet understood the fine line between being an editor with some power and simply performing secretarial functions for the profession.[76]

As exciting as pioneering may seem, women pioneers have a heavy burden. They experience isolation, especially from other women, partly because they are so few. They have periods of self-doubt. They are pressed into stereotypes by men and women. They are marginalized in various ways.[77]

But these women, and others like them in the first generation of sociologists did research and published despite the disadvantages under which they often worked.[78] They were ultimately recognized in the profession. S.D. Clark, in his historical overview of sociology in Canada, includes the work of Aileen Ross and Jean Burnet among the most important contributions to the body of knowledge in the discipline.[79] In March 1989, at the age of 86, Helen MacGill Hughes was honoured at the annual meeting of the Eastern Sociological Society.

Each of these women spent over 40 years as a professional sociologist.[80] Their lives reveal the passion and energy with which they pursued their work and made their contributions. Their self-understanding and retrospection on the meaning of the venture for women, for the discipline of sociology, and for society itself are part of our sociological heritage, and part of the history of women's participation in science.

II. BIOGRAPHICAL STUDIES

MARGARET GILLETT

The Heart of the Matter:
Maude E. Abbott, 1869–1940

The story of Dr. Maude Elizabeth Seymour Abbott is extraordinary, yet it contains many elements in common with those of other pioneering professional women of her day. Dr. Abbott was a distinguished medical researcher and teacher, a member of the Faculty of Medicine of McGill University in Montreal, who became world famous for her work on congenital heart disease and for her development of the medical museum as a medium of instruction. Her contributions to the writing of the history of medicine, and to the professionalization of nursing education, were also significant and widely acknowledged. During her career, she broke many barriers, scored many "firsts," won a number of awards ranging from gold medals to honorary degrees, participated prominently in international medical societies, had two scholarships and a lectureship founded in her name, was invited to the White House, was accorded honorary membership, among others, in the New York Academy of Medicine, and was greeted with affection by her colleagues and students. To record all this, a full-scale biography was published scarcely a year after her death. Such acclaim would seem to indicate unqualified recognition and success — and yet, and yet . . . .

Like the lives of many professional women of her day and ours, Maude Abbott's career was haunted by a reservation. She was, after all, a woman. Although she was famous abroad, she was not given academic promotion at home; although she was gregarious and hospitable, she was ultimately lonely; although she escaped from the anonymity that was the usual lot of her female contemporaries, she had to find refuge on the border of eccentricity.

The unusual aspects of her story began with her infancy. Maude was the daughter of Frances Elizabeth Seymour Abbott, whose husband, Jeremiah Babin, was a French-Canadian Protestant clergyman. The couple lived in the village of St. Andrews East, Quebec, about 30 miles from Montreal. In January 1867, Jeremiah Babin was accused of murdering his sister, a helpless cripple, who, in true Victorian gothic fashion, had been kept in the attic of his home, and whose body had mysteriously been found in a nearby river after the floods of the previous spring had receded. Although Reverend Babin was eventually acquitted, local feeling and circumstantial evidence were heavily against him. His wife, however, faithfully supported him throughout the long ordeal of his trial. Shortly before the trial she had given birth to a daughter, Alice, and two years later, to a second daughter, Maude. By then, Frances Abbott Babin "had suffered all she could endure and a few months later she died of pulmonary tuberculosis."[1] After these traumatic events, Jeremiah Babin took himself off to the United States and left his babies to be brought up by their widowed grandmother. She had their name legally changed to the maternal Abbott.

It is impossible to say how deep an effect this family tragedy had on Maude and Alice, but it must have left a residue of sorrow in its wake. However, it seems that the girls' childhood was essentially happy and their love for their grandmother very great. Alice proved to be musical; Maude was obviously intelligent, but she was not certain of her talents or her virtues, suffering the awful personal doubts of the teenager. She wrote in her diary:[2]

> I wonder what my life will be like and if I will have any opportunity to do something good or great with it. . . . How can anyone think anything nice about me? It must be that they don't know me well enough. (1 April 1884)

Then again three months later:

> When I come to turn myself over and pick myself to pieces, it is really awful how few lovable points I have in my character. I am half convinced I am clever . . . but my idea of cleverness is entirely different from what I am. (25 June 1884)

Dr. Abbott and friends in Scotland, ca. 1895. (From left to right) Jeannie,
Puddles the cat, Dr. Pace, Dr. Abbott, and Dr. McLean with Molly the dog.
Notman Photographic Archives, McCord Museum.

Both girls had their early education at home with a governess, not an unusual practice for children of their class at that time, yet Maude clearly wanted more. In 1884, at the age of 15, she wrote in her diary:

One of my day-dreams which I feel to be selfish, is that of going to school. I know Alice would like it herself ever so much, but I do so *long* to go . . . . Oh, to think of studying with other girls! Think of learning German, Latin and other languages in general. (March 1884)

On another occasion she wrote, "I don't think it's the other girls' society I want, or anything of the sort, but the good education I would love — how I long for one." (29 March 1884)

Later that year she resolved seriously:

If it ever does come to pass and I get my wish, I will try to keep my resolutions (1) to study hard and conscientiously (2) not to get wild etc., as many girls do (3) not to care for competition but for the real study and the benefit I will derive from it (4) to remember that I go to school for education, not for fun. (9 April 1884)

This intense yearning for education was characteristic of many young women of the era. (One such, M. Carey Thomas, later to be president of Bryn Mawr College, recorded in her diary a burning desire almost identical to Maude Abbott's.)[3] This ambition was both a cause and effect of the expanding educational opportunities for women in the 1870s and 1880s. In Montreal, the available options were the Montreal High School for Girls, which opened in 1875, or several private establishments for young ladies. Maude Abbott's dream came true within the year, for she was sent to a small school run by Miss Symmers and Miss Smith. She confided to her diary in December, 1884: "I have gone to school, so now I have a chance to keep those resolutions I made." But she added, "We are never satisfied. My next wish is to go to college and now I am wishing for that almost as ardently as I did last March for my present good fortune." (28 December 1884)

Happily for her, college too was now a possibility. Montreal's English-language institution of higher learning, McGill College, chartered in 1821, had opened its doors to women in October, 1884. This followed spirited efforts to gain entrance on the part of some girls from Montreal High, their spectacular matriculation examination results, and a sudden endowment for women's education by Donald A. Smith (later Lord Strathcona).[4] Thus, in 1885, after winning a scholarship, Maude Abbott was admitted to the McGill Faculty of Arts or, more accurately, to the Donalda Department for Women. She attended for three weeks, then, because there was a serious outbreak of smallpox in Montreal that fall, she returned to the safety of St. Andrews. The following year, she re-registered at McGill, and became president of her class of nine women. At that time, women were instructed by the regular professors, but were separated from male students. They were permitted to attend co-educational classes for honours work in their senior year, and were welcomed in some informal campus activities. Maude participated fully in student activities; she loved college life, confessing in her "Autobiographical Sketch"[5] of 1928 that "I was literally in love with McGill, or so the girls said. I have never fallen out of love with her since" — although there were times when she well might have.

In 1890, she attained the then-much-coveted B.A. degree, graduating as a gold medalist and simultaneously acquiring, as an insurance policy, a teaching diploma from the McGill Normal School. As class valedictorian, she made a speech that was the very model of sincere youthful exhortation, reminding the women students of their "duties and privileges," urging them to accept their individual responsibilities for the honour of the entire sex, begging them to "remember that at this early stage of women's education in Canada, you, as members of the advance-guard, are in your own persons to be pointed out as instances of its success or failure."[6] Maude Abbott's message yet applies, for women still have to prove themselves in new areas, and we still have to counter the stereotypic thinking that ascribes the shortcomings of one of us to all members of our "minority" group.

If Maude Abbott appreciated being a student at patriarchal McGill, and was grateful that women had been accepted in the Faculty of Arts, she was by no means content to leave it at that. She wanted admission to a field that continued to resist women's encroachments: medicine. This was a relatively unfamiliar professional area for women. The first M.D. degree to be earned by a woman was awarded to Elizabeth Blackwell at Geneva, New York, in 1849; the first Canadian doctor, Emily Stowe, got her degree from New York Medical College for Women in 1867; Stowe's daughter, Augusta, was the first woman to take a medical degree in Canada, and did so only in 1883 at Victoria College, Cobourg, Ontario. Medicine was commonly deemed inappropriate for "nice" young ladies, and many medical schools forthrightly refused to accept them. McGill's Faculty of Medicine is the oldest unit of the university — it existed independently before McGill actually functioned, was "engrafted" onto the college, and for many years remained a law unto itself. It did not welcome the idea of the female physician. In 1888, in the first valedictory address given by a woman at McGill, Grace Ritchie, a close friend of Maude Abbott's, had courageously defied official censorship of speech, and called for the doors of medicine to be opened. She was met with cries of "Shame!" and "Never!" and was forced to take her medical training elsewhere. When Maude Abbott asked her grandmother, "May I be a doctor?" she might well have received a similar answer. But, according to Abbott's recollection in her "Autobiographical Sketch," that wonderfully supportive woman replied, "Dear child, you may be anything you like."

As the time approached for her to begin her medical studies, Maude also found encouragement from some of the upper-class women of Montreal — even from some of the men and from the newspapers[7] — for her involvement in organizing the Association for the Professional Education of Women. Yet her high hopes were dashed. The faculty of medicine remained as Grace Ritchie had found it: impenetrable. Traditional arguments were advanced once more: the study of anatomy would produce hardening effects on the emotions; it would be impossible for any woman to pursue the long course in dissecting without losing her maidenly modesty and true womanliness, which are her essential charms; women were unsuitable for public life; their nerves were weak, their powers of endurance limited, their health uncertain; women should not unsex themselves by leaving their own domestic sphere for that of men. One professor threatened to resign, while another allowed that women "may be useful in some departments of medicine *but* in difficult work, in surgery, for instance, they would not have the nerve." "And," he added, "can you think of a patient in a critical case, waiting for half an hour while the medical lady fixes her bonnet or adjusts her bustle?"[8] Prejudice, sometimes camouflaged by "wit," carried the day, and Maude Abbott was also forced to study elsewhere.

Although she was actually invited to enter the medical faculty of the University of Bishop's College, a rival medical school, Maude still had difficulty getting permission to "walk the wards" at the McGill-dominated teaching hospital, the Montreal General. She described in her autobiography how public pressure — a "newspaper storm," and threats to withhold all-important private financing — finally forced her entry. She also noted how embarrassed she was by the publicity, and how lonely she was away from her women friends of McGill, isolated in an alien crowd of young men. Perhaps she was fortunate that her fellow students seem to have ignored her, for in other co-educational medical schools pioneering women were the constant butt of brutal "practical jokes," coarse language, and obscene graffiti. One woman pioneer wrote in her diary, "No one knows or can know what a furnace we are passing through these days at college. We suffer torment, we shrink inwardly we are hurt cruelly."[9] Maude may have had a comparatively easy time of it. She did not complain of discrimination in grading or awards — indeed, she again graduated with two high prizes — but she was very conscious of the fact that she was treated differently from the rest. She was either not asked to participate in class, or was given too much to do. She realized that she might have been "over-sensitive," but she found hurtful the apparently jocular remarks about "troublesome lady-students" by an apparently friendly professor. She was probably also aware of antipathy from a quarter from which she might have expected support.

The lady superintendent at the Montreal General, Nora Livingston, did not welcome the idea of women medical students. She was categorically against co-education, believing that "mixing of the sexes at lectures is bad and might give rise to complications, when the lady students get strong and brutal," and she rejoiced when the hospital decided to exclude them. When Maude was so grudgingly accepted, Livingston wrote in a letter to her sister, "Miss Abbott is to be admitted here. There is no way out of it. I am sorry, for she is aggressive, but she being the only one, will mind her p's and q's."[10] This raises a number of issues for consideration elsewhere: the relationship of nurses to doctors, the relationship of women to women of other professions, and the views of women who side with the patriarchy. Those who disavow as "aggressive" the women who hurdle the barriers make the task considerably more complex and infinitely more difficult.

In the nineteenth century and even later, it was not uncommon for North Americans to seek their graduate education and research training in Europe. Maude Abbott did this, spending almost three years abroad, studying with famous clinicians and bringing back knowledge, notes, and a collection of newfangled microscopic and lantern slides of medical specimens. She was accompanied on her trip by her sister Alice who, unfortunately, became very ill. The disease, so devastating for Alice, so heartbreaking for Maude, was manic depressive psychosis.[11] Although she survived for almost another 40 years, Alice remained a chronic invalid. She was a dear, but demanded responsibility that Maude alone had to bear. Their grandmother had died in 1890. Other members of the Abbott family included some distinguished personages, such as cousin Sir John, who became Prime Minister of Canada, but Maude had to make her own way in the world. That meant supporting herself and Alice.

On her return to Montreal in 1897, Dr. Abbott established herself in a private medical practice, but was soon drawn back into the McGill orbit. She tells how Dr. Charles Martin, of the McGill Faculty of Medicine, after a chance encounter, invited her to work part-time at the Royal Victoria Hospital, another McGill-associated institution. She became engaged in research, and produced a significant paper from a statistical study on heart murmurs. This had to be read to the Medico-Chirurgical Society by a male doctor, because women were excluded from membership, but it resulted in Abbott's being proposed and elected as the first woman member of that society. It also started her off on her way to fame. Before many years had passed, Dr. Maude Abbott was considered a world authority on congenital heart disease. In 1905, Dr. William Osler (1849–1919), one of Canada's most distinguished physicians and medical educators, who later became Regius Professor of Medicine at Oxford, invited this young woman to write the chapter on congenital heart diseases for the basic medical textbook he was preparing. This was a signal honour, and Maude Abbott was worthy of Osler's trust. His pleasure in the paper she produced was only exceeded by her delight in his letter of praise for its "extraordinary merit;" he deemed it "far and away the very best thing ever written on the subject in English — possibly in any language." For years, Dr. Abbott carried that glowing tribute with her in her handbag.[12]

Osler also set her off in another important direction. He encouraged her to take serious interest in the McGill medical museum. Despite her initial misgivings, she put her prodigious talents and energies to work, so that the course in pathology she developed using the museum became a voluntary,[13] then a not-to-be-missed, integral part of the McGill medical program. This was well before the era of TV and high-tech teaching aids, but Maude Abbott clearly understood how effective real objects and visual presentations could be in teaching. She also refined the system for classifying medical museum specimens, and produced a monumental catalogue of the McGill holdings. Before long, she found herself organizing the International Association of Medical Museums, becoming its secretary, and the editor of its journal. She held these positions for more than 30 years, breathing life into the organization, so that it was said that a meeting of the association without Dr. Abbott was like a performance of *Hamlet* without the Prince of Denmark.

Abbott also created an award-winning international medical exhibition, and wrote very successful histories of medicine in the province of Quebec and the profession of nursing, as well as a life of Florence Nightingale. The writing on nursing grew into a course at the McGill Graduate School of Nurses, while the text and set of slides she prepared for her lectures were published, and then adopted by many schools of nursing across North America. After the death of Sir William Osler in 1919, Abbott undertook the editing of a massive collection of medical research studies and essays in his memory. When another gigantic undertaking, *The Atlas of Congenital Cardiac Disease*, was completed, the publisher inscribed the first copy to Dr. Maude Abbott, "The Madonna of the Heart."

By this time, Abbott's fame was clearly established, so that any Canadian medical person travelling abroad was likely to be met with, "Ah, then you must know Dr. Maude Abbott."[4] She was one of McGill's most renowned staff members. But what kind of career did she have?

Dr. Maude E. Abbott, B.A. (McGill, 1890), C.M., M.D. (Bishop's, 1894), L.R.C.R.&S. (Edinburgh, 1897), M.D., C.M. (h.c., McGill, 1910), F.R.C.P.(C) (1931), F.R.S.M. (London, 1935), outlined her "progress" at McGill as follows:

> I was appointed to the McGill staff in 1899, with the title Assistant Curator of the Medical Museum, and was promoted to the full Curatorship in 1901. This was a teaching appointment, so that my name appears in the Medical Calendar in the line of ascent of the Teaching Staff from the year in this capacity. In 1905 I was made also research fellow in Pathology, and in 1912 Lecturer in Pathology .... I retained my post as Lecturer in Pathology from 1912 until the year 1924, when I was promoted by the Governors of the

University to the position of Assistant Professor of Medical Research. My appointment as Curator of the Medical Museum ran concurrently with the above posts.[15]

It is painfully obvious that this productive and well-respected scholar was advanced with spectacular slowness. The positions she was given were all peripheral, until the lectureship in pathology, which she was given after 13 years in the faculty. Even the assistant professorship, after another 12 years, was not in a regular department, but in a specially-created area with no real future. Still, to show that it was not entirely unappreciative of her worth, McGill took the unusual step in 1910 of awarding her the degree of M.D., C.M. *honoris causa*. That is, it gave her the medical degree it would not let her earn, awarding it on the basis of her "distinguished career as an undergraduate at Bishop's College and for her high reputation as a writer on medical subjects, especially on the subject of cardiac anomalies."[16]

Not surprisingly, other institutions sought out Dr. Abbott. During the First World War, she was offered an acting professorship at the University of Texas until the end of the fighting (when the men would be back), and an associate professorship thereafter. She did not accept that post, but, after considerable persuasion, she spent two years (1923–25) as professor and chairman of pathology at the Women's Medical College of Pennsylvania. Then she returned voluntarily to McGill, to her long-delayed assistant professorship. No man would have accepted this lowly status; no man would have been asked to. Why did she?

Her work, McGill, Montreal, and the care of Alice were obviously more important to Maude Abbott than her own career advancement. Yet, she had considerable professional self-respect, once refusing a job at a Montreal hospital because she would have had to work under one of her former classmates. She was afraid she would "get credit only when I asserted myself, which I find hard to do. I do not like the idea of doing higher work and being called only a second assistant, even for good pay."[17] Nor was she so much "in love with McGill" that she meekly accepted her lot. Over the years, she wrote many times to the chairman of pathology or the dean of the faculty requesting promotion, more security, additional assistance, or salary increases, complaining that "I am at the breaking point financially and in other ways."[18] Minor adjustments were made from time to time, but real promotion was denied. Explanations for decisions were not always given — except that McGill was chronically short of money — and since, in those days, lecturers and assistant professors did not have seats on the faculty, she was unable to argue her case at any collegial forum. A lone woman, she remained an outsider.

The years went by, and, as she approached 65, she wrote to the Principal of the university begging not to be subject to a new regulation requiring retirement at that age because

> I am still in the vigorous exercise of all my faculties and am actively engaged at the present time in the consummation of researches and publications of recognized importance, the results of my years of experience, and which cannot from their nature be relegated to or adequately carried on by anyone but myself. Interruption of these by my retirement at the present juncture would appear to be little short of a calamity.[19]

Like other McGill professors (including some prominent people, such as economist/humourist Stephen Leacock), Abbott was bitterly disappointed when the appeal was denied and the regulation enforced. She asked "one final favour: namely that I be retired with the status of Professor of Medical Research."[20] Again the answer was "NO," and the best the university could do was to grant her a three-month extension as assistant professor while attempting to soften the blow by awarding her a second honorary degree, the LL.D. (1936). She remains the only individual to have received two honorary degrees from McGill.

Since Dr. Abbott's work was of unquestioned merit, was it only because she was a woman that she was not promoted? Speculation about other reasons produces unconvincing results: (1) objections to her family history? This would be possible in a conservative milieu, but far-fetched here, as no one at McGill seemed to know that her father was an accused murderer, and this fact was not mentioned in any published biographical material until 1978. Furthermore, her maternal family, the Abbotts, were very highly respected; (2) conspiracy? During Dr. Abbott's 37 years at McGill, there were six deans of medicine and four principals of the university. It is very unlikely that they would all have agreed to suppress a particular individual; (3) personal dislike? Maude Abbott was generally on friendly terms with members of the faculty, as many letters, written tributes, and oral evidence indicate. Maude Abbott's lack of promotion can only be ascribed to the fact that she was an anomalous female scientist in a conservative male milieu.

While most of Dr. Abbott's colleagues liked her, a notable exception was Dr. Horst Oertel. She did not enjoy a happy working relationship with him, and they frequently clashed over museum policy. He was her contemporary, and a glance at his career pattern shows it was in considerable contrast to hers. As anyone who has ever attempted peer assessment knows, simple comparisons can be dangerously misleading, yet the differences in these cases are astounding. Dr. Horst Oertel was born in Germany in 1873 (Dr. Abbott in 1869); he received his M.D. from Yale in 1894 (the same year she earned hers from Bishop's); he undertook graduate studies in Europe for four years (she for three); after working at the Russell Sage Institute for Pathology, New York, and Guys Hospital, London, he came to McGill in 1914 as an assistant professor (a rank she did not achieve for another decade); he was named full professor and chairman of pathology in 1919, and later appointed to the prestigious Strathcona Professorship (distinctions never to be hers). The First World War helped the advancement of his career (as it might have hers, had she been willing to leave McGill). Oertel was made acting chairman when the incumbent left for military service, and was confirmed in this position after the war. He was apparently able to overcome considerable prejudice against him because of his name and German origins better than she could compensate for her gender. One professor resigned over Oertel's original appointment on the grounds that he was "a member of the enemy race."[21] However, the faculty resisted that pressure more decisively than it overcame ingrained antipathy to women in medicine. It promoted him, and merely retained her.[22]

Apart from Dr. Oertel and Dr. J.C. Meakins, chairman of the department of medicine, with whom she had a series of running battles concerning women's rights in the faculty, Maude Abbott's relationship with men was generally cordial. Like at least half of the highly-educated women of her generation, she never married, but she was by no means a man-hater; on the contrary, she "keenly enjoyed male society," and appreciated the help received from "the generous-minded men on the Faculty of Medicine."[23] It was remarked that the vast majority of the pictures around her rooms were of men, mainly professors and personages in medicine from Canada and abroad.[24] Indeed, she was something of a hero-worshipper. Pre-eminent among her heroes was Sir William Osler, whom she (and others) called the greatest clinical teacher of his time. His influence on her career has already been noted; his impact on her feelings can be seen in her "Autobiographical Sketch": "I shall never forget him as I saw him walking down the old Museum with his great dark burning eyes fixed full upon me." It may not be stretching too far to place a Freudian interpretation on her account of her first meeting with Dr. Osler. "And so he quietly dropped the seed that dominated all my future work," and on the last words of her autobiography: "Sir William Osler, whose keen interest in my work and broad human sympathy pierced the veil of my youthful shyness with a personal stimulus that aroused my intellect to its most passionate endeavour." Her editorship of the Osler memorial material, and the compilation of a complete Osler bibliography, were clearly labours of love.

Dr. Maude Abbott did not forget that women had supported her career — her grandmother, her teachers, Miss Symmers and Miss Smith, the rich matrons of Montreal who wanted to help her study medicine, Grace Ritchie, who had advised her how to get her ticket of admission to the hospital wards, Dr. Helen MacMurchy (co-founder with Maude Abbott and national corresponding secretary of the Canadian Federation of Medical Women), who thought she ought to be a fellow of the Royal Society of Canada.[25]

Although she worked for many years in an all-male environment, Abbott did not — as others in her situation have sometimes tended to do — join the patriarchy and become condescending to members of her own sex. Among her closest friends were such avowed feminists as Dr. Grace Ritchie England, and Professor Carrie Derick, who worked for the female franchise, birth control, and social reform. Her own efforts at liberation were more specifically confined to matters of her own immediate concern. She had little time for more. An editorial in a Montreal newspaper at the time of her death declared that she was "never what is popularly known as a 'feminist.' And yet she did much to advance the emancipation of women from the shackles of all sorts of limitations and prohibitions from which they suffered."[26]

Of course, the one person in her life to whom Maude Abbott was inextricably bound was her invalid sister, Alice. Throughout her very busy career, despite serious financial problems, regardless of health difficulties of her own, she always managed to find some time to visit St. Andrews, to send gifts, and to reply to Alice's letters. These communications add to the massive amount of evidence from many sources that Maude Abbott was generous, affectionate, and kind, or, as one admirer put it, "a beneficent tornado," who was constantly on the move, helping, giving parties, writing letters. The flurry of keeping up with friends near and far, old and new, kept her busy, but did not entirely disguise the fact that she lived alone in Montreal, nor that she seemed to have had no constant close companion and confidante with whom to share her troubles, frustrations, and triumphs.

Pioneering women professors in co-educational institutions, or any milieu where they first braved entry into a male domain, were by definition intruders, outsiders, not of the mainstream. Where they were few in number, they were bound to miss out on personally-and professionally-enriching collegiality; they could not belong to the "old boy network." Yet some were grateful, some proud, some humble, some felt a sense of wonder, a feeling of disbelief, that they had actually made it into the university. They felt their difference, even as they chose to ignore it and concentrate on the task at hand. Their male colleagues felt it, too, and quite frequently codified the gap with differential regulations of various kinds. Dr. Abbott's experience in being grudgingly employed by a university was not unique, but rather reflected a willingness of patriarchal institutions to accept females when there were exceptional circumstances or when there was something to be gained. Limitations imposed on these exceptional women no doubt reduced the precedent-setting effect they might otherwise have had.[27] As a case in point, Dr. Alice Hamilton, whose stature as an expert on industrial diseases was unsurpassed in the United States, in 1918 became the first woman appointed to the Harvard School of Public Health. She was hired because she was the leading expert in her field, but she was never completely accepted. Harvard's President Lowell explicitly stipulated that the appointment was not to be construed as a precedent for admitting women to the medical school, and he imposed three ridiculous limitations: Dr. Hamilton was not allowed into the faculty club; she was not allowed to participate in the academic procession at commencement; and she was not eligible for faculty tickets for the college football game! Dr. Hamilton, like many other professional women in similar circumstances, chose to overlook the trivial exceptions imposed upon her, but neither she nor Maude Abbott received the kind of acceptance an equally distinguished man would have had.[28]

Irrelevant distinctions based on gender are particularly difficult for young women to manage; older women may suffer less. Aging can have its compensations, through a growth in self-confidence, a stronger sense of identity, and perhaps a recognition that much of the academic politicking that goes on does not really matter — and also that it can adversely affect men as well as women. As Maude Abbott grew older, she acquired a degree of acceptance in the faculty of medicine, a special niche. She developed into a personality, and then became something of a character. The adjectives used to describe her changed from "plucky," "brilliant," "aggressive," and "touchy" in youth, to "gregarious," "indefatigable," "generous," "lovable," and "impossible" in later life. Over the years, she became busier, more short-sighted, more financially pressed, had more correspondence to keep up, had more difficulty dividing her time between Montreal and St. Andrews, had less time for herself, and less concern for such aspects of personal appearance as a stain on the front of her dress or the hem of a skirt held up by safety pins. The inevitable student-endowed sobriquet, "Maudie," she considered irksome and undignified at first, but came to accept as a sometime replacement for "Dr. Abbott" — although she still resented it when colleagues called her "Miss." Anecdotes were told about her — some of which she happily contributed herself.

She also became more absent-minded and accident-prone. There was something serio-comic about the famous Dr. Abbott's being hit by a taxi or a street car, but these accidents caused her physical pain and self-scrutiny reminiscent of her youthful, insecure self. In 1929, she wrote in her diary:

I have stood in the valley of the shadow and [was] almost killed. What a strange, awe-inspiring thought. A little more speed of the taxi, a little variation in the angle at which it struck me and the world would have swung on without me. The bright, beautiful world so full of people I care for and who care for me. Was it a warning against carelessness? Oh, my dear, *what* do you believe?[29]

The strategies for survival are many. Becoming a "character," embracing a mild form of eccentricity, is one of them — especially when, from the beginning, one is deemed to be deviant or different, and when the orthodox route to advancement is blocked. If Maude Abbott became slightly eccentric, it is no wonder. She worked in a very ambivalent professional world, where she was greatly admired but still remained "other." She was both larger than life and lesser; world famous and a figure of fun. She had support from significant men in high places — especially Osler — but she did not have a mentor, a champion who fought all the way for her, pressing her case for promotion. She was given important, but relatively small, opportunities, which she herself transformed into major accomplishments. Yet, in one of the host of affectionate and respectful tributes published after her death, on September 2, 1940, Charles Martin, who had first brought her back into the McGill orbit to do research, wrote that she was "a scholar at McGill who, with but few exceptions, had greater international repute and contacts than anyone in the Canadian profession," that she was a person with "vivid personality, with engaging traits of character to give an example to future generations."[30] Ultimately, despite the ambivalence, there can be no serious doubt that Dr. Maude E. Abbott ("Maudie") was genuinely different, special, an extraordinary woman who made a significant contribution to medicine and higher education.

M.F. RAYNER-CANHAM and G.W. RAYNER-CANHAM

Canada's First Woman Nuclear Physicist, Harriet Brooks, 1876–1933

In our accounts of scientific discoveries, it is those who attain the fame rather than those who do the work who are remembered. Yet some of those who toiled at the bench were remarkable scientists who themselves are worthy of remembrance. Harriet Brooks, one of Ernest Rutherford's first research students at McGill University, is one such forgotten scientist.

Born on July 2, 1876, in Exeter, Ontario, Brooks was the second of eight children of Elizabeth Worden and George Brooks. George Brooks was a commercial traveller for a flour company, and considerable hardship was involved in feeding and clothing the family on his salary. Because of his occupation the family moved frequently around Ontario and Quebec. Harriet's final years of schooling were spent at the Seaforth Collegiate Institute, in Seaforth, Ontario. In 1894, the year that she entered McGill University, the family made a final move to Montreal. Harriet Brooks was an outstanding student, winning a scholarship or award in each year of her studies, and it was the monetary scholarships that enabled her to cope with the costs of a university education.

The first two years of Brooks' studies at McGill were mainly devoted to mathematics and languages (Greek, Latin, French, and German), while the last two years were spent almost exclusively on physics. She graduated with a B.A. Honours in mathematics and natural philosophy in 1898. After graduation, Brooks became one of the first members of the research group directed by Ernest Rutherford, who had just arrived from England and was being hailed as an outstanding physicist. Brooks' initial work was on electricity, the subject of her first publication (1899)[1] and of her M.A. thesis (1901).[2] In 1899, Brooks was appointed non-resident tutor in mathematics at the newly-formed Royal Victoria College (RVC), the women's college of McGill University.

It was at about this time that Brooks' research with Rutherford changed to a study of the radioactive substance called "emanation," that was released from radium. Her work showed that the emanation was a gas (which we now know to be radon), with quite different properties from that of radium. This study, the first evidence that one element could change into another, was published in 1901.[3] A subsequent study on a comparison of the radiations from radioactive substances was published in the following year.[4]

In 1901, Brooks obtained leave from RVC to take a position at Bryn Mawr College as fellow in physics while pursuing studies towards a Ph.D. During that year, she was awarded a Bryn Mawr Fellowship to study at Cambridge University, England during 1902–03. With typical modesty, Brooks informed Rutherford of the good news:

> I'm afraid that your generosity in placing me as a collaborator where I am really nothing more than a humble assistant has rather imposed on the faculty of Bryn Mawr, for last night, they awarded me the European Fellowship and much to my satisfaction would prefer that I should make use of it at Cambridge. Of course I am just longing to be able to take advantage of it, the great difficulty is that I am afraid it may lose me my place at McGill and my experience down here has convinced me that there is no place where I want so much to be. It leaves so much to ask however that my place should be kept for me another year.[5]

Brooks added, "There are of course other difficulties to be met besides the ones I have mentioned money and the objections of my family for instance who will think me wholly out of my mind but I think I can overcome them."[6]

With the help of Rutherford, her position at RVC was kept open and it was arranged for her to work with another famous physicist,

Harriet Brooks, 1898.
Notman Photographic Archives.

J.J. Thomson, in the Cavendish Laboratory. Brooks exchanged letters with Rutherford quite regularly, describing in detail the work that she was doing and the problems that she had encountered. In these letters, she displayed a lack of self-confidence, as is illustrated by the following:

> I am afraid I am a terrible bungler in research work, this is so extremely interesting and I am getting along so slowly and so blunderingly with it. I think I shall have to give it up after this year, there are so many other people who can do so much better and in so much less time than I that I do not think my small efforts will ever be missed.[7]

Yet, comments made by Thomson, Rutherford, and others indicate that she was extremely skilled and very gifted in her field. For example, A.S. Eve, in a 1906 article on physics at McGill University, remarked, "Miss Brooks has published several papers on various radio-active phenomena, and this lady was one of the most successful and industrious workers in the early days of the investigation of the subject."[8]

After her year in England, Brooks did not return to Bryn Mawr to complete a Ph.D., but instead resumed her duties at her beloved RVC as non-resident tutor in mathematics and physics, at the same time rejoining Rutherford's research group. It is possible that she felt any further absence would result in the loss of her position at McGill. During this period at McGill, she discovered the recoil of the radioactive atom, a phenomenon that was to prove of great importance in the identification of radioactive isotopes. This research was published in *Nature* (1904).[9] In the same year, she also published some of the work performed in 1902–03 at the Cavendish Laboratory.[10] Brooks stayed only one more year at McGill, because she accepted a position as tutor in physics at Barnard College, the women's college of Columbia University, New York. Although the annual salary at Barnard was an improvement over that at McGill ($1,000 U.S. compared to $750 CDN), the main reason for her move was probably her romantic attachment to a physics professor at Columbia, whom she had met while at the Cavendish Laboratory.

At Barnard, most of Brooks' time was occupied by teaching advanced physics, and her life was relatively uneventful until the summer of 1906, when she became engaged to the professor, Bergen Davis. At that time, it was commonly accepted that women had to choose between a career and marriage. When Brooks wrote to Dean Laura Gill at Barnard to inform her of the impending marriage, Gill replied, "I feel very strongly that whenever your marriage does take place it ought to end your official relationship with the college."[11] Brooks' vehement response was perhaps unusual for the time:

> I think also it is a duty I owe to my profession and to my sex to show that a woman has a right to the practice of her profession and cannot be condemned to abandon it merely because she marries. I cannot conceive how women's colleges, inviting and encouraging women to enter professions can be justly founded or maintained denying such a principle.[12]

Brooks had a strong supporter in Margaret Maltby, head of physics at Barnard, who intervened on Brooks' behalf:

> I most sincerely hope [wrote Maltby] that you will not object to her continuing her work in the department. She is greatly interested in her research and teaching. She enjoys both and she is a very good teacher. I think I can sympathize with her thoroughly. Neither you nor I would like to give up our active professional lives suddenly for domestic life or even for research alone. I know of no woman to take her place — no one available who has the preparation and the personality and ability to teach, and the skill in physical manipulation, that she has.[13]

But Gill, quoting the view of the college trustees, replied, "The College cannot afford to have women on the staff to whom the college work is secondary; the college is not willing to stamp with approval a woman to whom self-elected home duties can be secondary."[14] In any event, for reasons that are unclear, the engagement was broken off. Brooks initially agreed to continue as tutor, but the following month resigned from Barnard.

Many of the letters from Brooks to Gill were written at the house "Summerbrook," in the Adirondacks. This address opened a new direction in her life, because Summerbrook was the summer residence of John and Prestonia Martin, two of the prominent Fabian socialists of the time. Also staying at the Martins at that time were Maxim Gorky, the Russian writer and revolutionary, his companion, Maria Andreyeva, and his secretary, Nikolai Burenin.[15]

It is not clear how Brooks met the Martins. Prestonia Martin advertised "Summerbrook" as a retreat for teachers, and it may be that

Brooks went there after her problems at Barnard. An alternative possibility is that Brooks met Andreyeva at a lecture the Russian woman gave in New York City. The writer John Dewey recalled: "A group of women had asked my wife if she would give the use of our apartment to Mme. Andreyeva to speak on the condition of women in Russia; a sensational newspaper reported that this was a reception to [sic] her, and the Barnard girls were the guests."[16]

Brooks stayed most of that summer at Summerbrook. Then, in October 1906, she travelled with the Gorky entourage to Italy, and stayed with them on the island of Capri. During that time, she must have made contact with Marie Curie, for a letter from Andreyeva to I.P. Ladyzhnikov in February 1907, mentions that Brooks was about to return to Paris, where she had been working with Curie.[17] It is not clear how long Brooks worked at the Curie Institute, but we do know that she was an independent researcher associated with André Debierne, an assistant and colleague of Marie Curie's. By the spring of 1907, Brooks was in London, England.

Curie invited Brooks to stay for the 1907–08 year, but Brooks decided instead to apply for a position at the University of Manchester in England. In her letter to Curie, Brooks wrote:

> Might I ask you to tell M. Debierne for me that I hope very soon to send him an account of the results of my work. I have been separated from my books, hence the delay. I wish to thank you both once again for your very great kindness to me while working with you.[18]

Although Brooks never published any of her work at the Curie Institute, we know that it involved a study of the emanation from the element actinium and that she also continued her studies on the recoil of the radioactive atom, for three subsequent articles from the Institute, two by Debierne, and one by Curie's research associate, Mlle L. Blanquies, cited Brooks' work.[19]

The position at Manchester was the John Harling Fellowship. This most prestigious post required the holder to devote the whole of one year to research. Rutherford wrote a reference for Brooks, in which he noted:

> Miss Brooks has a most excellent knowledge of theoretical and experimental Physics and is unusually well qualified to undertake

research. Her work on "Radioactivity" has been of great importance in the analysis of radioactive transformations and next to Mme Curie she is the most prominent woman physicist in the department of radioactivity. Miss Brooks is an original and careful worker with good experimental powers and I am confident that if appointed she would do most excellent research work in Physics.[20]

Brooks was still waiting to hear about the decision on the Harling fellowship, when she suddenly decided to terminate her physics research and marry Frank Pitcher, who had been a laboratory demonstrator at McGill University while she was a student. What were the choices that were open to her as a woman physicist? She could have continued as a research assistant, either with Rutherford at Manchester, or with Debierne in Paris. Progress of a woman to a senior science position at any university would have been impossible at that time. Alternatively, Brooks could have looked for an academic teaching position at another women's college in Canada or the United States. And while the doctorate was not yet a requirement for male physicists, as a woman lacking a Ph.D., Brooks could only have hoped for a position of lower rank.[21]

Moreover, as a single woman in her thirties, she must have felt societal pressure towards marriage. The difficulty she faced was aptly summed up by M. Carey Thomas, president of Bryn Mawr College: "Women scholars have another and still more cruel handicap. They have spent half a lifetime in fitting themselves for their chosen work and then may be asked to choose between it and marriage."[22] From the number of letters Pitcher wrote to Brooks, we know that his pursuit of her was very ardent. We also know that Mary Rutherford may have played a role as matchmaker, for she later wrote: "Kind regards to Mr. Pitcher. Mrs Gordon [Harriet's sister, Edith] evidently thinks I am responsible for him!"[23]

After her marriage in London on July 13, 1907, Brooks returned to Montreal with Pitcher. During the following years, they raised three children, two of whom died as teenagers.[24] Although Brooks gave up science, she remained active in a number of organizations, such as the Women's Canadian Club, of which she became honorary secretary, for 1909–10 and 1911–12, and president, for 1923–24. She was also a member of the scholarship committee of the Canadian Federation of University Women. In a presentation given to the McGill Alumnae Society in 1910 on Marie Curie, Brooks explained her views on women in science:

> The combination of the ability to think in mathematical formulas and to manipulate skillfully the whimsical instruments of a physical laboratory a combination necessary to attain eminence in physics is apparently one seldom met with in women. I may seem to run counter to generally accepted views in this but it has been my experience that men are as a rule much more skillful in the manipulation of delicate and intricate work than women.[25]

In her comments, Brooks is doing little justice to the performance of women scientists. There were a significant number of women nuclear scientists at that period, of whom Brooks herself was one of the most talented. In fact, with the obstacles to advancement in the physical sciences, it is more surprising how many there were rather than how few.[26] We now know that excellent women scientists have been ignored, while men scientists of the same calibre are remembered for their particular contribution. As Lois Arnold comments:

> How great is great enough? Apparently a double standard exists. In order to be included in science curriculum materials, men can be supergreat, great, or just successful scientists. But even successful women scientists who are recognized as having made a significant contribution in the eyes of their peers are not included.[27]

Harriet Brooks died on April 17, 1933, and she is buried in the Mount Royal Cemetery in Montreal. From accounts of her lingering illness, it would seem possible that she suffered from a radiation-related disease. Rutherford's obituary in *Nature* provides an excellent summary of Brooks' contribution to nuclear science:

> She observed that the decay of the active deposit of radium and actinium depended in a marked way on the time of exposure to the respective emanations and determined the curve of decay for very short exposures. This work, which was done before the transformation theory of radioactive substances was put forward, assisted in unravelling the complex transformations which occur in these deposits. With Rutherford she determined the rate of diffusion of the radium emanation into air and other gases. These

experiments were at the time of great significance, for they showed that the radium emanation diffused like a gas of heavy molecular weight, estimated to be at least 100.

She directed attention to a peculiar type of volatility shown by the active deposit of radium immediately after its removal from the emanation. In the light of later results of Hahn and Russ and Makower in 1909, it is clear that the effect was due to the recoil of radium B from the active surface accompanying the expulsion of an α-particle from radium A. This method of separation of elements by recoil ultimately proved of much importance in disentangling the complicated series of changes occurring in the radioactive bodies.[28]

Why has Brooks been overlooked by historians of science? She was repeatedly mentioned by Rutherford in his text and in his research papers, more so than his other students of the period. It seems clear that much of Rutherford's early work on radioactive decay, and particularly on radon, was performed by Brooks. Her role is recognized in the three major biographies of Rutherford.[29] Part of the reason why she has been overlooked in the history of the discovery of radioactivity may be that, as Rutherford remarked, it was years later that the significance of her experimental work became apparent. Alternatively, the lack of any previous study of this fascinating scientist may simply reflect our tendency to focus on the more central figures (mostly male) in the advancement of science. Obviously, justice needs to be done, for the life of Brooks, far more than that of Marie Curie, reflects what it was truly like to be a woman physicist at the turn of the century.

BARBARA MEADOWCROFT

Alice Wilson, 1881–1964: Explorer of the Earth Beneath Her Feet

Very briefly, at the end of her life, Alice Wilson became a celebrity. Journalists and photographers found inspiration in the story of this tall, white-haired woman, who, at the age of 80, was still clambering over rocks with her geological hammer. Famous, much-travelled, surrounded by admiring students — such is the image of Alice Wilson presented in 1962 by the National Film Board photostory. But what about the path that led to this pinnacle? How did Alice Wilson, born in the Victorian age in a small Ontario town, become the first female geologist in the Canadian government, and the first woman fellow of the Royal Society of Canada?

Alice Wilson's professional life was one long struggle: a struggle against ill health, a struggle for a higher education, and finally a struggle for the position within the Geological Survey of Canada to which her qualifications and experience entitled her. The chief obstacle in her path was the ingrained prejudice of her superiors. She was a woman daring to seek advancement in a field that had hitherto been reserved for men.

Alice Evelyn Wilson was born at Cobourg, Ontario, on August 26, 1881. She was the youngest child and only daughter of Adelia Kingston Wilson and Richard Wilson, a pharmacist. Richard Wilson loved the outdoors and taught his children how to survive in the woods. Years later, Alice referred to this early experience when she wrote to the director of the Geological Survey to request leave to attend graduate school. In an attempt to dispel the prevalent notion that women were not suited to field work, Alice wrote, "with reference to further field work of the more strenuous type I would like to point out that while not heavily built I am muscularly very strong, and from earliest childhood have been accustomed to an out-of-door life both with canoe and tramping."[1]

Intellectual curiosity of all kinds was encouraged in the Wilson family. Two of Alice's relatives were on the faculty of Victoria University, which, during Alice's childhood, was located in Cobourg. On one side of the family was John Wilson, professor of classics, and on the other, her maternal grandfather, William Kingston, professor of mathematics. It was from her grandfather, a geologist as well as a mathematician, that Alice first heard about the secrets that lie under the earth.

Alice's brothers, Alfred and Norman, showed a flair for science while still students at Cobourg Collegiate. Both went on to distinguish themselves: Alfred as chief consultant of mines for the government of Canada, and Norman as head of the department of mathematics at the University of Manitoba. In this atmosphere of scientific curiosity, Alice must have speculated about her future. Did she imagine, as she scrambled over rocks with her brothers, or listened to her grandfather explain the earth's formation, that she too could become a geologist? Probably not. In the 1890s there were few role models for women scientists. As Anne Montagnes points out in her excellent essay on Alice Wilson, Alice's mother had showed great mathematical promise as a girl, but had been discouraged from developing her talent by her father, Professor Kingston.[2] Alice might have discussed science at home, but at Cobourg Collegiate she followed the classical course. "I belonged to a generation," she later explained, "where educated people were supposed to have the classics.[3]

After matriculating with honours in classics, Alice entered Victoria College, University of Toronto, in 1901. She had decided to study modern languages and history, with a view to becoming a teacher. It is typical of Alice Wilson that she made full use of her skills in classical and modern languages after she became a geologist. She even reminded her superiors of these qualifications, in 1930, when applying for promotion at the Geological Survey, citing instances when she had used her knowledge of Latin grammar to help her colleagues.[4]

Fieldwork in the city — Alice Wilson and Jocelyn Legault examine
fossil imprint, Parliament Hill, Ottawa, Ontario, 1962.
Courtesy of Jocelyn Legault.

During her third year at university, Alice underwent some kind of crisis. Her academic record for 1904 indicates that she failed two courses, did not write the majority of her exams, and was given an aggregate mark in most courses. Anne Montagnes speaks of Alice's life-long battle with anaemia and the courageous humour with which she dismissed her disability.[5] At least twice during Alice's adult life, severe illness forced her to suspend all her normal activities for more than a year. The first such bout occurred in 1904.

A variety of emotional factors may have contributed to Alice's illness, including the death, in 1904, of her father, Richard Wilson. She may have been overfatigued as she pursued the rigorous honours curriculum in modern languages, while trying to satisfy her natural curiosity by attending lectures in science. She may have had doubts about her future. Did she really want to devote her life to teaching the rudiments of languages to young girls? Languages did not come easily to her; and she may well have felt that her analytical mind could be used to greater advantage in the sciences.

When Alice recovered from her long illness, she did not return to her studies. Instead, she found a job as clerk in the mineralogy department of the University of Toronto. For two years, she cared for and arranged the specimens in the departmental museum — training that stood her in good stead when she applied for employment in the Geological Survey of Canada.

The Geological Survey, a branch of the federal Department of Mines, was founded in 1842 to help the development of mining in Canada. The work of the Survey is to explore, map, and describe the geological formation of the country. In *Reading the Rocks*, Morris Zaslow explains how geologists within the Survey analyze different types of rocks and study the history of their deposition, in order to determine the areas where minable deposits are most likely to occur.[6] The Palaeontology Division of the Survey helps to determine the age of rock formations by studying the fossils found in sedimentary rocks.

In November, 1909, Alice found a temporary job in the Palaeontology Division of the Geological Survey, as museum assistant. The Survey became her permanent home. Even after her formal retirement, in 1946, she retained her office at the Survey, surrendering it only in 1963, the year before her death.

Alice was fortunate in her early years with the Survey. Percy Raymond, the invertebrate palaeontologist, noticing the interest that she took in her work, answered her eager questions about fossils, and encouraged her to study on her own. Far from thinking that custodial duties were the proper domain for a woman, Raymond advised Alice to complete her degree so that she could acquire professional status. Thanks to this enlightened man, Alice obtained paid leave of absence from the Survey. She returned to the University of Toronto in 1910, and graduated the following year with an Honours B.A. in modern languages and history.

On April 1, 1911, Alice was given permanent tenure at the Survey, and classified as IIB (skilled tradesmen or technical staff). Her salary, which had started at $800 was raised to $850. According to Zaslow, the salary schedule instituted in 1908 across the dominion civil service provided for a starting salary of $800 for Grade IIIB (clerical and labouring staff) and $1000.00 for Grade IIB.[7] Thus, Alice was described as technical staff, but paid as though she were a clerk. Until 1919, Alice's classification remained unchanged, while her salary increased by annual increments to $1,400.[8]

Under the sympathetic guidance of Percy Raymond, Alice's skill in the identification of fossils increased, and the scope of her duties enlarged. She longed to go on field trips, as the men did. Raymond encouraged her. Long expeditions were out of the question, since it would have been considered scandalous, in 1913, for a woman to camp out with a group of men. Having convinced the Survey that it would cost little to send her on short trips, Alice chose for her field work the relatively unexplored Ottawa-St. Lawrence Valley. This area of about 10,000 square miles is of great interest to geologists because it has a wide range of fossils from the Ordovician era. During this period, seven successive invasions of the sea deposited millions of tiny creatures that have since become part of the earth's crust.

For 50 years, from 1913 to 1963, Alice explored the Ottawa Valley, travelling by foot, by bicycle, and eventually, by car. She chipped fossils from the sedimentary rock, scrambling down quarries, or even swinging from a basket in a well shaft, in pursuit of her specimens. Then came hours of research and the preparation of reports with maps and meticulous drawings of the fauna. At times, she was obliged to suspend study of the Ottawa Valley, because of ill health or the pressure of other work at the Survey. In 1916, when the government requisitioned the Victoria Memorial Museum (home of the Survey) because fire had destroyed part of the parliament buildings, it was Alice who supervised the packing and storage of thousands of specimens, and who later took charge of the unpacking and rearrangement of the exhibits for display.

Whenever it was possible, however, Alice returned to her work on the Ottawa Valley. According to G.W. Sinclair, who succeeded Alice at the Survey, her fifty-year exploration of this area produced "a detailed map of the 5,500 square miles east of the Rideau Lakes, a descriptive geological memoir, and an impressive series of bulletins describing the fossils of the most important part of the basin, the Ottawa Formation."[9]

Achievements of this order would not have been possible without something more than the on-the-job training that Alice was receiving at the Geological Survey. With the support of Percy Raymond, Alice obtained a six-week leave, in the summer of 1915, to study at the Marine Biological Laboratory in Cold Spring Harbor, Long Island. While there, she worked on the comparative anatomy of simple marine organisms.

Perhaps it was the stimulation of this study leave, combined with the growing confidence of seeing her work appear in print,[10] that emboldened her to apply for leave to do her Ph.D. Eleven years later, when writing to Mabel Thom, of the Canadian Federation of University Women, Alice explained that her application was rejected and quoted R.W. Brock, Deputy Minister of Mines, who said, "Such work [field work] was given [her] to make it interesting, not that [she] should ever expect to go farther."[11]

Alice knew that advancement in the Geological Survey would be impossible without a Ph.D. By 1911, as Zaslow points out, the Survey was granting paid leave of absence to its most promising young geologists for the purpose of taking doctoral degrees.[12] Determined to attend graduate school, Alice made several further requests for leave between 1915 and 1926. She referred to these requests, without citing dates, in her letter of application for the traveling scholarship offered by the Canadian Federation of University Women. She added, "The grounds of refusal have been various, the fundamental reason has been that it would make a woman eligible for the highest positions in the Survey."[13]

Alice was obviously right in claiming that the Survey denied her requests for academic leave because of her gender, and not because of dissatisfaction with her work. In 1919, she was promoted to assistant invertebrate palaeontologist, the first woman to be given professional status in the Survey. Two years later, the Survey published the first of her many bulletins, *The Range of Certain Lower Ordovician Faunas of the Ottawa Valley with the Descriptions of Some New Species* (1921).

Alice's excursions in the Ottawa area whetted her desire to explore other areas rich in Ordovician fossils, in particular, the west shore of Lake Winnipeg. She would explore the shore by canoe and camp out, just as she had camped by Lake Ontario when she was a child. No doubt the need to show the Survey that a woman could undertake such strenuous and risky field work spurred her determination. But where was she going to find a suitable companion?

Luck favours the bold. At a French conversation course in Ottawa, Alice met a young teacher, Madeleine Fritz. Although Madeleine was only 23 and had a bare smattering of geology, Alice invited her on a fossil hunting expedition in the summer of 1920. More than 50 years later, Madeleine Fritz recalled that journey into the wilds of Lake Winnipeg: "Because it was the wilds, we saw nobody for six weeks except for the occasional Indian or fisherman."[14] They paddled a twenty-foot skiff, slept in a tent, and had several "hairy experiences."

The expedition changed the course of Madeleine Fritz's life. The young teacher who was hired by the federal government as "cook and canoeman" was so fascinated by fossils that she continued to study palaeontology, receiving her Ph.D. from the University of Toronto in 1926.

Alice Wilson had several obstacles to surmount before she could embark on her own Ph.D. The first was a serious illness that began in 1921 and lasted nearly two years. Presumably, this illness stemmed from the chronic anaemia that had afflicted her since childhood. On this occasion, Alice was forced to spend at least a year at the Clifton Springs Sanitarium in Clifton Springs, New York. In the correspondence between the Geological Survey and the sanitarium, mention is made of Alice's depression. Of course, she was depressed, and worried. In addition to anxieties about her health, she had financial problems. She was absent from the Survey for 19 months. After using up her sick leave, she was on half pay, and finally, for a period of ten and a half months, on unpaid leave. As her long illness ate into her savings, Alice must have wondered if she could ever afford to attend graduate school, even if she did eventually obtain study leave.

By October 1922, Alice was well enough to leave the sanitarium, and on December 16, 1922, she finally returned to the Geological Survey.

Two years later, she applied to Dr. W.H. Collins, director of the Survey, for an eight-month leave of absence in order to obtain her Ph.D. She suggested four possible thesis topics, all related to Ordovician fauna, pointing out that, since she would probably be working on these problems later for the Survey, an academic study of one of them now would make her future work more valuable.[15] Even though Alice's request was supported by Dr. E.M. Kindle, chief of the Palaeontology Division, Collins replied that he could not recommend leave, "at least with pay." Writing to Alice on December 29, 1924, Collins argued that since geological field work in Canada was rarely practicable for women, Alice's usefulness to the Survey would not be greatly increased by further study. He referred to the many days of sick leave Alice had taken since 1921, and concluded by mentioning the need for a substitute during her absence.

Replying on January 14, 1925, Alice stressed that her sick leave was not habitual, but confined to the years 1921 to 1923, and reminded the director that the question of a substitute was not raised when the other assistant palaeontologist applied for study leave. Arguing that her usefulness to the Survey was greatly enhanced by her study leave in 1915, Alice affirmed, "I am not working to the limit of my capacity."

Since the Survey would not grant her leave with pay, Alice tried another tactic: she asked permission from the Survey to apply for the annual scholarship, offered by the Canadian Federation of University Women. Permission was refused. Alice persisted; and in January, 1926, the Survey relented sufficiently to allow her to apply for the CFUW scholarship. In her letter of application to Mabel Thom, convener of the scholarship committee, Alice summarizes her long battle with the Survey to obtain study leave. She concludes:

> The obtaining of the degree would in all probability make no difference to the applicant, financially or in ranking of the present work, but it is the desire to create a precedent for any other woman who might fill the position under a later regime. . . . In the present instance the technical grading of the position for a woman is secured and it is desired to place it upon as high a footing as possible. If it is not possible to do that now it will probably be delayed many years, possibly another generation.[16]

As evidence of her ability, Alice included in her application copies of papers that she had published under the Geological Survey and elsewhere, and letters of support from Dr. Percy Raymond, head of palaeontology at Harvard, and Dr. Cumings, a specialist in Ordovician fauna, at Indiana University.

To anyone familiar with the slow grinding of academic committees in the 1980s, the efficiency and speed of the CFUW scholarship committee of 1926 is amazing. Within four weeks, the Committee managed to have the candidates' written work appraised by experts and to circulate the appraisals among its members, who were scattered across Canada. On March 1, Alice Wilson received a telegram informing her that she had won the CFUW scholarship for 1926.

Writing to wish Alice success in her studies, Mabel Thom affirmed, "I feel that the scholarship was designed to fit into the plans of such as yourself, who have done such splendid pioneer work, and by our help, can be put in a position to do so much for other Canadian women."[17]

On winning the one-thousand-dollar scholarship, Alice must have believed that the long-coveted opportunity for graduate study was within her grasp. If so, her euphoria was short lived. In replying to Mabel Thom, on March 7, Alice mentions that she may need a second year to get her degree, as her superiors are insisting that she complete the identification of the specimens collected by the field men before leaving for university. She adds that she has noticed "an amelioration of atmospheric conditions," since the announcement of the scholarship and hopes that "everything may straighten out."

On March 29, 1926, Alice wrote to Collins, requesting permission to transfer her Ordovician work to the university of her choice, for a period of six months. The letter suggests that Alice was doing everything possible to ensure that her period at the university would benefit the Survey as well as herself. Not only would she delay her departure in order to complete the identification of fossils for the field men, but she would focus her research on a problem already assigned to her by the Survey. Even these concessions did not satisfy her superiors. Kindle, the head of the Palaeontology Division, would not recommend leave with pay unless assured of a substitute during Alice's absence. Collins was even more determined not to grant Alice leave. Seizing on the technical description of her duties, supplied by the Civil Service Commission, he insisted that much of her work could not be transferred to a university. Writing to Alice, on April 9, 1926, Collins argued that the Palaeontology Division needed more staff for laboratory and museum work, not more researchers. While refusing Alice's request, Collins professed to "admire and sympathize with [her] desire for self-improvement."

The patronizing tone of that remark must have needled Alice Wilson. On receiving Collins' letter, she immediately wrote asking if an application for a six-month leave *without pay* would meet with his approval.

Again Collins refused. At this point, Alice could see only two alternatives: to hand back the scholarship, or to resign from the Survey in order to use it. She contacted the Canadian Federation of University Women to explain her predicament.

The executives of the CFUW were quick to support their candidate. At their request, Sir Robert Falconer, president of the University of Toronto, telegraphed the prime minister and the minister of mines, asking that study leave be granted to Alice Wilson.[18]

This unexpected appeal to the highest authority alarmed the Survey. The director wrote to Alice Wilson, asking to see the correspondence with the CFUW that prompted Sir Robert's telegram, and prepared a memo, outlining the history of her application for study leave. This five-page memo clearly reveals Collins' sexist attitude. Claiming that Alice Wilson was adequately educated for her present job, Collins argues that further education would only be appropriate if she were to perform the work of a field geologist. He concludes:

> Physically and sexually Miss Wilson is not fitted for any but the lightest sort of field work, and only in settled districts. An undesirable condition would be created by attempting to fit her for field duties.[19]

Despite Collins' reservations, the minister of mines decided that it would be advisable to yield to the political pressure of Alice Wilson's supporters and wrote to Sir Robert Falconer and to Susan Vaughan (President of the CFUW), saying that Miss Wilson's leave would be granted.[20] The important question of salary was not mentioned.

On learning that her leave was without pay, Alice again contacted her supporters in the CFUW. The women were anxious to help her, but the matter was delicate. Two members of the scholarship committee wrote to their members of parliament; other action was considered, including a further appeal to the minister and even the prime minister.[21] On reflection, however, Alice must have decided that it would be unwise to pursue the matter further. After all, she liked working for the Survey and wanted to return after she got her Ph.D.

Dr. Charles Camsell, deputy minister of mines, advised Alice that leave with pay "would involve extra expense to the country," because a substitute would be necessary.[22] Actually, the "question of a 'substitute' was a half truth," as Alice wrote to Mabel Thom.[23] In reality, the Palaeontology Division was short-handed and Alice's leave was being used as an excuse to hire somebody. Her absence would not handicap the division, since she had agreed to spread her leave over two years in order to handle the field identifications. Alice continued,

> Please don't think I am 'sore.' I am not, I feel that a real step has been made in getting leave at all, a precedent has been established which may be pushed further later. The very fact of the absolute refusal of leave shows without any comment of mine that they would have gone the limit to prevent it. We have gained the principle — mainly — for this time they have held on to the money and are comforting themselves with that.

Alice had won the right to use her hard-earned scholarship, but the director of the Survey had not changed his attitude. When he drafted the advertisement for the "substitute" who would replace Alice Wilson, Collins stipulated that the applicant should be "male."[24]

Alice Wilson was 45 in October, 1926, when she entered the University of Chicago. For her, graduate school was a revitalizing experience. In a letter to Mabel Thom (May 8, 1927), Alice speaks of the "very great stimulus" of working with people from all over the continent, and the "frank comradeship" of the graduate students, based on "mutual respect" and a "mutual state of impecuniosity."

Dr. Stuart Weller, head of palaeontology at the University of Chicago, describes Alice as "full of enthusiasm." Writing to Mabel Thom, on April 22, 1927, Weller adds, "Her previous work with the Canadian Survey gives her confidence in herself and she possesses the initiative to go forward with her research work in a highly satisfactory manner."

Unfortunately, Dr. Weller, an outstanding palaeontologist, died suddenly in 1927. Alice, who had chosen Chicago with a view to working under Weller, was obliged to complete her thesis under the supervision of a young assistant professor, Carey Croneis. Her thesis, entitled "The Geology of the Cornwall District, Ontario, Canada," made use of material that she had previously gathered during a survey of the

Cornwall area, conducted by the Canadian and American governments, before the deepening of the St. Lawrence River.[25]

In December 1929, Alice Wilson received her Ph.D. She had completed her course work and thesis in three years, a remarkable achievement considering the work load that she was simultaneously carrying for the Geological Survey. Despite the CFUW scholarship, the 12 months without pay sorely strained Alice's finances. It may have been for financial reasons that she delayed taking the final portion of her academic leave until the autumn of 1928.[26] Since she was dividing her leave in order to accommodate the Survey, her superiors agreed to pay her travelling expenses between Ottawa and Chicago — exclusive of her initial trip to Chicago and final return.

Another source of stress for Alice, while she was struggling to complete her thesis, was the death of her mother. Adelia Wilson died in March, 1929. For 47 years, Adelia had provided her daughter with encouragement and intellectual companionship. According to Anne Montagnes, the minds of the two women were so attuned that they could communicate their thoughts through aptly chosen biblical quotations.[27]

Private sorrow and professional neglect: the late 1920s and early 1930s were hard years for Alice Wilson. As she had predicted when applying for the CFUW scholarship, her doctorate made no difference to her status or remuneration at the Survey. Indicative of the attitude of her superiors was their mode of address: to them, she was still "*Miss* Wilson," whereas male geologists were addressed as Doctor.

As soon as she received her Ph.D., Alice applied for promotion from assistant invertebrate palaeontologist, a rank that she had held for 10 years, to associate invertebrate palaeontologist. On March 19, 1930, she renewed her application, outlining her qualifications in a letter to Dr. Collins and stressing that her present classification did not reflect her qualifications, work, or experience. Dr. Kindle, Alice's immediate superior, wrote to Collins (March 24, 1930), explaining why he could not support Alice's application. While both men agreed that Alice deserved a somewhat higher salary than the $2,520 she was receiving at the time, they objected to promoting her to associate palaeontologist, even though a vacancy at that level existed. Kindle, short staffed as always, wanted to confine Alice to museum work, while Collins insisted that Alice, as a woman, could not perform the required field work, and would consequently be overpaid. These two men went to the extraordinary length of proposing a new classification with the title "associate curator of palaeontology," and a maximum salary of three thousand dollars, in order to avoid promoting Alice to associate palaeontologist.

Alice recognized this stratagem for what it was, a grotesque attempt to keep her out of the higher echelons of the Survey, and to bar her from the field work that she so passionately enjoyed. The discussion of Alice's reclassification continued for over a year, culminating in a conference on July 7, 1931, attended by Dr. Collins, G.H. Gilchrist of the Civil Service Commission, and others. At the conclusion of the investigation, Alice criticized the department for its presentation of her case, pointing out that the "curator idea seemed to lead to a blind alley."[28]

Two months later, the Civil Service Commission decreed that it could not make any recommendation regarding Alice Wilson's promotion until the Treasury Board had determined the classification rates of technical and professional staff.[29] After 22 months of uncertainty, Alice had failed to win promotion or even a modest raise in salary. To be fair to Alice's superiors, we must remember that budgets were tight during the Depression, and that the Palaeontology Division was under-staffed. On the other hand, to expect Alice Wilson to devote most of her time to the cataloguing job that she had begun 20 years earlier, as an untrained clerk, was not only unfair, but a blatant waste of her talents and training.

The first show of appreciation for Alice Wilson's work came not from the Survey, but from the Conservative government. In 1935, Alice became a member of the Order of the British Empire. Whether or not this honour, combined with an invitation in 1936 to join the Geological Association of America, influenced the attitude of the Survey, Alice succeeded in changing her classification to assistant geologist, in December, 1936. She no longer had to contend with Dr. Collins, who had lost effective control of the Survey in 1933, and was, by 1936, a sick man.[30] The move to assistant geologist was a lateral one, resulting in a mere $60 increase in her annual salary, but it acknowledged the broad range of Alice's duties.

Once out of the Palaeontology Division, Alice advanced steadily, becoming an associate geologist, at a salary of $2,700 per year, in 1940, and a full geologist in 1945. Regulations required Alice to retire on her sixty-fifth birthday, August 26, 1946, but the records show that she continued to work at full pay ($4,080 per year) until May 26, 1947.[31]

Retirement, when it eventually came, made no difference to Alice Wilson. She continued to go to her office, as she had for 38 years. Released from her routine duties at the Survey, she was free to continue her work on the Ordovician fauna of the St. Lawrence Lowland, publishing her research in the *Bulletins* of the Geological Survey and in the *Proceedings of the Royal Society of Canada*.

To supplement her meager pension, Alice acted as consultant for oil companies, for the Ontario government, and for the government of Canada.[32] A report that she prepared for the federal department of transport, in 1953, led to a long argument over her fee. "I would be ready to do the work gratis," Alice wrote to L. H. Burpee. "But I am not prepared to underbid my profession."[33]

Since Alice's employment was only for 30 days, the sum involved was not large, but Alice, at 72, was still prepared to fight for a principle. On August 31, 1953, she wrote to Burpee to point out that, by withholding her pension for the month she worked, the federal government had reduced her fee to a pittance. She proposed a higher rate, concluding:

> I am afraid I have put you to more trouble than it may be worth to you but it is establishing a precedent which may be useful to other professional workers — and in the Government a precedent is as the laws of the Medes and Persians.

Alice's logic prevailed; through persistence, she succeeded in raising the rate of pay from $4,080 per year to $8,400.

In her so-called retirement, Alice took up another career, teaching. For 10 years, from 1948–49 to 1958–59, she taught a course in palaeontology at Carleton University. Discarding the ancient Cossack suit and knee-high boots that had long been her hiking costume for more conventional slacks and brogues, she led her students out to explore the rock formations of the Ottawa area. The energy and enthusiasm of this white-haired, frail-looking professor made an unforgettable impression on one young student, who said:

> We never understood how she could do all she did in a day, first to the Survey, then a two hour lecture with us, then back to the Survey, and then a field trip in the afternoon. She always let us browse a little first on a field trip to wear off our outdoors high spirits, but then she would start in describing fossils, making the

ancient creatures seem to smile they became so real. On the drive there and back she would lay out for us the whole history of the area.[34]

Alice Wilson had the gift of explaining complex scientific matters in language that everyone could understand. In 1947, she published a long-contemplated geology for children, entitled *The Earth Beneath Our Feet*. The Ottawa Field-Naturalists' Club so enjoyed their field trips with Alice, that they asked her to produce a permanent record for them. Her monograph, *A Guide to the Geology of the Ottawa District* (1956), outlines eight field trips, describes and illustrates various fossils found in the region, and briefly explains the geological formation of the Ottawa Lowland. To explain why geological faults occur, Alice suggests a simple experiment: "Take a small handkerchief, about eight inches square. Wrinkle up one half of it into miniature mountains but keep the other half flat maintaining the eight-inch edge. Tension becomes great in the unwrinkled part. It tears. Just so, the earth's crust!"[35]

In the last 20 years of her life, Alice was able to satisfy her longing to travel. Even in the difficult year of 1932, she managed to wangle 30 days leave from the Survey to visit the Bahamas and British Guiana. On this trip, as on all her travels, she collected samples of soil and fauna for her own research and for the Survey. On later trips, she sailed up the Amazon, flew over the Andes, and attended international geological conferences in England and Mexico. "Life is an adventure, and finding out things is an evolution," she told Kay Rex in an interview published in the *Globe and Mail* on February 25, 1960.

Honours came thick and fast in the last quarter of Alice's life. Frequently, she is cited as the first woman to attain a particular honour. Out of consideration for other women, Alice preferred to be known simply as a fellow of the Royal Society of Canada (a distinction she attained in 1938), rather than as the first woman fellow. In November, 1959, the Geological Survey held a reception at the Logan Club to celebrate her 50 years with the Survey. They surprised her with a handsome set of bookends and a paperweight carved out of marble from a quarry she herself had discovered. Finally, at the convocation of June, 1960, Carleton University made Alice Wilson an honorary Doctor of Laws.

In 1963, Alice gave up her office, much to the sorrow of her colleagues at the Survey, who knew how empty her life would be without work. But Alice Wilson was a realist: she was frail; her eyesight was failing; it was time to leave. On April 15, 1964, she died.

Did the honours and acclaim of her last years make up for the earlier hardship and neglect? Alice Wilson would have put it differently. For her, the privilege of working in an area that fascinated her and the knowledge that her efforts had helped open the field to other women made it all worth while. She never forgot the Canadian Federation of University Women, whose support, both financial and political, enabled her to obtain her Ph.D. and showed her gratitude by donating a fund, named in her honour, to provide for the further education of university women.

An analytical mind and acute powers of observation enabled her to make a real contribution to Canadian geology. Her maps of the Ottawa-St. Lawrence Lowland and her *Guide to the Geology of the Ottawa District* are still consulted by students.

In fighting for advancement within the civil service, Alice was keenly aware that she was helping to blaze a trail for other women. When asked in an interview to explain her attitude towards the "male-female equation" in her profession, she replied: "If you meet a stone wall you don't pit yourself against it, you go around it and find a weakness. And as with other problems, when you look at it in these terms, then you don't get so personally involved."[36]

The response is typical of Alice's tact and self-restraint. Courage, humour, tact, and resilience, these are the qualities that enabled Alice Wilson to triumph in a profession that had formerly been monopolized by men.

EDWINNA VON BAEYER

Isabella Preston (1881–1964): Explorer of the Horticultural Frontier

After the Second World War, a Japanese admiral visiting the United States was asked if there was a special attraction he would like to see — Niagara Falls perhaps? The admiral politely thanked his hosts, then said, "I would really like to travel to Canada and meet Isabella Preston." He was a lily enthusiast.[1]

Lilies were the main catalyst in Preston's transformation from an English immigrant to Canada with an interest in horticulture to a world-renowned hybridist. Not only did Preston originate nearly 200 hybrids in a 20 year period, she also successfully pursued a career which began late in life by today's standards, and which apparently did not encounter major impediments despite being within a male-dominated profession.

The Beginning: 1881–1912

The future hybridist began life as "a shy, little mouse," the youngest of five children in a prosperous middle-class family in Lancaster, England. Later in life, she stated that she probably had been "born with green fingers."[2] Her formal education was typical for a nineteenth-century girl of her class. She apparently was introduced to the popular game of tennis, but found it "a great waste of time when there was work to do in the garden."[3] At the age of 18 she matriculated. In 1906, when she was 25, Isabella took a short course at Swanley Horticultural College (a women's college), and this constituted nearly her entire formal education in horticulture.

In 1912, Preston's life was radically affected by her sister's decision, after their parents' deaths, to accept a position as music teacher at a girl's school in Guelph, Ontario. Margaret, a dynamic, outgoing type, persuaded Isabella to close up the family home and come with her to Canada for a year "to see if I liked the life."[4]

Guelph Interlude: 1912–1920

Isabella Preston arrived in Guelph, Ontario armed with a cultural background predisposed to horticulture, an enthusiasm for gardening, and an obvious determination to persevere. Horticultural fame, however, seemed far away. Her first horticultural job was on a fruit farm, picking raspberries, plums, and peaches. Preston, intent on studying horticulture "to find some means of cultivating this hobby,"[5] enrolled (at the age of 31) in the Ontario Agricultural College (OAC now the University of Guelph). British and North American women had been encouraged since the early 1800s to garden as an avocation, but not as a vocation. Family friends attempted to discourage Preston's interest. One friend who tried to direct her towards a more traditional female occupation said, "If you *have* to do something agricultural why not take up poultry?"[6] Undaunted, she began courses in the horticultural department under Professor J.W. Crow, in the fall of 1912. Following the objectives of the college (which was established in 1874 in response to a need for a practical school of agriculture), the department was oriented to specific, functional goals. Fruit and vegetable growing were a priority.

Women were not uncommon on the OAC campus by this time, although not fully evident in the horticultural and agricultural degree programs.[7] Evidently, Preston was not taken seriously by many of her fellow students — an attitude which changed considerably when they later dealt with her as the federal government's leading expert in ornamental horticulture.[8]

During her first semester at the college, she also laboured in the greenhouses earning 12 cents an hour.[9] By spring 1913, she no longer was taking classes. Professor Crow had hired her as a day labourer to look after an experiment he was running on a method of strawberry growing.[10] In time Preston also became responsible for the vegetable gardens and greenhouse maintenance: repotting, seeding, planting, and later, hybridizing.

Her first introduction into the mysteries of plant breeding occurred that year, as she watched Professor Crow emasculate and pollinate the flowers on dwarf pear trees. Until then, she had known nothing about this subject, but she remedied the deficiency by reading "all the books in the library" on horticulture and plant breeding.[11]

In the early 1900s, self-instruction in plant breeding was still possible for it was a relatively new science. The British tradition dated from the late 1700s, but sustained interest and practice was actually stimulated in 1899, when the Royal Horticultural Society held the first international hybridization conference.

Canadian plant breeding, pre-1900, was quite informal. There were dabblers in the new science, but most activity centred upon plant introductions, as agricultural department officials, nurserymen, farmers, academics, orchardists, and enthusiastic gardeners sought to introduce a greater range of hardy plants into our northern climate. The most intense activity centred on economic plants and crops, although by the late 1800s, there was a quickening of interest in hybridizing ornamentals.

By 1910 hybridization theory and technique had become quite sophisticated. Standards had been fixed, co-ordination and co-operation had increased, and writings on hybridizing had found wider circulation. A small army of amateur and professional hybridists had appeared, armed with the tools of the trade — tweezers, scissors, magnifying glass, small paper bags (for protecting the pollinated flower from insect interference), plant labels, notebook and pen.

Hybridists became more systematic in this work, usually specializing by working on a particular line: disease-resistant wheat, hardy hybrid tea roses, or red gladiolus. Information expanded on how and when to effect successful crosses, how to select the most promising seedlings, how to test under different conditions, and how to record the results.[12]

In this receptive atmosphere created by a small, but enthusiastic, circle of Canadian hybridists, Preston made her debut. She began in the OAC greenhouses by growing a variety of lilies from seed, then effecting as many different crosses as possible. She appeared to have a natural affinity for the flower, for her subsequent successful crossings were achieved without the modern technological tools of chromosome counts, cytology, etc.

When Preston began crossing lilies, the lily had not yet attained the pre-eminent position in the perennial border it enjoys today. Until the introduction of Preston's trumpet lily hybrid, there was a dearth of introductions into commercial circulation. Preston's accomplishment, however, was not an overnight feat. She crossed and reared hundreds of lilies between 1914 and 1917, suffering set-backs such as the death of all the seedlings planted out in open ground during the winter of 1917–18.[13]

On July 20, 1916, the historic cross was made — a cross which vaulted Preston into the front ranks of North American plant hybridists. *Lilium regale* — vigorous, disease-resistant and hardy — donated pollen to the seed-parent, *L. Sargentiae* — less floriferous, less hardy. The resulting seedlings were placed in a cold frame in November, 1918. Several blossomed in 1919.[14] The resulting hybrid was named *L. Princeps* — considerably taller, with large, fragrant white flowers and stronger-growing. Since it bloomed two weeks later than its parents, it was especially commended for extending the lily season. In 1923, after four years of trial, it was released to nurseries under the name *Lilium x princeps "George C. Creelman."* The OAC Horticulture Department named the lily after a popular OAC president. Thirty years later, the Creelman lily continued to be recognized, not only as a breakthrough, but also as an appropriate, often-used parent for contemporary hybrids.

The First World War curtailed Preston's ornamentals work. Her war-time efforts were greatly influenced by the "greater production" campaigns, which urged gardeners to grow as many vegetables as possible for home and army consumption. Plant breeding projects focussed on creating vegetable strains which would be faster-ripening, hardier, and resistant to disease and insects. The lilies had to wait.

Consolidation of Career: The Ottawa Years — 1920–1948

After the First World War interest in ornamentals was renewed, resulting in a call for new varieties, colours, and forms to enhance our gardens. The long war period had stimulated a longing for beautiful flowers and gardens — symbols of peace and repose. After the war, professional horticulturalists, who had experienced great difficulty in obtaining plant material during the war, called for more Canadian grown and originated material.

The Dominion Experimental Farms System was a leader in the resurgence of ornamentals research and breeding. The centre of activity was Ottawa's Central Experimental Farm (hereafter CEF), in the Horticulture Division led by William T. Macoun (1869–1933), son of the famous botanist, John Macoun. As Dominion Horticulturist, Macoun oversaw the work of the horticultural departments in the System's 24 farms and stations.

Macoun responded to the need for an expanded range of ornamentals by searching for someone to undertake the experimental work. He was unhappy with a previous assistant, who had had "neither the eyesight, disposition or the ambition to do this work."[15] The success of Preston's Creelman Lily, the solid work she had done under Crow's tutelage, and her obvious talent for ornamental breeding brought her to Macoun's attention. Preston described her transition from self-taught researcher to centre-stage hybridist quite simply: "Dr. Macoun was looking for someone to do breeding work with ornamental plants so I applied for the position. I wanted to discontinue working with vegetables which I had to do during the war. Dr. Macoun gave me a list of plants and told me to see what I could do with them."[16]

This modest statement concealed the fact that Macoun suggested she work on six different genera he chose as less likely to duplicate the efforts of other plant breeders. The genera were: lily, rose, lilac, Siberian iris, columbine, and flowering crabapple — quite a challenging range. Most breeders would specialize in one or perhaps two genera, as the work involved and the slow acquisition of information on timing, technique, and cultivation could be enough for one person's lifetime. Preston's main objectives were to breed material hardy enough to endure northern prairie winters, and ornamental enough to beautify farms, ranches, towns, and cities.

Preston occupied a unique position in the Ottawa bureaucracy. When she entered the federal civil service in 1920, women were not favoured employees. They traditionally occupied the lower bureaucratic levels — clerks, stenographers, etc. Advancement almost never occurred. Women who married were expected to resign. In general, women were not considered suitable for, or capable of, employment at higher, more responsible levels.[17] In fact, Preston was doubly unique: she was participating in an (as yet) unrecognized profession, as well as invading a male-dominated vocation. Men held key positions in horticultural societies, and were major contributors in plant breeding circles. They also operated the majority of Canadian nurseries and greenhouses. The first woman president of the influential Horticultural Societies of Ontario Association, Mary Yates, was elected only in 1920; Mary Eliza Blacklock, one of our first nurserywomen, established Rowancroft Gardens only in 1914.

The Department of Agriculture was not exceptional in its hiring policies toward women. Although Preston made her appointment seem effortless, it was not. She actually began working at the CEF on May 1, 1920, at 50 cents an hour, as a day labourer — one of the lowest grades in the Department. By November, Macoun requested that the director of the CEF (E.S. Archibald) create a new position in the Division of Horticulture — "specialist in ornamental horticulture" — to be filled by Preston. She was highly recommended, in turn, by Archibald for her "energetic" work in breeding and labelling ornamentals, her "excellent training and an excellent record as a Hybridist at Guelph," and her "real love for the work," a "qualification so very difficult to discover in Assistants."[18] Archibald's praise was qualified by his further admission: "To be frank we have been on the lookout for trained men capable of filling these vacancies and carrying on the work as it should be done, and have failed to locate promising men who would consider coming at the minimum of the classification."[19] The department feared that the men who applied at this scale would be relatively untrained, and would soon leave for better-paying jobs.

The director did rewrite the educational qualifications to suit Preston's unique background. The original stipulation for a university graduate in botany was reduced to an educational equivalent of high school graduation, with training in botany, and four years experience in plant breeding at an agricultural college or experimental station. During the 1920s, hiring self-taught personnel, although not as prevalent as in prior years, was not unusual. Many of the first Department of Agriculture officials were self-taught enthusiasts. For example, William Saunders, the first director of the Experimental Farm System, was a druggist in London, Ontario, who became prominent through his experiments in fruit-raising and insect study on his own experimental grounds. W.T. Macoun rose through the ranks at the farm — from day labourer to Dominion Horticulturist, responsible for the progress of Canadian horticulture. Preston, like her superior, became a professional on the job, rather than as part of an academic program of study.

Preston enthusiastically began working on May 1, 1920. She set out into the CEF gardens that first summer, with her tweezers, labels, and notebook. Sitting on her favourite low stool, she meticulously recorded the day's crosses, working her way through the lily, rose, crabapple, lilac, and columbine collections. She chose seed parents and pollen parents; watched the pollen ripen until it was just right for fertilization, and effected the cross, and then painstakingly tied labels on each stem. Then she waited and watched until seed pods matured, and she could collect the viable seed. This intense summer of enjoyable work became the foundation for her subsequent hybridizing efforts.

Preston may have worked steadily, but the mills of the bureaucracy ground very slowly, for she did not receive a permanent position as "specialist in ornamental horticulture" until September 9, 1922. Although the duties remained the same (plant breeding, labelling the collection, writing for public information, record keeping, and exhibition judging), the position was declassified from an assistant's pay scale (beginning at $2,400) to the new position of "specialist" starting at $1,400.[20]

Horticultural Interests

One of the subjects of Preston's first breeding programs was the lilac. From the mid-1800s, the field in hybrid lilacs had been led by the French. Preston's 1920 crosses, however, put Canada on the lilac "map." Following Macoun's suggestion, she crossed *Syringa reflexa* (pendulous, compact, narrow pink flower clusters) with *S. villosa* (smaller, erect flower clusters) — both hardy in Ottawa — with the hope of creating a hardier floriferous variety suited to prairie cultivation. She was so successful that nearly 300 seedlings resulted from the cross,[21] of which 50 were originated and named after Shakespeare's heroines, from Adriana, to Portia, to Volumnia. Designated as *Syringa prestoniae*, the shrubs were registered and released for commercial distribution in the 1930s. These hardy, showy lilacs, with semi-pendulous flowers in many

Isabella Preston with lilies, Georgetown, Ontario, ca. 1956.
Photo by Sandy Best, National Archives of Canada NA-136938.

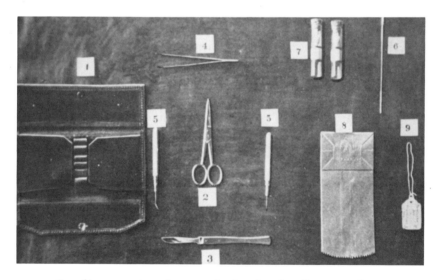

Set of instruments and accessories for plant breeding operations:
1) case for instruments; 2) scissors; 3) scalpel; 4) tweezers;
5) needle-holders; 6) camel's hair brush; 7) small glass bottles;
8) manila paper bags; 9) tags with cord.
Courtesy of Edwinna von Baeyer.

shades of purplish pink, were rapid growers and free from disease and insect pests, but unfortunately not fragrant.

With Preston's arrival at the CEF, the rose breeding program, which had ended with the introduction of Dr. William Saunders' hybrid rose "Agnes" in 1897, commenced anew. Preston dreamed of producing a climber, which could be "left over the arches and pergolas all the year, and in a few seasons cover the supports with masses of bloom like they do in the Old Country."[22] Also on her wish-list were winter-hardy roses and hybrid teas, which would keep their colour during hot, dry Canadian summers. "Everyone," she once declared, "who has a garden wants roses in it and there is no reason why they should not have some."[23]

Preston began by crossing *Rosa rubrifolia* and *Rosa rugosa*. The rugosas were especially prized by northern breeders for their hardiness and resistance to disease and insects. Between 1928 and 1940, she originated 28 hybrids, ranging from single to double flowers, pink through dark purple hues, and bushes to climbers. Preston had begun bravely in 1922 by announcing, "A new rose cannot be made in a day, but we hope to live long enough to produce a rose as good in its place as Marquis Wheat and Melba Apples are in their[s]."[24] But, for some reason, the rose program did not elicit the same level of enthusiasm and attention as her others, and in 1946, she sadly noted that her roses "have been rather neglected owing to wartime conditions."[25] Unlike her other plant originations, none of her roses ever won an award.

Before the 1920s, when Preston began working with *Iris sibirica*, very little work had been done on this Central European native,[26] which was hardy, easy to grow, and lacked insect troubles. By 1924, Preston had 92 seedlings blooming from the first summer's crosses — all in various shades of blue. Never a negativist, Preston commented spiritedly, "our wish for a tall white Siberian iris has not yet been realized, it will come . . . "[27] Between 1928 and 1936, she made 23 originations from one cross, naming them all after Canadian rivers. "Ottawa" and "Gatineau" won Awards of Merit from the Royal Horticultural Society, and today are recognized as significant contributions to the species. In fact, "Ottawa" was the first Canadian iris to win an international award.

Preston's work with hybrid "Rosybloom" crabapples was also initiated in 1920. Named by W.T. Macoun for a group of hybrids originated at the CEF before Preston's tenure, they were significantly improved by her further crossings. Few flowering trees and shrubs, let alone those with purple foliage, were hardy in Ottawa and northwards. Preston's work was hampered neither by weather nor the limitations of science, only by the general public. While she waited to harvest the seeds, fruit-loving visitors picked the hybridized fruit. She was thankful that, at least, the topmost fruit could not be reached. Despite the predation, a group of highly ornamental trees resulted, bearing deep rose or pink, fairly fragrant flowers, bronze purplish leaves, and fruit that varied in taste, colour, and size. Between 1928 and 1940, Preston originated 33 hybrids, named after Canadian lakes (Erie, Muskoka, Okanagan), which caused excited interest across the country. "Athabasca" and "Simcoe" won Awards of Merit from the Royal Horticultural Society in 1936 and 1940.

Professional Duties

When Preston was not in the garden, she was writing, usually during the winter. During her 26 years at the CEF, she wrote prodigiously. Part of her writings were devoted to answering horticultural queries from the general public and fellow enthusiasts. She might detail the specifics of crossing lilies, or new plant material proven hardy at Ottawa, or she might simply detail the successes and failures of a certain line of inquiry. A later preoccupation, especially during the 1950s, when she and a handful of others were organizing the North American Lily Society, was correspondence with various horticultural committees.

She corresponded with all the major breeders in Canada, the United States, and Britain who were interested in similar plants. She was unfailingly helpful and informative. One breeder, Percy Wright of Sutherland, Saskatchewan, wrote: "You are one of my heroes, not only because you have been successful in a line which I should like to be successful in, but because of your long record of helpfulness and human sympathy."[28]

When Preston was not writing letters, she was churning out articles on a variety of horticultural topics, especially "how-to" articles focussing on plant cultivation. Many of these articles were published in Canada's foremost horticultural magazine, *The Canadian Horticulturist*, later *Canadian Horticulture and Home Magazine*. She would also write announcements of new annuals, perennials, or shrubs entering the market, often to be published in *The Canadian Florist*. In magazines and annual reports, such as *The Gardeners' Chronicle, American Rose Annual*, and the British or American *Lily Yearbook*, Preston published pieces detailing her new originations, or reports on a particular line in her breeding programs. She also wrote one- to three-page plant bulletins, unsigned press articles, and, for others to deliver, a series of radio talks for CKCO, Ottawa's first private radio station.

In addition to her two books on lilies, published by the Orange Judd Company in 1929 and 1947, Preston authored major CEF booklets on roses, annuals, and perennials. Her lily books were praised for their appreciation of the home gardener's need for understandable instructions and of the restrictions imposed upon urban gardeners. Both books were the only ones ever written in Canada on lilies.

All her writing was characterized by clear, unadorned, concise prose. No rhetorical flourishes or fancy metaphors cluttered the information she was so happy to impart. Yet, there was a controlled zest in her writings, which was also present in her speech. A.R. Buckley, former curator of the CEF Arboretum, recalled that "she could talk your arm off on certain subjects." Discussions with fellow enthusiasts often sounded as if they were all conducted in Latin.[29] In fact, Preston could be quite definite ("a stickler for detail") about Latin usage. She much preferred to use the correct Latin plant name, but, in her popular writings, often used the common English name. However, she was not above a bit of proselytizing. In recommending the book *Annuals*, by the British author, Roy Hay, she noted, "The translations and explanations of the botanical names will help the reader to realize that these difficult names mean something and so will be more easily memorized."[30]

Preston could be quite assertive in her opinions which ranged from the proper manner of staking delphiniums to advice on childraising and tea making and which were usually voiced in a soft, but decisive, tone.[31] Yet, she was quite a shy, reticent woman, with an absolute terror of giving public speeches. At the height of her fame, she was asked by the North American Lily Society to speak at an annual meeting. She told her niece: "Good gracious, I couldn't possibly do that, you know. I should die of fright." When she was awarded Ontario's prestigious Carter Medal in 1937, her acceptance speech was pointedly short: "It's a great honour to receive this beautiful medal and I wish to express my thanks and deep appreciation."[32]

Much happier imparting her horticultural knowledge to individuals and informal groups, Preston was comfortable leading tours through the CEF's ornamental gardens, answering questions and pointing out things of interest. She took notables (Lady Byng, Princess Alice), enthusiasts (lily growers, nurserymen), and diverse groups around the gardens. She was rather miffed with one encounter: "Scotch school girls came . . . The Canadian lady in charge talked all the time & made it impossible to give any useful information to the other members of the party."[33]

Preston had a vested interest in the success of her tours, for it was also her responsibility to see that the ornamental gardens were properly maintained and the plants correctly labelled. The ornamental gardens and test plots were important not only for testing new plants, but also for providing a wide choice of plants for the breeding program.

Preston also seemed to be in charge of the Macoun Memorial Garden — a combination of perennials, lily pond, and memorial to her late supervisor. She was also involved in other plant projects, such as in the testing of annuals, perennials, trees, and shrubs. She also gave advice to aid in the war effort during the Second World War. In 1942, she was given a unique assignment: to devise a list for the RCAF of plants suitable for camouflaging aircraft hangers.[34]

Preston was quite protective of her gardens. In the late 1930s or early 1940s, while wandering through the gardens one afternoon, she spied a man picking flowers for a bouquet. He supposedly was Jean François Pouliot, a Liberal M.P., whose family was prominent in the political life of Canada. When she ordered him to stop, he merely said, "Do you know who I am?" Allegedly, she tartly replied, "I don't care if you are the King of England, you are not to pick my flowers."[35]

Assertive, likeable, fair, and truthful — these qualities characterized Preston, who because of these traits, and her knowledge, was often in demand as a flower show judge. Many CEF officials travelled to the multitude of horticultural exhibitions and flower competitions to judge entries. However, in contrast to her supervisors, Preston was not very deeply involved in horticultural organizations. She did belong to the Ottawa Horticultural Society, and did judge, but she evidently drew the line there. Or perhaps, she did not want to be relegated to the ladies' committee or be in the horticultural "spotlight." From the late 1920s until the early 1930s, she was secretary of the Ontario Horticultural Societies Association's Committee on Names and Varieties. The purpose of this committee was to bring new, noteworthy, or less-well-known varieties to the attention of the association. And in 1937, Preston was asked to join the Canadian Horticultural Council's Subcommittee of its Ornamental Gardens Committee.

Usually, the fact of her sex did not enter her professional life. But it did cause a comic incident during one of her trips. The Trappist monks at Oka, Quebec, needed horticultural advice, and requested a visit from a CEF horticulturist. Preston was sent. When she stepped off the Oka ferry, the monks who came to meet her were horrified, for the monastery was off-limits to women. It had never occurred to them that the expert would be a woman. But rather than embarrass her, they walked her around the outside of the monastery, asking inconsequential questions about some plants on the boundaries, then sent her back across the Ottawa river.[36]

A more successful excursion occurred in 1922, when Preston advised Prime Minister Mackenzie King on a landscape design for his summer property in the Gatineau Hills, north of Ottawa. He appealed to W.T. Macoun for someone from the farm to "look over my Kingsmere property with a view of making suggestions for its beautification."[37] Dutifully, Preston and T.F. Ritchie (head of the Vegetable Gardening Section) went out to Kingsmere and drew a rough plan with a list of shrubs and trees for planting.

The Lilies

Preston's favourite flowers, lilies, had not been forgotten amid the pressures of her office work, and the competition from her other breeding programs. Like most hybridizing efforts, her lily hybrids were not an overnight success. Between 1920 and 1932, Preston effected 222 different lily crosses, which resulted in nearly one thousand seedlings. Out of these seedlings, only 313 were successfully raised into blooming plants.[38] This was only the beginning. Out of hundreds of seedlings, after years of testing only the best would be registered. This is what happened with the lily seedlings produced from a cross made in 1929. The original cross involved *L. Davidi var. Willmonttiae* (in the Turks-cap group) and a seedling raised at Ottawa of *L. dauricum* (an Umbellatum-type) a very wide gap to bridge, which many breeders would have said could not be done.

The resulting 40 seedlings varied in colour in the orangey-red spectrum; the deep red tones were especially prized, as it was an uncommon lily colour. The tendency of the hybrid's flowers to face outwards was also highly praised. Between 1934 and 1939, seven of the original 40 seedlings were introduced. The hybrids were named after seven stenographers who worked for the Horticulture Division, and thus became known as the "Stenographer Lilies." They were lauded for their resistance to disease, their adaptability to ordinary garden soils, their hardiness, their floriferousness, their ease of propagation, and their beauty. For many years after, the "Stenographers" were used by hybridizers as breeding material for improved strains of lilies.[39] Preston said she was particularly happy with the interest the lilies aroused in lily growers around the world. She was also very gratified "to know that they do well in the colder sections of Canada where few lilies had been grown before."[40] Future notable lilies originated from crosses within and outside the Stenographer group.

By the 1940s, Preston had achieved recognition outside of horticultural circles, as *Chatelaine, Canadian Horticulture and Home Magazine, Canadian Homes and Gardens,* and various newspapers ran profiles of her. Even Vita Sackville-West, the famous British writer and ardent gardener, who had never met Preston, added to her reputation: "I picture Miss Preston to myself as a lady in a big straw hat, going round with a packet of labels, a notebook, and a rabbit's tail tied to a bamboo stick."[41]

Awards were given by her peers, and places of honour were reserved for her at head tables at horticultural conferences. Her hybrids collected not only individual honours, but also honours as breeding material, as more and more hybridists used and publicized their use of Preston originations. Although very proud of her achievements, Preston was adverse to personal publicity. Once, while attending the Philadelphia Flower Show with her niece, she quickly advised her, "Don't say a word to anyone who I am or they'll all flock around me."[42]

The lilies were her last great contribution to Canadian horticulture. Much of her work had been stymied by the war and the reduced labour pool. By the time life and horticulture began returning to normal, it was 1946, and Preston was 65.

Georgetown: The Final Years — 1946–1965

On December 1, 1946, Preston closed her office for the final time. The following month, she left for England, and remained for a year to see if she wanted to settle there. But she discovered that after living in Canada for 35 years, she could no longer tolerate the English climate, nor the fuel and food shortages in post-war Britain.[43] She returned to live in Georgetown, Ontario, because "I want to die on British soil." The advantages were many: friends from the OAC had settled there, Sandy Best, a well-known lily enthusiast and breeder was close by, and the town was two climate zones down from Ottawa, making it possible to grow a wider range of material. And Georgetown being in the eastern part of the country, it was easy for her to travel to her American relatives for holidays.

Preston bought a small wooden house on a large lot that had a lot of space for gardening. She had it all to herself, not subject to any bureaucratic restrictions. She had once written to the famed Manitoba horticulturist, Frank Skinner, that she "had a great desire to have a garden of lilies of my own"[44] and now she did. She organized her garden almost as a miniature Horticulture Division garden. A large space on the east side of her house was devoted to her lilies and iris, and seedlings of the crosses she never ceased to make. All the plants in this section were neatly labelled, grown in straight rows, and recorded in detail[45] — the work habits of a lifetime were not easily discarded.

The garden on the west side of the house was given over to ornamental garden beds, where Preston grew perennials, annuals, and Preston lilacs. She remarked that she had never met anyone who did not like lilacs until she moved to Georgetown. While she was planting a few of her hybrids, a watchful neighbour announced, "I hate lilacs, I always tear them up." Preston, true to form, instantly retorted, "You wait until you see mine."[46] She also grew flowering crabapples, roses, vegetables, and fruit.

Although retired, she maintained ties with the Horticulture Division into the 1950s. The summers of 1947 and 1948 found Preston in Ottawa for short visits, helping the ornamentals staff with the breeding program — they had not found a replacement for her.[47] Later contact and questions were restricted to letters. She also continued to be prominently active in lily groups, such as the North American Lily Society, which she helped establish.

Her life in Georgetown was quiet, given to her garden, visits from relatives and friends, occasional trips to nearby horticultural conferences, and the reaping of rewards. In 1950, at the age of 69, she received the prestigious Lyttel Cup from the Royal Horticultural Society, for "good work in connection with the genus *Lilium*." She commented, rather uncharacteristically, that "I felt like standing on my head!"[48] Despite the many honours she received, Preston was not "awards-proud," and often had forgotten where they were when curious visitors asked to see them.

In 1956, an enduring honour was awarded to her. Friends and colleagues in the North American Lily Society established the "Isabella Preston Trophy" in recognition of her work in the improvement of lilies. The sterling silver cup, embellished with three-dimensional lilies clustering around the base, continues to be awarded to the best stalk in the show.

That trophy can still be won, her medals can be touched, and her award citations can be read in pre-Second World War horticultural journals; unfortunately, many of her originations live on only in photo collections, bloodlines of contemporary hybrids, and in dying memory. Plant breeding is an ephemeral art. A selected few of her crabapples still bloom at the Experimental Farm. A couple of her Siberian iris continue to be sold by nurserymen. Her lilacs survive in home gardens and the catalogues of a few nurseries. Her "crown," her lilies, have nearly disappeared from private gardens and commercial distribution. However, her legacy to the lily world does live on. She pushed the horticultural frontiers forward, stimulating later breeders to venture even further into the unknown, to create new, improved varieties with different colours, forms, heights, and stronger resistance to disease and pests. Certainly, our gardens were enriched by her talent, determination, and courage to persevere.

At her death she was characterized as "the dean of hybridists" and "the grand lady of Canadian horticulture," but Preston's niece saw another side: "She was a grand old girl, she had a lot of spunk, a lot of character, I guess that is what it is, in her face, in her body, in her bearing, there was character"[49]

RALPH H. ESTEY

Margaret Newton:
Distinguished Canadian Scientist

Margaret Newton, Canada's most illustrious female scientist to specialize in studies of the cause and control of plant diseases, was born in Montreal on April 20, 1887, the daughter of Elizabeth Brown and John Newton.

Margaret's formal education began with four years in a traditional little red schoolhouse at North Nation Mills, Quebec, not far from Plaisance, where for a number of years John Newton worked on the farm of his father-in-law. When John, a university graduate from England, realized that his earnings as a farm laborer were insufficient to maintain a home of the desired standard, he got a job in Montreal with a firm of box manufacturers and lumber merchants.[1]

As a consequence of that move, Margaret attended school in Montreal for four years. This was followed by a move back to Plaisance, which interrupted her high school attendance half-way through the four-year course. After two more years in a country school, she accepted an invitation to teach in a one-room school at Ste. Amadée, although she lacked the formal qualification to do so.

Margaret enjoyed teaching, and decided to become fully qualified. To do this, she studied for two years at the Collegiate Institute in Vankleek Hill, Ontario not far from Plaisance, but on the opposite side of the Ottawa River, and obtained a teacher's certificate from the Normal School in Toronto.

Now fully qualified, Margaret taught school in Lachine, Quebec, for three years, and then for one year in the same little school in which she had begun her own formal education. During those four years of teaching, she paid off all her debts, and saved enough money to enable her to go to university without becoming a financial burden on her family.

Initially, Margaret's objective was to obtain an arts degree, so she enrolled at McMaster University. However, before completing a full year of the arts program, she decided to study agriculture at McGill University's Faculty of Agriculture, Macdonald College, in Ste. Anne de Bellevue, Quebec. Doubtless, she had been influenced in this decision by her brother, whom she had visited when he was a student there.

When Margaret Newton applied in 1914 for admission to the degree course in agriculture, she was not immediately accepted, although her credentials showed that she was academically well qualified. The reason for this hesitation on the part of the college officials is not known, but it may well have been because the women who had been accepted the previous year were not doing very well.

In September, 1913, Lord Kitchener's niece, Mary Kitchener, together with Katie Broad, and a woman whose name is not known (because the names or initials of at least two others in the registration list could be of either women or men), registered for the degree course in agriculture. They, and about 60 men, are in the group photo of the Class of '17, and the class historian proudly proclaimed that theirs was the first class in agriculture to admit women.[2] For various reasons, the three women, and nearly half of the men dropped out of that class before the end of their second year. Certainly some of those dropouts were related to the fact that the First World War had begun.

If there was any reluctance on the part of the staff at Macdonald College to accept Margaret Newton, it must have soon vanished, because once there, she proved to be a brilliant student. She became a class leader, and won the Governor General's bronze medal for highest standing at the end of the second year.[3]

It wasn't easy. Margaret encountered a number of problems and irritants that the men in her class did not have to face. One was that at first, the laboratories were closed to her in the evenings. She was told that study in the laboratories after the evening meal was restricted to male students. Margaret did not tolerate that situation for very long. She, with the full support of Prof. W.P. Fraser, complained to the dean of the college. She was soon granted permission to work or study in the laboratories in the evenings, and whenever they were not being used for class teaching. In winning that concession, she ran into another problem that was directly related to her sex. Women students were required to return to their residences before ten o'clock at night.[4]

It was during her second year in agriculture that Margaret became so interested in Prof. Fraser's course, and his research on the fungi that cause rust diseases in plants, that she decided to make plant pathology her chief field of study.

It was this interest in plant rusts that prompted her to attend the March 14, 1916, meeting of the Quebec Society for the Protection of Plants (QSPP), to hear a talk on a rust disease of white pine trees, and to join that Society as its first woman member. She had been recommended for membership by William Lochhead, professor of biology at Macdonald College, who from the beginning had been very supportive of Margaret especially when for several months in her second year she was the only woman among 50 or more students.

In September of that year, another woman, Pearl Clayton Stanford, from the Nova Scotia Agricultural College, joined the third-year class of degree students in agriculture at Macdonald College. She and Margaret soon became close friends, and although Pearl was majoring in horticulture, and had relatively little interest in plant pathology, she accompanied Margaret to an autumn meeting of the QSPP, and was accepted as a member at that time.[5]

Besides being an excellent student, Margaret Newton was an active participant in the Debating Society. She was also president of the class Literary Society for 1916–17, a year in which the two women dominated activities, as Pearl was the society's vice-president. It was also the first time any class had won twice, the Robertson Shield for debating, and, with Margaret on the team, the first time a woman had ever represented an agricultural class on the platform.

Margaret continued to be a class leader until she graduated with a B.S.A. degree in 1918, the first woman to complete all the requirements for a degree in agriculture at Macdonald College. She shared, with Pearl Stanford (who had done part of her studies in Nova Scotia), the honour of being the first women in Canada to earn a degree in agriculture.[6]

In the summer of 1917, Prof. Fraser left Margaret in charge of his collection of fungi and his research on the rust disease of grasses, while he went to western Canada to survey the rusts and other diseases of wheat. Part of Margaret's work and responsibility during his absence was to inoculate his collection of grasses, including wheat, with spores of the rust fungi that he collected and sent to her.

The following summer, Fraser made arrangements with the federal Department of Agriculture for Margaret to go to Manitoba and help him with his work on grain diseases. Her chief task was to determine the relationship, if any, between the stem rust on wheat and the rust on other kinds of grass. That work, which included greenhouse studies at the Manitoba Agricultural College, was under the direction of the Brandon laboratory of the Government of Canada's Division of Botany.[7] During that summer in Winnipeg, Margaret experimented with the use of adhesives on glass slides to catch air- borne spores, especially those of the rust fungi.[8]

While Fraser was negotiating with federal authorities to get Margaret on the payroll for work with him in Manitoba, Dr. Charles E. Saunders, Dominion Cerealist at the Central Experimental Farm, Ottawa, visited her at Macdonald College to see for himself what this young woman was doing. He was so favourably impressed, that he asked her to consider joining him in his work of breeding and selecting superior varieties of grain after she received her bachelor's degree. He also gave her a head of his relatively new Marquis wheat. Out of curiosity, Margaret planted several of the grains and inoculated the resulting plants with spores of wheat stem rust.

To her surprise, she discovered that some of the inoculated leaves did not display the normal rust reaction. She repeated the inoculations twice more, and got the same result each time. When Fraser returned, she explained to him exactly what she had done, and showed him the results. At first he was perplexed, but it wasn't long before both he and Margaret were convinced that the rust fungus must be composed of more than one pathogenic strain or race. This, as far as they knew, was a new and revolutionary discovery in the long struggle for control of rust on grain. The remarkable feature of this apparent breakthrough is the fact that it was accomplished by an undergraduate student working virtually alone at Macdonald College.

When Fraser informed the dean of agriculture at the University of Minnesota of this phenomenal discovery, he was told that a Minnesota man, Dr. E.C. Stakman, had made a similar discovery. Nevertheless, the dean was so surprised by what this relatively isolated Quebec

Margaret Newton receiving Outstanding Achievement Award
of the University of Minnesota from E.C. Stakman, 1956.
Courtesy of R.H. Estey.

student had done, that he asked Fraser to encourage her to come to Minnesota for graduate studies and continue her rust research under the guidance of Dr. Stakman. At that time, Margaret didn't have enough money to seriously consider such an enticing prospect, but Prof. Fraser, who saw great potential in Margaret, began exploring sources of funding for her.

Because of her exceptional research accomplishments as an undergraduate student, Margaret continued her grain rust investigations at Macdonald College and obtained a master's degree in 1919. In the absence of Prof. Fraser, who had accepted a position in Saskatchewan, her thesis, "The Resistance of Wheat Varieties to *Puccinia graminis*," was written under the nominal supervision of Professors H. Mackay and Wm. Lochhead, although virtually all of the work had been done under Fraser's direction.

At about the time that Margaret was writing her master's thesis, Dr. W.P. Thompson, head of the department of biology at the University of Saskatchewan, and a distinguished pioneer in the application of science to the solution of problems in plant pathology, had found that one of his new varieties of wheat proved to be highly resistant to rust in Saskatoon, but was susceptible to the disease in Rosthurn, less than 80 kilometers away. When he asked Prof. Fraser if he could explain this unexpected phenomenon, Fraser told him that both Dr. Stakman and his student, Margaret Newton, had shown that the rust fungus occurred in more than one strain or biologic form, and that the strain in Rosthurn was probably different from the one in Saskatoon. This logical explanation so intrigued Thompson, that he asked Fraser if he could persuade this remarkable student to work for him.

In the meantime, Margaret had been notified that she could study and work for a doctorate in Minnesota, under Dr. Stakman's supervision, with financial assistance from the Honorary Advisory Council for Scientific and Industrial Research of Canada, the forerunner of the National Research Council. When Dr. Thompson learned of this, his determination to have her work with him did not lessen. He made a number of telephone calls, including one to Stakman in Minnesota, and arranged that Margaret would work with him in Saskatoon for six months of each year, while working the other six months with Stakman. Thus, in three years, she would spend the 18 months at Minnesota which were required by that university for a doctorate. Although Margaret realized that such an arrangement would delay her degree by nearly a year, she agreed to Thompson's overall plan, because it provided an opportunity for her to work with Fraser, Thompson, and Stakman, three widely-recognized leaders in the field of grain rust research.

In compliance with the first phase of Thompson's plan, Margaret went to Saskatoon where, for a few weeks in 1920, she was assistant plant pathologist on the staff of the recently-established Dominion Laboratory of Plant Pathology at the University of Saskatchewan, whose officer in charge was Prof. W.P. Fraser.[9]

From the beginning of Margaret Newton's doctoral program, Dr. Stakman was very cooperative. He made a special trip to Saskatoon to see an outline of her proposed experiments, and to discuss her work with Fraser and Thompson. This was technically necessary, because to satisfy the degree requirements of the University of Minnesota, Prof. Stakman had, at least nominally, to supervise her research for a thesis. Stakman also speeded up Margaret's research by providing Fraser with seeds of the different host plants that had been most satisfactory in his work of identifying discrete strains of the stem rust fungi in Minnesota.[10]

For her second stint in Saskatoon, Margaret was appointed instructor of botany in Thompson's department of biology at the University of Saskatchewan, where she did some teaching in addition to research.

Her unique association with Fraser and Thompson in Saskatoon, and Stakman at the University of Minnesota, continued until she obtained a Ph.D. degree from the latter institution in 1922, with a thesis titled, "Studies in Wheat Stem Rust (*Puccinia graminis tritici*)." This was a two-part thesis reflecting the two major aspects of her studies and research. One part dealt with the 14 biologic forms of wheat stem rust that she and Fraser had found in western Canada, and which had also been found in the United States. The second part was a study of the rust fungus in the tissues of resistant and susceptible host plants.

After obtaining her degree, the first Ph.D. earned in an agricultural science by a Canadian woman, she took a holiday in Europe. Then, as Dr. Margaret Newton, she returned to the University of Saskatchewan to continue her rust research in cooperation with Fraser and Thompson. Initially, she was again appointed instructor, but was soon promoted to the rank of assistant professor in the department of biology.[11] While at the university, she worked on research with strains of stem rust on wheat and on wild grasses, the effect of light and temperature on rust-spore germination, and the relation between the size of the stomata on the grasses and rust resistance.[12] She also taught plant physiology, and assisted Professor Thompson with his teaching, especially the laboratory portions of his courses. In addition, she tutored student veterans of the First World War, who were finding it difficult to keep up with their classmates in biology.

In 1924, when the Honourable W.R. Motherwell, Federal Minister of Agriculture, was in Saskatoon, he asked Dr. Newton if she would go to Winnipeg to take charge of research on physiological specialization in the cereal rusts in a new rust research laboratory that was to be constructed on the campus of the University of Manitoba. Dr. Newton was reluctant to leave Fraser and Thompson, and the cooperative work in which they had been so successfully engaged at Saskatoon. However, she was beginning to find that the teaching responsibilities there were taking more and more of her time from research. This factor, together with the planned new facility at Winnipeg, as well as the assurance that she could have a technician or research assistant of her choice, made the Winnipeg offer too good to refuse.

When Dr. Newton went to Winnipeg in the summer of 1925, she was the most highly-trained grain rust specialist in Canada, and had more experience with research on the rust fungi than any other member of the staff. Her choice of Thorvaldur Johnson, one of her most brilliant former students, to be her assistant in Winnipeg, was very fortunate, because Johnson soon became a competent colleague and himself a widely-acclaimed authority in rust research. The list of Dr. Newton's publications shows that she enjoyed the support and active collaboration of several very capable colleagues, in addition to Johnson, during the 20 years of her research at Winnipeg.[13]

By 1929, the year in which she joined the Canadian Phytopathological Society as a charter member, the results of Dr. Newton's work were receiving international recognition. Botanists, plant pathologists, and geneticists from foreign countries were visiting her laboratory. One of the latter was the renowned Russian geneticist, Nikolai Vavilov, who spent several days at the Winnipeg research station. While there, he invited Dr. Newton to join his group in Leningrad, where she would be able to work with plant breeders and have the opportunity to visit Turkestan, the presumed original home of barberry bushes, an alternate host for the wheat stem rust. She would also have all the necessary facilities, and the help of technicians, for a comprehensive study of specialization in the grain rusts of the U.S.S.R. Vavilov's offer also included the promise of a salary equivalent to about $10,000, a fabulous amount for a Canadian scientist in the 1930s.[14] Although such an offer must have been flattering and otherwise very enticing, Margaret realized that she was already in the newest and best laboratory in the world for rust research, and that she had a superb technician. There was also the question of whether she would have to resign from her position with the Canadian government before being put on the payroll of a foreign government, and the possible difficulty of getting money out of Russia. After due consideration, Dr. Newton politely declined Vavilov's offer. Even so, when E. Cora Hind, the noted Canadian agricultural writer on the staff of the *Winnipeg Free Press*, visited Russia, Vavilov told her that he had not given up hope of persuading Dr. Newton to join his rust research group.[15]

Although Dr. Newton never joined Vavilov's staff, she did visit Russia in 1933, and, in compliance with Vavilov's request, discussed (with a number of scientists there) her methods of isolating, inoculating, and identifying physiologic races of the wheat rust fungi. She refused all payment for her work and advice.[16]

In Canada, Dr. Newton's rust disease surveys, and her epidemiology work, took her to many widely-separated places, such as Churchill, Manitoba, and Hay River in the Northwest Territories, where trains and boats were the only feasible means of transportation.

Among her personal letters, now in the archives of the University of Victoria, are copies of letters to and from Dr. Stakman regarding the identification of rusts she had sent to him, and others she had sent to Dr. George B. Cummins of Purdue University. There is also a letter from the editor of the journal *Phytopathology*, dated January 7, 1932, thanking her for being an associate editor for three years, and one from Dr. Stakman congratulating her for discovering urediospores and teliospores of the rust fungi in tissues of barberry bushes.

Dr. Newton took an active part in meetings of the International Botanical Congress that were held in Amsterdam, in 1935, and it is on record that she seconded a motion by Dr. Stakman recommending changes in the terminology pertaining to the rust fungi.[17]

Perhaps because she was one of the few women scientists in Canada in the 1930s, and felt compelled to excel in the world of men, Dr. Newton tended to undertake several research projects at the same time, and to publish a certain number of papers each year, regardless of whether the research on which they were based had or had not been completed.[18] In contrast to this, her principal collaborator, Dr. T. Johnson, who had been awarded a Ph.D. by the University of Minnesota in 1930, wanted to complete each project before publishing the results. The minor friction caused by her pushing and his holding back was never serious enough to interfere with their harmonious working relationship and continued friendship. It was, however, another one of the irritants with which she, a mild-mannered woman, had to contend in her struggle for success. In his praise of Dr. Newton following her retirement, Johnson commented on this aspect of their respective personalities, and added, "In addition to a warmth of personality which won her many friends, she had a great capacity for work and more ambition than most people I have known. She had to a remarkable extent the quality often referred to as 'drive'."[19] When Johnson himself was awarded an honorary degree by the University of Saskatchewan, Dr. Newton sent him a congratulatory note. In his thank-you letter to Margaret, he wrote, "As the years pass, I realize more and more how much I owe to my collaboration with you. I understand now, what I did not fully understand before, that my attitude towards research is something I acquired from you."[20]

Dr. Newton's remarkable "drive," combined with the help of able colleagues, resulted in the publication of more than 40 papers on the rust fungi and one on mildew fungi; she also wrote an unpublished manuscript on the "net blotch disease" of barley, and had a number of articles published with the annual reports of the Dominion Botanist. She participated in research that was fundamental to the understanding of the rust fungi, while investigating the genetics of physiologic races, the segregation and recombination of genetic factors, and the variability in the disease-producing capacity of rust races with environment, and their role in the production of rust-resistant varieties of grain. When Dr. Newton started her research, stem rust of wheat was the major crop hazard in western Canada; it caused average annual crop losses in the prairie provinces of at least 30 million bushels. By the time Dr. Newton retired, the losses from wheat rust were negligible. She played a major role in the conquest of that disease.

In consequence of such outstanding studies on the rusts, Dr. Newton was elected fellow of the Royal Society of Canada in 1942, and became the second woman to be so honoured. Adding to that honour, the Society awarded her its Flavelle Medal in 1948, because her rust studies had, as the citation states, "established a body of information on those phases unparalleled in the literature of plant pathology."[21] She was the first woman to receive that medal, and the first graduate of an agricultural college to be so decorated. Honours and awards were not new to Margaret Newton. She had won prizes, scholarships, and medals throughout her educational and research career. She was a member of the Agricultural Institute of Canada, the American Phyto-pathological Society, and Sigma Xi, and an honorary member of Sigma Delta Epsilon, the society for graduate women in science. Shortly after her retirement, she was made an honorary member of the Canadian Phytopathological Society, of which she had been a charter member.

As a delegate to the International Botanical Congress in Sweden, in 1950, Dr. Newton was further honoured by being presented to King Gustav VII. Later that year, she was a Canadian representative at meetings of the International Federation of University Women, in Basel, Switzerland.

In 1956 the University of Minnesota presented her with its Outstanding Achievement Award, an honour that is restricted to former students who have attained eminence and distinction in their work. In 1964, the University of Victoria, in British Columbia, recognized her scientific achievements by naming one of its residences Margaret Newton Hall.[22] Two years later, Dr. Newton served as the official representative of the University of Minnesota at the ceremony for the investiture of a chancellor of the University of British Columbia[23] and in 1969 the University of Saskatchewan awarded her an honorary LL.D.

Margaret Newton came by her brilliance quite naturally. She was one of five children in a brilliant family, all of whom obtained Ph.D. degrees in various aspects of the agricultural sciences. Her sister, Dr. Dorothy (Newton) Swales, the only surviving member of the family, is a well-known botanist and long-time member of the academic staff of McGill University, who, following her retirement, was appointed honorary curator of the university herbarium.

Unfortunately, Margaret Newton paid a high price for her achievements. The pressures under which she laboured, and her prolonged close work with the spores of fungi, aggravated a long-standing respiratory problem to such an extent that she was forced to retire in 1945. In retirement, in Victoria, British Columbia, she remained the same slim, well-tailored woman with beautifully coiffured hair that she had been for so many years in Winnipeg. She was active in various woman's organizations, and maintained a garden that was a model of well-kept beauty.

Dr. Margaret Newton, who to this day is acknowledged as Canada's most distinguished and productive woman plant pathologist, died in Victoria, British Columbia on April 6, 1971.

KAILASH K. ANAND

assisted by ANITA K. ANAND

Cypra Cecilia Krieger and the Human Side of Mathematics

According to Dr. Cathleen Morawetz, director of the renowned Courant Institute of Mathematics, New York Univeristy, Cypra Cecilia Krieger was "the most capable woman mathematician of her time in Canada."[1] That Krieger has an important position in the history of Canadian women in mathematics cannot be questioned. She was the third person to receive a Ph.D. in mathematics (1930) from a Canadian university (Toronto).[2] Moreover, she was the third Canadian woman to obtain a doctorate in mathematics anywhere in the world.[3]

Although Krieger published in prestigious journals and worked hard as a university teacher, she never progressed beyond the position of assistant professor at the University of Toronto.[4] Like many other women in science, she was simply not promoted. It was difficult for a woman scientist in her time to attain a senior position in any organization. To a large extent, unfortunately, this remains true today.

Cypra Cecilia Krieger was born in Poland in 1894, one of five children of Sarah and Moses Krieger. Her father was a merchant. She finished secondary school in Poland, then attended the University of Vienna for one year, specializing in mathematics and physics. In 1920, she was brought to Toronto by her brother, Sam, who had preceded her. She immediately set out to overcome her first handicap: a complete ignorance of English. After taking some private lessons, she enrolled at the

University of Toronto, where she completed her B.A. (1924). As an undergraduate student, she supported herself by working at an inn in Muskoka during the summer months.[5]

She then began graduate work at the University of Toronto, taking courses in "modern elliptic function," "minimum principles of mechanics," "theory of sets," and "theory of numbers."[6] She completed her M.A. in 1925, and promptly began working towards her Ph.D. Krieger's advisor was W.J. Webber, the chief contributor to the development of graduate studies in the mathematics department, University of Toronto. Webber was a brilliant young pioneer in the field of modern analysis and lectured on the theory of functions and calculus.[7] The latter was the inspiration for Krieger's Ph.D. thesis, entitled "On the Summability of Trigonometric Series with Localized Properties — On Fourier Constants and Convergence Factors of Double Fourier Series."[8] Due to her impressive academic success, she held the position of instructor while working on her Ph.D in 1928–29, and became lecturer of mathematics and physics in 1930. After 12 years, she was finally appointed to the position of assistant professor in 1942. This was the highest academic position she would attain during her tenure with the University of Toronto's department of mathematics. The injustice of this did not escape her.[9]

Dr. Krieger taught an average of 13 classes a week, with the number of students in each class ranging from six to 75.[10] Such a schedule obviously left little time for research. In spite of this, she published a number of important papers: "On the Summability of Trigonometric Series with Localised Properties,"[11] "On Fourier Series in Two Variables and On Questions in the Theory of Sets,"[12] and "On Fourier Constants and Convergence factors of Double Fourier Series."[13]

She worked on a translation of Professor W. Sierpinski's book on *General Topology*, and its sequel, in whatever time she could spare from teaching and the preparation of lectures — often in the evenings.

> This publication by the University of Toronto Press . . . led to the organizing of the Mathematical Exposition Series in 1940. This was a technical journal of mathematics. Later Sierpinski's *General Topology* was also translated by Cecilia and it appeared as No. 7 in the series in 1952.[14]

The *University of Toronto Monthly* of March, 1934, pointed out the importance of this venture: "Her translation . . . makes the whole work available to mathematicians generally . . . Professor Sierpinski is probably the leading authority on the subject of Aggregates."

When asked by a local newspaper about a mathematician's idea of relaxation, Krieger mentioned music, literature and theatre. She had no hobbies and was not interested in sports.[15] Not surprisingly, her work was an all-consuming occupation.

During the 1930s and 40s, in addition to her busy career, Krieger had considerable family responsibilities. Her unmarried sisters lived with her. As they were not employed, her salary evidently supported them. Moreover, the Krieger sisters helped a family of Jewish refugees during the Second World War. It is obvious Cecilia Krieger was a very warm and caring person. University of California professor Alex Rosenberg, and his sister Edith remember her fondly. Edith recalls, "the Krieger sisters . . . virtually adopted us when we arrived in Canada."[16]

Krieger married Dr. Zygmunt Dunaij, a physician and Holocaust survivor, in 1953 when she was 59 years old. Why did she wait so long? Family responsibilities may have led her to postpone marriage. It could also have been the uncertainty of keeping her job, such as it was, if she married. It was a well-known fact at the time that a woman had to choose between a career and marriage.

Cecilia Krieger, although officially retired in 1962, continued teaching until 1967. Her husband died in 1968, and this may have triggered her return to academic work. She was indefatigable, setting an enviable record of achievement. She started teaching at Upper Canada College in 1968 and continued until her death in August 1974, at the age of 80.[17]

Krieger was "a miracle of modesty, disclaiming any particular credit for her work and denying that she had done anything unusual".[18] We know, however, that she touched many lives favourably. She was a great and dedicated teacher, and one of the most able mathematicians of her time. Cathleen Morawetz attributes her own entrance into higher mathematics and her subsequent decision to stay in the field to Krieger's encouragement and support.[19] Dr. Morawetz's father, Professor Synge (himself a mathematician), confirms this impression, saying "she [Krieger] encouraged my daughter . . . to work for a degree in Mathematics and Physics in Toronto and then proceed to graduate studies in the U.S.A."[20] When, in 1934, Krieger was questioned as to the position of women in the study of mathematics, she replied, "It is a subject on which it is very difficult to generalize. It really depends on the individual. To be sure, so far the greatest work has been done by men, but that does not mean that women will not make their mark."[21]

Dr. Cecilia Krieger certainly did not achieve as much recognition as she would have had she been a man. The fact remains that she was a member of the highly visible, male-dominated department of mathematics at the University of Toronto. It is obvious that she accomplished an admirable amount, despite a plethora of obstacles ranging from language handicaps to the simple fact of her sex. And despite the odds, she made her mark.

JANICE BEAVERIDGE

Getting a Job Done and Doing It Well: Dr. Blossom Wigdor, Psychologist and Gerontologist

Not many scientists, and even fewer women scientists, enjoy the distinction of official recognition and public acclaim — especially while they are still active and contributing to their profession. In April, 1989, Blossom Temkin Wigdor, Ph.D., director of the Centre of Gerontology at the University of Toronto, received the Order of Canada for "working tirelessly to foster research and education in the problems of aging, and to improve the circumstances of the elderly."[1]. According to Wigdor, directing the Centre (formerly Programme in Gerontology) since 1979 has been a satisfying expression of her life-long interest in people and the human life-cycle. She built the program into a multi-disciplinary research centre, which brings together experts from diverse fields to study all aspects of aging. This essay will focus on influences from her family and education, and will identify some of the choices and turning points which were important to her success. It will describe her clinical and academic career as a pioneer in the field of gerontology in Canada, and will focus on some conditions influencing the course of her career, particularly at McGill University.

Early Life

Blossom Temkin Wigdor was born on June 13, 1924, in Montreal, where she and her younger sister were raised by Russian Jewish immigrant parents. During her early years in Outremont schools she had the benefit of small classes and good teachers. As a student who performed well in physics and chemistry, she won scholarships which helped to pay for her high school education. Her family had a lasting influence. Wigdor's ability to work hard and set her own high standards began early with her mother, Olga's, exacting demands, although Blossom knew she would not be satisfied to follow her mother's example of staying at home.[2] Her father, Solomon Temkin, provided a stimulating intellectual environment, and encouraged the education of his daughters. His influence on his older child was particularly strong, and he encouraged Blossom to attend university and to plan a career. So, early in life, she learned that exceptional performance and hard work would be prerequisite to a university education. The Temkins were part of a large influx of Jewish immigrants, mainly from Austria, Poland, Roumania, and Russia, who poured into Montreal during the interwar years. The Jewish population expanded into what was described in 1939 as a "large, comparatively heterogeneous and widely scattered, yet solidly integrated, self-conscious community."[3] The children of these immigrants

> enrolled in McGill in ever-increasing numbers; 25 percent of the students in the faculty of Arts, 15 percent in Medicine, and 40 percent in Law were Jewish. As the official historian of McGill has noted, the university, "liberal as its traditions might be, was not ready for such a change in its constituency and measures were taken towards the end of the 1920s and 1930s to control the influx of Jewish students." A quota system was employed in Medicine, while in the Arts Jewish students required a higher matriculation standard than others.[4]

Blossom Temkin proved her ability by achieving a score of over 800, when the minimum entrance requirements for Jews was set at 750, in contrast with 600 for non-Jews. She started at McGill in 1941, with ideas about a career in chemistry but, since she was undecided whether to take a B.A. or B.Sc., she chose a double arts and science program, beginning with chemistry, physics, Latin, French, English and mathematics. During the Second World War, many male students and instructors left for service in the armed forces, and this led to increased female enrolment in university. Blossom found herself increasingly interested in people, and began to focus her studies on psychology, sociology, and economics. She received intellectual stimulation from particular mentors and collaborators, such as Forrest Laviolette, a social psychologist, and B.S. Kearstead, a British economist, who stimulated her thinking about scientific aspects of social change, while Dr. Frances Alexander, a clinical psychologist and one of very few women professors at McGill in the early 1940s, provided Blossom with an important role model.

On May 30, 1945, two weeks before her twenty-first birthday, Blossom graduated with a B.A. The following day she married Leon Wigdor, a chemical engineer. Like most of her contemporaries, she never considered staying single, and like them she expected to have children. Leon's attitudes provided encouragement and support early in their marriage, a crucial time for women to make career decisions. He was a non-conformist, who had an unconventional view of women and relationships, and he shared Blossom's view of marriage as a partnership.[5]

Blossom decided to study medicine at McGill, but was told by the registrar that the university would not even accept her application because the integration of returning veterans resulted in a considerable increase of the student population. Many years later Blossom recalled that the registrar was a man well known for his racial, religious, and gender prejudices.[6]

The Wigdors left for Toronto in 1945. Blossom stayed at home for a few months, but it soon became clear that life at home was not going to offer her much satisfaction. Her interests were academic, and she realized that she wanted to study human behaviour — over the entire life span. So she applied to, and was accepted into, the master's program in psychology at the University of Toronto.

Enrolment policies at the University of Toronto were less exclusive then they were at McGill. Because of this Blossom felt more welcome. Moreover, at the University of Toronto women had very much been a part of research in psychology and had produced outstanding work in laboratory and applied studies.[7] During the war, women had formed nearly half of the faculty in the psychology department;[8] but during the post-war years, the position of women faculty members diminished "with the influx of men into the profession, the re-orientation of the discipline to experimental psychology, and the intensification of discriminatory attitudes and practices in the field."[9]

As a young wife and graduate student in Toronto, Wigdor accepted without question the traditional domestic responsibilities of cooking and housework. She spent time with her husband during the evening, then worked until late into the night on her thesis, completing her master's degree in psychology in one year.

Wigdor found practical application for her interests in clinical psychology well before formal clinical programs existed. The pressures of veterans returning in large numbers, which had barred her entrance into medical school, now gave her the opportunity for employment with the Department of Veterans' Affairs (DVA). Later, her association with veterans hospitals would direct her career towards gerontology.

In 1946, Dr. William Line, director of personnel selection in the Canadian army and a professor at the University of Toronto, asked Wigdor to do psychological assessments of returning veterans for the DVA. She took courses in the United States in special assessment techniques, and began her professional career with the DVA at the Christie Street Hospital. When her husband was transferred back to Montreal, in 1947, Blossom was able to transfer within the DVA and she began a 32 year association with Montreal veterans' hospitals and homes for the aged.

Blossom Wigdor soon saw the need for further studies, and applied again to McGill, this time for a Ph.D. in psychology. She was accepted. The DVA allowed her some study leave, and in 1949 Blossom started to work on her doctorate. At the time Dr. Donald O. Hebb became chairman of McGill's department of psychology and a new period of growth was underway. Wigdor was a student in Hebb's first Montreal seminar, as mentioned in the introduction to his *Organization of Behavior* (1949), a book that "brought new interest to the neural bases of behavior," and "opened new avenues of research," with a new concept of cell assemblies in the brain.[10] This was the book that later led to pioneering research on sensory deprivation and intelligence testing. Wigdor found Hebb's work exciting, and credits Hebb with fostering in her a new sense of scientific inquiry into physiological psychology.

Wigdor found encouragement for her work both at McGill and at the hospitals. She enjoyed the clinical work and, because of her advanced training, was in great demand. In 1948 the federal government established programs to fund mental health training and provided bursaries for students and salaries for faculty. Child development was capturing attention for research and funds. Wigdor's studies included an examination of intelligence testing and intellectual change and development. A turning point came when Dr. Hebb pointed out to her the opportunities at the veterans' hospitals to study numbers of older men, and suggested that she focus her studies on the later years of life. Thus began her research on aging, the subject that would become her lifelong specialization. In 1952, she was one of four women at McGill to receive a Ph.D. in psychology (along with Brenda Milner, who went on to achieve distinction as a neuropsychologist). Wigdor then began teaching part-time in the clinical psychology program at McGill.

Home and Family

Dr. Wigdor successfully managed both her career and family life, but not without sacrifice. When her son was born in 1956, after 11 years of marriage, she took only the summer months off to be with him. Although she relied on domestic help to achieve a loving, stable home atmosphere, there was no question that her family came first and, when choices had to be made, it often meant concessions in her work. As a result, she published less and her career progressed more slowly than was otherwise possible. In a recent interview, she stressed that

> men make their biggest contributions in their early years — the contributions that determine their careers — and that's just the years women want to be child-bearing. It may only be 10 years out of your life but those are very critical years in terms of academic achievement or research. People put out their *magnum opus* in their early thirties. There are basic things that come out of their Ph.D. theses and that is where they focus their energies.[11]

From 1942 to 1979, Dr. Wigdor held two jobs in Montreal. She worked full-time for the DVA as a psychologist and consultant. She was also a part-time lecturer at McGill in the Applied Psychology Centre and, later, assistant professor and associate professor in the department of psychology. The applied and teaching paths were not equally rewarding.

Clinical Practice

Dr. Wigdor generally felt full acceptance as a professional in the hospitals where she did counselling and consulting work for the DVA. She served as consultant in psychology at Maimonides Hospital and Home for the Aged (1954– 1967) and the Jewish General Hospital, and was senior consultant in psychology at the Queen Elizabeth Hospital (1963–1974). In 1961, Wigdor was appointed chief psychologist at the Queen Mary Veterans' Hospital in Montreal, and in 1965, director of the psychological research unit. She was one of the few professional women working in Montreal hospitals, and co-workers at times had difficulty perceiving her as a woman. She heard comments like, "She's not a woman, she's a psychologist."

Academic Career

After graduating with her Ph.D. in 1952, Dr. Wigdor's part-time career at McGill University progressed from lecturer (1952– 1965), to assistant professor (1966– 1972) and associate professor (1972–79). She continued her research, conducted seminars in psychology for nurses, medical staff and graduate students, and served as chair of the Graduate Faculty Committee on Aging. Although on the surface it appears that her academic career progressed well, it is clear that there was a considerable time lag in advancement: 11 years as lecturer and nine years as assistant professor before her appointment to associate professor in 1972. Her natural aspiration for an appropriate position as full professor would be realized only when she left McGill for the University of Toronto in 1979.

Why did Wigdor's advancement at McGill not meet her expectations? Why did a position at McGill, appropriate to her education and extensive experience, remain just beyond her reach? Her progress may have been deliberately blocked, or it may have been simply a matter of heavy competition for few positions. While her son was young, Wigdor was not able to channel her full energies into research and publication. If we look, however, at women in the academic environment during the three decades of her employment at McGill, other factors emerge as possible influences.

Wigdor was not inclined to challenge prevailing attitudes of her time, and after she received her Ph.D. she did not encounter obvious discrimination in her work in Montreal hospitals and homes for the aged. The exception occurred in 1965, when she applied for a position within the DVA as advisor to the Assistant Deputy Minister of Veterans' Affairs, Treatment Services, in Ottawa. Wigdor later learned that there had been opposition to her appointment, because she might have had to travel in the company of a male superior, but after some delay she got the job, and went on to hold the position until 1978.

During this same span of 27 years, Wigdor concentrated on her work, and was not at first particularly aware of any bias against women at McGill. She never believed that there was any organized feeling against women, but over issues of promotion, she felt the "subtle pressures of tradition" in that university, which "have something of a conspiratorial force."[12] Margaret Gillett claims that the nineteenth-century view of women as basically different intellectually and in their social role (in service and obedience to men), although modified and modernized, was still alive and well at McGill in the 1980s.[13]

Wigdor found that Dr. Hebb, chairman of the psychology department, encouraged her work, but she recognized that he did not know how to deal with female students, and that, in fact, Hebb was uncomfortable with them.[14] One could reasonably conclude that he was also uncomfortable with staff members who were female; he was, like many other "well-respected, kindly men who could be charming, helpful and encouraging to women they knew personally or individually, but [who] in the last analysis . . . threw their prestige and authority onto the side of tradition."[15] Hebb's real views are evident in his response to the 1971 "Report of the McGill Committee on Discrimination as to Sex," in which he stated: "the record shows that a small proportion of women are outstandingly good and must be recognized, but . . . women on the average are much less productive of original research . . . [and] . . . bound to get less promotion in a university that values research."[16] When Hebb claimed that males are more likely to "add to the university's reputation by doing and publishing significant research,"[17] he was, in fact, supporting salary and promotion differences. By that time he was chancellor of McGill, and this added considerable weight to his opinion. Such a view could not help but create difficulties for women who were struggling for promotion and wage parity.

Gender and racial discrimination often appear together, and may be indistinguishable. McGill's international reputation as a liberal and open academic institution should not be allowed to mask a history of institutionalized racial prejudice. This cannot be ignored as a possible influence on Wigdor's career. Evidence of racist sentiments in hiring academic staff appears in a 1939 letter written by Dr. J.J. O'Neill,

> I think it would be a bad mistake to bring Dr. . . . onto the staff, primarily on account of his race. For some of those of his race who are, or have been, on the staff, the conditions have been trying, not only for them, but for those who endeavoured to fit their families and friends into the general social structure. I have come to the conclusion that no matter how desirable the person may be, it is better from the University standpoint to avoid any such engagements.[18]

Policies restricting enrolment of Jewish students, even without official sanction by faculty or senate,[19] "had succeeded in reducing the number of Jewish students to 12.1 percent in the Arts, 12.8 percent in Medicine, and 15 percent in Law"[20] before these restrictive practices were supposedly ended during the war.[21] Since "we can be entirely sure that discriminative laws *increase* prejudice,"[22] it is quite certain that racist sentiments affected attitudes of influential people at least through the 1950s and 1960s, and that they continued to have a detrimental impact upon both faculty members and students.[23]

Another factor that influenced the course of Wigdor's career relates to an issue which had long affected departments of psychology at McGill and other universities: whether the discipline should be regarded strictly as an academic science, focusing on experimental research, or whether it should incorporate research on practical problems.[24]

From the time psychology at McGill emerged as a separate department in 1924, the department had emphasized experimental psychology over applied aspects of the discipline. Dr. Hebb acknowledged the need to train students in practical applications of psychology, however, and he set up the Applied Psychology Centre in 1952.[25] Between 1952 and 1965, Dr. Wigdor lectured part-time at the Applied Psychology Centre, while she continued to work for DVA. The Applied Psychology

Centre expected staff to work in non-academic settings, in order to maintain their professional orientation.[26] Although part of the department of psychology, the Centre was run as a separate, semi-autonomous unit, offering master's programs in clinical, industrial, and counselling psychology, and personnel courses for business organizations. In practice, relations between scientific psychology and applied psychology at McGill were later called "ideologically divisive,"[27] and the arrangement was labelled "administratively unsound."[28] According to Edward C. Webster, director of the Applied Psychology Centre (and chairman of the department from 1958 to 1964), Hebb was not willing to be involved with the applied program himself; because of Hebb's growing international reputation and increasing influence on staff and students, this view began to prevail in the department.[29] Hebb was interested in producing a small number of research professionals, and he did not want applied psychology students coming into his research program.[30] In Webster's view, "too many things that involve personal status and development are stacked against those who really attempt to produce practitioners within a Department."[31] The Centre was disbanded in 1965, and its resources were merged with the department. Wigdor continued to work at McGill in the department of psychology, and also for Veterans' Affairs. Although she was promoted soon after, her association with the Applied Psychology Centre cannot have favoured her.

Wigdor enjoyed the intellectual challenges of academic life. Like other professional women at McGill, she seemed to be "reasonably content and unlikely to 'rock the boat.' "[32] Like them, she believed that working hard and doing well would produce recognition. It became apparent, however, that recognition and promotion did not automatically follow merit in the university system. Wigdor eventually realized that she and other women of her time generally did not know how to get promoted. Only when she learned that one of her former male students intended to ask for a promotion from assistant professor to associate professor did she realize that she had to take a similar initiative. In discovering that she had to actively seek promotion, Wigdor learned what many women find difficult: how to assert themselves in a male-dominated system. However, being assertive, combined with years of experience, was not enough to assure her success when she tried to change her status from part-time associate professor to full professor.

Wigdor's experience confirms the difficulties women scientists have experienced converting their scientific accomplishments into adequately-paid professional positions commensurate with their capabilities.[33] To a large extent, such difficulties stem "from science's association with the university system, which had remained a bastion of male-dominated, exclusive loci of knowledge reproduction."[34] In this environment, "old expectations that women should be agreeable rather than assertive," as Gillett suggests, "together with simple condescension, may create an atmosphere more strongly conducive to conformity to the stereotype than blatant prejudice or rank injustice."[35]

The Paths Converge

Wigdor is one of the many women at McGill "who had the determination (without apology) to achieve their full intellectual potential,"[36] and, in the mid 1970s, she was well established in her career in Montreal. By the late 1970s, she found pressure building to make a change: the Queen Mary Veterans' Hospital was changing from a DVA hospital to a chronic care hospital under provincial jurisdiction, and her contract would end with this transition; she was unable to obtain a full-time position with McGill as professor; her husband had sold his business and was interested in returning to Toronto; and she was ready for a move if it were to offer appropriate advancement. That opportunity appeared when Wigdor discovered that the University of Toronto had funds to begin a program in aging, the field in which she had been working. After a period of negotiating, in 1979, Dr. Wigdor accepted a full-time position as director of the new Programme in Gerontology, the first of its kind in Canada. This immediately provided her with status as full professor of psychology with the rank of dean. Under her direction, the program grew to employ more than 30 scientists, ranging from cellular-molecular biologists to researchers in clinical medicine, sociology, anthropology, economics, psychology, and nutritional science, and to offer graduate courses across the spectrum of relevant disciplines.

Dr. Wigdor, a warm and attractive woman, attributes her success to consistent hard work, and an environment which encouraged her to achieve. She enjoyed the intellectual stimulation of her academic life, always with an active concern for human health and well-being. She learned the value of planning and the importance of negotiating important issues such as salary. Experience taught her that choices, necessary for women in a scientific career, are often difficult, and require personal sacrifice. Unlike most women of her day, marriage and child-bearing did not deter her from having and pursuing professional goals. She successfully managed a family and a career, something that was unusual in the 1950s.

Wigdor's interest in people led her to specialize in gerontology when the elderly were a small proportion of the Canadian population, and their needs and problems were not widely appreciated. She is a pioneer in Canadian gerontology, a charter member and founder of the Canadian Association of Gerontology, the first editor of the *Canadian Journal on Aging*, and a member of the National Advisory Council on Aging. Appointments to the Science Council of Canada (1973–79) and the Canadian Geriatric Research Council (1980–86) were recognition of her scientific contributions. She was appointed a member of the Canadian Association of the Club of Rome, and awarded the 1975 YWCA Woman of Achievement Award. She is a fellow of the Canadian Psychological Association, a member of the American Psychology Association, the Gerontology Association of America, and other professional associations. Dr. Wigdor also has an impressive list of academic and research publications, including articles in *The Journal of Gerontology* (1977), the *Handbook on Mental Health and Aging* (1980), and the *Canadian Gerontological Collection* (1977). She also wrote *Planning Your Retirement* in 1985, and co-authored *The Over Forty Society* with David K. Foot in 1989. This is a book which responds to the growing public interest in aging, and which highlights issues that will face the baby-boom population in their pre-retirement years. The 1980s were challenging to Wigdor — she struggled to raise enough funds to continue and expand the gerontology program. The period was personally satisfying — she attained autonomy and status. She is a woman of remarkable capacity for work and achievement, with a love of learning and interest in people, whose focus on goals enabled her to overcome barriers of which she was largely unaware. Receiving the Order of Canada, along with the ensuing flood of congratulations, added to the pleasure that came from her work, and caused her to reflect on her life. She said: "I think that I have been very fortunate .... It was a question of trying to get a job done and hoping it was done well."[37]

III. CONTEMPORARY CONCERNS

LOUISE LAFORTUNE

translated from the French by Nancy Schumann

On Being a Woman and Studying Math

Today, women, like men, can enrol in math or science at the university level. There is no discrimination in the admission process. But are there still hard-to-identify prejudices, behaviour patterns, and attitudes that influence women's career choices? Do these prevent them from reaching higher levels even after they have begun in these fields? Do women still face difficulties similar to those faced by women mathematicians in the past? A backward glance upon my own path in mathematics has made me realize that the position of women in mathematics is not as equal as it may seem. In the following pages, I will try to support this claim by discussing some of my own experiences in education, at work, and in my social life. Before presenting these facts, I will identify the general context in which I lived and studied, as well as events which gave rise to my interest in the situation of women in math.

I was born in Montreal, in 1951, the younger of two children. My father, a physician, died when I was nine years old, and my mother had to return to work as a secretary. Therefore I had to take care of myself and make my own decisions. I was forced to become independent and this, in turn, influenced my future behaviour. My early independence later allowed me to withstand pressure, and eventually choose mathematics as my field of study. I went to a mixed elementary school of the Montreal Catholic School Commission, where classes were not mixed, however. I did my four years of secondary classical studies in a French-language public girls' school, where the teaching was largely done by nuns of the Sainte Croix community. I was then admitted to the health sciences program at CEGEP Rosemont, within the recently created CEGEP (college) system in Québec, on the condition that I complete certain math and science prerequisites during the summer and first term, thus avoiding high school Secondary Five, which was not mandatory at the time. In 1970, with my CEGEP diploma in hand, I entered the math program at the Université de Montréal, graduating in 1973 with my B.Sc. in math.

My own interest in the situation of women in the workplace comes mainly from my union involvement. In the milieu FNEEQ-CSN (Fédération nationale des enseignants et enseignantes du Québec) up to 1980 women did not have a place, and it is even questionable whether they have a place today. Because I wanted to explore the question more deeply, in 1982 I enrolled at the Simone de Beauvoir Institute (Concordia University) and took several courses in women's studies. As a result of these two experiences (my union involvement and women's studies), I began to examine my own reasons for choosing a career in a discipline traditionally reserved for men; I wanted to know the history of women who had worked in mathematics. I registered in the faculty of education at the Université de Montréal and completed a master's thesis on the history of women mathematicians.

If I think back to my math experiences in elementary school, second grade stands out most clearly in my mind. The teacher often gave us math exercises to do in class. I solved the problems quickly. Since there was really no one to compete against, I simply tried to out-do myself, and had fun trying to beat my own records. At one point, the teacher did not know what to do to keep me busy, so she suggested I ask my mother for knitting needles and yarn. No sooner said than done! I arrived at school with my supplies, and while the class was doing math exercises, I spent a good portion of the time learning to knit. I made my first vest in second grade.

For many years, I thought that I had been lucky to be able to learn to knit as well as to learn math. Now I realize that my particular talents in math were not encouraged and developed (except for being able to count stitches on a knitting needle). It is true that knitting kept me occupied, but it did not allow me to fully develop my potential in math. I still have a hard time imagining boys keeping themselves busy by knitting in math class! I wonder if my teachers, male and female, had

Louise Lafortune in the process of demystifying
mathematics to women, Montreal, Quebec, 1989.
Photo by Guy Beaupré.

the talent necessary to stimulate my interest in math, or was it inconceivable at that time to encourage girls to excel in scientific fields?

In high school, my reputation for having a "gift for math" was quickly established. I was the one the other girls turned to when they weren't able to do their homework or prepare for an exam. Even today, when I meet former classmates, they are not surprised that I am a math teacher.

Looking back at my high school days, I get the feeling that the image I projected created a distance between my fellow students and myself. They needed my assistance, of course, but for academic questions, for my intellectual contribution. I felt important, but it was a one-sided relationship, for there was little concern on their part for what I was experiencing on an emotional level. I was the rational female mathematician who had the right answer, and who did not need others. Slowly, I moulded myself to the social image associated with mathematics, a discipline which is considered objective, and which must be approached rationally, without emotion. It is a masculine image in that it projects values generally associated with men. If I wanted to continue in a discipline which I loved, and in which I wanted to be taken seriously, I had to conform to this model as much as possible.

As my late father was a physician, my family pushed me toward medicine. So in 1968 I enrolled in CEGEP in the health sciences. I did, however, make sure I chose the most advanced courses in physics and math, in order to be able to switch from health to pure sciences at the right moment. I found that I still loved math as much as ever, and I decided that after CEGEP I would go into pure mathematics at the Université de Montréal.

Today, I see several reasons why it took me so long to reach this decision: the fear of being prevented from studying mathematics, of disapproval, and of being isolated. Finally, I was afraid of being influenced by social pressures which would most likely discourage me, and my not being able to resist them. In some ways, I was protecting myself. While at CEGEP, I was not even thinking about a career in math. I liked "doing math," and the rest, it seems to me, was not very important. I never consulted a career advisor, male or female. What would they have suggested to a girl in 1968–70? Would they have dared to suggest I go into engineering or physical sciences? Today, I am aware that it was better for me to choose on the basis of my own likes and dislikes, and not on the basis of advice from a person influenced by the social pressures of the time. I believe that such an influence would have shaken my determination, and thus led me to change my direction.

At university I was a model student who attended all of my classes and who never handed work in late. My fellow students noticed that my course notes were clear and at their request I began to take notes using carbon paper in order to be able to distribute copies to them. I ended up not waiting for the boys to ask me for class notes; I usually made 10 copies in order to meet the requests of fellow students who were absent.

I also remember groups of boys who would spend their spare time playing bridge. I always loved playing cards and wanted to join these groups. I wasn't very familiar with the game, so I spent a lot of time watching them play. The first time I was asked to play, I didn't hesitate, and in spite of my spotty knowledge, I said I knew how to play. For me, that was the only way to get into the group. In the beginning, it wasn't easy; they tripped me up on all my mistakes. I had to learn quickly; above all, I had to discover the mistakes that others made in order to show I was good enough to play.

In retrospect, it is clear that I had two choices: I could go to classes, study every evening, spend my free time in the library, and get very good grades, like the majority of girls or, like the boys I knew, I could choose to go to classes and study as little as possible. I would not do quite as well, but I would have fun. I chose to try to fit into the boys' group. I soon found out that, in order to be accepted, I had to behave in a certain way. I thought that if I acted as their secretary, they would allow me to join in their fun. Being "one of the boys" was a kind of camouflage; did I become similar to the people who pretend that they are able to succeed without hard work? In trying to be accepted into this "male milieu," is it possible for women to keep their identity? Must they make the differences between the sexes an abstract idea? Must they play the men's game?

In 1973, at the age of 22, I got my first job as a mathematics teacher at the CEGEP du Vieux Montréal earning $6000 a year. In addition to my teaching, I agreed to write the final draft of the class notes which the teachers (male, naturally) of the department had produced. They told me I had good handwriting! I did not see how I could refuse to do this and still be re-hired the next year. For them, I was surely a very good math secretary. I knew what exponents, square roots, trigonometric functions were. I could even check and correct the computational errors of these "conceptual mathematicians." One might think that I got this "secretary's" job because I was the last one hired, but this was not the case. A male part-time teacher worked at designing the course notes, while another female full-time teacher served as secretary, in addition to doing her own regular work. In contrast to my student years, when I felt appreciated for my mathematical ability, I felt slighted in the workforce because I was a woman.

In CEGEP André-Laurendeau where I now teach, I have noticed that some of my male colleagues would come to discuss math problems with me *only* if there was no one else in the department at the time. But as soon as a male colleague arrived, the problem would suddenly disappear, only to reappear on the male colleague's desk. I have even had something literally taken out of my hands while I was reading it.

It is easy for me to see why I ended up losing interest in solving advanced math problems. At one point, I even began to doubt my own mathematical ability. Today, to my great surprise, I find myself wanting to delve deeper into mathematical ideas; I enjoy playing with math again. Nonetheless, my objectives are very precise: to examine the mathematical work of women mathematicians through history, to find ways of demystifying math, particularly for women, and to help "mathophobes" (people experiencing math anxiety) to increase their self-confidence in this field. My unusual background in both classical studies and pure sciences especially equips me to meet these objectives.

In recent years, I have regained confidence in my ability to study math at an advanced level, and although I am currently working on my doctorate, I do not like the fact that math is still male-dominated. Even if I believe that more women should take math courses and go into scientific fields, and even if I may help them move in that direction, I cannot help thinking that it will not be easy for them to be truly accepted and still maintain their female identity in a field that is to this day heavily influenced by male stereotypes. I have come to realize that women in mathematics are perceived differently from men in mathematics. I have tried to observe people's reactions when I say that I am a math teacher. I have even tried an experiment in the seduction games played in cafés and bars. I have elicited very different reactions when I have announced I was a math teacher than when I said I was a secretary. The truth provoked surprise and a certain backing off by the other person. All of a sudden I became less interesting. I felt that I was seen as a "normal" woman only if I lied. Would male math teachers elicit this same surprise in women? Judging by my discussions with some women, women's reaction is rather one of curiosity and interest. Try to imagine men's reactions to an ad in the personal column of a newspaper that reads: "female mathematician, single, 37, seeks an available man."

Now I realize that during my studies I was not aware of discrimination. I did not think about having to overcome obstacles which were different from the ones men had; wanting to succeed was enough. If I had been fully aware of all these difficulties, it would have been very hard for me to remain in that masculine setting which did not really accept me.

I also realize that in attempting to mould myself to the social image associated with math I, in fact, isolated myself from female company. To be competitive in the men's world meant to be the best, often at the expense of others. By not conforming to the image of the female student who does an enormous amount of work to succeed, I was reinforcing the male image of success without effort, and the existence of a so-called "gift" in math. Is it possible to stay in this masculine world without becoming isolated?

I think that my own experience shows the importance of having female role models in math with which girls can identify. Only an increase in the number of women in scientific careers, and/or in the teaching of math or science at advanced levels, will change the masculine social image associated with these fields, and encourage more girls to enter them.

Moreover, professionals in education should develop strategies which take into account attitudinal differences with regard to math. Such an approach would have a greater chance of reaching girls, who do not really relate to the way math is currently presented: as competitive, rational, objective, rigid, lacking in emotion. We should challenge girls who choose traditionally feminine careers under the pretext that they are not able to succeed in math. Encouraging, approving, stimulating, and listening can help us to know the real reasons which motivate them to select such programs, and to help them to perhaps re-orient their choices.

BETTY COLLIS

Adolescent Females and Computers: Real and Perceived Barriers

GENDER DIFFERENCES IN ACCESS TO COMPUTERS

School Participation

Computer use in schools is strongly established throughout Canada, with virtually all secondary schools and the majority of elementary schools having installed computers by 1985.[1] Extensive school computer initiatives have been made in Ontario,[2] Manitoba,[3] and Alberta.[4] As of March 1987, Alberta had the fifth lowest student-computer ratio of any province in Canada or state in the United States, and the second-greatest number of computers in schools, exceeded only by California.[5] However, despite the number of computers in schools, there is consistent evidence that females make less use of the technology than do males. This is particularly so with regard to participation in computer science courses at the secondary level.[6] National assessments in the United States compared male and female enrolment in secondary school computer programming courses in 1978 and 1981–82. These assessments found approximately twice as many males as females enrolled in these courses in 1978, a difference that remained constant during the four-year time period through 1982.[7] Although "computer programming" has come to be replaced by "computer science" as a senior secondary elective course, the same disproportionate enrolments of males and females continue to be documented.[8] If completion of secondary school computer science courses increases the likelihood of continued work with computers after secondary school, either in university, other postsecondary training, or the workplace, then the long-range implications of male-dominated computer science courses in secondary school may be substantial.

These gender differences in participation are also seen at the junior secondary level, although the ability to make choices about participation is limited at these grades.[9] Male to female ratios in these studies typically range from 5:1 to 2:1. Finally, in elementary grades, several studies also report significant gender differences in "computer class participation."[10] Teachers at all grade levels identify boys, rather than girls, as the students most actively involved with school computer use.[11] For example, when teachers in a national American survey were asked to indicate the sex of the three students most involved with computers in their schools, 74 percent of the elementary teachers and 78 percent of the secondary teachers cited a male as the first student named and overall indicated males twice as often as females.

Extracurricular Usage

Gender differences in extracurricular computer use are also well established.[12] In a study done in several Ontario schools 10 times as many males as females used computers during extracurricular time.[13] Boys outnumber girls three to one where computers are used either before or after school and, at the "typical middle school" in a 1985 national survey of 2,331 American schools, only 15 percent of the extracurricular users of computers were females.[14] Males consistently outnumber females in enrolment at computer camps, and at computer-related courses outside of school and, as costs and age increase, the proportion of females decreases.[15] Although video game arcades have declined in popularity, they were and continue to be strongly identified with male users.[16] Finally, home use of computers is reported to be more likely for adolescent males than for adolescent females.[17]

Attitudes

Gender differences in adolescents' attitudes toward computers have been reported in a number of studies, with adolescent males consistently more positive than adolescent females.[18] The author interviewed

156 grade eight and grade 12 students to develop an item pool of statements relating to attitudes toward computers and computer users. The instrument developed from this item pool was subsequently administered to nearly 3000 grade eight and grade 12 students, the majority of the populations for those grades in two British Columbia school districts. Results from this study and subsequent replications of the study include the following:

1. Sex differences in attitudes toward computers are strongly established by grade eight.
2. Males are consistently more positive about using computers than are females, and more likely to express interest in and pleasure in using a computer.
3. Males and females agree that males are most likely to be the computer users in their households, and that "mother" is the least likely person in their households to have any interest in using a computer.
4. Females are more likely than males to associate social and academic stereotypes with computer users.[19]

Why Be Concerned About These Differences in Attitude and Participation?

It is not important or feasible that all adolescents have positive attitudes toward technology, or participate in computer science courses in secondary school. If females were underrepresented in computer classes and in informal experiences with computers because of disinterest based on thoughtful decision-making processes on their parts, the situation might not be of serious concern to educators, especially now that early predictions of school computer literacy experiences being critical to future job prospects have been qualified.[20] However, a number of research studies indicate that inequities and barriers to access, and not thoughtful well-informed decisions, are involved. Females stay away from computers because their options become prematurely limited, either by themselves or by others.

They believe that working with these machines is appropriate for bright males, but not for them, that they indeed are "not cut out for computers," and that efforts they might make would be repaid with both social embarrassment and personal frustration . . . .

Females expect they won't do well, won't enjoy the (computer) contact, and have no need for it.[21]

As personal expectations frequently become self-fulfilling, it is critical that educators respond to any influences that may relate to the stunting of academic achievement and self-esteem.[22] What are the influences that serve to erect or reinforce barriers between many adolescent females and constructive computer experiences in schools?

A CONCEPTUAL MODEL TO PREDICT ADOLESCENT FEMALES' COMPUTER ACCESS

Models To Predict Participation

A number of models have been developed to predict female participation and achievement in various school subjects.[23] All include perceptions of self-efficacy and personal relevance, as well as perceived expectations of significant others as predicators. Some researchers have attempted to build a prediction model of influences on female utilization of school computer resources.[24]

Apparently there are five "problem areas" that influence secondary school students' computer access: (1) attitude-related, including motivational and self-concept variables; (2) software-related; (3) hardware access and "human interface" problems; (4) academic, including interest and success in certain computer-related courses; and (5) social, perceptions of peers and of home environments.[25] School policy, software selection, student encouragement, and the role of family and peers are also considered critical components.[26] A recently developed causal model includes the interactions between task characteristics; cultural milieu; teacher, student, and family characteristics; and various domains of expectations.[27]

Based on analyses such as these, we propose a model with three dimensions as an efficient predictor of adolescents' access to constructive experiences with computers. The model has potential predictive and explanatory value, and can also serve as a framework for intervention strategies. A study involving researchers from British Columbia, Alberta, and Quebec is being conducted (1986–87) to test the model, with data from adolescents in rural, isolated, and urban areas in various regions of Canada. As of March, 1987, over three thousand grade 11 students from eight urban areas in Canada have been involved in the study. The three dimensions of the predictive model may be described as: (1) school policies and practices, (2) social expectations, and (3) personal factors. The dimensions, while distinct, are not independent.

1. *School-related Policies and Practices*

(a) *Policies relating to academic pre- and corequisites.*

The majority of utilization of secondary school computer resources occurs within the context of computer science or computer studies courses.[28] These courses frequently require mathematics prerequisites, have a mathematical orientation, and are taught by instructors who were originally mathematics teachers at the school.[29] Little opportunity exists to use school computers outside of this mathematically-oriented computer science framework, although business education students may have their own lab.[30] More recent American data show only 13 percent of secondary school computer use occurs outside computer science courses or business education courses.[31] Data from a British Columbia survey show the same pattern of limited opportunities for computer use in secondary schools, with students' choices typically limited to computer science (with senior mathematics pre- or corequisites), or word processing, in business education courses.[32]

The American surveys also document a revealing statistic. As secondary schools acquire more computer equipment, the new resources are typically not used to expand access to more students, but, instead, to provide more extensive access to those already involved in computer science courses. In terms of inequities and barriers, this represents a systematic exclusivity that focuses computer opportunities on capable mathematics students. This in turn serves to disfranchise the majority of students, for whom mathematics is neither a strong subject nor an interest, and this group includes proportionately more females than males.[33] Thus, the typical secondary school practice of allowing computer science teachers and courses to dominate use of school computers and to insist on mathematics prerequisites for access to these courses is a real and effective barrier to computer use for many females.

(b) *Practices relating to a limited view of computer use.*

Computer science and studies courses involve a narrow view of computer applications relative to the many valuable uses that can be made of computers in the secondary school setting. Computers can be used in English classes to support composition, and as tools for functional writing done in a social context.[34] They can be used in science classes as data-capturing and display tools and as vehicles for the presentation of various types of simulations of scientific processes.[35] They can also be used in social studies, as tools for the accessing and organizing of information, and the display of information in graphic form,[36] and in art and music courses for the support of new types of creative expression.[37] These and many other applications are available now for the secondary school. They do not require any substantial infusion of new equipment, or reorganization of instructional timetables. Their incorporation has the potential of providing interesting and relevant computer experiences for a much larger group of students than those who are now interested in computer science courses.[38] In particular, word processing in an academic context rather than in the vocational context of business education courses has special potential for female students, in that females are frequently more self-confident about themselves as writers and communicators in English courses than as participants in mathematics, science, and computer courses.[39] However, the typical secondary English, science, social studies, or mathematics teacher makes no use at all of school computer resources.[40] Thus, by school practice, probably based on a lack of awareness of the breadth of instructional uses of computers possible in all subject areas, the majority of adolescent females are never given any opportunity to use school computers in instructional settings where they could develop their awareness of the computer as a relevant tool, especially for language-related tasks. Through this omission, adolescent females as well as males are deprived of access to many valuable aspects of constructive computer usage.

(c) *School policies with regard to the location of computers.*

The most typical pattern for hardware organization in secondary schools is to cluster the majority of the school machines in a single computer laboratory.[41] This may inadvertently result in the creation of more barriers for female students. The secondary school computer lab has become associated with males.[42] Computer labs frequently become locker-room type environments that are unattractive to most females (and to many male students as well).[43] In addition, computer labs often become the responsibility of the computer science teacher, whose students absorb as much access time as they are allowed.[44] Together, the computer teachers and students may be perceived as an elite group around whom others are not comfortable.[45] Schools could mitigate many of the problems associated with computer laboratories by rotating access to the lab and responsibility for the lab among teachers in different disciplines, or by limiting the lab access of computer science students to certain time blocks. However, these strategies rarely occur. School policy, or lack of policy, with regard to location of and access to hardware perpetuates a major barrier to equitable and relevant computer usage for females.

(d) *School practices with regard to the organization of learning.*

A final area in which school practices fail to relate to the interests and preferences of many female students involves the type of learning environments usually organized for computer use and computer-related assignments. Computer-related assignments frequently involve programing or program design done independently by each student, or as individual keyboarding practice in business education word-processing courses. However, there is evidence that many female students prefer cooperative learning situations to individual or competitive situations.[46] Grade eight social studies students were assigned to three groups, all of which made use of a computer simulation within the context of a two-week unit on map reading and navigation. One group was told to work cooperatively, with their final grades based on an average of each group member's marks. Another group was told they would be graded on a competitive, norm-referenced basis within their group. The third group was told their grades would reflect only their individual work, and would be based on criterion-referenced standards, rather than any sort of comparison with their classmates. Males in the competitive condition expressed a more positive attitude toward computers after the treatments were concluded than did any of the other male or female groups. However, females in the cooperative condition accomplished more work and achieved higher scores than did females in the competitive and individualistic conditions, and students in the cooperative condition (male and female) completed more work and correctly answered more items than did students in the other two groups. In addition, students in the cooperative condition nominated more female classmates as desired future work partners than did students working competitively or individually. Students in the individualistic condition ended the experience "liking computers" less than any of the other students. These results suggest that cooperative learning experiences involving computers have both social and achievement-oriented benefits for adolescents, and may "equalize status and respect" for female group members.[47] Thus, the typical secondary school practice of expecting students to work individually at computer terminals does not exploit a learning environment that is attractive and productive for many female students.

2. Social Expectations

(a) Computers and masculine associations.

It is well established that gender-typed labeling of school subjects is related to students' achievement and participation in those subjects.[48] Furthermore, expectancy of success in a task is also related to an individual's perception of its gender-appropriateness for him- or herself.[49] Because of this, it is particularly significant that the computer domain is strongly identified as being a masculine one. A 1986 Canadian study found that three- to six-year-old children already associate computers with boys rather than with girls.[50] Several others found that young children perceive computers as more appropriate for boys than for girls, and that this impression increases with age.[51][52]

The computer-male association is reinforced by the marketplace. In large-circulation computer magazines males dominate the articles and illustrations.[53] Men appeared twice as often as women, and were overrepresented as managers and experts, whereas women were overrepresented as clerical workers or observers.[54] It is not surprising that magazines display this type of gender difference with regard to computer use in the workplace. Men are more likely than women to be involved in computer use at a managerial or expert level, while females who use computers at work are more likely to be using them under someone's direction and for clerical tasks.[55] In the home, males are the predominant computer users,[56] and the director of educational marketing for Apple Computers was quoted in 1985 as saying, "The buyers of Apple computers are 98% male. We do not feel that women represent any great untapped audience".[57]

Secondary students have absorbed this message of computers being in a male domain. Female students are significantly more likely than males to endorse a stereotype of a computer user as being a bright male who likes mathematics, but is not particularly attractive socially.[58] Many others document a male association attached to computer use for secondary school students.[59] This gender typing is likely to erect or maintain a barrier that will inhibit the development of computer-related competencies in many adolescent females.

3. Personal Factors

(a) *Lower self-confidence.*

It has long been documented that females express lower levels of self-confidence than do their male peers. Women are less likely than men to believe they have the ability to do university work, even though they earn better secondary school grades. A survey of graduate students in science, engineering, and medicine at Stanford University showed that even the women in this group were "less self-confident and assertive than their male counterparts."[60] Another study found females to have significantly lower self-concepts in mathematics than did their male peers, even though the females had significantly higher achievement levels in mathematics than the males.[61]

With this inclination to express lower levels of self-confidence, it is not surprising that females have been found to be significantly less self-confident than their male classmates with respect to computer use.[62] Heightened anxiety levels can create another barrier to adolescent females' constructive involvement with computers.

(b) *"We can, but I can't"*

There is an interesting extension that can be made to the examination of females' self-confidence with regard to computer use. The only computer-attitude items on a 1984/86 survey to which females responded in a more positive manner than did males were those which described the ability of "women in general" to be competent computer users. Females in both grade eight and grade 12 strongly agreed with all statements about females in the abstract being as computer-competent as men (while males were inclined to disagree). However, as soon as the females were asked to assess their own competencies and self-confidence with regard to computers, they shifted in their attitudes. The typical adolescent female respondent felt that women in general are capable, but that she, as an individual, is not likely to be a competent computer user. This "We can, but I can't" paradox may represent the collision of two different sets of cultural messages, and may have psychosocial implications for contemporary adolescent females that range well beyond computer work.[63]

A similar finding has recently appeared in a Labour Canada survey of the career aspirations of Canadian school children. There was a definite trend among the grade one to eight students surveyed. The students saw the development of a greater participation rate of women in traditionally male careers (interestingly, there was no similar trend for men toward traditional "women's work"). However, when girls were asked to indicate their own career aspirations, they tended to choose "women's jobs" rather than predominately-masculine professions.[64]

> It was as though girls did not apply to themselves their general belief in the equality of the sexes. Many of them seemed to be saying, "Yes, women can become doctors, but I expect to be a nurse."[65]

This "We can, but I can't" paradox has the potential to be a formidable barrier to equitable computer access for adolescent females, no less powerful because it is self-imposed.

(c) *Perceived irrelevance of computer work.*

Computer activities in schools may hold little appeal to females because the females do not see any personal relevance for computers in their own lives, present or future.[66] One major reason for this may be that adolescent females still are less career-motivated than males,[67] forming career goals at a later age than males[68] and, as a result, they may be less concerned about the importance of developing a strong base for further professional or vocational growth. In a Canadian sample, girls still "picture their adulthood as consisting of being mothers with small children" and further assume they will have husbands to support them.[69]

Even Grade 8 girls of 14 years of age did not consider the possibility of their having to be in remunerative employment to support themselves or their children. There do not seem to be any unmarried mothers, deserted wives, widows, or divorcees among the imaginary women Canadian schoolgirls expect to become.[70]

This "Cinderella" perspective[71] has the potential to translate itself into a major barrier, a barrier of disinterest that can thwart motivated effort with computers in schools for adolescent females — "If it's for boys, anyway, and isn't very interesting, and I'm never going to need it, why bother?" Until girls realize that they will in all probability have to be breadwinners, not just "cakewinners," it is likely that more males than females will continue to involve themselves in computer opportunities in secondary school.

RECOMMENDATIONS

Intervention Strategies

As of 1986, there are at least seven large-scale intervention programs focusing on the reduction of barriers to females' utilization of school computers.[72] All of these programs are based in the United States. Most involve materials for parents and teachers, as well as descriptions of computer activities that are felt to be attractive to both boys and girls. However, similar intervention programs for females in mathematics and science have long been in existence, but have apparently not made large-scale impacts on female interest and participation in these subjects.[73] It is unrealistic to expect isolated intervention programs to have any sustained impact on the formidable assortment of barriers between secondary school females and equitable, constructive use of school technology. However, some recommendations do seem important.

1. Expand computer use in secondary schools beyond the computer science/computer studies courses so that *every* student has repeated opportunities to use computers as appropriate tools within the context of his or her ongoing school activities. Emphasize language and communication applications in order to capitalize on the positive attitudes females have about themselves and language.[74] Build this

orientation into teacher-training programs and teacher inservice so that teachers see the computer as a tool within a curriculum context rather than as an object of study in itself.[75]

2. Monitor the computer laboratory environments in schools so that all students have equitable access to the resources even if this means that some computer science students will have less access than they currently do. "Let the herd instinct work for you"[76] by structuring cooperative computer activities for pairs or groups of students.

3. Counsel adolescent females to more realistic expectations of the importance that work is likely to have for them in their adult lives. Articulate and discuss the "We can, but I can't" paradox and the "Cinderella" expectation, and help the students identify the impact of these psychological constructs on their current and future academic decisions.

This last point is especially important. We as educators must share some of the responsibility for the barriers of perceived inadequacy that thwart female students. We have let male mathematics teachers become the computer educators in our secondary schools. We have allowed the content of school computer experiences to be weighted with mathematics and have minimized or ignored the central importance of language and communication in professional computer use in the workplace. We have allowed a few male students to dominate the school computers. More fundamentally, we have allowed females to grow up feeling they are inadequate. We have not reacted when we see them limit their options by erecting barriers marked "appropriate behaviour — for a girl," and "not appropriate — for a girl." We have not communicated to them the importance of work, with or without a technological component, to their future financial and psychological health, nor have we communicated the extent to which the level of this health will relate to their ability to feel self-confident and productive in a technologically-dominated society.

Removing some of the barriers to appropriate technological interaction will be a major challenge for both educators and students. Not removing them may lead to results too serious to ignore.

N. NEVITTE, R. GIBBINS and P.W. CODDING

The Career Goals of Female Science Students in Canada

Introduction

The observation that there are few women career scientists in western industrialized countries is now a commonplace one. Most of the systematic evidence brought in support of the case is drawn from Britain, the United States, France, and Sweden, but there is little reason to suspect that Canada departs markedly from this trend. An analysis based on 1976 census data establishes the general point; it indicates that the percentage of women candidates who received degrees in engineering, mathematics, and the physical sciences was too small to be measurable.[1]

Admittedly, the ratio of women to men in the scientific community has probably improved marginally in the last 25 years. For example, in 1960–61, women made up to 0.9 percent of the full-time university teachers in engineering and applied sciences; by 1980–81, their proportion had crept up to 1.3 percent of the full-time teaching staff. Similarly, in 1960–61, 3.9 percent of all full-time university teachers of mathematics and applied sciences were women; that increased to 4.7 percent by 1980–81.[2]

These incremental shifts in the gender composition of the academic scientific community have been mirrored by similar changes in the non-academic scientific professions over roughly the same period.[3] What has changed far more dramatically, however, is the increased awareness of the broader significance of the issue. The matter was succinctly put at a 1980 workshop on the science education of women, where it was argued that the gender discrepancy in science education has "profound economic and political consequences in a world where the impact of science and technology is becoming increasingly significant."[4] It is the realization that such discrepancies engage broad issues of gender equality, as well as questions related to the potential loss of scientific talent, that has added urgency to researchers' efforts to seek out explanations for why so few Canadian women pursue scientific careers.

While the evidence indicating the small size of the female scientific community is hardly controversial at all, the prevailing *explanations* for such a gender gap continue to hover in the realm of speculation. Indeed, the only firm conclusion that can be drawn from the relatively sketchy research literature is that *there is no single compelling line of explanation*. Three general lines of reasoning are deployed to explain why there are so few women scientists.

First, there is the argument that there are motivational differences between boys and girls; young males are more highly motivated than their female counterparts to pursue science subjects in school. Essentially, the motivational explanation places emphasis on the voluntaristic dimension of behaviour. If motivations are seen as the springboard of preferences, then it is but a short inferential step to arrive at the conclusion that gender discrepancies in enrolment in various fields of educational endeavour represent an indirect measure of gender differences in motivations. In this respect, the available Canadian data seem to match the findings in a number of other western industrial societies. In general, girls have a lower enrolment in science than boys in high school, and within the science curricula, boys massively outnumber girls in the hard sciences, such as math, physics, and chemistry. Only in biology do girls match or outnumber their male counterparts.[5] Some researchers, however, are not persuaded that differences in enrolments are a true measure of gender differences in science motivation. In this vein, Steinkamp and Maehr's recent comprehensive American study (1984) represents one impressive attempt to assess directly science motivations. They reached two significant conclusions. First, they found gender differences in motivational orientations at the elementary and secondary school levels to be very small, and they reason that such differences, by themselves, cannot be a primary explanation for female underrepresentation in science professions.[6] Second, they also found that gender differences in motivational orientations towards science tend to decrease with age.[7] What is problematic, of course, is that it is difficult for any students, females included, to return to science, even if their motivation to pursue science increases as they move through the life-cycle. Perhaps more so than in other disciplines, science education is cumulative in nature — participation in advanced science depends upon earlier grounding in science. Consequently, the high proportion of "seepage" of females away from basic science training at an early stage in school careers results in a substantial permanent loss to the potential pool of female scientific talent.

A second line of reasoning looks to biological differences between males and females. This avenue of speculation, one that was popular in the 1970s, hypothesizes that there are biologically inherited gender differences in quantitative ability, visual-spatial ability, and field articulation — all areas that are regarded as the essential tools of "scientific thinking."[8] The plausibility of the biological explanation, however, has been seriously challenged on several fronts. First, the evidence supporting the biological hypothesis is, at best, very weak; at worst, it is contradictory. As Kimball has pointed out,[9] even if the data are read very generously, the amount of gender-related variance which could be explained by biological inheritance, as with the motivational hypothesis, is too small to account for the relative underrepresentation of females in science. But beyond that, controversy revolves around the interpretation of the data. Is it possible to separate causes from symptoms? To put the matter differently, can the apparent gender differences in scientific aptitudes be wholly attributable to endogenous biological factors? Or, alternatively, can such differences be attributed to exogenous social factors? Other data also pose difficulties for the biological line of argument. For example, the biological hypothesis cannot easily explain the fairly substantial evidence indicating that those females who do pursue science academic programmes tend, on average, to outperform their male counterparts in the classroom.[10] Nor does the biological hypothesis travel well across cultural and national boundaries; it does not readily account for the relatively large proportion of female professional scientists found in Eastern European countries.[11]

The third line of explanation, one that focusses on socialization factors, has gained ground, perhaps because of the weaknesses and limited explanatory range of the first two explanations. At the heart of the socialization explanation lies the view that the way young girls are socialized is crucial — that the values that surround them and the expectations of them encourage and cue them to pursue particular educational choices. In turn, those educational choices set the pattern for career paths. Thus, the particular cultural milieu provides a structured context of expectations, and within that milieu, parents, peers, and other agents shape in significant ways the nature of appropriate male/female roles.[12] Canadian researchers, like their counterparts elsewhere, argue that girls, unlike boys, are discouraged from, or at least not encouraged to pursue science, and that counselling received in junior high and high schools compounds the problem.[13] It is also suggested that there is stereotyping and a lack of sufficient female role models among scientists;[14] and it is contended that there are gender biases in curricula and that teaching methods may convey, subtly, different expectations regarding what girls can achieve.[15]

The socialization line of inquiry has substantial *prima facie* appeal. Unlike other approaches, it offers a multivariate explanation, one that draws upon a large, well-established literature grounded in social psychology and as such it provides a more comprehensive perspective that can account for cross-cultural variation. For analysts who see explanation as a first step in the process of redressing the problem of gender imbalances in recruitment to scientific careers, the policy ramifications for the socialization explanation are not very promising. In providing a socially integrated view of the problem, a socially integrated solution is implied, one that calls for a comprehensive shift in social values.

Problem and the Research Strategy

Despite basic differences in theoretical perspectives, researchers usually concentrate on one particular aspect of the problem, namely the question of why so few females get *into* the starting blocks of science careers. As a result, much of the research effort is directed towards the study of gender differences in science enrolments in the *early* phases of academic training. However, the small size of the female scientific community is not solely determined by gender differences at the entry point of science training. If that were the case, then the number of women in the science professions would be roughly proportional to the number of women graduating from universities with science degrees. Aggregate data suggest not only that there are gender discrepancies in early enrolment in academic science courses, but also that there are significant gender differences in the rates of exit from science.[16] Although apparently qualified females are more likely to leave the science community than are their male counterparts, we know very little about this aspect of the general problem. The aim of this paper is to examine the nature of this "seepage" at a late decision point, that is, at the time when female senior science undergraduates are making career choices.

There are a number of practical reasons why senior female science undergraduates should be targeted for analysis. Most obviously, this group is strategically significant in the sense that it consists of those women who are the most immediate, serious contenders for science careers. They are the pool from which future role models will be drawn. Any information about why some of these women choose to continue in science and why others do not is potentially useful, as it may serve as a policy guide for those interested in pursuing remedies for gender imbalance, remedies that are less ephemeral than a general call for a change in social values and which, although more limited, may have a better chance of success. Unfortunately, much of the available evidence about the "defection" of women from science at this critical juncture tends either to be narrowly focused on a single group, such as engineers,[17] or is anecdotal.[18] Although useful, this evidence is limited. It is by expanding the analysis to encompass a broader and more representative segment of the target group that we can move towards a more systematic assessment of the problem.

A second feature of the target group carries implications which can best be appreciated in the context of the preceding discussion of conventional explanations of the problem. Our target group consists of women with sustained training in science, so we can assume that they have overcome such obstacles as "learned helplessness," "math anxiety," and the putative biological and motivational factors. We can assume, too, that they have been able to deal with those socialization factors that drew others away from science during early confrontations with the science disciplines. By focussing our analysis on this target group, we are, in effect, applying a set of approximate controls for those factors that explain why females fail to enter the science academic discipline. Furthermore, direct comparisons between this target group and its male cohort helps us to isolate the gender significance of those variables particular to the late stage decision point. This strategy not only allows us to discount generational and life-cycle effects, but also it enables us to determine whether such variables as social background and performance are relevant to women's career choices in Canada as they are in other national settings.[19]

Data

This examination of gender differences in career choices of science undergraduates takes place through the secondary analysis of survey questionnaire data that were generated for other purposes.[20] The data are drawn from a 118-item questionnaire completed in 1983–84 by final-year undergraduate university students at nine regionally dispersed Canadian universities.[21] The data set has a number of features that make it particularly useful for this analysis. First, the research design of the original project called for purposive stratified sampling of the student population, with the result that an equal number of males and females were contacted within each of four academic disciplines: science, humanities, social sciences, and business/commerce. This strategy produced a matched sub-sample of males and females within the senior undergraduate science community. Second, the questionnaire mail-out was large enough (about 1,288 cases), and the response rate strong enough (about 53%), to yield a sufficient number of cases in our target group (N = 204) for meaningful analysis.[22] Third, the questionnaire solicited basic background socio-demographic data from respondents as well as evaluations of their academic performance, and an open-ended segment of the questionnaire invited respondents to indicate their career goals. The questionnaire then, combines two essential characteristics: it is sufficiently precise for testing hypotheses about gender differences in career goals and, should such differences emerge, it is sufficiently broad to allow for a reasonable search for correlates of those differences.

A. GENDER AND CAREER GOALS

We have indicated that in the original study, the data were generated by sampling equal numbers of male and female undergraduates within four broadly defined academic disciplines. Beyond that, the questionnaires were distributed *randomly* within each of those broad disciplines so there was, for example, no attempt to match a female mathematics major with a male mathematics major. Consequently, we would anticipate that the balance between male and female respondents across the subdisciplines of science would reflect, roughly, the sub-disciplinary gender balance within the whole science undergraduate community. Table 1 provides a summary picture of the target group that will be the focus of our analysis, and it indicates the gender distribution of science students grouped by discipline within science.

In general, Table 1 provides additional evidence indicating significant differences between males and females in fields of study within science. Engineering students are predominantly male; males outnumber females in the "hard" sciences, that is, mathematics and the natural sciences; and those females who are in science tend to be concentrated in areas relating to bio-medical sciences. A more detailed gender breakdown of the bio-medical science category shows that biology is a "female domain," in that women students outnumber their male counterparts by a ratio of about 2:1, but there is approximate gender parity within the field of medical sciences.

Table 1: The Gender Distribution of Science Students

GENDER	FIELD OF STUDY				TOTAL
	BIO-MEDICAL SCIENCES	MATH/NATURAL SCIENCES	ENGINEERING	$\bar{x}\%$	N
Male	40.3%	58.1%	79.3%	57.8%	118
Female	59.7%	41.9%	20.7%	42.2%	86
	(100)	(100)	(100)	(100)	204

Source: Nevitte-Gibbins Canadian Youth Elite Equality Survey, 1983.

Our concern is not to join others in speculations about whether female students are drawn to academic areas that have to do with "life and nurturing" and males to those fields that deal with "how inanimate things work." Rather, we want to explore the question of whether there are differences between the career aspirations of male and female undergraduates who are already within the same sub-disciplines of science academic programmes. The question can be put in the form of the following null hypothesis: if goals are gender-neutral, then we would expect to find no differences in the career aspirations of male and female respondents within each field of science. The data presented in Table 2 (A through D) address this hypothesis.

Table 2A provides an overview of the career choices indicated by male and female science students. The five broad categories indicated there are constructed from responses to the question: "What are your career goals after you get your degree?" Unlike menu-driven questions that present respondents with a choice from a fixed list of options, open-ended questions provide no response cues but, as a result, responses can be too ambiguous or general to be useful. In this instance, a number of respondents indicated simply that they wanted "to get a job," or "to do something in my field." It is hard to say whether students responding in this way regard their undergraduate degree as a terminal qualification, or whether they intend to continue in science. For the purposes of this analysis we regard such indeterminate responses as "noise," and we relegate them to the category "job in field." Other responses provide a far more definitive basis for interpretation. Overall, women science students are about four times more likely than their male counterparts to enter such "nurturing" careers as social work or missionary work. Obversely, males are about seven times more likely than their female counterparts to use their science degree as a springboard to "do something in the business world," as one respondent put it.

Table 2: Student Career Goals By Area of Study

GOALS

		NURTURING	EDUCATION	BUSINESS	SCIENCE/RESEARCH TECHNOLOGY	JOB IN FIELD	(SEEPAGE RATE)[*]	N
(A) *All Science Students*								
Male	(100)	2.9%	17.3%	9.6%	52.9%	17.3%	(29.8%)	104
Female	(100)	11.5%	20.5%	1.3%	34.6%	32.1%	(44.9%)	78
								182
(B) *Bio-medical Sciences*								
Male	(100)	8.0%	16.0%	4.0%	44.0%	28.0%	(40.0%)	25
Female	(100)	12.2%	29.3%	2.4%	24.4%	31.7%	(46.3%)	41
(C) *Math-Natural Sciences*								
Male	(100)	2.8%	27.8%	11.1%	27.8%	30.6%	(44.4%)	36
Female	(100)	14.8%	11.1%	0.0%	29.6%	44.4%	(59.3%)	27
(D) *Engineering*								
Male	(100)	0.0%	9.3%	11.6%	79.1%	0	(11.6%)	43
Female	(100)	0.0%	10.0%	0.0%	90.0%	0	(0.0%)	10

* "Seepage Rate" is calculated as the percentage of the sample that aims to pursue neither further education nor science/research and technology.

Source: Nevitte-Gibbins Canadian Youth Elite Equality Survey, 1983.

What is of most interest in Table 2A are the distributions within the remaining new categories: "further post-graduate education," and "science, research and technology" for it is those two groups that most unequivocally contain the students who plan to remain in science. Taking these two categories together, the data indicate that male students are less likely than females to defect from the science community at the graduation decision point. The summary calculation of the defection, or seepage, rate expressed in the last column of Table 2 is a conservative estimate, for we isolate only those male and female science students who have not *explicitly* indicated that they intend to pursue a science career path. According to this gross measure, our data show that the overall seepage rate among women science students (44.9%) is about 50 percent higher than the seepage rate among male science students (29.8%), and this difference is a statistically significant one (at p < .01).

It is by unpacking the aggregate data summarized in Table 2A that we can develop a more detailed picture of how gender correlates with the structure of career choices within the undergraduate science community. Tables 2B, 2C, and 2D break the aggregate data down into three subsamples that correspond to the three academic disciplines within science: bio-medical science, math/natural science and engineering, and a comparison of three subsamples highlights some interesting interdisciplinary contrasts regarding females' career aspirations. Perhaps the most striking data are represented in Table 2D, which indicates that the career choices of female engineering undergraduates are atypical in at least two respects. First, none of the female engineers responding to our survey indicated that they planned to pursue a "nurturing" career. Indeed, the overwhelming majority indicated a preference for a science or research and technology career path. Second, and perhaps more surprising, is the fact that according to our criteria establishing seepage rate, none of the female engineering undergraduates aim to defect from the science career path. This perfect retention rate is striking in the extreme, but these data should be read very cautiously because our sample contains only 10 female engineers.

The remaining respondent pools are relatively robust, and a comparison of Tables 2B and 2C points up other significant gender differences in career goals, differences that have not been reported elsewhere. We have already pointed out that, unlike other subdisciplines of science, bio-medical sciences cannot be easily characterized as a male-dominated domain. Aggregate population statistics on undergraduate enrolments at Canadian universities indicate that of the female students in science, the largest proportion are attracted to this field, and our sample mirrors that broader trend; female respondents outnumber their male counterparts in this subdiscipline. Table 2B indicates that nearly 30 percent of the female bio-medical science students plan to further their education in the field; they are about twice as likely as their male counterparts in the field to do so. Of all the male science students, those in the bio-medical sciences have the highest seepage rate (40%), but the point worth emphasizing is that this seepage rate is still lower than that of their female counterparts in the same field.

These findings contrast rather dramatically with the distribution of career choices between male and female students in math and natural sciences, as shown in Table 2c. In the bio-medical sciences, subsample males were much more likely than females to pursue "science, research, or technology" career paths, but in the math/natural sciences sub-discipline, the proportion following this career path is roughly evenly balanced along gender lines. However, a far larger proportion of this subgroup of male seniors (27.8%) compared to their female counter-parts (only 11.1%) reported planning on further post-graduate educa-tion, and it is this difference that is largely responsible for the females' higher seepage rate from the science community.

The initial step in the data analysis provides further support for the general trend that could be inferred from a careful reading of aggregate census data, namely, that there *are* significant gender differences in the recruitment of senior science undergraduates to the science commu-nity. A more detailed examination of individual level data, however, enables us to illustrate the significant subdisciplinary variation in these seepage rates for Canadian science students. In addition, we can identify two gender-based trends with respect to the direction of seepage: (1) with the exception of engineering students, women are consistently more likely than men to leave science for "nurturing" careers, and (2) in all instances, across all subdisciplines within science, female students are systematically less likely to regard "business" as an attractive career option.

An overview of the subdisciplinary variations in seepage rates throws into bold relief the atypical structure of the career goals of engineering students, both male and female. We have emphasized the need for caution in drawing firm conclusions on the basis of such a limited sample of female engineering students, but evidence of unusually low seepage rates in this subsample remains an intriguing finding neverthe-less. We could speculate that in pursuing an undergraduate degree in engineering, these students, more unequivocally than their counter-parts in other areas of science, have already crossed the threshold of a professional career path, a career path that provides unusually clear expectations about career rewards and professional norms, and which fully engages students in reinforcing anticipatory socialization. But to confirm such an analysis would call for other data, data that could both identify engineering bound students at an earlier decision point, and probe the motivations of these candidates.

B. ARE CANADIAN WOMEN SCIENCE STUDENTS DIFFERENT?

While our data do not permit us to delve into the specific incentives that encourage women to pursue science, nevertheless we are in a position to search for background factors that may be unique to such a group. To conduct such a search, we followed standard exploratory scanning procedures: the science sample was divided according to gender, and the two groups were then compared along an array of approximately 20 standard social, cultural, economic, and demographic indicators. That data sweep revealed statistically significant differences between male and female science students with respect to father's occupation. Our principal finding in this regard is that female science undergraduates are significantly more likely than their male counterparts (p. < .05) to have fathers in scientific or technological occupations. Beyond that, what is clear from the more detailed breakdown of our data presented in Tables 3A through 3D, is the extent to which father's occupation operates as a structuring variable that not only differentiates female from male science students, but also clearly differentiates female science students from females in other academic disciplines.

Furthermore, standard statistical tests indicate that father's occupation is a stronger correlate of daughter's degree program than is father's education. Moreover, when biology students are excluded from the female science sample, the results are even more striking. A comparison of Tables 3C and 3D shows that father's occupation is a background variable that decisively distinguishes female students in the "hard sciences" from females in the social sciences, and in this instance as well, occupation correlates more strongly than does father's education.

We find no Canadian literature reporting such evidence, but reports of similar findings in Britain speculate that it is the encouragement of fathers, along with teachers, that is significant to women's academic and career choices. The precise line of reasoning that links father's occupation to female students' academic and career aspirations, however, is neither a particularly clear nor compelling one. The question of why father's occupation and "encouragement" should be more relevant than say, mother's occupation, level of education, or "encouragement" is not an issue that has been either systematically addressed or persuasively answered. Our attempt to explore this issue through a comparison of mother's and father's occupation yielded too few instances of working mothers to pursue a meaningful analysis. This finding is itself significant, because it suggests the importance of a generation gap. Presumably, as more mothers routinely enter the workforce and pursue sustained careers, such a comparison would be an increasingly meaningful one. It is in the context of the absence of two careers that the occupational experience of fathers becomes especially meaningful; it becomes the only conduit for precise images and expectations regarding career paths. In this instance, we can speculate that fathers who have scientific and technological careers in a sense demystify science for their progeny, both male and female, but especially female. At bottom, such a line of speculation borrows from the socialization argument, and suggests that familial contextual factors and role models are relevant at career decision points as well as during earlier decision points that relate to selecting the field of academic study.

C. DOES PERFORMANCE MAKE A DIFFERENCE?

The chance of achieving high-flying scientific careers, of course, is not solely determined by background socio-structural factors such as father's occupation; it depends, at least in part, upon how well students perform academically. Available evidence suggests that generally within the academic setting, women science students perform at least as well, if not better, than their male counterparts. The very best university science graduates are an especially important national resource, for they constitute the critical pool from which tomorrow's senior scientists will be drawn. If any group is likely to lead the way for women in science, and provide role models for the next generation of women scientists, it will be this one. The chances of breaking the current gender mould of the senior science community hinges upon the career choices of the very best female science students. In this context, the question to which we now turn becomes a crucial one: does the level of academic performance make a difference with respect to career goals?

Table 3: Father's Occupation & Education: Female Students

(A) *Father's Occupation For Female Students in Science and Social Science*

Female Students' Degree Program

FATHER'S OCCUPATION	SCIENCE	SOCIAL SCIENCE	x̄%
Science/technology	28.0%	14.3%	20.1%
White collar	57.4%	57.1%	57.2%
Blue collar	14.6%	28.6%	22.7%
	(100)	(100)	(100)
			N = 194

CHI squared significant at p < .05

(B) *Father's Education for Female Students in Science and Social Science*

Female Students' Degree Program

FATHER'S HIGHEST EDUCATION	SCIENCE	SOCIAL SCIENCE	x̄%
Some high school or less	22.0%	38.4%	31.4%
High school grad	26.0%	19.2%	22.1%
Some university or other post-secondary	26.0%	27.3%	26.7%
University grad or post-grad	26.0%	15.1%	19.8%
	(100)	(100)	(100)
			N = 172

CHI squared not significant at p < .05

(C) *Father's Occupation for Female Students in Non-Biological Science and Social Science*

Female Students' Degree Program

FATHER'S OCCUPATION	NON-BIOLOGICAL SCIENCE	SOCIAL SCIENCE	x̄%
Science/technology	26.8%	13.2%	17.5%
White collar	63.4%	56.0%	58.3%
Blue collar	9.8%	30.8%	24.2%
	(100)	(100)	(100)
			N = 132

CHI squared significant at p < .01

297

(D) *Father's Education for Female Students in Non-Biological Sciences and Social Science*

Female Students' Degree Program

FATHER'S HIGHEST EDUCATION	NON-BIOLOGICAL SCIENCE	SOCIAL SCIENCE	x̄%
Some high school or less	13.9%	40.1%	32.3%
High school grad	27.8%	19.5%	22.0%
Some university or other post-secondary	27.8%	26.8%	27.1%
University grad or post-grad	30.5%	13.4%	18.6%
	(100)	(100)	(100)

N = 100

CHI squared not significant at p < .05

Source: Nevitte-Gibbins Canadian Youth Elite Equality Survey, 1983.

In reviewing the general career goals of the entire student science sample, we indicated earlier that the seepage rate of female science students exceeded that of their male counterparts (Table 2). Table 4 elaborates these data by dividing the target group according to self-reported academic performance.[23]

Table 4: Career Goals And Academic Performance

(A) *"Top" Academic Performers: Career Goals*

GENDER	(N)	NURTURING	FURTHER EDUCATION	BUSINESS	SCIENCE/RESEARCH TECHNOLOGY	JOB IN FIELD	SEEPAGE RATE
Male	(70)	1.4%	18.6%	8.6%	51.4%	20.0%	30.0%
Female	(44)	15.9%	11.4%	0.0%	43.2%	29.5%	45.4%

(B) *"Average" Academic Performers*

GENDER	(N)	NURTURING	FURTHER EDUCATION	BUSINESS	SCIENCE/RESEARCH TECHNOLOGY	JOB IN FIELD	SEEPAGE RATE
Male	(33)	6.1%	12.1%	12.1%	57.6%	12.1%	30.3%
Female	(34)	2.9%	32.4%	5.9%	23.5%	35.3%	44.1%

Source: Nevitte-Gibbins Canadian Youth Elite Equality Survey, 1983.

There are several significant findings that emerge from this breakdown of the data. First, a comparison of Tables 4a and 4b indicates that the general finding that males have a lower seepage rate than females is a trend that holds true regardless of academic performance. But what is striking from a comparison of the "seepage rate" marginals is the finding that there are significant differences in the seepage rates for female science students. Given that performance is an essential ingredient of career success for senior scientists, we might expect that the very best female students would, *ceteris paribus*, be more likely to plan on staying within the science community. The evidence presented in Table 4, however, contradicts such an expectation. The data show that the very best female science students are *more likely* than their "average" performing counterparts to defect from science, and, in fact, it is the top academic performing female science students who report the highest seepage rate of any of the groups under consideration. A more detailed picture of the structure of that "seepage" can be fleshed out by a comparison of the career goals of all four groups.

The impact of performance on the career goals of male science students can be summarized fairly easily. Top male performers are less likely than average performers to turn to nurturing or business careers. Instead, they are more likely, about 50 percent more likely, to indicate that further education is an immediate career goal. If this pattern of career goals is regarded as normal, then the impact of performance on the goals of female science students would have to be regarded as perverse, for the prevailing pattern for their female counterparts is almost precisely the opposite. Although our sample is fairly small, the best female science students are about *five times more* likely than average performers to seek "nurturing" careers, and, perhaps most astonishingly, average performers are about three times more likely than top performers to plan on pursuing further post-graduate education. The best performers are more likely to see jobs in science, research, and technology as a career option, but none view business as an attractive career goal.

Table 5: Students Continuing Education

FIELD OF STUDY	GENDER	
	MALE	FEMALE
Social science	16.9%	23.2%
Science	17.3%	20.5%
Non-biological science	17.7%	10.8%
x̄%	17.3%	18.16%

Source: Nevitte-Gibbins Canadian Youth Elite Equality Survey, 1983.

These findings are easier to describe than to explain. We are not suggesting that further post-graduate education should be a domain limited to only the very best students. But if further post-graduate education is a necessary stepping stone in the career paths of senior scientists, then from the point of view of maximizing the chances of getting the very best scientific talent into the science community, the proportion of superior female science students aiming to pursue that career path is alarmingly low. The scope of that loss is most serious for female science students in non-biological science, according to the data presented in Table 5.

The most telling tale that emerges from this exploratory analysis is the one that reveals itself by indirection. Academic ability alone is not a sufficient condition for propelling talented science students towards full-fledged science careers; it is the combination of ability and aspiration that is crucial. These data unequivocally indicate that the most able female science students are significantly less likely than males to use their early success in science as a launching pad for careers within the science community. The clear implication is that the problem of the shortage of female scientists is not just a matter of early socialization, "math anxiety," or "learned helplessness." The problem is also that the most able female science students, students who have already overcome the legion of real or imagined obstacles to entering science, still do not see science careers, on the whole, as an attractive career option.

Conclusion

Much of the research aimed at explaining why there are so few female scientists in Canada has focused on gender differentials in science enrolments during the early stages of academic training. We have argued that the preoccupation with that focus may have deflected attention away from another significant aspect of the problem, namely, the "seepage" of women from science at a later decision-point. The aim of this paper has been to explore the scope and nature of this seepage through the secondary analysis of a gender-stratified sample of senior undergraduate students at nine Canadian universities. In doing so, three avenues of investigation were undertaken: (1) an assessment of gender differentials in the career aspirations of science students; (2) a search for social, economic, and cultural correlates that distinguish female science students from their male counterparts; and (3) an evaluation of the impact of academic performance on career goals. Our data indicate first, that there are substantial and statistically significant differences between male and female students with respect to career aspirations. Second, the data scan of socio-demographic background variables revealed that father's occupation consistently distinguished female science students from their male counterparts. Finally, the data show that academic performances does indeed have a significant impact on the career goals of science students. That impact, however, is counter-intuitive for all of the groups under consideration: it was the very best female science students who were found to be least likely to plan further post-graduate education.

Had our research findings indicated no gender differences in the seepage rates from the scientific community at the last decision-point, then we could reasonably infer that the problem of low numbers of women in science is rooted in the early socialization process. Given the gradual increases in female enrolments in high school courses over the last two decades, we could have concluded, optimistically perhaps, that the solution to the problem was already in motion, and that gender equality in this respect would be "just a matter of time." However, our findings provide no grounds whatsoever for such optimism. The quasi-experimental design approach to the research problem, that is, the focus on the matched gender sample of students already in science, is an approach that minimizes the force of the socialization argument that is common in research literature in this area. The general lack of socio-demographic correlates may also suggest that the early stages in the learning/socialization process may not be all that important for the target group studied here. If the socialization argument is set aside, then the central question that emerges is: why do women, especially the top performing women, defect from science at a greater rate than their male counterparts? That is the question that must be addressed by future research. This article directs attention to the critical nature of the late stage decision-point, and in that respect, it establishes the contours of the issue, but our data do not allow us to dig beneath the surface of responses about career goals. Nevertheless, in establishing the contours of the problem, and in focusing on the central question, we can suggest the kind of research strategy that could inform a policy response to the problem.

We suggest that at least three sorts of research questions can be usefully pursued. First, what factors encourage women to go into science? What expectations do they carry with them regarding careers within science? And, do those expectations shift during the course of their science training? Second, what are the operating incentive structures of female science students at the point of making career choices? And, what factors are decisive in encouraging some to choose a science career path? Third, for established female scientists, what factors, looking retrospectively, were critical in making their career choices? And why were those factors critical? It is by addressing these issues that we can gain further insight into the importance of father's occupation and whether, for instance, gender disparities in science can be explained by voluntary career shifts, lack of role models, or such factors as the anticipation of blocked mobility.

Of course, whether the issue of gender imbalance within the science community is "a problem" at all is a matter of perspective. We have suggested that it can be seen as a problem on at least two counts. There is the general social question of gender equity and the increased marginalization of women in a workforce that demands increasingly scientific literacy. Quite aside from the social dimension of gender sympathies, there is also the question of how to increase the supply of an important national resource. If only about 10 percent of the best female students in the "hard" sciences is considering post-graduate education in science, then notwithstanding our gender sympathies or politics, it is clear that we are under-utilizing scientific talent. From this perspective alone, it would be short-sighted of policy makers to ignore half of the potential resource pool. Regardless of which perspective is taken, any proposed policy response has to rest upon a much more focused, systematic, and substantial understanding of the dynamics of late point career decision making.

RACHELLE SENDER BEAUCHAMP
and SUSAN A. MCDANIEL

Women Inventors in Canada: Research and Intervention

What is an inventor or an invention? In this essay, we use the definition of the Canadian Patent Act, which considers a patentable invention to be a new or improved product or process or a new application of an existing product or process. An invention must be technically feasible — it must "work" — and it must be novel enough so as not to be an "obvious" extension of a previous invention.

In this essay we only consider patentable inventions, because this is how the term is widely used, both in academe, and in business and government. Most scholars who study inventions and inventors rely exclusively on patent office data. Similarly, economists and statisticians generally use such data to measure the level of innovation in a given country.

However, there are some ambiguities and difficulties in defining invention, which should be recognized at the outset. In particular, the line between "invention" and "discovery" (the uncovering of *pre-existing* knowledge) is often a fuzzy one. As any scientist can attest, the two are, in practice, inextricably linked. A new discovery, such as the structure of DNA, is dependent on many inventions, such as x-ray diffraction instrumentation, and, in turn, generates other inventions.

In recent years, the legal definition of invention has been greatly broadened, and this has further eroded the distinction between invention and discovery. For example, when one of us (R.S.B.) was a graduate student in molecular biology in the late 1960s, bacterial mutants were considered "discoveries." Today, such bacteria, and even fragments of their DNA, are routinely patented. In the United States, plants and animals (mice) are patentable in some cases, as are drugs.

In this essay, we have used the term invention in the new and broader sense. Some of the examples used may be on the "fuzzy border" between invention and discovery, but we believe that all are, arguably, patentable by today's criteria.

In Canada, the stereotypical inventor is an eccentric man tinkering alone in an ill-equipped basement laboratory or garage workshop on an idea that might never see the light of day. The inventor is an outsider, someone not totally accepted or acceptable, a person whose creativity refuses to be channeled into more desirable or familiar directions.

If the male inventor is something of a pariah, the female inventor bears a double stigma, both as an inventor and as a woman. According to most of the literature on inventors, as well as the popular perception, women are not supposed to invent at all.[1] Clearly, women and their inventions have received little attention in history books or the news media.

With the increasing scholarship in feminist history, however, some fascinating examples of women's inventions are now coming to light.[2] One study suggests that prehistoric women were inventors, in that "gathering food was an early critical invention and an important step in the divergence of the hominid line."[3] This was largely women's work. Similarly, women have been credited with developing the earliest domesticated plants.[4]

Even in historical times, women were often "hidden" inventors. For either legal or commercial reasons, because they could not "own" a patent, or because they felt that a patent in a woman's name would not be taken seriously,[5] women often did not patent in their own names. For this reason, the number of patents listing a woman as inventor is probably considerably smaller than the actual number of women inventors. Nevertheless, patent office records are, overall, the best sources available for identifying women inventors.

In reviewing such records, it is clear that inventions by women frequently reflect the necessities of womens' lives, for example, patents on dishwashers, sewing machines, irons[6] and beds.[7] A particularly sobering reflection on women's lot in life is the large number of bed pan patents.

Rachel Zimmerman, 17, of London, Ontario,
inventor of a computer for the handicapped.
Courtesy Women Inventors Project.

But women's inventions are by no means confined to the domestic sphere. According to Stanley,[8] 20 percent of the machines patented by women in the United States between 1790 and 1888 were non-domestic in application, for example, an apparatus for raising sunken vehicles, a steam generator, and a pump.

Women have been particularly important inventors and innovators in the fields of biochemistry and pharmacology. Prehistoric women developed many herbal remedies,[9] and mediaeval peasant women bound mouldy bread over wounds centuries before Alexander Fleming discovered that a substance produced by the *Penicillium* mould killed bacteria.[10] To this day, women physicians and scientists continue to make important contributions in the biomedical area. Indeed, of the 10 Nobel prizes awarded to women in science, five have been in physiology and medicine, with Rosalyn Yalow, the inventor of the radioimmunoassay, and Gertrude B. Elion, the co-inventor of a variety of therapeutic drugs, being two notable recent recipients.

As these examples illustrate, women obviously have the drive, creativity, and ability to invent successfully, but there are still relatively few women anywhere who receive patents on their inventions. According to the Canadian Patent Office, less than one percent of Canadians receiving a Canadian patent are women; in the 1988–89 fiscal year, 99 out of 17,245 (0.6%) of the patents issued were issued to women.[11] In the United States, the figure is somewhat higher; approximately eight percent of American patents have the name of a woman as inventor.[12] In both cases, the figures are rough approximations based on guesses as to the gender of inventors, as neither patent office keeps records of the gender of patent holders.

Together with our colleagues, we set out to explore the reasons for the paucity of women inventors, and to develop an intervention program which would encourage innovative Canadian women to develop their ideas. In this essay, we review our research on the lives of contemporary Canadian women inventors. What are the challenges and barriers these women face, and how do social and gender structures impinge on their lives so as to render them invisible, or to denigrate their work? After attempting to answer these questions, we discuss the experience of the Women Inventors Project in helping women inventors to surmount some of the obstacles.

Background

A social structure that undermines the legitimacy of women's experiences as innovators overwhelms the attributes of any individual woman inventor.[13] When the dominant society focusses on men, men's ideas, and men's understanding of the world, we are given "a one-sided standpoint [that] comes to be seen as natural, obvious and general."[14] A deep-seated sexist ideology, that says that only what men do matters[15] has profound and negative effects on women. It also structures society's reaction to women's creativity and innovation, making their achievements insignificant or invisible.

Women who come into work or professions that have been established and shaped by men in both content and form, tend to be seen as inadequate in comparison to men. They are immigrants to foreign cultures.

Science and technology are the epitomy of such a male culture. As Evelyn Fox Keller[16] and many others have pointed out, science was, from its beginnings, conceptualized as a specifically masculine endeavour — the quest for simple and often hierarchical relationships, the search for mastery over nature (the latter often seen in feminine terms), and the distant, objective, and rational stance of the scientist. Women scientists, such as Rosalind Franklin in DNA research,[17] Ursula Franklin in metallurgy, Lynn Margulies in evolutionary biology, Barbara McClintock in genetics,[18] Barbara Wright in embryology, and Ruth Hubbard in biology of gender, who have provided innovative conceptualizations of scientific problems, have had an uphill battle to gain acceptance.

Much of the literature (by men) implies that women are incapable of high-level creativity. It is argued that women are *biologically* prevented from full development of creativity because of their natures, which are seen to centre on reproduction and childrearing. Given such pressures, it is not surprising that women often rechannel their creative urges into more acceptable forms. "One cannot help but wonder how much female creativity is, and has been, channelled into . . . creative living, ranging all the way from interior decoration (sometimes called nest making) to how to live for a month on an income that leaves almost nothing for food."[19]

Yet, "creativity associated with personal home decoration and personal appearance is less esteemed in our society than creativity which designs new machines or produces esthetic works for public consumption."[20] As Cockburn (1986) suggests, women have largely been excluded from the crucial role of tool-maker, and thus often lack the technical expertise so valued in the public realm. Domestic creativity is discounted, as is women's creativity in the more public worlds of science and art.

A Study of Contemporary Women Inventors

For the purpose of this study, we interviewed 21 women who had registered their inventions for an assessment by the Canadian Industrial Innovation Centre in Waterloo. Most were "independent" inventors, who worked on their inventions at home, and most were at an early stage in developing their ideas — they had not yet marketed or even patented their inventions.[21]

We employed an open-ended interview schedule, in which we asked about the process of inventing in the women's own terms, how and why they got into it, how they saw themselves and how others reacted, how they dealt with the reaction of others, the challenges they faced as inventors, and the multiple roles they occupied.

The 21 women who participated in the study were diverse in every respect. They ranged in age from 24 to 66, with a mean age of 42.6. Sixty-one percent (13) of the respondents had had some post-secondary education, but some (10%) had had only grade 11. Most of them (76.2%) were married at the time of the interview, with equal numbers cohabiting, divorced, and widowed. Ten percent were never married. Two-thirds of the respondents had children, while 20 percent (4) did not. For three additional respondents, it was not known whether or not they had children. At the time the women were involved in inventing, 43 percent (9) had children still at home. The majority of respondents (76%) were employed outside the home at the time of the interview, with the remainder seeing themselves as homemakers, or not in the labour force. The latter category includes a student, a retired person, and a person on long-term disability. The range of occupations represented was impressive: a food services worker, sales clerks, a bank teller, an artist, a singer, a business consultant, a marketing analyst, a special education teacher, a university professor, a teaching assistant at a university, and a nursing supervisor.

Tables 1 and 2 reveal some of the complexities involved for our sample in the process of invention. For the vast majority of women (81% plus) we interviewed, inventing was done at home (Table 1). This should not be interpreted as meaning that their inventions were all domestic, however. Table 2 shows the tremendous diversity in types of inventions on which the women worked. One third of them, however, were involved in working on inventions to improve domestic life.

The most striking finding of the study was the fact that the women inventors interviewed had so internalized the myth that women are not inventors that they denied their own experience. Only a small percentage (23%) would label themselves as inventors; a typical comment was, "I would not say that I was an inventor. My invention was an 'out of the blue' sort of thing. Inventors create a lot of things that are more technical than mine." Most strongly denigrated their work, calling it "silly" or "just making do." They kept their inventing quiet, "I have never told anyone that I invent on the side . . . . " In striking contrast was their appreciation of others: they were quick to label the men in their lives (father, husband, son) as inventors.

It appears that many of these negative perceptions of the women's own experience are tied to the invisibility and denigration of home-based work in general, and the lack of a recognized connection between the private realm of the home and the public sphere, where events of "importance" are seen to transpire. Inventing is considered by many of the women to be an extension of the homemaker's role, and this connection is reinforced by the fact that a majority of their inventions (67.5% of the women contacting the Innovation Centre) were in the "personal/household" category, as compared with 18 percent for inventions by males.

There were also other common elements in the women's experiences. A major barrier for most was the financial one. Developing an invention is usually very costly: North American patents alone cost at least $5,000, and that is just the start. In addition to the barriers faced by male inventors in raising this kind of money, women inventors also face gender-related obstacles. For example, several studies of Canadian women entrepreneurs have found that women make heavy use of their own finances in business start-ups, because they have difficulty in getting funding elsewhere.[22]

Time is also a gender-specific problem for women inventors; in juggling the demands of homemaking and childcare with work outside the home and with inventing, many women were coping with three full-time jobs. The difficulty is not only a general lack of time, but also the lack of quiet time for thinking and creating. A typical comment was, "it's hard . . . . not to be left by myself. You know, to really do what I want to do. I'm not just free as the breeze."

Another challenge, again related to working at home, was isolation. Many inventors lacked family support ("My husband was the greatest doubter, definitely"), and almost all lacked a peer group, for advice and moral support, and the business and professional contacts needed to develop their ideas. In the words of one, "I'd say contacts [were the biggest problem]. I have the idea but I don't know who would have the technology, who would have the knowledge of who else I should contact. I think it's just getting over that stuff . . . because this is one that stalled me." Many expressed the view that they didn't know where to start. Most felt that "more women would invent if they knew of other women inventors."

The Women Inventors Project

In the past decade, a variety of educational programs designed to encourage young women to continue with math and science courses in high school and enter "non-traditional" occupations have been instituted. The Lawrence Hall of Science, University of California, Berkeley, has been a pioneer in this work, but many Canadian school boards have been active as well.[23]

Unfortunately, there is much less programming available for adult women involved or interested in "non-traditional" fields. Prior to the inception of the Women Inventors Project, no one had ever tried to develop a program for women inventors, even though the Canadian government (and many other groups) have professed a strong interest in encouraging innovation, and even though it was clear that existing support programs for inventors (such as the Canadian Industrial Innovation Centre in Waterloo) were not reaching women effectively. In fact, historically, only five percent of the Innovation Centre's clientele had been female.

As mentioned already, our interviews with women inventors had clearly identified concerns and problems common to most. Some of these, including isolation, lack of self confidence, and the need for information and referrals to reliable professionals, appeared amenable to an intervention program. Therefore, one of us (R.S.B.), together with Lisa Avedon, designed an educational and support program for women inventors. The organization which resulted —the Women Inventors Project—began operations in November, 1986, with funding from the federal and provincial governments. It is the first program in North America aimed specifically at women inventors.

The Project's initial mailing list of less than 100 was comprised of women inventors who were either clients of the Canadian Industrial Innovation Centre in Waterloo, or holders of a Canadian patent. Through personal referrals and media publicity, that number has grown: as of January, 1989, there were over one thousand inventors on the mailing list, and about 250 women have attended one or more workshops sponsored or co-sponsored by the Project.

The women involved with the Women Inventors Project have developed a wide variety of inventions, including a novel three-way mirror for applying eye make-up or contact lenses, an electronic car mileage recorder, a collapsible prawn trap, a pacifier holder, and artificial intelligence software (see summary in Table 2). In addition to the work with adult women described here, the Project has developed and tested a workshop on inventing for grade 10 girls. Inventions by students have included a solar-heated rabbit hutch, a folder for organizing sheet music, and a handbag organizer.

To help women inventors and innovators overcome the barriers they encountered, the Women Inventors Project designed a workshop which fills a three-day period, or which can be broken down into shorter workshop units. The content includes information and resource materials relevant to the launching of an invention and information on networking strategies. The training format was refined in two three-day programs for 51 women from across the country, all at some point in the invention process.

The women inventors who participated in the Project's initial three-day workshops found that they learned and worked most effectively when there were opportunities to relate personally to workshop leaders, develop a sense of community with other women in the group, and see the relevance of workshop materials to their personal projects. This is a relational learning style.[24] In order to enhance the quality of the training, the workshops were especially designed to include time for one-on-one conversing between workshop leaders and participants, hands-on prototype building, role models the women could relate to, displays of the women's inventions, and brainstorming situations from the women's own experience. Much peer learning — learning from each other's experience — occurred during the training; some of the women found this to be the most stimulating part of the sessions.

In a follow-up study of workshop participants, carried out about a year later, all the women interviewed accorded high scores to the training received.[25] As compared to the women inventors in the earlier study, there was a dramatic difference in self-perception. While over 80 percent of the original sample had poor self confidence (as evinced by the fact that they saw their own "lack of ability" as a major barrier), 83 percent of the workshop participants rated their self-confidence as good or very good.

In order to widely disseminate the workshop experience, the information covered and the experiences of the participants themselves, were summarized and published as an inventors' manual, *The Book for Women Who Invent or Want To*. Unlike most material for inventors, the book was written simply and clearly, using non-sexist language. Interestingly, we have found that demystifying technology *for women* also makes it more accessible to many men, as indicated by the fact that we have sold many books to, and have had very favourable feedback from, male inventors.

In parallel with the distribution of the book, the Project has helped to establish networks of women inventors in several Canadian cities. These networks provide "moral" support for otherwise isolated inventors, run workshops, and even work on inventions as a collective. The Project also publishes a newsletter for inventors, to enable women in more isolated communities to keep up to date; it also works with teenage girls.

Conclusion

In our research into the lives of contemporary women inventors, we have found that they face many of the same obstacles and barriers as do women in other male-dominated professions. They must balance the constraints of primary responsibility for home and family with careers, the parameters of which are established by men, for men. They face challenges in being taken seriously by their families, friends, and

313

neighbours. They feel the stigma of being in a field that is unusual in general, but particularly so for women. They are reluctant to see themselves as inventors, because they experience ghettoization of their work into areas thought to be appropriate for women. In short, meshing the roles of inventor, mother, and worker is far from straight-forward.

A further problem faced by many women inventors is the isolation of working at home without colleagues for support and companion-ship. As with housework, this isolation means that women inventors lack a peer group by which to measure their accomplishments. They also lack business and professional contacts to help their inventions come to fruition. Home-based inventors may feel the particular sense of alienation from the public sphere that has characterized homemak-ers for decades.

Yet, home-based creative work has its positive aspects as well. Possibilities exist for balancing paid work with family responsibilities that so far are few in the workplace. The late 1980s was a time of rapid growth in a number of home-based industries, although this work is often poorly paid with limited opportunities for the workers to help each other to organize. The 1980s saw a rather dramatic growth in the numbers of successful women entrepreneurs and business people, many of whom work out of their homes. Many new women entrepre-neurs find this work a viable option to the lack of opportunity women face as salaried workers. It may be that women inventors could increase in numbers in the future for some of the same reasons that have contributed to the increase in women entrepreneurs. Indeed, many of the most successful women inventors are entrepreneurs as well —they have taken their own products to market.[26] Unlike many women involved with science and technology, they are in the fortunate position of being able to work, at least to some extent, autonomously and outside of male-dominated organizational hierarchies.

Women inventors may be pioneers in another sense as well. They provide one model of women coping independently with technology, and hint at the type of transformation process suggested by Franklin,[27] Menzies,[28] and others. As one woman inventor, Deborah New, says, "I went to an engineering department in Cambridge but they couldn't work on it (my invention) for me. So I decided to go ahead and learn enough electronics to do it myself. And that's where it became a reality, on my kitchen table at home."

Table 1: Location of Inventing

	PERCENT	NUMBER
Home	81	17
Work	10	2
Home and Work	5	1
Unknown	5	1

(T = 21)

Table 2: Women's Inventions, By Category

	CIIC[1] GROUP		WIP[2] GROUP	
	PERCENT	NUMBER	PERCENT	NUMBER
Environmental	5	1		
Recreational	14	3	17	4
Teaching Aid	10	2	9	2
Medical	10	2	17	4
Domestic/Personal	33	7	30	7
Chemical	5	1	4	1
Electronic/Computer			13	3
Mechanical			9	2
Not Known	24	5		

1 Canadian Industrial Innovation Centre, Waterloo. T = 21.
2 Women Inventors Project (group attending the Project's first workshop). T = 23.

JOAN PINNER SCOTT

Disadvantagement of Women by the Ordinary Processes of Science: The Case of Informal Collaborations

In organizations like science, which apparently function on 'objective' gender-neutral principles, gender roles are pervasive, and gender patterning is produced both by discriminatory events and by the much more numerous ordinary processes. In recent years, feminist scholars have become aware, "of the gender subtext of the impersonal,"[1] and found that organizations that appear to be impersonal and gender neutral are in reality pervaded by gender. This gives rise to a new research question: How and why can we look at a gender-patterned organization and continue to believe the myth that both the organization and its work are gender-neutral?

My work, as part of the equality project in the feminist critique of science,[2] aims at both a detailed understanding of the ordinary processes of science and of how those processes operate in resisting the entry and the normal advancement of women in the sciences. The problem of women in science is much larger than one of numbers, but that is the place from which this essay begins.[3] Research which documents how resistance to the advancement of women in science occurred, could be useful to women who wish to confront it.

I saw faculty women as likely to be good informants for a qualitative study, the findings of which could be suggestive for both action and future research. These results would not be applicable to the whole population of faculty scientists, but could provide categories for future quantitative work, the results of which could be more generally applicable. My study might also be relevant to other so-called "non-traditional jobs."

I chose biosciences for this study of the ordinary practices of science, firstly because I am a member of a biology department. The deep divisions between university science departments might have threatened the frankness of the interviews if another science had been selected.

The data for the study come from in-depth taped interviews, informal conversations, and a variety of documents including cvs. At the interviews I asked informants about current work and their careers. I did not refer to gender in my questions, but almost all informants raised topics with a gendered component. Faculty interviewed were members of departments of biology, botany, zoology, plant and animal science, and microbiology, both in and outside of medical schools. The second reason that I chose bioscience was confidentiality, which is important in this population where everyone knows everyone else, and careers are at stake. In bioscience departments, in contrast to say physics, chemistry or engineering there are a reasonable number of women from which to draw a sample. If one were interviewing women from the smaller pools characteristic of the other sciences, confidentiality would be a much greater problem. I also changed the names of informants and their institutions and specialties, to protect confidentiality. It was for the same reason that only I transcribed the tapes.

This essay is one section of a larger study which focuses on the experiences of some of the 85 women and 1137 men, in tenurable faculty positions in bioscience in 27 of the larger Canadian universities.[4] Their careers span the period from 1945 to the present. The study explores the ordinary processes of science, such as the importance of mentors; getting started in a career; getting the first career position in a normal career; the ways that some women were channelled from a normal career; the organization of research work at different funding levels; the 'gatekeepers,' their opportunities and solidarity; and the topic of this essay which is collaboration in publication between scientists in two or more laboratories.[5]

The study focuses on the experiences of those women who were members of faculty. There are of course many other women working in these bioscience departments as lecturers, instructors, instructional assistants, laboratory instructors, demonstrators, technicians, research assistants and associates and many have Ph.D.s. Their experiences would say as much or more about how the situation of women in science was produced, as do the experiences of faculty women. In fact, some of their experiences are included in this study, because the careers of the faculty women informants often included periods spent in the above mentioned non-faculty positions. Future research might explore career development processes among these non-faculty women.

From the total population of 85 women, assistant, associate, and full professors, I made a randomly selected short list. I visited five cities and interviewed 20 of the women on that list. From the total of 1,137 men in those positions I selected a similar list, of whom I have interviewed 12. Those women and men make up the sample.[6]

The informants received their Ph.D.s at 27 years of age, on average, with the range extending to 36 years for women and 31 for men. Based on the frequency of their representation in the sample, it was easiest for white men to get faculty appointments. Then in order of frequency came Asian and Indian men, white women and then Asian women. Pakistan, India, Japan, Korea, China, the United Kingdom, Canada, the United States, and Germany are among the countries in which they were born.

In the sample, most of the Canadian-born women did Ph.D.s in Canada while most Canadian-born men did theirs in the U.S. Post-doctoral fellowships were held by two-thirds of the men but only one quarter of the women, and four women took teaching-only jobs after the Ph.D. Two of these women took two part-time teaching jobs simultaneously, which suggests that they were both involuntary part-time workers, doing part-time work because they had not been offered the full-time work that they sought. One quarter of sample women did research assistantships or associateships instead of post-doctoral fellowships, but only one man did and he was from Asia. One woman took a sequence of two research assistantships, both of which were "honorary" i.e., unpaid positions. There is a long history of women taking unpaid positions in science.[7]

Collaboration — An Ordinary Process of Science

Collaboration usually means that two or more scientists work together on, and claim credit for, a publication. There are two distinct types of collaboration: between investigators in one laboratory, and between investigators in two or more laboratories. Within one laboratory, collaboration usually means the production of a paper by some members of the team, often graduate students with varying amounts of assistance from the principal investigator, and its publication under the name(s) of the student(s) involved, plus, almost always that of the principal investigator. It is a routine part of the work within any laboratory and is probably the major source of the papers which make up scientists' publication records. The principal investigators are often described as "independent," which suggests that they alone do all the work and should receive all the credit for work which appears under their names. However, depending on the size of the grant, each has a team of graduate students, post-docs, technicians, etc., and much of the work, not only the manual work but even the reading and the thinking up of modifications to experiments, is done by team members. In these collaborations it is always clear who is the senior and junior author and the division of credit tends to reflect that, regardless of who did the work. The principal investigator is dependent on other people, largely women, both inside and outside of the university, who do many necessary and skilled tasks. Those people are rarely recognized as making any contribution to science, although their work is part of that claimed as the scientist's.

This essay deals only with collaboration between laboratories which is not routinized as is collaboration within the same laboratory. This less formally established and potentially more flexible type of collaboration is revealing with regard to both the ordinary processes of science, and to their different effects on women and men. The relationships between collaborators in different laboratories do not arise from existing organization, and they require a special initiative from one or other of the scientists involved. Within one laboratory the relationships are based on the formal institutional positions of professor, student, etc. In collaboration between scientists in different laboratories the relationship both originates and is negotiated informally by, the participants. In this type of collaboration, the entitlement to credit is more ambiguous than in collaboration within one laboratory. Here we look at the effects of participant's gender on such collaborations, and analyze and compare man-man, man-woman, wife-husband, and woman-woman collaborations.

The issue of which individual "owned" the project ran through descriptions of this type of collaboration. Informants said, "my grant, my project, my idea," "the project is clearly mine," and "I think I could have applied on my own, totally on my own." The significance of this concern with ownership is that it means entitlement to credit for ensuing publications which is the basis for future granting and reputation of the faculty scientist. Such claims may occur because of the ambiguity of entitlement to credit in collaboration between laboratories.

Man–Man Collaboration

Three men had experience of collaboration between two laboratories. As time went on, reputations of various kinds were being made by them and for them. Junior members worked very hard but received little credit, and were increasingly anxious about their own reputations as independent scientists (Barry, Nicholas, and Harry).

Barry was a young pre-tenure professor who had been appointed only after he had raised his first year's salary by writing a joint grant application with his future chairman, whose research interests overlapped with his own. He was three years into his job and was developing his own laboratory while continuing to collaborate with his very productive chairman. He was anxious about how much his reputation was being harmed by people assuming, wrongly, that the work of his own lab was actually coming out of the lab of his chairman. Barry suggested that people will "make decisions" or "get impressions" whether they have all the facts or not.

Nicholas was one of seven faculty who were a jointly funded group led by the man who had been his Ph.D. supervisor. He had joined the group more than a decade ago, just as it was being put together, after he finished his training. Nicholas noted that many people who had worked with his leader and had continued working on the same problems, even in competition with him, "have found it difficult to get themselves taken seriously," and he also feared that if he sought funding as an individual he might receive it only occasionally.

Harry was at about the same stage in his career although he appeared to be in an accelerating phase. Grants were increasing as was the size of his team, and he was very concerned with keeping everyone fully occupied. Harry collaborated in an especially profitable way. Through collaboration he gained services worth up to $20,000 annually, and ideas from people at a government lab, and yet he described the project as "clearly mine," thus claiming entitlement to all of the credit.

These three men were in relationships which offered support and motivation for productive work with others and yet were also sources of anxiety. Collaborations were organized mainly by differences in access to funding between the faculty involved. Other significant differences were age, rank, position in department, and research interests. Ordinarily the senior of two male collaborators progressively gained power relative to the junior one, especially where there were differences in grant size, age and rank to begin with. In all but one of these cases, there was anxiety that the senior partner would profit at the expense of the junior. The injustices feared and experienced by the junior men were never described as produced intentionally. Rather they were seen as impersonal mistakes of the system. There was also said to be a similar tendency in the publishing system which discriminates, again impersonally, against "new" people.

Collaborative relationships between laboratories were generally, as described above, between men. They involved growing differences in reputations, as the junior did a large proportion of the work and often saw it credited to the senior. The system was impersonally unjust to the junior member whose reputation as an autonomous researcher was relatively underdeveloped. The ordinary practice of collaboration between laboratories produced an informal hierarchy which was much like the formal hierarchy within any one laboratory.

What about collaborative relationships involving the few faculty women? Since only seven percent of the faculty scientists were women, when women collaborated, of necessity, they usually collaborated with men. Were the roles similar to those between men? How did collaboration of women with unrelated men compare to those with husbands, and also to those rare collaborations between women? How did science resist the advancement of women through collaboration between two laboratories?

Woman–Man Collaboration

Helen was a very successful mid-career woman who had broken her engagement to be married when she decided to go to graduate school. She identified collaboration as *the one* area of a scientific career where being a woman had made it more difficult. She illustrated the difficulty by saying that she found that she worked harder than "most people" and that two "people" with whom she had tried to collaborate "didn't come across."

Ninety-three percent of her potential collaborators were likely to be men so it can be safely assumed that by "people," she meant males, and that it was in collaborations with two male faculty members that she had been expected to do the majority of the work. In effect, they had tried to make her fulfil the role of the junior in a collaboration.

Helen had produced nearly 20 papers, in just over a decade, in collaboration with a man who was "an absolutely superb technician." He was the second author on a number of the papers. She said, "We had a very successful relationship." From the way that credit was claimed it is clear that he did not make her into the junior. Interestingly, she advised women not to have a chip on their shoulders, saying that while we may want to change the social context in which we live, we also have to live in it and must not be so antagonistic as to alienate the majority of people. Again, "people," can only mean men.

Years after Nancy's collaborations with a man, she discovered that her contribution had been improperly evaluated by a granting committee. Nancy had entered into collaborations

> because they were appropriate and I wanted to do certain things. ... Those collaborations went very well so I was actually astonished in 197– when I saw some reviews of a grant which I had put into a granting agency (earlier). A referee actually said that my publication record was very impressive, however all publications that were done with Dr. Black, for example, had to be discounted because they were clearly not my papers. So I have not been very anxious to collaborate any more because if I am going to be judged in collaborations with men as only being willing hands, then I'm really not interested.

She explained that in this collaboration, "it was I who initiated . . . I who planned the experiments." She suggested that when women carry out collaborations with men it was assumed by the grant panels evaluating papers that the women were doing something, "at the behest of the men." As in the case of Helen, Nancy was being placed permanently in the position of the junior collaborator, even though it was Nancy who had initiated the work.

The granting panels were composed almost entirely of men. This was to be expected given the proportions of women science faculty, but special arrangements could have been made, although they apparently were not, to ensure representation of women on every panel. Informants did refer to a special requirement that francophones and geographic regions of the country be at least represented, although they criticized it. Their criticism was based in the idea that attention to representation of any group necessarily put quality in jeopardy. They seemed unaware that this implied that it was impossible to achieve excellence and at the same time have a fair representation of, for example, francophones, and say Newfoundlanders and, of course, women.

Whereas Helen could and did find a satisfactory male collaborator who did not make her into the junior, it was not possible for Nancy to find an alternative granting panel, let alone one which would evaluate her as something other than "willing hands." Also, by the time Nancy knew that her work had been inappropriately evaluated it was too late to change that part of her own career. All she could do was to avoid collaboration with men in the future.

The experiences of Helen and Nancy show that it was very easy for women to be cast in the role of juniors, but with no prospects of advancement to a senior status. In fact, in collaboration with men women could easily become permanent juniors.[8]

Wife–Husband Collaboration

Sandra and her husband had had similar qualifications and research specialties; they had met in the labs at graduate school, which has long been a very common pattern. Some years later when they moved to Canada, Sandra entered the country as a family-class immigrant rather than as an independent scientist. A promise was made, at her husband's interview, that there would be a job for her. Both received job offers but while his job entitled him to apply for grants, Sandra's was without this entitlement, and at another university in the same city. The anti-nepotism rules[9] were used to justify her job being outside of her husband's department. Sandra was offered work as a demonstrator. Other demonstrators were also faculty wives, and some others, like her, had Ph.D.s. Sandra observed that it was always the wives who were given the subordinate positions and that the university was getting a very good deal out of these women.

Sandra passionately wished to do research but she could not apply for her own grants from a demonstrator's position, and so she was forced to do research for a project "owned" by another scientist. Like many other wives before her she worked on her husband's projects in the summers. By working on somebody else's project she was disadvantaging herself for making grant applications in the future, even if she could get an assistant professor's position, because as she said, "everything I had put out was really coming out of my husband's lab." Because she could not do a piece of research on her own, she lost "the confidence that I would get any money." She said that because she was not doing, "something totally on my own" she felt, "under some kind of pressure," and said "my feeling about my own ability did not improve."

The combination of her loss of confidence and the practices of grant committees who would translate her publishing record into that of a "dilletante" meant that she could not have a future with independent status where credit for her work would translate into grants for her projects. Simultaneously the work she contributed to the credit of her husband would translate into larger future grants for him. The harder she worked the greater the power difference between them could become. Having been in the junior role for a while she was seen by granters as someone intrinsically and permanently incapable of the senior or autonomous role. She was seen as unable to do the whole process of conceptualizing, managing and executing the work. She lost the self-confidence which informants repeatedly said was essential for women in science, and as she said, it put her, "under some kind of pressure."

Lynne, Sarah, and Judith were married women who, between them, had a total of 115 papers, of which only five were published with their husbands. They had all experienced set-backs in their own careers when moving for their husband's careers. Subsequently Lynne and Sarah had moved, with their husbands, explicitly to positions where the women could have careers that were on the same level as their husbands. Judith had moved away from her husband and divorced him in the process of establishing her own career.

The three women were conscious that their own projects might easily be seen as their husband's and that their credit could easily be redirected so that they, the women, could become seen as incapable of independent work in the future. To prevent this easy slide into subordinate status in the eyes of grant committees, they felt that women should not change their names upon marriage; never or only very rarely, publish in the same research area as their husbands; never or rarely, publish with their husbands and then not permit the woman's name to be systematically placed in the second author position.

Clearly married women were disproportionately subject to loss of status as scientists especially upon moving for their husband's careers and in the collaboration process. Sandra's career became subordinate through the immigration process, and that subordination was then amplified by the university that first employed her. Although she finally obtained a position from which she could apply for her own grant, a combination of how her publication record was viewed by granting panels and her loss of confidence prevented her from achieving autonomous status.

From the list of precautions above we are given a sense of the slippery slope which often led to permanent junior status for these married women while their husbands' reputations were enhanced.

Woman–Woman Collaboration

Knowledge of the problems experienced by women with male collaborators, whether or not the women were married to them, might lead women to deliberately seek collaboration with other women. However it was likely that potential collaborators would be geographically very distant which made working together difficult. Nancy deliberately set up a collaboration with a woman in Europe, but it "ground to a halt," within a few years of the sabbatical in which it started because "doing experiments across the ocean is very difficult."

However there were two examples of successful collaboration between two women. At an early stage of her post Ph.D. career Anne had the title of "Visiting Professor." This usually means that she would be working on her own project but she described herself as in fact working on the project of a senior professor. She was an unofficial advisor to the graduate students of her professor, Dr. Edwards. When a question arose in the work done by Anne and Dr. Edwards, they thought that a Dr. Carol Flower would be able to help them. Dr. Edwards asked Dr. Flower's Head of Department about it. The two men set up a meeting between Dr. Flower, who was really the expert, and Dr. Edwards. He was too busy and sent Anne. The two women discovered that they both had the same ideas about how to explore the question from their different perspectives. They went ahead and collaborated in the research. Within the hierarchy, these two subordinates, whose positions required them to give their time to other people's projects, met and began research on a project of their own. This led to 14 collaborative papers over seven years. Anne described it as a "close" collaboration and as "a true collaboration, in fact we just alternated the names on papers. The person who was the first author was not necessarily the person who did most of the work, although it tended to be pretty equal."

At the beginning of this collaboration the project was available for the two senior men, but by the ordinary processes of delegation, and the exceptional situation that two women were both scientifically and geographically close enough, the project became theirs. Apparently the two Ph.D. women did not have senior and junior roles. While Anne admits that the amounts of work they did was not always reflected in their alternated order of names on the paper, it was "pretty equal."

Barbara had a long and important collaboration with a female technician during an extremely busy period when her several children were young and she had heavy administrative responsibilities in the department. In recognition, she credited the technician, by making her co-author of a number of the papers.

Collaborations between two women were necessarily rare and made difficult by distance, but they could offer a great deal and also be free of the hierarchies typical of science.

Conclusion

This inquiry into some examples of collaboration between scientists of two or more laboratories provides a new understanding of a small part of the ordinary processes of science. Between men informants, collaboration between two laboratories, involved a status difference which generally grew larger during the life of the relationship. The junior man was at risk of receiving inadequate credit and doing the majority of the work, while the senior man's reputation was likely to grow more than his contribution warranted. Junior men could try to establish themselves as autonomous scientists and thus escape from junior status although it might be risky and difficult. Collaboration between laboratories reproduced the same hierarchical patterns seen more formally within each laboratory's team.

The study also shows how those processes were operated in resisting the normal advancement of women. Collaborative relationships involving women were of necessity usually between women and men and they were built on the same basic hierarchical pattern as those between men, except that women were more frequently cast, often permanently, into the junior's role. This was true of women collaborating with men who were not their husbands, and even harder to avoid and less remediable for women who collaborated with their husbands. This was not due to simple chauvinism of the husbands but was an outcome of the institutional responses to women, especially to those who had not escaped being categorized by the institutions as wives. It happened in a way that seemed to follow objective and gender-neutral principles. Like the women, young men were also ill treated as juniors, but while most men escaped from it, a significant fraction of women spent many years, and sometimes their whole careers in that status.

A long productive collaboration between one woman informant and her male technician was an exception to this usual process of making the woman in a woman-man collaboration into a permanent junior.

The hierarchical pattern of senior and junior found in formal laboratory teams and, informally, in the ordinary inter-male collaboration does not seem to have been expressed in collaborative relationships between women informants. Obviously it was unlikely that there would be many appropriate women in the system and where there were and they found each other, women collaborators had problems including those of distance. However two women informants had productive relationships with other women which lasted several years. One of these was an equal relationship with a colleague and the other was that of a faculty member with a woman technician.

Over time, the differential progress of men and women through this one part of the ordinary processes of science contributed to reproducing the historic pattern of the advancement of women in science. No women reached the top of the hierarchy, and the senior men made different kinds of job offers to women and men. Thus men in high positions shaped the funding process, did not take the junior scientists involved in collaboration seriously, created and implemented "anti-nepotism" regulations, etc.

While my previous quantitative work on science subject choice and achievement in females in high school provided occasions for expression by some men of resistance to the entry of women into science, perhaps this work can be useful to women as a tool for change and as a source of stimulation for other researchers.

MARGARET-ANN ARMOUR

Canadian Women and Careers in Chemistry

"Our most precious commodity is people."[1] Such a sentiment is common to the several reports which have appeared recently on the health of research in chemistry in both Canada and the United States.[2] Yet, the profession of chemistry has not been successful in attracting women in any numbers into its ranks. And this in spite of the fact that the proportion of Canadian university degrees in chemistry granted to women has risen markedly in the last 20 years. In 1970, 15.6 percent of bachelor's and first professional degrees were awarded to women; by 1985 that number had risen to 35.8 percent. Many more women than before are continuing to post-graduate studies in chemistry. In 1970, 12.7 percent of master's degrees were awarded to women in 1985, 31.3 percent. However, the most dramatic increase has been at the Ph.D. level. Only 2.4 percent of doctoral degrees went to women in 1970; in 1985 that figure was 21.7 percent. An interesting statistic for comparison is the proportion of women *enrolled* in bachelor's, master's and Ph.D. programs in chemistry. For 1985–86, these figures are 34.4 percent, 33.2 percent and 20.2 percent respectively. Therefore, when compared with the degrees actually *awarded* to women in 1985, it becomes clear that women are being slightly more successful than men in obtaining bachelor's and Ph.D. degrees, and only slightly less successful than men at the master's level.[3] It is also worth noting how similar these figures are to those for the United States. According to the American Chemical Society's Committee on Professional Training, in 1985, women earned

329

35.3 percent of the bachelor's degrees, 32.3 percent of the master's degrees, and 19.9 percent of the doctorates in chemistry.[4]

How do the Canadian women obtaining chemistry degrees fare in the workplace? Few figures are available on the numbers and seniority of women chemists who have careers in government and industry; perhaps this is a reflection of how few there are. Data on the percentage of teaching female staff at Canadian universities are available from Statistics Canada. These show that women make up just under five percent of the chemistry faculty, a figure which has not changed over the past 10 years.[5] In fact, as early as 1965–66, 4.7 percent of the full-time university teachers in the mathematical and physical sciences were women.[6] Further, only about 10 percent of the membership of the Chemical Institute of Canada, the society which represents chemists, chemical engineers, and chemical technologists, is female. An indication of the level of positions held by women chemists can be gained from the annual salary surveys of members of the Institute.[7] Table 1 lists, for the years 1983–87, the ratio of the average salary of the survey's female respondents to the average salary of all respondents. From this table, it can be seen that, in each year, the women respondents earned less than 70 percent of the average salary of all respondents. This is strong evidence that very few women are found in the upper ranks of their employment sector. It can be argued that this is at least partly owing to the fact that women have only relatively recently been obtaining Ph.D. degrees in chemistry in significant numbers, and therefore have not had the qualifications to allow them to reach the most senior levels. If, as might be expected from the undergraduate and graduate student data already presented, many of the factors affecting the careers of women chemists in Canada are not dissimilar to those discovered in the United States, the figures also conceal other influences.

Comprehensive surveys of all its female members have been conducted by the American Chemical Society in 1975, 1980 and 1985.[8] The data suggest that an increasing fraction of Ph.D. degrees in chemistry will be earned by women, so that the percentage of professional women chemists will increase. The major employers of women chemists have been educational institutions. However, the 1985 survey found that women employed by Ph.D. granting institutions are promoted at a slower rate than men, and even when sorted by level of experience, it still takes women longer to achieve tenure. When salaries are matched by degree, rank, experience, and type of institution, women are still 10 percent below men. This factor is most likely also influencing the salary levels of academic women chemists in Canada.

One trend which is identified from the 1985 survey is of considerable interest to Canadian women chemists. This is a movement of doctoral women chemists out of academe and into industry, where starting and continuing salaries for women are now almost competitive with those of men. For example, in 1975, 22 percent of women with Ph.D. degrees in chemistry worked in industry, while by 1985, this figure had risen to 36 percent. In contrast, in 1975, 54.4 percent of women Ph.D.s were employed in academe, compared to 39 percent in 1985. In 1985, 33 percent of men holding doctoral degrees in chemistry were in academe, a figure which had changed little over the previous 10 years, while 55 percent were employed in industry. In Canada, the ratio of opportunities for chemical careers in government and industry compared to those in academe is much smaller than in the United States. Neither government nor industry has been notably supportive of innovative research. For example, in 1987, the Ontario government, with 40 to 50 thousand employees, listed 200 jobs in the scientific category. Intensified interest in research in biotechnology and high technology should lead to an expansion of basic research in industry. However, at the present time it seems unlikely that the trend for women chemists to choose jobs in industry over those in educational institutions, which is observed in the United States, will appear in Canada. (This trend leads to the expectation that the distribution of men and women among the different employment sectors of academe, government/non-profit, and industry, could be similar by the year 2000.) Also likely to affect this distribution in Canada is the fact that, over the past 10 years or so, there has been little expansion or movement of chemistry faculty. Thus, there have been few academic positions available. This has led to an increasing average age of the professoriat, and an expected retirement of 25–40 percent of the faculty before the turn of the century. Universities are becoming more sensitive to the need to try to increase the proportion of women in faculties in which they are markedly under-represented. As a result, many Canadian universities are actively recruiting women to their teaching staffs, especially in the sciences.

With the employment picture looking more promising than it has for several years, why is it that women still represent only one-fifth of those completing Ph.D. degrees in chemistry?

A study at the University of Alberta showed that, over a 10 year period from 1971 to 1982, female students performed as well as, or better than, their male peers in undergraduate science and math courses, including chemistry.[9] Thus, the young women are as capable academically of moving into graduate studies as the young men.

Many factors have been identified as influencing young women's career choices; these are described elsewhere.[10] We will discuss here only those which affect the choice of career at the post-secondary level, and the achievement of success in that career.

The small proportion of professional female chemists means that there are few role models for young women. Further, according to Dr. Anne Alper, executive director of the Chemical Institute of Canada (CIC), the women who are in the chemical profession are not very visible.[11] Taking the CIC as an example, although about 10 percent of the members are women, they are not represented in proportion as presenters of papers, invited speakers, award winners, or holders of high-profile positions. Since the absence of high-profile role models is one reason why young women do not choose careers in chemistry, women presently in the profession must network effectively with their colleagues, both male and female, to bring their names to the forefront.

Many studies have shown that young women are socialized to underestimate their abilities, and that they often do not apply for positions for which they judge themselves to be insufficiently qualified.[12] Not only must women review their self-imposed inhibitions, but society's perception of women has to change. Fundamental social changes are required, such as the acceptance of child-care as a parental, not just a maternal, responsibility. As an indication of its awareness of the need for such changes, in 1987 the CIC board passed a motion allowing a member of either sex, who is staying at home to raise a family, to pay fees at the graduate student rate for up to seven years. At the present time, this rule is likely to affect more women than men.

Professional societies have an important role to play in increasing awareness of inequities, and raising the profile of women in the profession they represent. One of the oldest examples of such an initiative is that of the American Chemical Society, which in 1927 established a Women Chemists Committee. The objectives of the committee have been five-fold: to serve as a forum for the problems of women in chemistry, and to develop concrete recommendations regarding these problems and their solutions; to provide a means of increasing and improving the participation of women chemists in the society at both national and local levels; to stimulate the active interest of women chemists in the society; to try to increase the membership of women chemists in the society; and to promote the attendance of women chemists at local, regional, and national meetings. There are many local sections of the committee, which are the centres of action, and a national newsletter is published.

Many initiatives are now being taken in Canada to encourage young women to pursue careers in science, to provide a supportive network for women currently in scientific careers, and to raise society's awareness of the advantages of having more women involved in policy-making decisions in the sciences.[13] An example of an initiative from a university is York University's Women Investigating Science Horizons (WISH) program. Eighteen young women in grades nine and 10 spend a month during the summer in laboratories and self-development workshops. The program is described as an "apprenticeship" aimed at encouraging female students to consider careers in the sciences. At the University of Alberta, WISEST (Women in Scholarship, Engineering, Science and Technology), a committee of the vice-president, research, organizes a summer research program for grade 11 high school students. Each summer since 1984, about 25 students have spent six weeks working in research groups, the girls in the faculties of science and engineering, and the boys in the faculties of home economics and nursing. Not only does this broaden the career choices of both girls and boys, but it has also made faculty aware of the enthusiasm and ability of young women to do research in the sciences and engineering.

There are societies across the country, all with similar mandates: to encourage women to enter the sciences, provide a supportive network of women in the sciences, and try to solve some of the problems common to women in science. Names and addresses of these societies are listed in Table 2. All of the groups hold meetings at regular intervals, and all produce a newsletter for members. Many are active within the schools in their area, and have members willing to speak to interested community groups.

It has to be admitted that so far the many initiatives to bring women to the forefront in science, engineering, and technology have succeeded only in increasing the proportion of women completing a university education in these fields, and obtaining a beginning job in industry or becoming assistant professors. As is obvious from the figures for academic staff and salary levels over the past five years, little progress has been made in increasing the participation of women at senior levels. Time away from the laboratory to raise a young family affects both the obtaining of tenure and movement through the ranks.[14] Women still suffer from systemic discrimination,[15] although serious efforts are being made by educational institutions to provide equal opportunities for women and men.[16] Further, the awareness of chemists in the workforce of how few of their colleagues are female is being increased, and the issue is being debated and discussed openly. This growing consciousness may slowly give rise to the fundamental social changes which will result in women becoming full partners in the field of chemistry.

Why is it so important to have a larger proportion of women in the sciences in general, and in chemistry in particular? Women's career choices have to be widened to include jobs which require scientific and technological training; Canadian society needs to use all of its brain-power, it's our most valuable natural resource; and finally, science needs women. The different approach women could bring to science was described by Ronald Leger, director of the Canadian International Development Agency, in his address to the Third World Academy of Sciences Conference on the "Role of Women in the Development of Science and Technology in the Third World," in Trieste, Italy, in October 1988. He stated, "I believe the majority of women do see and feel reality in a way different from most men; of course, there are exceptions. But because of gender and because of historical and social conditions, I believe women tend to view the world in a more holistic way, and more spontaneously see and feel interdependence. They also have the capacity to create bridges more easily than empires, hierarchies and walls."[17] The infusion of women with this breadth of concern into decision-making roles can only benefit the chemical profession.

Table 1
Salary Ratios Of Female Chemical Institute of Canada Members

YEAR OF SURVEY	TOTAL NUMBER OF RESPONDENTS	% OF RESPONDENTS WHO WERE FEMALE	AVERAGE FEMALE SALARY AVERAGE SALARY OF ALL RESPONDENTS
1983 (6)	2317	6.7	0.655
1984 (7)	1997	6.3	0.699
1985 (8)	875	8.9	0.688
1986 (9)	2194	7.8	0.695
1987 (10)	2032	9.0	0.695

Table 2
Names And Addresses Of Canadian Societies
for Women In Science And Engineering

Society for Canadian Women in Science and Technology (SCWIST)
P.O Box 2184
Vancouver, B.C.
V6B 3V7

Association of Women in Engineering and Science (AWES)
P.O. Box 6912
Postal Station D
Calgary, Alberta
T2P 2GI

Women in Scholarship, Engineering, Science and Technology (WISEST)
c/o Dr. M.A. Armour
Department of Chemistry
University of Alberta
Edmonton, Alberta
T6G 2G2

335

Canadian Association for Women in Science (CAWIS)
P.O. Box 6054
Postal Station A
Toronto, Ontario
M5W IP5

Women in Science and Engineering — National (WISE)
P.O. Box 6067
Postal Station A
Toronto, Ontario
M5W IP5

ANNE INNIS DAGG

Women In Science — Are Conditions Improving?

A survey I carried out in 1981 of women Ph.D. scientists in Canada[1] showed that:

1) many such scientists could not find work in science even though a variety of Canadian academics were urging that more graduate students in science be trained;

2) in the natural sciences, between one and eight percent of university professors of all ranks were women; women were rare or non-existent in the higher ranks; some universities had no women science professors of any rank; and the percentage of trained women available was always much greater than the percentage of women hired as university teachers;

3) many women scientists had retrained or planned to retrain so that they could obtain work;

4) most of the women questioned had worked steadily at some job, usually full-time, since obtaining their Ph.D.s; and

5) many had experienced sexual discrimination while studying at university and/or at work.

Of the 162 University of Toronto women science Ph.D. alumnae who graduated between 1950 and 1981, 66 responded to the questionnaire I circulated.

In this paper, I shall consider the status of Canadian women Ph.D.

scientists who have graduated since 1981, when my earlier work was carried out. I shall look at the percentage of women enrolling in and obtaining Ph.D.s in science programs at Canadian universities; the number of women science professors currently at Canadian universities; and the information obtained by questionnaire from recent Ph.D. graduates in scientific subjects from the University of Toronto.

Ph.D. Science Programs

Despite the effort universities are thought to be making to attract women to graduate work in science, the percentage of women enrolled has increased little over a recent five-year period (Table 1). In no discipline has it increased by over two percentage points between the years 1982–83 and 1986–87, and in physics it has not increased at all.

For Ph.D. degrees granted over the five years 1982 to 1986, the percentage of women graduates has not increased markedly, and in several disciplines (biology and chemistry) has even declined recently (Table 2).

An average Ph.D. student enrolled in any one year (Table 1) probably expected to graduate, on average, about two years later (Table 2). Comparing such groups in Tables 1 and 2, it is evident that women in physics have done well compared to men, but that more women proportionately in biology, chemistry, and geology have been enrolled than have graduated several years later. The discrepancy between the percentage of women enrolled in graduate programs and the percentage of women awarded a Ph.D. is even greater in some social sciences, such as psychology and sociology.[2]

The percentage of students obtaining first degrees in science who are women is often considerably larger than the percentage obtaining Ph.D.s (Table 3, cols. 3 and 4). This is true in biology and chemistry, the sciences most favoured by women. In physics and geology, the ratio of men to women is almost the same in bachelor's degrees and in doctorates. Women are uncommon in both these disciplines; perhaps those who are dedicated enough to enter them at all, are dedicated enough to carry their studies all the way through graduate school. As well, compared to biology and chemistry, there are few low-level jobs as technicians and research assistants to attract bachelor's and master's students.

There are various reasons why women don't study science at university, either at the undergraduate or at the graduate level. Most importantly, society perceives science as a masculine subject, so that women are subtly steered away from it by their teachers, friends, and families; as well, few scientists are seen to be women, so women students feel that they may never find good jobs in science to reward their years of hard work at graduate school.

Women students are probably also discouraged by the sexism that exists in universities, especially in graduate schools. At Simon Fraser University, a survey of university women revealed that 61 percent of graduate students had been sexually harassed, usually by faculty members.[3] Students may find it difficult to work in a predominantly male atmosphere, are sometimes excluded from study groups, sometimes receive less money for their work, seldom have women professors as role models or mentors, and may not be encouraged, as male students are, to excel.[4]

Women Science Professors

My 1981 survey of women science professors at Canadian universities showed how few women were employed at any professorial rank (Table 3, col. 1). Of these few, more were at lower than at higher ranks. No discipline had more than five percent full professors who were women, and some had no women full professors at all.

A mail survey of science deans carried out in January 1989, concerning women faculty currently in Ontario universities indicated that most universities have hired women professors in science since 1981, but that they are still rare (Table 3, col. 2). One university, Laurentian, had none in 1981 and had none in 1989. For the 12 Ontario universities which responded to the survey,[5] the percentage of women faculty members increased in nearly every discipline (Table 3, cols. 1 and 2). Despite these gains, the current percentages of women are still abysmally low. For biology, in which about half of undergraduates and a quarter of graduate students are women, the percentage of women faculty members is only 13 percent. For the other science disciplines, the percentage of women undergraduates is at least six times greater than the percentage of women faculty. Universities often argue that they have hired few women faculty members because few were available. Yet Table 3 (cols.

2 and 3) shows that the percentage pool of trained women scientists is in every discipline nearly twice as great, and usually much greater, than the percentage of women professors.

This low number of women science professors means that women students will often not aspire to be university teachers, because the chance of succeeding is obviously so slim. It also means that few of the many trained women in science find jobs in universities, and that science will continue to be taught from a male perspective, with exciting new feminist theories and research possibilities ignored.

The survey of Ontario science deans showed that presently few women scientists (3%) are full professors, with little change in the past seven years. This is unfortunate, because it is the full professors who have the most power in departments when it comes to such things as who will be hired, who will be given tenure and promoted, who will participate in the important university committees, and who will decide what direction the department and university should take.

Information from Questionnaires

In December 1988, I sent out the questionnaire in Appendix A to the University of Toronto Ph.D. women graduates (1982 to 1988) in scientific disciplines. These were in graduate studies division III (physical sciences) and division IV (life sciences). A total of 183 women received the questionnaire (52 others were returned because of incorrect addresses). They were mailed from the University of Toronto to ensure anonymity, and 80 women returned them to me giving a return rate of 44 percent. The number of women scientists has increased markedly in recent years; at the University of Toronto, 162 women earned Ph.D.s between 1950 and 1981, while 235 did so between 1982 and 1988.

Available Work in Science

Virtually all the women who returned the questionnaires were working in science, usually full-time (Table 4). Many had had little difficulty finding a post-doctoral position, but a few women felt they would have a much harder time finding permanent work. A few women worked part-time, but this was usually their choice. Several women were not working for pay, either because they were studying for a further degree or (one) because she was a homemaker.

This was a marked improvement over the 1981 survey, which had revealed that many women had been unable to work in science because no one would hire them, and one-quarter had retrained or were willing to do so in order to find satisfying work.

Most of the recent graduates were working at universities either as teachers or in research (Table 4). Many were also working for government or in hospitals, and some for industry. A few ("other") had returned to studying or were self-employed.

Sexual Discrimination

The questionnaire asked if the respondent had experienced sexual discrimination as a graduate student (15% replied yes) or while at work (25% replied yes). These values are somewhat lower than those found in the 1981 survey, but some of the women in the earlier group had a lifetime of experience to report on, unlike the recent graduates. In addition, nine of the women in the 1988 survey said they had not experienced sexual discrimination, then went on to detail discriminatory incidents that had affected them, but which they perceived as unimportant and not worth counting.

In this survey, 18 women complained of sexism at the University of Toronto. Five said they had suffered harassment, one so severely that she had to transfer to another unit to be able to continue her studies. Her harasser thought women were lesser beings than men and was constantly trying to get rid of her. Another harassed woman said she had trouble graduating after she rejected her professor's advances; she felt her work had to be twice as good as that of her male peers. A third woman was harassed for two years by her thesis supervisor after he made a "very messy pass" at her.

Other women complained of different sexist behaviour. Some men made it clear by their sexist comments that they did not think women belonged in science. One woman believed the older faculty men questioned her sincerity, implying that science was a hobby for her rather than a career. One had her rear squeezed at a Ph.D. committee meeting; she had also been present at a conference where some male faculty members made a big deal about "oral exams" given to female

341

graduate students. Two graduate students were denied funds because they had husbands to look after them financially, while one new faculty member felt she was underpaid because she was a woman.

Some complaints about sexist treatment were more nebulous. Several women felt ignored or negatively patronized, including one who believed Jewish women were especially disregarded. One felt that her male supervisor and mostly-male Ph.D. committee expected undue deference from her because of her gender. Another watched interesting projects and new research go to male postdocs rather than to her; she felt that she was regarded as a den mother or diplomat. Her ideas were spontaneously dismissed at first, unless they coincided with those of the male postdocs. Only one woman said she was actively encouraged in her studies.

Sexist treatment also occurred when some of these scientists began working as researchers and professors at other universities. One woman was passed over for a number of tenure-stream positions, even though departments sometimes said they were actively looking for women faculty, and at least one department had no woman among its faculty of 20 or 30. One scientist saw little hope of promotion and several noted a double standard for women and men — one was called a "beautiful marker" by a professor. A third felt patronized because her ideas were often disregarded. The most angry woman worked at an American university, where her older male superior admitted discriminating against women employees in hiring and promotion. He talked about "the lack of aggression in females" which meant they lacked affinity for the Harvard system. He said "Let's face it . . . if you give female rats testosterone, they become more aggressive." This woman made a very good impression in an oral presentation to a group of Japanese investors, but her superior dismissed her efforts, saying "there are not many blondes in Japan." This woman knew of five male postdocs, but no female postdocs, in her lab who had been promoted to assistant professor; one woman had been promoted, but only to instructor. Only a few women university teachers complained of being underpaid, although statistics show that virtually all women earn less than men with comparable jobs and abilities.[6]

Scientists who work for government also suffered from discrimination. One woman earned far less than a man with comparable qualifications and responsibilities; another had difficulty being hired; others felt they were treated less seriously and expected to behave in different ways than men. One woman in the Ontario government worked with peers who felt they had a right to review her work. Her boss felt uncomfortable with the two women he supervised, treating them in a more petty manner than he did the men. Another woman objected to the men's club atmosphere that pervaded her workplace. Business discussions took place in the men's room, and out-of-town trips involved business socializing at "strip-joints." One woman was so enraged by her treatment in a federal government service that she considered going public with her grievances. She did not do so because she knew of another woman Ph.D. who had done this and had never been allowed to work in her field again.

Two scientists who were hired by hospitals had specific complaints. One was not given short-term funding because, as an older woman, she was not expected to obtain agency funding. The other, working in Toronto, had a superior who said openly that he did not believe women with children should be in research, because they did not have the time to devote to it. This man was powerful enough to negatively affect the careers of many women.

Eleven women mentioned sexism at their unspecified workplaces. One worked with an openly sexist man, who made rude comments and derided her scientific ability because she was a woman. One had trouble with a few men working under her because they would not carry out her instructions adequately. A third had a boss who was uncomfortable relating to women, while a fourth had to delay starting work because she was pregnant. Other random comments mentioned being underpaid, having to be deferential to men, struggling to get co-operation from co-workers, being patronized, putting up with sexist remarks, and feeling left out by "the boys" at work.

Life Style

A total of 70 percent of the questionnaire respondents were married or living with a partner. Most of them (60%) had no children, while 12 percent had one child, 13 percent had two children, five percent had three children, and one woman had four children. Only two respondents mentioned working part-time or not for money so they could care for their families.

Half of the respondents (49%) said they would be willing to move if they were offered a job that they wanted elsewhere, one-third (34%) said they would not, and the rest were unable to commit themselves one way or the other. Almost all the women who were unmarried and without children expressed willingness to move away from their present home if their work necessitated this.

The starting pay earned by these women ranged upward from $19,200, which was what one woman, hired in 1988, was earning in a post-doctoral position in chemistry (Table 5). The highest starting salary was $54,000 for a woman in engineering. Engineering and pharmacology offered the highest average starting salaries, and chemistry and physics the lowest. Many of the wages earned were below starting salaries of students with bachelor's degrees.

Conclusions

Based on information gathered about Ph.D. studies, we see:

1) Few more women compared to men were earning Ph.D.s in science in 1986 than had been five years earlier. However, the number of women obtaining Ph.D.s in this period was far greater than that in the preceding 30 years.
2) Many undergraduate women study biology and chemistry in university, while fewer study physics and geology. However, women in physics and geology are more likely to go on to do Ph.D.s.
3) There are proportionately more women professors at Canadian universities than there used to be, but their numbers are still low. The percentage pool of trained women scientists is much larger than the percentage of women science professors. Almost no women scientists are full professors.

Responses to questionnaires sent to women who have recently received their doctorates in science indicated that:

1) Virtually all respondents have found jobs in science, although these are often very low-paying post-doctoral positions.
2) Almost all the respondents are working full-time in science, usually at universities, but also for government and industry.
3) Nearly one-sixth of the questionnaire respondents said they had experienced sexual discrimination when they were graduate students,

while one-quarter reported such discrimination at work.

4) Most of the women who replied lived with a partner, and 40 percent had one or more children.

5) Half of the women respondents were willing to move if their work were to demand it.

6) Starting salaries for the respondents were often very low ($20,000), but ranged up to $54,000. Engineering and pharmacology commanded the highest average wage, and physics and chemistry, the lowest.

Table 1
Percentage of Women (Full-and Part-time) Enrolled in Doctoral Science Programs at Canadian Universities from 1982–3 to 1986–7

	1982-83	1983-84	1984-85	1985-86	1986-87
Biology, Botany and Zoology	27%	26%	29%	30%	29%
Chemistry and Biochemistry	22%	22%	22%	22%	23%
Physics	7%	6%	7%	7%	7%
Geology	15%	16%	18%	18%	17%

Source: Statistics Canada, Universities: Enrolment and Degrees. Annual Catalogue 81–204, Table 10.

Table 2
Percentage of Women Among Doctoral Candidates Awarded Ph.D.s in Science at Canadian Universities from 1982 to 1986

	1982	1983	1984	1985	1986
Biology, Botany and Zoology	27%	25%	23%	26%	23%
Chemistry and Biochemistry	16%	16%	18%	22%	19%
Physics	12%	7%	8%	8%	10%
Geology	9%	11%	7%	15%	19%

Source: Statistics Canada, Universities: Enrolment and Degrees. Annual Catalogue 81–204, Table 22 or 21.

Table 3
Percentage of Recent Professors, Ph.D. Graduates, and Bachelor's Graduates in Science Who are Women

	PERCENTAGE FACULTY WHO ARE WOMEN IN CANADIAN UNIVERSITIES 1981 (DAGG, 1985)	PERCENTAGE FACULTY WHO ARE WOMEN IN 12 ONTARIO UNIVERSITIES 1989 (PERSONAL SURVEY)	PERCENTAGE OF PH.D.S GRANTED TO WOMEN 1986 (STATS CAN, 1988)	PERCENTAGE OF BACHELOR'S DEGREES AWARDED TO WOMEN 1986 (STATS CAN, 1988)
Biology, Botany and Zoology	7%	13% (N = 41.5)	23%	52%
Chemistry and Biochemistry	2%	6% (N = 14)	19%	41%
Physics	1%	1% (N = 3.5)	10%	13%
Geology	1%	3% (N = 5)	19%	20%

Table 4
Results of Questionnaire Survey of Women Ph.D. Scientists, 1982–1988

	NUMBER OF RESPONDENTS	JOB HARD TO GET? NO	WORKING FOR PAY FULL-TIME	PART-TIME	NO	EMPLOYER UNIVERSITY	GOV'T OR HOSPITAL	INDUSTRY	OTHER
Medical Science	20	94%	70%	15%	15%	89%	6%	6%	—
Biology	16	77%	94%	—	6%	50%	25%	—	25%
Psychology	10	71%	80%	10%	10%	56%	44%	—	—
Chemistry/ Biochemistry	8	100%	88%	—	12%	50%	—	38%	12%
Engineering	7	71%	86%	14%	—	57%	29%	14%	0
Pharmacology	6	100%	100%	—	—	50%	33%	17%	—
Physics/ Astronomy	4	100%	100%	—	—	25%	50%	—	25%
Geology	3	33%	67%	23%	—	67%	—	—	33%
Other*	6	67%	83%	17%	—	67%	—	—	33%
	80								

"Other" included two women from computer science, and one each from dentistry, mathematics, sociology, and criminology.

Table 5
Starting Salaries in 1988 Dollars* of
Women Ph.D. Scientists —x $1,000

	AVERAGE STARTING SALARY	LOWEST REPORTED SALARY	HIGHEST REPORTED SALARY	NUMBER OF SALARIES AVERAGED
Medical Science	$33	$20	$49	15
Biology	$31	$20	$44	7
Psychology	$32	$24	$44	7
Chemistry/Biochemistry	$28	$19.2	$35	7
Engineering	$41	$29	$54	5
Pharmacology	$38	$24	$47	5
Physics	$30	$24	$36	4
Geology	$31	$26	$35	2
Other	$32	$21	$50	4

*Inflation per year was calculated at 4%.

Appendix A
Questionnaire Sent to University of Toronto
Women Ph.D. Scientists

Questionnaire for Women Scientists

1. What year did you receive your Ph.D.? . . . .

2. In what science was it? (geology, chemistry, etc.) . . . .

3. After you received your Ph.D. was it difficult to find a job?
Comment:

4. Since obtaining your Ph.D., have you worked as a scientist
full-time? . . . . part-time? . . . . not at all? . . . .

5. Are you employed by a university? . . . . industry? . . . .
government? . . . . other? . . . .

6. If you have not been working full-time, was this by your choice?
Yes . . . . . No . . . .

7. Did you experience sexual discrimination as a graduate student at university?
Yes . . . . . No . . . . . If yes, please give details:

8. Did/do you experience sexual discrimination while working?
Yes . . . . . No . . . . . If yes, please give details:

9. Are you married or living with a partner? Yes . . . . . No . . . . .

10. How many (if any) children do you have? . . . .

11. Would you be free to move away if offered a job elsewhere?
Yes . . . . . No . . . . .

Optional: What was your year of starting work . . . . . and the full-time salary
you received (to the nearest $1,000) at that time? . . . .

Thank you for your help. Please return in the enclosed envelope. Please add any
comments on the back of this page.

Return to:
Dr. Anne Innis Dagg
Independent Studies
University of Waterloo

KAREN MESSING

Feminist Studies into
Genetic Hazards
in the Workplace

Since 1978, our research group, initially involved in parasexual genetics of imperfect fungi, has been doing research on genetic effects of workplace conditions, usually at the request of unions. This re-orientation has involved changes in our conception of how research is done, evolution of our thoughts on objective and subjective data, and a general increase in our level of aggressiveness toward the official institutions of science.

This article was written to describe some of our experiences, since we are not aware of publications in this area by other scientists with similar experiences. Being trained in genetics rather than sociology of science, I have not made a study of how researchers in occupational health and safety deal with the warring interests in the field. In any case, documentation of such experiences is rendered difficult by the fact that the actors involved may be unwilling to be quoted, as well as by traditional difficulties in finding out what happens behind the closed doors of peer review committees, union meetings, and boards of directors. I cannot judge how far our experiences are typical, although they are certainly not isolated.

From 1975 to 1983, our laboratory was involved in studying the genetics of *Metarhizium anisopliae*, a mosquito pathogen. We were funded at a modest but increasing level by the usual federal and provincial sources, and published at a steady, respectable rate. In 1976,

349

the Université du Québec signed an agreement with the two major Quebec trade unions, the Confédération des syndicats nationaux (CSN), and the Fédération des travailleurs du Québec (FTQ), which provided that the university would respond to requests for educational and research services from the unions, and that such services would be regarded as belonging to the professors' job definition.[1]

Shortly thereafter, we received a request to determine the genetic risk in a refinery in which workers were exposed to a radioactive dust. To our surprise, the workers' questions did not have simple answers, and we were forced to learn, experiment with, and eventually apply state-of-the-art techniques. The activities initiated by this request became increasingly time-consuming, and have now taken over the laboratory. Due to the university-union agreement, we have been able to obtain university grants and released-time to enable us to work on these projects.

Our group, consisting of one university professor and two under-graduate volunteers, met first with the union executive. They described to us the manufacturing procedures, which were very unclear to us, both because of our technical inadequacies, and because no one had ever explained to the workers where their jobs fit into the refining process. We were able to gather that there were particular sites which were very dusty, and that the dust was radioactive. It was not until two years later, when the union was finally able to negotiate our visit to the plant, that we could confirm that dust levels were extremely high, and this despite the fact that (coincidentally?) the preceding Saturday the factory had been swept for the first time in its 27 years of existence.

We also learned that there was a government report on contamination in a sister plant, and that the report listed various chemicals. The union had been promised a copy several months before; it was to receive it three years later, after the completion of our study. We were told that radioactivity levels had been measured with a Geiger counter, and found to be less than the legal limit. We could not understand why a Geiger counter measurement of environmental gamma radiation was relevant to the determination of risk to workers who breathed and ate dust, thus incorporating alpha emitters permanently into their bones.

Therefore, our situation with regard to exposure data was as follows: we knew that there was some radioactive contamination in the dust, but in the absence of personal and appropriate environmental dosimetry, we could not determine the level of contamination; we knew that there were contaminants other than radioactivity, but not which or how much. We had no access to the workplace, and no familiarity with industrial hygiene techniques, nor any money with which to hire experienced personnel. Since our contact was exclusively with the union, which had no lever on the employer, it was impossible for us to get the kind of information the employer had. On the other hand, we were the only resource available to the union confronted by this problem.

The workers asked us to explain the consequences of exposure to radioactivity, and we spoke of cancer and of reproductive effects. The workers could not tell us about the possible incidence of cancer; they knew that various workers had left the plant due to illness, but not what the illness was. However, of the four members of the executive who had had children, all had had at least one child with a congenital problem of some kind, from congenital heart defect to club foot. The wife of a fifth was pregnant with twins (she subsequently gave birth to a child with a tracheo-aesophageal fistula).

This moment of the first encounter with the executive was very upsetting, as can be imagined. We were shocked, because to us genetic research had been something abstract, and they were shocked because, as one later told us, "I have worked all my life in this crummy plant to keep my family safe and healthy, and now you're telling me that I gave my son his heart problems."

As scientists we could not affirm that there were genetic risks associated with the workplace based on the sample of 5/5. We therefore turned to other scientists with experience in human genetics to help. For example, at the birth of his second malformed child, one member of the executive had been told by the genetics counselor at a local hospital, "These things just happen, we'll never understand them. But they could not be associated with your work." We called the hospital many times, trying to reach this doctor, known as an expert in the field, and eventually to reach any one in the service, but our calls were never returned. In 1982, after our report had come out, the doctor finally called us: he had been retained by the employer, and was threatening us with a lawsuit on their behalf.

We called the genetics service of another hospital, to see whether anyone would undertake a study of the workers. The service would not do a study, but offered to examine the newborn with the tracheo-aesophageal fistula to see whether she or her parents had chromosomal anomalies. The test was negative, but this did not enable us to conclude that the baby's problems were unrelated to the workplace, since not all chromosomal anomalies are visible.

We talked to the head of a large department of human genetics, and he informed us that offspring of *male* workers could not be affected by working conditions. On being asked why, in that case, he injected male rather than female mice when he studied mutagenesis, he responded that it was strange, wasn't it. (This fairly common scientific error is made less often now that many workplace exposures have been shown to affect male reproduction.)[2]

In general, the local genetics community clearly was reluctant to get involved; it made us think of New Yorkers watching a mugging. We learned quickly not to use the word "union," but even "workplace" sufficed to induce a negative reaction. (We have subsequently met the same response from a dozen scientists, who refused us when we asked them to testify in a court case involving compensation to an infant allegedly malformed by *in utero* solvent exposure.)[3]

Not finding anyone else to do the study, we got a tiny grant from our university for a study of chromosome aberrations among 15 workers and 15 controls, and for development of a questionnaire on workers' reproductive outcomes. We were extremely nervous about doing this, since in our work with fungi we would never have agreed to use a technique about which we knew so little. However, once it was clear that participation was to be anonymous, the scientific community was very helpful: an epidemiologist generously offered to help us write the questionnaire and check the results, and a cytogeneticist taught us how to check for chromosome aberrations. This test, different from that for chromosomal anomalies, looks for chromosome breaks in a random sample of white blood cells of adults. The numbers of breaks are counted and compared to those found among an appropriate control group. Chromosome breaks are thought to be an indicator of genetic damage. The union arranged to introduce us to 15 of the most exposed workers, a sample size adequate for studies of chromosome aberrations, since many cells from each subject can be studied.

With the help of two undergraduate summer students, we analyzed the chromosomes and read the questionnaire results. The chromosomes, coded "blind," yielded a significant difference between exposed workers and controls of the same sex and similar ages selected from university personnel and their relatives. However, this test is not unambiguous, and we did not have perfect confidence in our results, owing to our own inexperience.

A well-known researcher from another country offered to check our results. He came, took samples, and returned with them to his laboratory, promising us to send the results. After a few months, workers received letters (in English, which they found confusing) saying their tests were all negative. When we phoned, we were told that the letters resulted from a secretary's error, and that the tests had not yet been done. We asked the scientist to prepare a letter in French explaining the error, but this was never done. A few months later, he called to say that he had still not completed the analysis, but would like to have permission to put a picture of one of the workers' chromosomes in a textbook, since he had never seen a chromosome so badly damaged. We never heard from him again, and the workers were badly confused by this incident, in which their needs and our credibility were not taken seriously.

The questionnaire results were suggestive, since there appeared to be a very large number of congenital malformations, but not all workers had responded, so that the sample might have been biased toward those with problems.

We therefore reported these very partial and tentative results to the union as evidence that a problem might exist, and suggested that a grant be sought for a complete study using trained personnel. In a fit of anger against the company, union representatives slapped our report on the bargaining table during negotiations. The company immediately contacted a well-known geneticist, who called us asking for our slides, and wanting to know where we got our funding. Having in mind the kinds of differing interpretations of chromosomal aberrations with which the citizens of Love Canal had had to contend,[4] we referred him to the union. He did not contact the union, but proposed, for $100,000, to do a study for the company. Management then offered to settle with the union for $50,000, to be put into renovations of the ventilating system of the plant, if the union would keep our report confidential, and if we would not pursue our study. The union agreed.

Our reaction was mixed. We found $50,000 for ventilation, which should have been installed years before, small compensation if indeed children had been born with malformations because of the working conditions. On the other hand, we were glad that our report had served a purpose, since it is rare that a scientific study results in an improvement in working conditions. As scientists, we were disappointed not to be able to publish, or to pursue the study further. We were left with unsatisfied curiosity because we do not know to this day whether there was a serious exposure to genotoxic agents at this plant. We also didn't understand why the company's geneticist continued to be well respected in scientific circles (e.g., president of a major scientific association), while accepting money from management to be used as a bargaining chip, while we were regarded as untouchables because of a *non-lucrative* relationship with unions.

Since that time, we have been involved in several studies. We had found the technique of looking for chromosomal aberrations to be too hard on the eyes of our laboratory workers, and too susceptible to differing interpretations. We, therefore, have been involved with applying to occupational exposures another method of measurement of genetic damage, in which we have more confidence. We have measured mutant frequencies in lymphocytes of hospital patients[5] and workers[6] exposed to ionizing radiation, and have received grants from several sources to work in this area. We have been supported to work on fundamental biological parameters of our test, effects of radiation on cells in culture, and molecular characterization of mutant cells.

But these are not the only activities of our research group. With my colleague, Donna Mergler, a neurophysiologist, we have formed a group which studies health effects of women's working conditions,[7] reproductive outcome of hospital workers,[8] and working conditions and health effects among slaughterhouse workers and solvent-exposed workers.[9] I can thus compare the responses of colleagues to various types of research proposals. It has been interesting to compare the treatment grant requests receive when they are about ways to improve genetic control of mosquitoes, or those of our current studies which involve only cells in culture, with that afforded requests for funding to study genotoxic or neurotoxic effects of working conditions.

It is, of course, difficult to separate the effects of granting agency policy, composition of specific peer groups, quality of the proposal, and prejudice against unions when examining responses to various grant proposals. What *is* clear, is that there is no granting agency in Canada which has a priority to fund research initiated by unions or other community groups in order to respond to needs defined by them. The closest approach to such a granting agency is Quebec's Institut de recherche sur la santé et la sécurité du travail (see below), which requires employer approval for all studies, even those in which no entrance into the workplace is involved.

In general, we got a negative response if we said we were going to treat information from non-scientists as we would treat "hard" data. Our group now holds over $400,000 in grants from agencies outside our university, and none of it is for any study involving any type of questionnaire on working conditions, although we submitted six such requests. When the studies have not been rejected outright, the parts involving questionnaires have been cut. We have unfortunately no idea how to gain information on working conditions without use of questionnaires, since employers are reluctant to let even non-union-affiliated researchers onto their property to do direct observation during working hours, and since workers are usually people who know most about their true, rather than ideal, working conditions.

If it is stated that workers need and want desperately the answer to some question, this is a reason for a study not to be funded, on grounds of bias, although such reasoning is not applied to university-industry joint projects, which are actively encouraged by granting agencies.[10] We have been trying for four years to fund a study on reproductive outcome, which was requested by a union of one thousand workers, designed with them, and addresses questions of daily concern to them. But when the study is explained, scientists tend to react negatively to this aspect, since subjects of a study are not supposed to have a stake in the results. We think, on the other hand, that a really effective way to ensure good-quality data is by involving the subjects in the study, since they have much less interest than the researcher in biasing the data. After all, it is in the interest of a scientist to find an interesting workplace risk to health in his or her study, but the person who has to work there the day after is happier when no risk has been shown.

Workplaces do not lend themselves to scientific study, in the eyes of many scientists. It is considered more accurate to model the workplace in the laboratory, and then state all the differences between the model and the real situation. See for example, the literature on how to assay genotoxic effects,[11] or the classic ergonomic studies on load lifting, all of which were done in the laboratory, with workers modelled by college students or army volunteers.[12]

In fact, humans do not lend themselves to scientific study, according to many scientists. When I spent a sabbatical year in a highly-regarded research institute, examining mutant frequencies in blood cells of people exposed to ionizing radiation, and exploring methods for differentiating radiation caused from other DNA damage, the most frequent comment I received on my project was that it would be much better to do it with Chinese hamster cells. When I replied that I was interested in living human blood, which circulates, and varies in its exposure to radiation in ways that cells in culture don't, people replied that it was impossible to control all the parameters affecting human blood, and that work with isolated cells was more reliable.

Thus, the closer we were to questions asked by workers, the less likely we were to encounter a sympathetic response from other scientists. But it was not only the content of projects which offended other scientists. My colleagues and I have frequently been in a position to hear more personal comments on each others' grant applications. For example, one of us included in her résumé, in an application for work on radiation effects, co-authorship of a 100-page booklet on radiation in the workplace, published jointly by the unions and the university. This single reference led to the remark, "Why does she bring up the unions everywhere (sic) in her application?" In contrast, a member of a committee considering a grant request for work with cells in culture in collaboration with a hospital staff, said, "Oh, now she's a good little girl!"

We were told by a biochemist, member of a committee which considered a grant request by another one of us, "Someone asked, 'Isn't she the one who has a relationship with unions?' Of course, that didn't influence our [negative] decision, but it made a funny atmosphere around the table." In contrast, the chairman of a major Canadian epidemiology department regularly does paid consulting for companies, and we have not heard of this influencing negatively his considerable ability to obtain grants. He recently accepted money from a company to critique a project proposed by the union, and then was selected by a granting agency to review the same project for funding. (Funding was refused.)

Consequences

Our experience can be taken as an example of the pressure which is exercised on non-conforming scientists, and especially those who "mix" other than middle-of-the-road politics with their scientific

356

endeavours. Donna Mergler describes pressure on her group to abandon studies of the neurotoxic effects of solvents;[13] doctors at the Ontario Workers' Health Centre have been asked to choose between their university appointments and their participation in a labour-sponsored organization.[14] A labour-initiated study at the National Institutes of Occupational Safety and Health (NIOSH) in the United States, on the effect of VDTs on pregnancy was stalled by labour-management conflict for so long that the proposed control group started using VDTs, making the study impossible. The researcher subsequently resigned from NIOSH.[15]

Consequently, unions in joint labour-management committees or adversary situations have unequal access to highly-trained, and especially, to highly-respected, scientific resources. This is so, not only owing to unions' unequal ability to pay for resources, but also because a scientist who testifies for, or works with, a union automatically loses prestige with the very group the union is trying to impress: judges, juries, and public opinion.

The difficulties we have experienced affect our ability to do certain projects, and even our desire to become involved in questions posed by workers. It is a tremendous disruptive force on our group. We now know how to write grants and get them funded. But we are honest people, and we don't use funds for work they weren't intended for. Thus, we feel pressure to do work far from the central concerns of workers. If we were not at a university which has set up mechanisms to recognize, and to some extent support, this kind of work, I am afraid we would have turned exclusively to *in vitro* studies by now.

Compensations

Quebec now has a research institute, the Institut de recherche en santé et en sécurité du travail, where funds are distributed for work in occupational health by a committee composed of four union representatives, four management representatives, and five scientists. Through this organization, several union-based or union-associated projects, including ours, have now been funded. Through working on the various committees, some union people have become quite sophisticated about how science works, and what kinds of projects can be funded. Management and labour to some extent agree on the necessity of a practical approach, and one that answers questions posed in the workplace. Thus, we have more financial and institutional support than is usual for a progressive university group, and are able to be a bit less fearful of repression than some of our colleagues.

In spite of our disconcerting, and occasionally frightening, experiences, we make an overall positive evaluation of the scientific advantages to us in doing union-initiated research.

One consequence of listening to workers' formulations of problems is that one comes across new ideas. It was in an educational session with radiology technicians that I was asked whether stress on the job could influence the number of radiation-induced mutations. This question is quite meaningful to workers in a context of extensive personnel cuts, but at first glance, nonsensical to scientists trained to one agent — one lesion mutagenesis. However, it started me on a reflection on the many possible workplace influences on genotoxic effects, which has led to new hypotheses, and incidentally to several grants.

Donna Mergler and Nicole Vézina were led by workers to examine the effects of cold exposure on menstrual problems, the first North American study in this area.[16] Jean-Pierre Reveret, Donna Mergler, and I were led by workers' questions to examine working conditions in women's employment "ghettos," leading to some original reflections on the biological justifications for such ghettos.[17]

In addition, one is unlikely to encounter much scientific competition when one responds to workers' questions, because of the prejudices mentioned above. We hope, of course, that this advantage will disappear as scientists and granting agencies become more sensitive to workers' concerns. Finally, we find that the opportunity to produce some effect, however minimal, on the parameter we are studying, enriches our professional lives.

GILLIAN KRANIAS

Women and the Changing Faces of Science

Science has three faces. In the life of an individual, science can be a profession; in the search for truth, it is a method of furthering understanding; and in the world of social and economic interests, it rears its head as an unwieldy institution. Recent feminist studies and critiques have touched on all these aspects. In her study, "The Relationship Between Women's Studies and Women in Science," Sue Rosser indicated that women in science respond to the women's movement first in their personal lives, later, through their research approaches, and finally, in the way they teach science, the most public activity of scientific institutions.[1] It is unfortunate that Rosser neglects to consider further aspects of science as an institution, such as the structure of research teams, as well as their funding and publishing channels. Perhaps these are often the last aspects to change, and thus, few interesting cases exist that could be studied. One such case, I was delighted to discover, is the work of Karen Messing and the Groupe de recherche-action en biologie du travail (GRABIT) at the Université du Québec à Montréal (UQAM). The work of this group serves as an example of where feminist science can take us.

When feminists (especially those of us who are not professional scientists) talk and write about a feminist science, we are often not sure to what extent our speculations are feasible. Most of us do not envision a single new profession, method, and institution replacing the old; instead, we hope for a diversity of approaches, each appropriate to its specific time, place, and the people involved. Within that context, my study has limitations, but it can also provide some fruitful insights. In the following pages, I will explore and compare feminist theoretical writings with the reality of Messing's practice as a feminist scientist working with a feminist research team. I will consider, in turn, each of the three faces of science: the institution, the method, and the profession.

The Institution

Science has grown up into a vast institution, tightly woven into our contemporary socio-political and economic fabric. As Elizabeth Fee points out:

> This modern context for the production of scientific knowledge demonstrates the difficulty of developing a specifically feminist science. The problem of the liberation of women would first have to become a major social concern, with the necessary social resources devoted to its solution.[2]

The work of Messing and her colleagues has not involved such large-scale transformations of science as an institution, but GRABIT has managed to make a small dent in the great machine.

Messing co-directs GRABIT along with her colleague, Donna Mergler. Within UQAM's department of biology, Messing and Mergler have effected many changes. When Messing was hired in 1976, she and Mergler were the only full-time women faculty members. Together, they lobbied for more women to be hired. Today, women constitute approximately one third of the full-time faculty in the UQAM biology department, and they have a significant impact on its direction. This "opening up" of the department allowed Messing, in 1978, to create an undergraduate course called "Biologie et condition feminine" the first course of its kind in North America. Responsibility for teaching the course has since been shared with others, but the curriculum emphasis remains the same: the course explores biological studies of sex differences, and looks at how the results of certain studies have been used to oppress women. Thus, UQAM's biology department has changed, becoming "more feminist" than most. The truly radical transformations, however, have occurred within GRABIT.

GRABIT is a feminist institution, if the term is not contradictory. Eighty percent of GRABIT researchers are women, and the six men in the group are feminists. According to Messing, GRABIT researchers do not make decisions solely on the basis that "we are feminists, therefore . . ." Nonetheless, a feminist awareness affects most aspects of their scientific practice. Messing writes:

Because of their sex and class, the large majority of scientists are less likely than the general population to be interested in such topics as the occupational exposures that present a risk to the nursing mother, alternate (non-hormonal) treatments for the discomforts of menopause, how a woman can give herself a safe (and, where necessary, secret) abortion, what work postures increase the likelihood of menstrual cramps, and how a low-income family can provide itself with nutritious meals. On the other hand, there is plenty of research supported by drug companies, on drug therapy for menopausal women, by government on what racial and income groups have most abortions, by employers on the relationship between women's physiological cycles and productivity, and by private charity on how to prevent a rich fat-laden diet from causing heart disease.[3]

GRABIT's priorities are fundamentally radical, because researchers focus on evaluating workers' health risks and suggesting preventative, non-medical solutions, and because their projects deal primarily with women's health problems, within women's employment ghettos. Even the way researchers select a given problem implies a new organization of science. Through a protocol signed in 1976, UQAM offered to put its scientific resources at the disposal of Quebec's two major unions — the Confédération des syndicats nationaux (CSN) and the Fédération des travailleurs du Québec (FTQ). In fulfillment of this commitment, all GRABIT's research projects have either been directly suggested by unions, or have arisen out of GRABIT's discussions with workers. "We listen to people," says Messing. "It is easy to take questions and ideas from workers but that's not the way research projects usually get developed."[4]

Of course, one cannot forget that intimately tied to any research team's choice of topic are concerns about funding. The necessarily subversive nature of research supporting the interests of the oppressed means that GRABIT cannot appeal to the biggest funders of science, the military and industry, for support. GRABIT researchers have found that the more they interest themselves in people's daily experience, in concrete working conditions, the harder it becomes to obtain funds.[5] This is the gloomy side of feminist science. Fortunately, the Institut de recherche en santé et securité du travail du Québec (IRSST), a research division of the Workers Compensation Board whose board and scientific panel include worker representatives, funds more than two-thirds of GRABIT's annual budget of approximately $370,000.[6]

But feminist thought pushes beyond demands for a shift in research priorities! It aims for distinct changes in the structure and functioning of a research team as well. As Ruth Bleier states:

> Recognizing that different people have different experiences, cultures, and identifications . . . feminist science would aim for cultural diversity among its participants, so that through our diverse approaches we would light different facets of the realities we attempt to understand.[7]

GRABIT is beginning to reflect the ideal of a more heterogeneous science. Messing says that she and Mergler have made no conscious efforts to recruit researchers from a variety of backgrounds, but the open nature of the UQAM environment and the structure and focus of GRABIT have attracted and welcomed individuals often excluded from scientific institutions. "GRABIT researchers reflect class backgrounds from the daughter of a working class alcoholic to the daughter of a doctor," says Messing.[8] One of GRABIT's senior researchers is a Bolivian refugee; a political prisoner at the age of 18, she came to Canada without a cent. One of the team's male researchers, who is pursuing a master's degree by studying the effects of ionizing radiation on hospital workers, was a hospital worker himself before he joined GRABIT

Still, there remain obstacles, even within GRABIT, for many aspiring scientists. Although within Messing's lab everyone either has or wants children, mothering is not easily compatible with research. Messing says:

> The Canadian NSERC fellowships for gifted students have an absolute limit of two years in which to obtain the Master of Sciences degree. While maternity leave (unpaid) is granted, no

The GRABIT, 1988. Karen Messing and Donna Mergler
(first row, second and third from left).
Photo by Jacques Munger.

provision is made for a slower rhythm of work once the mother returns to the laboratory or field. If she takes longer than two years for the M.Sc., she can get no Ph.D. support.[9]

Women can get discouraged easily, Messing feels, partly for realistic reasons and partly because "we're brought up to think we're no good anyway."[10]

"We must strive for more humane working conditions for all of science's practitioners," writes Marion Namenwirth.[11]

GRABIT strives to foster such an atmosphere. Within the labs, relationships are humane and supportive; personal responsibilities and difficulties outside the job are respected and understood, not slighted. GRABIT's warm team spirit has been critical to the progress and success of its innovations, especially since the group is not in the mainstream of the scientific community.

The Method

In a science designed by women . . . subjects would tend to be viewed in their larger context, with greater attention to the linkages between different levels of organization, and between different aspects of the same subject. It is the WHOLE, complete with all its details and idiosyncracies and individualities that is important in a female worldview.[12]

GRABIT researchers treat the work environment as a whole. In order to do so, each of their projects integrates laboratory work with alternative methods of investigation, primarily questionnaires and discussions with subjects. These alternate methods actively involve research subjects in the investigative process. Thus, they challenge the long-entrenched subject/object dichotomy of traditional scientific methodology, as do many feminist critics.[13] As Hilde Hein suggests: "those who aspired to understand the world more fully would be admonished to become more fully integrated with it; not to separate themselves and stand apart from it."[14]

In many of GRABIT's projects, the dissolution of the subject/object barrier has helped researchers gain access to a more complete picture of the health factors affecting a particular group of workers. In a study of the effects of radiation exposure on hospital technicians, discussions with the subjects revealed to Messing and her colleagues that:

(1) We could not neglect the risk of accidental, fairly high exposures, since many [technicians] reported that doctors did not wait for them to leave the side of the patient before turning on the radiation;(2) Dosimeter readings, on which we had counted, had been informally checked by the technicians, many of whom had doubts as to their accuracy;(3) The most important health symptom reported by these workers was a very great feeling of exhaustion, associated with recent extensive cuts in the workforce which in many places had halved the numbers of workers available to do the same job, and left them "on the front lines" to face the often angry patients.[15]

Similarly, questionnaires help GRABIT researchers identify occupational health risks that have been traditionally overlooked (i.e. exposure to solvents, to cold, lack of mobility). In women's employment ghettos, health risks are usually not as spectacular as those within traditionally male work environments; but they can be equally, if not more, dangerous and debilitating.[16] Questionnaires can reveal complex conditions that scientific instruments alone cannot detect. For instance, many parameters influence a worker's perception of cold:

The degree of humidity, the amount of physical mobility permitted by the task, and the possibility of performing the task while wearing adequate protective clothing such as warm gloves. A thermometer will not measure all this; yet these factors contribute to the physiological state of being cold.[17]

In response to the complexity of people's working situations, Donna Mergler has been developing new statistical methods to facilitate the simultaneous analysis of compound health factors.

In the past, scientists have preferred to perform experiments within the confines of a laboratory, and later excuse any discrepancies between their results and reality.[18] In contrast, GRABIT's approach begins with the complexities of concrete situations. This involvement, or *engagement*, often illuminates aspects of a problem that laboratory researchers would never think to question.[19] Thus, GRABIT's method of action-research often works to minimize bias. At the same time, Messing admits that "there are no guarantees."[20]

Marion Namenwirth has stated:

> I would like to see scientists confront head-on the probability of cultural bias and distortion in choice of research problems, use of language for formulating and describing what ought to be studied, choice of experimental design, methods of data collection and analysis, and the evaluation and interpretation of the results. All these should become matters for introspection, for critique and discussion within research groups, and for open acknowledgement and analysis within the discussion sections of research papers.[21]

Messing and her colleagues argue that possibilities for bias "should not be used to say that studies where subjects are aware are useless."[22] Nevertheless, bias distorts scientific truth, so GRABIT researchers always carefully evaluate the neutrality of the research method they choose to use for a given problem. If any doubts arise, they look for ways to eliminate them.

For example, during a study of the effects of radiation exposure on offspring, GRABIT researchers had chosen questionnaires as an effective tool for gathering much of their data. In view of this choice, a question was raised concerning whether those women who had experienced problems might be more encouraged to answer the questionnaire than others, and whether they might exaggerate any abnormalities. To minimize this uncertainty: (1) Messing took care to explain, in letters to the potential respondents, the importance of a random sample of workers; (2) the research team made sure to include questions concerning more "objective" data, such as birthweight, to back up qualitative variables; and (3) laboratory studies were performed, to complement the questionnaires, and to act as a check on their accuracy. After further reflection and debate, the researchers concluded that workers, if biased at all, were more likely to respond conservatively, because "they did not want to be told that there was a problem when there wasn't or even if there was (since they didn't want their health to be endangered)."[23]

Perhaps the most encouraging feature of GRABIT's methodology is that, because it involves research subjects at every step of the process, from the choice of a topic to the evaluation and application of results, subjects feel more responsible for the research results and respond to questions more carefully. The result is a better understanding of reality.

The Profession

Experience has taught us that being a feminist scientist implies more than simply being a woman scientist. (In fact, you don't even *have* to be a woman!) The career of a contemporary feminist scientist also differs considerably from what we might dream it ultimately could be. Today, one is more-or-less isolated within a largely hostile environment. Messing, drawing from her own experience, is quick to emphasize that seeking out and teaming up with other feminists is the first step to achieving substantial changes within any discipline. Isolation can be the worst enemy to the career of any scientist. Without the moral, psychological, and scientific support of Donna Mergler and the rest of the GRABIT team, Messing says she would have left science long ago.[24]

Although Messing's profession is only at the doorstep of change, the current directions of this change reveal new professional options that a feminist approach to science would, most likely, further expand:

> There is more than one way to practice science. For some people the traditional "all day and night, every day in the lab" may be best. For others, a totally different time schedule and approach may lead to other valuable insights.[25]

In Messing's life, priorities outside the lab compete equally for her time. "I recently gave a talk 'How Does it Feel to Have Two Heads,'" she says.[26] Earlier in her career, Messing brought up two children. Today, she is writing more and more for non-scientific, usually feminist, audiences. Like many contemporary feminist scientists, Messing is concerned with demystifying science and challenging its traditional bias. "To me," writes Messing, "feminism is to some extent just being fair and intelligent."[27] But this kind of dedication involves struggle. Whether alone in the lab, holding discussions with research subjects, or writing for a public audience, Messing will continually face new challenges.

> [Science's] goal [is] not prediction per se, but understanding; not the power to manipulate, but empowerment — the kind of power that results from an understanding of the world around us, that simultaneously reflects and affirms our connection to that world.[28]

Messing and her colleagues use scientific knowledge to empower the oppressed. When GRABIT performs research, says Messing, "we identify not only the effects, but also the means for correcting problems."[29] In addition, Messing and Mergler act as resources to courses for union members, wherein they offer workers tools for systematizing their own knowledge (for example, measuring instruments, lab tests, and scientific interpretations). Through her work with GRABIT, Messing has developed a keen awareness for the implications of her research. This may be the most radical change that a feminist approach brings to the professional side of science.

Conclusion

The experiences of Messing, Mergler, and the GRABIT team allow us a glimpse, through one window, into the world of feminist science. Although the effects of a feminist approach to science are bound to differ from one discipline to the next, we can all gain new insights from the GRABIT experience. Feminist research teams eliminate the isolation of feminist scientists working alone against the mainstream. GRABIT feminist team approach affects both the choice of projects and their methodology, which integrates laboratory work with other methods of investigation. The GRABIT team not only identifies and analyzes problems, it also identifies solutions and uses its scientific knowledge to effect social change.

We may be a long way from overhauling the mighty institution of science, but the "cottage industry" of feminist knowledge production[30] can have far-reaching repercussions. As feminist critiques evolve, we can hope that increasing numbers of scientists and research teams will experiment with feminist innovations to the institutional, methodological, and professional structures of science. These changes, in turn, will affect the future of our planet.

Selected Bibliography

Women and Science, General

Abir-Am, P. and D. Outram. eds. *Uneasy Careers and Intimate Lives: Women in Science 1789–1979.* New Brunswick, N.J.: Rutgers University Press, 1987.

Alic, M. *Hypatia's Heritage: A History of Women in Science from Antiquity to the Late 19th Century.* London: The Women's Press, 1986.

Ainley, M.G. "Field Work and Family: North American Women Ornithologists, 1900–1950," in Abir-Am & Outram, pp. 60–76.

Amram, F. "Women's Work Includes Invention." *Proceedings of the First International Conference on the Role of Women in the History of Science, Technology and Medicine,* Veszprém, Hungary, 1983, pp. 1–5.

Astin, H.S. *The Woman Doctorate in America: Origins, Career and Family.* New York: Russell Sage Foundation, 1969.

Aysenberg, N. & M. Harrington. *Women of Academe: Outsiders in the Sacred Grove.* Amherst: The Unviersity of Massachussetts Press, 1988.

Bardell, E.B. "America's Only School of Pharmacy for Women." *Pharmacy in History* 26 (1984):127–133.

Beard, M.R. *Woman as a Force in History.* New York: Collier Books, 1946.

Bernard, J.S. *Academic Women.* University Park: Penn. State University Press, 1964.

Bleier, R. *Feminist Approaches to Science.* New York: Pergamon Press, 1986.

Bose, C., P. Bereano, and M. Malloy. "Household Technology and the Social Construction of Housework." *Technology and Culture* 25 (1984):53–82.

Brody, J. "Patterns of Patents: Early British Inventions by Women," in E. Vamos, ed. *Women in Science: Options and Access.* Budapest: National Museum of Science and Technology, 1987, pp. 1–12.

Cole, J., and S. Cole. *Social Stratification in Science.* Chicago: University of Chicago Press, 1973.

Conroy, M.S. "Women Pharmacists in Nineteenth and Early Twentieth-Century Russia." *Pharmacy in History* 29 (1987): 155–164.

Cowan, R.S. *More Work for Mother: The Ironies of Household Technology from the Open Hearth to the Microwave.* New York: Basic Books, 1983.

Dagg, A.I. *Harems and Other Horrors: Sexual Bias in Behavioural Biology.* Waterloo: The Otter Press, 1983.

Easley, B. *Science and Sexual Oppression: Patriarchy's Confrontation with Woman and Nature.* London: Weidenfeld and Nicolson, 1981.

Epstein, C.F. *Deceptive Distinctions: Sex, Gender, and the Social Order.* New Haven & London: Yale University Press, 1988.

Glazer, P.M. and M. Slater. *Unequal Colleagues: The Entrance of Women Into the Professions, 1890–1940.* New Brunswick, N.J.: Rutgers University Press, 1987.

Gornick, V. *Women in Science: Portrait from a World in Transition.* New York: Simon & Schuster, 1983.

Hafter, D. "Artisans, Drudges, and the Problem of Gender in Pre-Industrial France." *Annals of the New York Academy of Sciences.* (1985):71–87.

_____ . "Women's Use of Technology in 18th Century Rouennaise Guilds," in Vamos, pp. 13–28.

Harding, S. *The Science Question in Feminism.* Ithaca, N.Y.: Cornell University Press, 1986

_____ . and J. O'Barr, eds., *Sex and Scientific Inquiry.* Chicago: The University of Chicago Press, 1987.

Keller, E.F. "The Anomaly of a Woman in Physics," in S. Ruddick and P. Daniels, eds., *Working it Out.* New York: Pantheon Books, 1977, pp. 77–91.

_____ . *A Feeling for the Organism: The Life and Work of Barbara McClintock.* San Francisco: W.H. Freeman and Co., 1983.

_____ . *Reflections on Science and Gender.* New Haven, Conn.: Yale University Press, 1985.

Kidwell, P.A. "Women Astronomers in Britain, 1789–1930." *Isis* 75 (1984): 534–546.

Koblitz, A.H. *A Convergence of Lives. Sofia Kovalevskaia: Scientist, Writer, Revolutionary.* Boston: Birkhauser, 1983.

Kohlstedt, S.G. "In From the Periphery: American Women in Science, 1830–1880." *Signs* 4 (Autumn 1978):81–96.

Kramarae, C., ed. *Technology and Women's Voices: Keeping in Touch.* New York & London: Routledge & Kegan Paul, 1988.

Lafortune, L., ed. *Femme et Mathématique.* Montreal: Editions du remue-menage, 1986.

_____ . *Quelles différences? Les femmes et l'enseignement des mathématiques.* Montreal: Edition du remue-menage, 1989.

Landes, R. "A Woman Anthropologist in Brazil," in Peggy Golde, ed., *Women in the Field: Anthropological Experiences.* 2nd edition. Berkeley: University of California Press, 1986, pp. 119–139.

McDaniel, S., H. Cummins, and R.S. Beauchamps, "Mothers of Invention? Meshing the Roles of Inventor, Mother, and Worker." *Women Studies International Forum* 11 (1988):1–12.

McGaw, J.A. "Women and the History of American Technology: A Review Essay." *Signs* 7 (1982): 798–828.

Meitner, L. "The Status of Women in the Profession." *Physics Today* 13 (1960):116–21.

Merchant, C. *The Death of Nature: Women, Ecology and the Scientific Revolution.* San Francisco: Harper & Row, 1980.

Merchant, C. "Isis' Consciousness Raised." *Isis* 73 (1982):398–409.

Mosedale, S. "Science Corrupted: Biologists Construct 'The Woman Question.' " *Journal of the History of Biology* 11 (1978): 1–55.

Morantz-Sanchez, R.M. *Sympathy and Science: Women Physicians in American Medicine.* New York: Oxford University Press, 1985.

Mozans, H.J. *Woman in Science.* Cambridge: MIT Press, 1974. [Originally published in 1913].

Namenwirth, M. "Science Through a Feminist Prism," in R. Bleier, pp. 18–41.

Nice, Margaret M. *Research is a Passion With Me.* Edited by Doris H. Speirs. Toronto: Consolidated Amethyst Communications, 1979.

Ogilvy, M.B. *Women in Science: Antiquity through the Nineteenth Century.* Cambridge, Mass.: The MIT Press, 1986.

Osen, Lynn M. *Women in Mathematics.* Cambridge: MIT Press, 1974.

Opfell, O.S. *The Lady Laureates: Women Who Have Won the Nobel Prize.* Metuchen, N.J.: Scarecrow Press, 1986.

Rose, H. "Beyond Masculinist Realities: A Feminist Epistemology for the Sciences," in Bleier, pp. 57–76.

Rosser, S. "Good Science: Can It Ever Be Gender Free?" *Women Studies International Forum* 11 (1988):13–19.

Rossi, Alice. "Women in Science: Why So Few?" *Science* 148 (1965): 1196–1202.

Rossiter, Margaret W. *Women Scientists in America: Struggles and Strategies to 1940.* Baltimore: Johns Hopkins University Press, 1982.

———. "Sexual Segregation in the Sciences: Some Data and a Model." *Signs* 4 (Autumn 1978):146–151.

Rothschild, J., ed. *Machina Ex Dea.* New York: Pergamon Press, 1983.

Sayers, J. "Feminism and Science — Reason and Passion." *Women Studies International Forum* 20 (1987):171–179.

Shapley, D. "Obstacles to Women in Science." *Impact of Science on Society.* 25 (April/June 1975):115–123.

Seth, M. "Women's Contribution to Technological Innovation: Product and Process," in Vamos, pp. 177–197.

Schiebinger, L. "The History and Philosophy of Women in Science: a Review Essay." *Signs* 12 (1987):305–332.

_____ . "Maria Winkelmann at the Berlin Academy: A Turning Point for Women in Science." *Isis* 78 (1987):174–200.

Sudarkasa, N. "In a World of Women: Field Work in a Yoruba Community," in Golde, pp. 167–191.

Vetter, Betty. "Women in the Natural Sciences." *Signs* 1 (1976): 713–720.

Warner, D.J. "Science Education for Women in Antebellum America." *Isis* 69 (1978): 58–67.

_____ . *Graceanna Lewis: Scientist and Humanitarian.* Washington, D.C.: Smithsonian Institution Press, 1979.

_____ . "The Women's Pavilion," in R. Post, ed., *1876: A Centennial Exhibition.* Washington, D.C.: National Museum of History and Technology, Smithsonian Institution, 1976, pp. 163–173.

Weisstein, N. "How Can a Little Girl Like You Teach a Great Big Class of Men? . . ." in Ruddick & Daniels, pp. 241–250.

White, Martha S. "Psychological and Social Barriers to Women in Science." *Science* 170 (1970):413–416.

Zimmerman, J., ed. *The Technological Woman: Interfacing with Tomorrow.* New York: Praeger Publishers, 1983.

Zuckerman, Harriet and J. Cole. "Women in American Science." *Minerva* (1975):82–102.

Canadian Women

Ainley, Marianne G. "D'assistantes anonymes à chercheures scientifiques: Une rétrospective sur la place des femmes en sciences." *Cahiers de recherche sociologique* 4 (April 1986):55–71.

_____ . "Women Scientists in Canada: The Need for Documentation." *Resources for Feminist Research* 15, 3 (November 1986):7–8.

_____ . "A Family of Women Scientists." *Bulletin of the Simone de Beauvoir Institute* 7, 1 (1986):5–10.

_____ . "Femme et Mathématique: Quelles Actions Prendre?" *Bulletin d'association mathematique du Québec* 27 (October 1987):25–26.

Arena, F. "Présence des femmes en science et technologie au Québec." *Cahiers de recherche sociologique* 4 (1986):33–53.

Canadian Woman Studies/les cahiers de la femme 5 (Summer 1984).

de la Cour, L. "The 'Other' Side of Psychology: Women Psychologists in Toronto from 1920 to 1945." *Canadian Women Studies* 8 (1987):44–46.

Dagg, A.I., and P. Thompson. *MisEducation: Women & Canadian Universities.* Toronto: OISE, 1988.

Derick, Carrie M. "Professions Open to Women," in *Women of Canada: Their*

Life and Work. National Council of Women of Canada, 1900, pp. 57–62.

Dodd, Dianne. "The Canadian Birth Control Movement: Two Approaches to the Dissemination of Contraceptive Technology." *Scientia Canadensis* 9 (June 1985): 53–66.

Dunbar, Moira. "Women in Science: How Much Progress Have We Really Made?" *Science Forum* 32 (April 1973): 13–15.

Edwards, Mrs. O.C. "Professional Training," *Women of Canada: Their Life and Work*, pp. 63–73.

Ellis, Dormer. "Canadian Women in the Engineering Profession." *Proceedings of the First National Conference for Women in Science Engineering and Technology*. Vancouver, 1983, pp. 135–142.

Estey, Ralph. "Margaret Newton: Distinguished Canadian Scientist and First Woman Member of the Quebec Society for the Protection of Plants." *Phytoprotection* 68 (1987): 79–85.

Ewan, Gail. "Agnes Higgins, Nutritionist, 1911–1985, and the Montreal Diet Dispensary." *Resources for Feminist Research* 15, 3 (1986):48–49.

Franklin, U. "Will Women Change Technology or Will Technology Change Women?" CRIAW *papers* 9 (1985).

Gaskell, J. and A. McLaren, eds. *Women and Education: A Canadian Perspective*. Calgary: Detselig Enterprises Limited, 1987.

Gillett, Margaret. *We Walked Very Warily: A History of Women at McGill*. Montreal: Eden Press, 1981.

Gillet, Margaret and Kay Sibbald, eds. *A Fair Shake: Autobiographical Essays by McGill Women*. Montreal: Eden Press, 1984.

Gjedde, Albert. "The Emancipation of Miss Menten." *The Journal of Cerebral Bloodflow and Metabolism* 9 (1989):243–46.

Griffiths, N.E.S. *Penelope's Web: Some Perceptions of Women in European and Canadian Society*. Toronto: Oxford University Press, 1974.

Houle, Ghislaine. *La femme et la société québecoise*. Quebec: Gouvernement du Quebec, 1975.

Lasvergnas, I. "Contexte de socialisation primaire et choix d'une carrière scientifique chez les femmes." *Recherches féministes* 1 (1988):31–45.

Mergler, D. et al. "The Weaker Sex? Men in Women's Working Conditions Report Similar Health Symptoms." *Journal of Occupational Medicine* 29 (1987):417–421.

Messing, K. "Do Men and Women have Different Jobs Because of Their Biological Differences?" *International Journal of Health Services* 12 (1982): 43–52.

———. "The Scientific Mystique: Can a White Lab Coat Guarantee Purity in Research on the Nature of Women?", in M. Lowe and R. Hubbard, eds., *Women's Nature: Rationalizations of Inequality*. New York: Pergamon Press, 1983, pp. 75–88.

Messing, K. & J.P. Reveret. "Are Women in Female Jobs for Their Health? A Study of Working Conditions and Health Effects in the Fish-processing Industry in Quebec." *International Journal of Health Services* 13 (1983): 635–647.

Mioduszewa, B. "Careers for Women in Mining: A Canadian overview." *Geology* 5, 8. (1977):498–499.

Mitchinson, W. "Medical Perceptions of Female Sexuality: A Late Nineteenth Century Case." *Scientia Canadensis* 9 (1985): 67–81.

Montagnes, Anne. "Alice Wilson, 1881–1964," in M.Q. Innis, ed., *The Clear Spirit: Twenty Canadian Women and their Times.* Toronto: University of Toronto Press, 1967, pp. 260–278.

Mura, R. "Sex-Related Differences in Expectation of Success." *Journal for Research in Mathematics Education* 18 (1987): 15–24.

Morrison, Carolyn. "Options for Women in Geography: Some Experiences Shared." *Canadian Geographer* 26 (1982): 360–366.

Pinet, Janine. "La femme et la science." *Atlantis* 3 (Spring 1978):96–115.

Pringle, James. "Anne Mary Perceval (1790–1876): An Early Botanical Collector in Lower Canada." *Canadian Horticultural History* 1, 1 (1985):7–13.

Sheinin, Rose. "Women in Science: Issues and Actions." *Canadian Woman Studies/les cahiers de la femme* 5 (Summer 1984): 70–77.

———. "Jeanne Manery Fisher: Scientist, Feminist: a Model of Excellence." *Bulletin of the Canadian Biochemical Association* (December 1987).

Sheinin, Rose & L. de la Cour. "Canadian Women Medical Scientists of 1870–1911: A Made-Invisible Canadian Product." *The Crucible: Journal of the Science Teachers' Association of Ontario* 18 (January-February 1987): 34–38.

Smith, Lorraine C. "Canadian Women Natural Scientists — Why Not?" *The Canadian Field Naturalist* 90 (1976):1–4.

Stephenson, Patricia. "Allie V. Douglas" and "Mildred K. Nobles," in "Hidden Voices: the Life Experiences of Women Who Have Worked and Studied at Queen's University." Queen's University Oral History Project, 1980.

Waxman, S.B. "Dr. Emily Stowe: Canada's First Female Practitioner." *Canada West* 10 (Spring 1980): 17–30.

Contributors

MARIANNE GOSZTONYI AINLEY studied industrial chemistry in Hungary. After twenty years as an "invisible" chemist in Sweden and Canada, she became interested in the history and sociology of science, obtained an M.Sc. from the Institute d'histoire et sociopolitique des sciences, Université de Montréal (1980) and a Ph.D. in the history and philosophy of science from McGill University (1985). She has published articles on the history of ornithology in *Living Bird* (1979–80), *Tchébec* (1981, 1982), *Picoides* (1986), *Scientia Canadensis* (1988) and the proceedings of two international congresses, and on women scientists in *Cahier de recherche sociologique* (1986), *Resources for Feminist Research* (1986), and in *Uneasy Careers and Intimate Lives* (1987). She teaches a course on "Women, Science, and Technology" at the Simone de Beauvoir Institute, Concordia University, where she is an Adjunct Fellow. She is currently completing a biography of Canadian zoologist, Dr. William Rowan (1891–1957), editing with John Sabean the correspondence of Louise de Kiriline Lawrence and Doris H. Speirs, and working on *The Overlooked Dimension: Canadian Women and Scientific Work: 1890–1960*.

KAILASH K. ANAND is an associate professor of mathematics at Concordia University, Montreal, where she has taught since 1962. She received her B.Sc. and M.Sc. in India and her Ph.D. in mathematics from the Courant Institute of Mathematical Sciences, New York University, in 1980. She has published several papers in the areas of differential equations and the history of mathematics, and has recently become interested in the history of Canadian women mathematics. Dr. Anand is married and has three grown children.

MARGARET-ANN ARMOUR was born and educated in Scotland, where she obtained Bachelor and Master of Science degrees. She worked as a research chemist in the paper industry before obtaining a Ph.D. in physical organic chemistry from the University of Alberta in 1970. Since 1979, she has been supervisor of the undergraduate organic chemistry laboratories at the University of Alberta. She is currently serving as assistant chair of the department of chemistry.

Dr. Armour is the author or co-author of three laboratory manuals, and thirty-seven papers on chemical education, hazardous waste disposal, and women in science. She sits on the University's Biosafety Committee, chairs the Department of Chemistry Safety Committee and is a member of the Chemical Institute of Canada, the American Chemical Society, and the New York Academy of Sciences.

Dr. Armour is vice chairperson and convenor of WISEST, a committee of the vice-president (research) on women in scholarship, engineering, science and technology, and past-president of the Academic Women's Association. She is a member of the board of St. Stephen's College, University of Alberta, and of the EX TERRA Foundation.

RACHELLE SENDER BEAUCHAMP holds a doctorate in molecular biology and has taught and researched in that field. She has also worked as a project scientist in occupational health and as a technology analyst. At present, she is co-director of the Women Inventors Project. She has received numerous awards for academic achievement, including election to Phi Beta Kappa, and a Medical Research Council Postdoctoral Fellowship. In 1987, she received a special award from the United Nations' World Intellectual Property Directorate for her "invention" of the Women Inventors Project. She is also the co-founder and past president of the Canadian Association for Women in Science.

JANICE BEAVERIDGE is a mature student at Laurentian University who, after many years in secretarial and administrative work, has returned to school. She is interested in aspects of social psychology and how women are affected by the organization of business systems. She has lived in Alberta, British Columbia, Northwest Territories, and Quebec.

CLARA M. CHU is a doctoral candidate, School of Library and Information Science, University of Western Ontario. Her research interests include the history of communication, growth and diffusion of knowledge, and the information-seeking behaviour of scholars. She was technical editor for the project which led to the publication of *Science and Technology in Canadian History: A Bibliography of Primary Sources to 1914.*

ROBERT J. CLARK is associate professor of curriculum studies, Faculty of Education, University of Western Ontario. He is interested in Ontario history, particularly the history of the pharmacy profession in Ontario.

PENELOPE W. CODDING is a Heritage Medical Scholar and professor of chemistry and of pharmacology and therapeutics at the University of Calgary. Her research interests include the study of the interaction of pharmaceutical agents with biological receptors, and the development of design strategies for new therapeutic agents. She has an active interest in the participation of women in science and the development of programs to encourage female students.

BETTY COLLIS studied mathematics and the teaching of mathematics in the

United States (Ph.D. Stanford University), and was associate professor in the department of psychological foundations at the University of British Columbia. In 1988, she was appointed the first woman associate professor at the University of Twente, the Netherlands, one of three Dutch universities focusing on science and engineering. She has been involved with computers in education, and has given talks and published papers on school computers and equity issues.

GAIL C. COULAS recently received her Ph.D. in sociology from McMaster University. She is interested in the sociology of occupations and organizations, with emphasis on women in pharmacy.

ANNE INNIS DAGG is academic director of the Independent Studies Program of the University of Waterloo. Her graduate work was in the genetics of mice and the locomotion of large mammals. Since then, she has done research on giraffes, camels, urban biology, and sexist biology, among other things. Recently, she has also been doing work on issues involving women. Her latest book (with Patricia J. Thompson) is *MisEducation: Women and Canadian Universities* (OISE Press, 1988).

LYKKE DE LA COUR is currently completing an M.A. in history at the University of Toronto. Her research interests include women's history, Canadian history, and the history of medicine and psychiatry and she has published two articles in *Canadian Woman Studies* on women's experiences in the life sciences.

DIANNE DODD recently completed her Ph.D. at Carleton University, with a thesis on "Delivering Electrical Technology to the Ontario Housewife, 1920–1939: An Alliance of Professional Women, Advertisers and the Electrical Industry." Dr. Dodd has also published articles on the Canadian birth control movement of the 1930s. She is currently on a post-doctoral fellowship with the Hannah Institute for the History of Medicine, conducting research into the career of Helen MacMurchy, M.D., an active promoter of infant and maternal welfare in the 1910s, 20s, and 30s.

RALPH H. ESTEY, B.Sc. (Agr.), B.Ed., M.Sc., Ph.D., D.I.C., fellow of the Linnean Society, fellow of the Canadian Phytopathological Society, and honourary member of the Quebec Society for the Protection of Plants, is now an emeritus professor of McGill University and a writer of Canadian agricultural history.

JOYCE A. FERGUSON is a lecturer in the faculty of pharmacy at the University of Toronto. She recently completed her Ph.D. and is interested in drugs and the elderly, and geriatrics and pharmacy practice.

ROGER GIBBINS received his Bachelor of Arts from the University of British Columbia, his M.A. and Ph.D. degrees from Stanford University. He is currently professor and head of the department of political science at the University of Calgary, where he has worked since 1973. Professor Gibbins has written extensively on western Canadian politics, constitutional developments, and

Senate reform. Recent works include: *Meech Lake and Canada: Perspectives from the West (ed.); Conflict and Unity: An Introduction to Canadian Political Life and Regionalism: Territorial Politics in Canada and the United States.*

MARGARET GILLETT Ed.D., LL.D., is Macdonald Professor of Education at McGill University, and founding director of the McGill Centre for Research and Teaching on Women. For more than twenty years, she has been active in women's affairs on campus, teaching women's studies, helping to initiate a survey on women, contributing to the establishment of the Senate Committee on Women, and writing the first history of women at any Canadian university. This work, *We Walked Very Warily: A History of Women at McGill* (1981) has been supplemented by *A Fair Shake: Autobiographical Essays by McGill Women* (1984), which she co-edited with Kay Sibbald. The most recent of her eight books is *Dear Grace: A Romance of History* (1986). The book is based on letters to Grace Ritchie, a pioneer woman student at McGill (B.A. 1888), and close friend of Maude Abbott and Carrie Derick, whose biographies Dr. Gillett presents here.

SUSAN HOECKER-DRYSDALE, Ph.D., is associate professor of sociology, Concordia University, Montreal, Quebec, where she teaches courses in sociological theory and women's studies. She is currently completing a biography of Harriet Martineau (1802–1876), first woman sociologist (British), and is working on *The Sociology of Harriet Martineau.* She lives in Montreal with John Drysdale, also a sociologist, and their son David who is pursuing biology/environmental studies.

ROY W. HORNOSTY is associate professor of sociology at McMaster University. He is interested in sociological theory, history of sociology, and the sociology of work, with emphasis on occupational ideologies and feminization.

GILLIAN KRANIAS presently works as public education coordinator with a community based environmental organization in Toronto. She obtained her B.A. from Concordia University (1988), where she focused on studying the relationship between science, society and the environment. Her continuing work aims to encourage individuals in identifying and acting upon a sense of responsibility for the well being of the human community and planetary environment — all from a feminist perspective.

LOUISE LAFORTUNE is a researcher and teacher of mathematics at CEGEP André-Laurendeau, Montreal. She is also the provincial co-ordinator of MOIFEM (Mouvement international pour les femmes et l'enseignement mathématique). After a B.Sc. in math (1973), she became interested in the history of women mathematicians, and completed an M.Sc. in 1988. She published a research report "L'enseignement des mathématiques aux adultes: étude des methodes pédagogiques et des attitudes des enseignants et enseignantes." (1988), and edited *Femmes et mathématique* (1986), and *Quelles différences* (1989).

BERTRUM H. MACDONALD is assistant professor, School of Library and Information Studies, Dalhousie University, Halifax. He holds graduate degrees in the history of science, and library and information science. His current research interests focus on publishing history and the dissemination of information in Victorian Canada. He was assistant director for the project which led to the publication of *Science and Technology in Canadian History: A Bibliography of Primary Sources to 1914.*

SUSAN A. MCDANIEL, Ph.D., is a professor of sociology at the University of Alberta. Previously, she was on faculty at the University of Waterloo and, in 1981, was a recipient of that university's Distinguished Teacher Award. She was also the first recipient of the Thérèse Casgrain Research Fellowship in 1987–88. In 1988, she was honoured as Professional Woman of the Year in Kitchener-Waterloo, Ontario. She is the author of two books and more than sixty scholarly articles. Her work is in the areas of women's issues, aging, and childbearing and reproduction.

BARBARA MEADOWCROFT is an Adjunct Fellow at the Simone de Beauvoir Institute, Concordia University. She has a Ph.D. in English Literature from McGill University. She is working on a project about Montreal women artists, and has published an article on Ethel Seath and the catalogue essay for the Mabel Lockerby Retrospective Exhibition at Gallerie Walter Klinkhoff, Montreal.

KAREN MESSING is professor of genetics at the Department of Biological Sciences at the Université du Québec à Montréal and co-directs, with Donna Mergler, the GRABIT, which does research on workplace effects on health. She received her Ph.D. from McGill University in 1975, and studied genetics of fruit flies, yeast, and fungal pathogens of mosquitoes before turning to effects of workplace pollutants on the genes of workers. She was a founding member of the Interdisciplinary Research Group in Feminist Studies at the Université du Québec à Montréal in 1977. With Donna Mergler, she initiated and taught the first course on Biology and Women in North America, in 1972. Since 1981, she has done research on women's occupational health: workplace-induced reproductive damage, biological effects of women's traditional work, and the question of biological bases for the sexual division of labour in the workplace.

NEIL NEVITTE is professor of political science at the University of Calgary. His current research interests relate to politics and value change in advanced industrial states, and, with Roger Gibbins, he is completing *New Elites in Old States* (Oxford University Press, forthcoming 1990).

DIANA PEDERSEN was educated at the University of British Columbia and Carleton University, receiving her Ph.D. in history in 1987. She has published several articles on women's history, and the uses of photography as historical documents. She has taught at Queen's University, and has done contract work for the National Archives of Canada and the Museum of Civilization. She is currently employed as assistant professor of history at the University of Western

Ontario.

MARTHA PHEMISTER was educated at the University of New Brunswick and Carleton University, where she developed her interests in visual history and art history. She has worked as a museum consultant and as an archivist for the Ottawa City Archives and the Documentary Art and Photography Division, National Archives of Canada. She is currently working in the Architectural History Branch, Canadian Parks Service.

MARLENE F. RAYNER-CANHAM, B.Sc. (Waterloo) is an instructional assistant in physics at Sir Wilfred Grenfell College, Corner Brook, Newfoundland. Her main interest is the history of women in science; she has co-authored a review on Maria Goeppert-Meyer, and has recently co-authored a full biography of Harriet Brooks, which she hopes to publish. She is currently researching other women nuclear scientists.

GEOFFREY W. RAYNER-CANHAM, Ph.D. (Imperial College, London) is a Professor of Chemistry at Sir Wilfred Grenfell College, Corner Brook, Newfoundland. He has published extensively in the field of chemical education, and has received two national awards for chemistry teaching. He is the senior author of a pair of Canadian high school chemistry textbooks, and has also written several historical studies of science, and co-authored a biography of Harriet Brooks.

JOAN P. SCOTT is a member of the Biology Department of Memorial University of Newfoundland, Canada, who regularly teaches undergraduate and graduate courses in Women's Studies. Her new course on Women and Science has recently been approved for inclusion in the Women's Studies Minor degree at Memorial. She is on leave from the university for two years, 1988–1990, as a Research Analyst at the Canadian Advisory Council on the Status of Women, in Ottawa. She is also finishing a Ph.D. thesis on the careers of women and men who are bioscience faculty in 27 of the larger Canadian universities.

NANCY SCHUMANN is a teacher of French, English, and special education. She received her B.A. in French from Bucknell University, and her M.A. in French from Middlebury College, Vermont. She enjoys nature, birdwatching, and the arts.

ROSE SHEININ, a fellow of the Royal Society of Canada, was a professor in the department of microbiology, faculty of medicine, and vice-dean of the school of graduate studies at the University of Toronto. She is currently academic vice rector at Concordia University. Dr. Sheinin has long been interested in women in science and technology, and, in addition to her numerous scientific articles, has published papers on the history of women in medicine in Toronto.

ERNST W. STIEB is professor and associate dean, faculty of pharmacy, University of Toronto. He is interested in the history of professional, cultural, and technical aspects of pharmacy; historical study of pharmacy organizations, education, journalism, and legislation.

EDWINNA VON BAEYER is an Ottawa writer specializing in landscape history. Among her works are *Rhetoric and Roses, A History of Canadian Gardening, 1900–1930*; *Ontario Rural Society 1867–1930, A Thematic Index of Selected Ontario Agricultural Periodicals*; and *A Selected Bibliography for Garden History in Canada*. She has also written numerous articles for newspapers, magazines and journals on historical topics and contemporary issues in her field, and has recently completed a manuscript on William Lyon Mackenzie King's years on his Kingsmere country estate.

Notes and Acknowledgements

Ainley • Last in the Field?

ACKNOWLEDGEMENTS

Research for this article was supported by a pilot project grant from CRIAW (1984), a post-doctoral fellowship SSHRC (1985), and a SSHRC Strategic Grant (1986–88). I thank David Ainley and Mary Baldwin for their encouragement and support. I am grateful to Robert Michel, Nellie Reiss, Ann Habbick (McGill), Sharon Larade (University of Toronto), Joan Burke (ROM), Gertrude MacLaren (University of Alberta), and many others for helping me obtain information, and to all the scientists who answered my letters and/or agreed to talk about their own, or their colleagues' experiences.

NOTES

1. On early Canadian natural history, see George Basalla, "The Spread of Western Science," *Science* 156 (May 1967):611–621; Carl Berger, *Science, God and Nature in Victorian Canada* (Toronto: University of Toronto Press, 1983); M.G. Ainley, "From Natural History to Avian Biology: Canadian Ornithology, 1860–1950," Chapter 1, unpublished Ph.D. thesis, McGill University, 1985; Suzanne Zeller, *Inventing Canada: Early Victorian Science and the Idea of a Transcontinental Nation* (Toronto: University of Toronto Press, 1987); the professionalization of a discipline has often been considered by historians and sociologists of science as a measure of its maturity. Among the many useful sources on disciplines and professions, see: J. Ben-David and A. Zloczower, "Universities and Academic Systems in Modern Societies," *Archives européennes de sociologie* 3 (1962):45–82; J.D. Beer and W.D. Lewis, "Aspects of the Professionalization of Science," in K.S. Lynn et al, eds., *The Professions in America* (Boston: Houghton-Mifflin, 1965), pp. 110–130; G. Lemaine, ed., *Perspectives on the Emergence of Scientific Disciplines* (Paris: Mouton, 1976); E. Mendelsohn, "The Emergence of Science as a Profession in Nineteenth Century

Europe," in K. Hill, ed., *Management of Scientists* (Boston: Beacon Press, 1964), pp. 3–48; D. Outram, "Politics and Vocation: French Science, 1793–1830," *The British Journal for the History of Science* 13 (1980):27–43; N. Reingold, "Definitions and Speculations: The Professionalization of Science in America in the Nineteenth Century," in A. Oleson and S.C. Brown, eds., *The Pursuit of Knowledge in the Early American Republic* (Baltimore: The Johns Hopkins University Press, 1976), pp. 33–68; R.A. Stebbins, "The Amateur: Two Sociological Definitions," *Pacific Sociological Review* 20 (1977):583–605; R. Kargon, *Enterprise and Expertise: Science in Victorian Manchester* (Baltimore: Johns Hopkins University Press, 1978).

2. Lorraine C. Smith, "Canadian Women Natural Scientists: Why Not?" *The Canadian Field Naturalist* 90 (1976):1. Smith refers to nineteen women honoured by an exhibition at the National Museum of Natural Sciences in 1975, International Women's Year; she also lists a few others who made "significant contributions" to natural science studies in Canada.

3. Zeller mentions some of the early known women scientists. As most of them did not publish in their own names, but rather, sent specimens and descriptions to other naturalists, their work became incorporated into general scientific knowledge.

4. See Basalla.

5. Ibid.; see also Trevor H. Levere and R.A. Jarrell, *A Curious Field Book: Science and Society in Canadian History* (Toronto: Oxford University Press, 1974).

6. P.L. Farber, *The Emergence of Ornithology as a Scientific Discipline, 1760–1850* (Boston: D. Reidel, 1982), p. 10.

7. J.L. Baillie, "Naturalists on Hudson Bay," *Beaver* (December 1946):36–39; Ainley.

8. Native women were familiar with plants and animals. They snared birds and mammals and prepared animal skins. See Sylvia Van Kirk: *Many Tender Ties: Women in Fur Trade Society, 1670–1870* (Winnipeg: Watson & Dwyer, 1980).

9. Sir. W.J. Hooker, *Flora Boreali Americana* (London: Henry G. Bohn, 1829–40), 2 vols.; R.A. Jarrell, "The Rise and Decline of Science at Quebec," *Histoire Sociale/Social History* 10 (1977):77–91; J.S. Pringle, "Anne Mary Perceval (1790–1876), an Early Botanical Collector in Lower Canada," *Canadian Horticultural History* 1 (1985): 7–27. On American women botanists and their correspondence with Darlington and Torrey, see S.G. Kohlstedt, "In From the Periphery: American Women in Science, 1830–1880," *Signs* 4 (1978):81–96.

10. Pringle, p. 9.

11. M.M. Whiting, "Early Collection of Plants in Prince Edward Island," *Kew Bulletin* 3 (1948): 236.

12. Zeller, p. 233.

13. Marion Fowler, *The Embroidered Tent: Five Gentlewomen in Early Canada* (Toronto: House of Anansi, 1982), p. 52.

14. Ibid., p. 67.

15. Père Louis-Marie, "L'herbier de la soeur Marie-de-Sainte-Amelie, s.c.," *Annales de l'acfas*, 7 (1941):97; Copies of the Bernard Boivin papers at the Herbier Louis-Marie, Laval University (originals at the Hunt Institute of Botany, Pittsburg), contain much information on Quebec nuns who were botanists.

16. Zeller; also see D.E. Allen, *The Naturalist in Britain: A Social History* (London: Penguin Books, 1978).

17. W.C. King to T.W. Tru, 20 December 1892, Smithsonian Institution Archives, RU 192, Permanent Administrative Files. Unfortunately, no record of Charlotte Flett King's major collection was found in the Smithsonian Institution Archives. Roderick Macfarlane, retired chief factor of the Hudson's Bay Company, several times mentions "Mrs. W.C. King" as a collector around 1890, in his "Notes on the Mammals and Birds of Northern Canada," in Charles Mair, *Through the Mackenzie Basin: A Narrative of the Athabasca and Peace River Treaty Expedition of 1899* (Toronto: William Brigs, 1908), pp. 153–448. The only personal information on Charlotte Flett King came from a reference in her husband's file, at the Hudson Bay Company Archives, Winnipeg, which indicates that his "usefulness to the Company has been hindered by being married to a Native of interfering manners," HBCA, A. 12/FI 30/3, Judith Beatty to Author, 18 December 1985.

18. Moira O'Neill, "A Lady's Life on a Ranche," *Blackwood's Edinburgh Magazine* 163 (January 1898):1–16; C.S. Houston, "The Wemyss Sisters: Saskatchewan's First Lady Birdwatchers," *Blue Jay* 39 (March 1981): 25–29; Marion E. Moodie file, Glenbow-Alberta Institute Archives; P.A. Taverner — Wm. Rowan correspondence; Elsie Cassels — Wm. Rowan correspondence, William Rowan papers, University of Alberta Archives (hereafter UAA).

19. William Coleman, *Life Science in the 19th Century: Problems of Form, Function and Transformation* (Cambridge: Cambridge University Press, 1977); P.L. Farber, pp. xv–xxi; "The Transformation of Natural History in the Nineteenth Century," *Journal of the History of Biology* 15 (1982):145–52.

20. See Zeller.

21. On Canadian women's early education, see Margaret Gillett, *We Walked Very Warily: A History of Women at McGill* (Montreal: Eden Press, 1981), pp.1–18; Although no specific work exists on science education in Canada, information on this subject can be found in the general histories of Canadian universities. Most of these were written, however, before women's education and science education were considered as separate analytical categories.

22. M.W. Rossiter, "Sexual Segregation in the Sciences: Some Data and a Model," *Signs* 4 (1978):146.

23. E.M. Spieker, "Memorial to Grace Anne Stewart (1893–1970)," pp. 1–2. Copy, Department of Geology Files, UAA.

24. Allen to Stewart, 17 June 1924, J.A. Allen Papers, UAA; in the U.S., women had been teaching geology at women's colleges (1890s) and working on various state geological surveys since the first decade of the twentieth century.

25. Oral History Interview, B–74–0022, University of Toronto, 1973.

26. The only other woman in paleontology at the Royal Ontario Museum (which was affiliated with the University of Toronto) was Margaret Howell, the secretary of the department. Later, as Margaret H. Mitchell, she became a well-known volunteer investigator in ornithology.

27. Joan Burke, personal communication.

28. Later, this museum formed the basis of the Victoria Memorial Museum, established in 1911, the precursor of the National Museum of Canada. For a history of the Survey, see Morris Zaslow, *Reading the Rocks* (Toronto: Macmillan, 1975). Zaslow, like many other historians, does not deal with gender issues at the Survey. In fact, he ignores Alice Wilson's long-standing problems with the administration.

29. Digby J. MacLaren, FRSC. "Helen Belyea, 1913–86," *Transactions of the Royal Society of Canada* Series v, Vol. II (1987): p. 199.

30. Ibid., p. 200.

31. Interview with J.D. Aitken, 19 June 1987.

32. P.S. Warren to W.H. Johns, 12 January 1954, Department of Geology Files, (UAA).

33. Ibid.

34. Interview with Kyra Emo, 2 May 1989.

35. Joan Dicky, who worked for Shell (1954–58), also "retired" to be married. In contrast to the oil industry, soft-rock geology, the mining industry would not hire women, because miners remained superstitious about women descending into the mine shafts. Interview with Dorothy Wyer, 2 May 1989.

36. G. Donnay, "Preface," *Directory of Canadian Women Geologists*, McGill University, 1984, p. ii.

37. Pat Townshend, personal communication; correspondence regarding proposed salary scale and personnel, between G.W. Scarth and Dean J.J. O'Neill, Scarth to O'Neill, 15 February 1939; Muriel V. Roscoe to C. James, 3 January 1941, RG 2, C. 97, McGill University Archives (MUA).

38. Interviews with Roscoe, July 1986, August 1988. On Roscoe's wardenship at Royal Victoria College, see Margaret Gillett, pp. 194–202.

39. Ralph Estey, personal communication.

40. F.H. Montgomery to B. Boivin, 8 February 1976, Boivin papers, Herbier Louis-Marie, Laval University.

41. Oral History Interview, B-78-0003, University of Toronto. During the war, like most other botanists at the university, Forward gave up her own research to conduct milkweed and dandelion investigations, part of the Canadian government's effort at research into natural rubber.

42. L.M. Hunter, CV, Canadian Federation of University Women papers, National Archives of Canada, NAC, MG 28, I 196.

43. R. Buller to H. Gussow, 7 October 1932, PAC, MG 30, B104, Gussow Papers, correspondence 1932–37.

44. Esther Fraser, "Silver and Other Organisms," *New Trail* 32 (1976):5–7.

45. Ibid., p. 7; interview with Silver Keeping, 18 July 1985.

46. G.W. Scarth to Dean J.J. O'Neill, 25 July 1938, MUA, RG 2, C. 62.

47. Vicky Marcoc, "Education of Quebec Women in the 1920s, 1930s, and 1940s," unpublished paper, 1989.

48. CV, CFUW files, NAC.

49. In 1886, the "Experimental Farm Station Act" of the federal government received royal assent, and five experimental stations were established across the country. The Central Experimental Farm was located in Ottawa, and James Fletcher was appointed botanist and entomologist. On Faith Fyles, see W.J. Cody *et al, Systematics in Agriculture Canada, at Ottawa, 1886–1986* (Biosystematics Research Centre, Agriculture Canada, Historical Record Series No. 28 (1986):11.

50. Ralph Estey, personal communication.

51. Patricia Stephenson, *Hidden Voices.* (Catalogue of Abstracts of Oral History Recordings, 1980), p. 22; Estey, personal communication.

52. Cody *et al.,* p. 38.

53. Ibid.

54. Ibid.; Estey, personal communication.

55. J. Ginns, "Irene Mounce, 1894–1987," *Mycologia* 80 (1988):608.

56. Estey, personal communication. The exact career path (advancement and pay) is difficult to determine. Personnel records of government employees are kept only for "important people," such as directors, or other public persons "judged to be of historical value." Moreover, "records of an individual are not available to a third party until twenty years after their death." Privacy Act, section 3 M. By some miracle, five file cards labelled "Personnel Index" pertaining to Dr. Irene Mounce survived in the Department of Agriculture papers at the NAC; these list the content of files no longer in existence, and give some information on her advancement and pay.

57. "Presidential Address — Fifty Years of Canadian Zoology," *Transactions of the Royal Society of Canada* Section IV, II (1917):1–14.

58. D.B. McMillan, "Battle, Helen, Irene," *The Canadian Encyclopedia* 2nd edition, Vol. I (Edmonton: Hurtig Publishing, 1988), p. 186; interview with Helen Battle, 13 June 1985. Unfortunately, Battle's papers got "lost" when her office was cleared out after retirement. Dr. Barbara Bain, personal communication.

59. Dixie Pelluet, interview with author, 16 July 1986. On 9 July 1984, Professor Judith Fingard of Dalhousie University also interviewed Pelluet; see her "Gender and Inequality at Dalhousie: Faculty Women Before 1950," *Dalhousie Review* (Winter 1984–85):687–703.

60. Pelluet to A.E. Kerr, 25 November 1952, Dalhousie University Archives (DUA), MS-1-3-C-381.

61. Interview with Joan Marsden, 28 November 1986.

62. Joan Marsden, "A Good Place For Me," in Margaret Gillett and Kay Sibbald, *Fair Shake: Autobiographical Essays by McGill Women* (Montreal: Eden Press, 1984), p. 130.

63. Helen I. Battle, "Zoology in Canada in Retrospect," *Le Naturaliste Canadien* 91 (1964):183.

64. McGill University Calendars; interview with Joan Marsden.

65. UAA, Zoology Department Files. Most of Hughes' problems were owing to the Depression, when men and women had their pay cut back, and many people, including Canadian civil servants, lost their jobs. Hughes' department head, Dr. William Rowan, also suffered. He received no salary increase on his appointment to full professor in 1931, and, like other academics at that time, he saw his pay actually reduced, and then frozen for a number of years.

66. Robert Newton to John Macdonald, ca. March 1946, Department of Zoology File, UAA.

67. Scientists became fascinated with the complexity of marine organisms following the 1872–75 Challenger expedition to the deep seas. Biological stations for the detailed study of such organisms were established in several countries. On Canadian marine biology and fisheries research see K. Johnstone, *The Aquatic Explorers: A History of the Fisheries Research Board of Canada* (Toronto: University of Toronto Press, 1977); Frances Anderson, "The Demise of the Fisheries Research Board of Canada: A Case Study of Canadian Research Policy," *Scientia Canadensis* 27 (December 1984):151–56; A.W.H. Needler, "Biological Station, Nanaimo, B.C., 1908–1958," *Journal of the Fisheries Research Board of Canada* 15 (1958):759; J.L. Hart, "Biological Station, St. Andrews, N.B. 1908–1958," *Journal of the Fisheries Research Board of Canada* 15 (1958): 1127–1161. An "in-house" history of the Board and its personnel is H.B. Hachey, "History of the Fisheries Research Board of Canada" MS Report Series (Biological) no. 843. On American women and marine biological work, see M.W. Rossiter, *Women Scientists in America: Struggles and Strategies to 1940* (Baltimore: Johns Hopkins University Press, 1982),pp. 47–49, 58.

68. Canadian women published papers on taxonomy, distribution, physiology and biochemistry, as well as the physical and chemical factors present in marine environments.

69. G.M. Watney to author, 11 November 1985.

70. Ibid.

71. V.S. Black to author, 15 February 1986.

72. Leim to Principal Morgan, 19 August 1936, RG 2, C 63, Department of Zoology, MUA.

73. Interview with Delphine Maclellan, 19 August 1988.

74. Cody *et al*, p. 60.

75. Ibid., pp. 61, 62.

76. In the United States, the Department of Agriculture established a Division of Economic Ornithology and Mammalogy in 1886. In Canada, in spite of government interest in the study and protection of birds and fur-bearing animals, ornithology became important only after birds were found to be excellent environmental indicators (the post-DDT period).

77. Royal Ontario Museum Archives (ROM), J.H. Fleming Papers, H.H. Mitchell to J.H. Fleming, 20 September 1921.

78. F. Bradshaw, in *Annual Report of the Game Commissioner*, Department of Agriculture, Province of Saskatchewan, 1922, p. 57.

79. K.E. Ball to author, 7 March 1983; 6 April 1983. Ball's grandfather was W.E.

Saunders, the noted London, Ontario, naturalist. As a child, Ball spent much time in the field with him. On career opportunities in ornithology, see my "La professionnalisation de l'ornithologie américaine, 1870–1979," unpublished M.Sc. thesis, Université de Montréal, 1980.

80. V.C. Wynne-Edwards to A.L. Rand, 20 May 1946, National Museum of Natural Sciences (NMNS). Wynne-Edwards was not trying to put down women; in fact, he was quite supportive. His letter simply echoes the prevailing attitude at the time.

81. Francis R. Cook, "Editor's Addendum" to Bill Gummer et al., "A Tribute to Violet Humphreys, 1919–1984," The Canadian Field Naturalist 100 (April-June 1986), p. 279.

82. See my "D'assistantes anonymes à chercheures scientifique: une rétrospective sur la place des femmes en sciences," Cahier de recherche sociologique 4 (1986):55–71; Ann Shteir, "Botany in the Breakfast Room: Women and Early Nineteenth Century British Plant Study," in Pnina Abir-Am and Dorinda Outram, eds., Uneasy Careers and Intimate Lives: Women in Science, 1789–1979 (New Brunswick, N.J.: Rutgers University Press, 1987) pp. 31–43.

83. Hanna Papanek, "Men, Women and Work: Reflections on the Two-Person Career," in Joan Huber, ed., Changing Women in a Changing Society (Chicago: The University of Chicago Press, 1973), pp. 90–110.

84. "Mrs. Fantham," n.d. typescript attached to a letter from L.W. Douglas to J.J. O'Neill, 21 February 1938. RG 2, C63, Zoology Department, 1938–39, MUA.

85. O'Neill to Brittain, 12 November 1937.

86. O'Neill to Douglas, 22 February 1938.

87. Ibid., 8 March 1938.

88. I am grateful to Dr. Mary Needler Arai, granddaughter of Edith Berkeley, for information and documentation on her grandmother's life and work. The October 1971 issue of the Journal of the Fisheries Research Board of Canada is dedicated to Edith and Cyril Berkeley.

89. Interview with Mary Needler Arai, 11 August 1985; interview with A.W.H. Needler, 22 July 1986.

90. Torontoniensis, 1924, p. 22.

91. See my "Margaret H. Mitchell," in Martin McNicholl and John Cranmer-Byng, eds., Historical Perspectives on Ontario Ornithology [forthcoming].

92. Ottawa Naturalist 29 (1915–16):14–18, 21–29.

93. Ainley, Ph. D. thesis, pp. 166–67.

94. D.H. Speirs, personal communication.

95. Ainley, Ph.D. thesis, pp. 170–73.

96. NAC, CFUW, File on Fellowship Committee, MG 28, 1196, Volume 10.

Chu and MacDonald • The Public Record

ACKNOWLDEGEMENTS

An earlier version of this paper was presented at the fifth Kingston Conference on the History of Canadian Science and Technology, Ottawa, Ontario, October 1987, and published in *Scientia Canadensis* 12 (Fall/Winter 1988): 75–96.

NOTES

1. Studies which bridge the gap in the historical treatment of women in Canadian science and technology include: Marianne Gosztonyi Ainley, "Canadian Women Natural Scientists 1900–1950: A Pilot Study," paper read at the fourth Kingston Conference on the History of Canadian Science and Technology, Kingston, Ontario, October 1985; Marianne Gosztonyi Ainley, "Women Scientists in Canada: The Need for Documentation," *Resources for Feminist Research* 15,3 (1986): 7–8; Diana Pedersen and Martha Phemister, "Women and Photography in Ontario, 1839–1929: A Case Study of the Interaction of Gender and Technology," *Scientia Canadensis* 4,1 (1985): 27–52. Philip C. Enros, comp., in his *Biobibliography of Publishing Scientists in Ontario Between* 1914 and 1939 (Thornhill, Ont., 1985) identifies women scientists; Sheila Bertram, comp., *Women in Pure and Applied Science Bibliography* (Edmonton, 1987) is a bibliography of approximately 2,500 entries, and includes Canadian coverage, primarily of works on modern women. It is frequently updated, and may be obtained by writing to Dr. Sheila Bertram, Dean, Faculty of Library and Information Studies, University of Alberta, Edmonton, Alberta, T6G 2J4.

2. R. Alan Richardson and Bertrum H. MacDonald, *Science and Technology in Canadian History: A Bibliography of Primary Sources to* 1914 (Thornhill, Ont., 1987).

3. We recognize that because we focus on the publishing history, women whose only contributions were through building natural history collections, or whose work was subsumed by others, are excluded.

4. The *Bibliography* does not include medical publications (except as noted) because other reference works have covered that area. See, for example, Charles G. Roland, *Secondary Sources in the History of Canadian Medicine: A Bibliography* (Waterloo, Ont., 1984), and Charles G. Roland and Paul Potter, *An Annotated Bibliography of Canadian Medical Periodicals, 1826–1975* (Toronto, 1979).

5. The identification of women authors was conducted by selecting appropriate names from the author catalogue of the *Bibliography*. This catalogue lists the authority (or standardized) name of each author and any variant name(s) by which an author may be known. A variant name acts as a "cross-reference," directing a user to the authoritative form of an author's name, under which all the works by that author are listed. For example, all works by JULIAN DURHAM

are grouped under the standardized heading HENSHAW, JULIA WILMOTTE, 1869–1937.

6. Name dictionaries included: E.G. Wythycombe, *The Oxford Dictionary of English Christian Names* (Oxford, 1945); Charles Earle Funk, *What's the Name, Please? A Guide to the Correct Pronunciation of Current Prominent Names* (New York, 1936); and C.O. Sylvester Mawson, *International Book of Names* (New York, 1942).

7. The subject about which authors were writing sometimes helped us to determine the sex of an author whose name was "indeterminate"; however, since information on the exact time women began to publish on specific subjects is not available, subject information could not always help resolve the problem.

8. Ainley, "Canadian Women Natural Scientists, 1900–1950"; Ainley, "Women Scientists in Canada."

9. Enros.

10. Jonathan R. Cole and Harriet Zuckerman, "The Productivity Puzzle: Persistence and Change in Patterns of Publication of Men and Women Scientists," in Marjorie W. Steinkamp and Martin L. Maehr, eds., *Women in Science* (Greenwich, Conn., 1984), p. 217. (Advances in Motivation and Achievement, v. 2).

11. Lady of the Principality, *The History of Wales: Containing Some Interesting Facts Concerning the Existence of a Welsh Tribe Among the Aborigines of America. Arranged as a Catechism for Young Persons* (Shrewsbury, 1833).

12. Anna Brownell Jameson, *Winterstudien und Sommerstreifereien in Canada* (Braunschweig, 1839), 3 vols.

13. Eliza Maria Jones, *Dairying for Profit; or, The Poor Man's Cow* (Montreal, 1892); *Lecture on Co-Operative Dairying and Winter Dairying* (Montreal, 1893).

14. Harriet Sheppard published using the name "Mrs. Sheppard." She was the wife of William Sheppard, and one of the founders of the Literary and Historical Society of Quebec. Her name was confirmed in W. Stewart Wallace, *The Macmillan Dictionary of Canadian Biography* (Toronto, 1978), rev., enl., and updated by W.A. McKay, 4th ed.

15. As far as we know, women were involved in a limited number of scientific fields. Lois Barber Arnold, in *Four Lives in Science: Women's Education in the Nineteenth Century* (New York, 1984). notes that "as far as scientific fields are concerned, American women were found almost exclusively in the fields of natural history and the biological and medical sciences throughout the nineteenth century." Sally Gregory Kohlstedt, in her paper "In from the Periphery: American Women in Science, 1830–1880," *Signs* 4,1 (1978); 81–96, found that of the women interested in science in the early nineteenth century, there were more in natural history and agriculture than in the physical sciences, a fact that applied to men as well.

16. Helene Cummins, Susan A. McDaniel, and Rachelle Sender Beauchamp, "Women Inventors in Canada in the 1980s," *Canadian Review of Sociology & Anthropology* 25,3 (1988): 393.

17. Eliza Maria Jones, *Laiterie payante, ou, La vache du pauvre* (Trois Rivieres, 1894); Jameson; Cora Elisabeth (Robinet) Millet, "Du pâturage du trèfle et de la luzerne," *Agriculteur; journal officiel de la Chambre d'agriculture du Bas-Canada* 13,3 (1860): 56–8. 18. Although *Agriculteur* was the only French language Canadian journal that figured in our study, other Canadian French language journals appear in the *Bibliography*, such as *Le naturaliste canadien* and *Abeille canadienne, journal de littérature et de sciences.*

19. Katharine Jeanette Bush (b. 1845) received the first doctorate in zoology awarded to a woman by Yale University, in 1901. Anna Botsford Comstock (1854–1930), an entomologist, received a B.S. from Cornell University in 1885, and an honourary doctorate from Hobart College, Geneva, N.Y. She also became the first woman on faculty at Cornell University (department of entomology). Ruth Holden (1890–1917), a botanist, was a student at Radcliffe College. Carlotta Joaquina Maury (1874–1938), a geologist, studied at Radcliffe College and University of Paris, and received a Ph.B. in 1896, and a Ph.D. in 1902, both from Cornell University. Ida Helen Ogilvie (1874–1963), a geologist, received an A.B. (1896 or 1900) from Bryn Mawr College, and a Ph.D. in 1903 from Columbia University. Jennie Maria (Arms) Sheldon (b. 1852), a geologist, was a special student at MIT between 1877 and 1881 for at least two years, and also a special lab student at the Boston Society of Natural History. Erminnie Adele Smith (1836–1886), an anthropologist, graduated from Emma Willard's Troy Female Seminary (New York) in 1858, and also studied in Germany and won the undergraduate prize for geology and mineralogy at Vassar College. Anna Murray Vail (b. 1863), a botanist, studied privately, mostly in Europe.

20. Baker's thesis and publications were on the aesthetics of light and colour; Benson's thesis was on "The Rates of Reactions in Solutions Containing Ferrous Sulphate, Potassium, Iodine and Chromic Acid." See Judy Mills and Irene Dombra, *University of Toronto Doctoral Theses, 1897–1967* (Toronto, 1968), p. 131, p. 24.

21. Further discussion on Menten's work is found in John Walkley and Chris Hewer, "Maud Leonora Menten: Her Contributions to Biochemistry," paper read at the fifth Kingston Conference on the History of Canadian Science and Technology, Ottawa, Ontario, October 1987. *The National Union Catalogue Pre-1956 Imprints* provides two spellings of Menten's middle name, Lenora and Leonora.

22. Although the categories were not always clear-cut, the educators were Emma Sophia Baker, Clara Cynthia Benson, Harriet Brooks, Anna Botsford Comstock, Mattie Rose Crawford, Clara Eaton Cummings, Carrie Matilda Derick, Elizabeth Frame, Clara E. (Speight) Humberstone, Margaret Macdonald, Annie Louise Macleod, Carlotta Joaquina Maury, Maud Lenora Menten, Ida Helen Ogilvie, Mary McKay Scott, and Jennie Maria (Arms) Sheldon; the assistants were Katharine Jeanette Bush and Alice Cunningham Fletcher (museum assistants), Faith Fyles and Annie L. Saunders (Department of Agriculture, Ottawa). The literary authors were Marie Adelaide Brown, Helen Mar Johnson, Helen M. Merrill, Susanna Moodie, Amelia MacLean Paget, and Catharine Parr

Traill (also a botanist). The journalists include Julia Wilmotte Henshaw (also a botanist and geographer), Ella Cora Hind, and Rosalind Watson Young (a scientist turned "volunteer investigator.") Women on editorial boards were Alice Cunningham Fletcher, Mary Basset Hodges, Mary McKay Scott, and Anna Murray Vail. Helen Henman was secretary of the Thornbury Horticultural Society (Ontario).

23. Pnina G. Abir-Am and Dorinda Outram, eds., *Uneasy Careers and Intimate Lives: Women in Science, 1789–1979* (New Brunswick, N.J., 1987); Arnold; Kohlstedt; Margaret W. Rossiter, *Women Scientists in America: Struggles and Strategies to* 1940 (Baltimore, 1982).

24. For example, Henrietta F. Buller, wife of Edmund R. Buller (writer on apiculture); Faith Fyles, daughter of a naturalist; Lucy Lawson, first wife of George Lawson, a botanist; Dolores Gonzales Leon, wife of Luis G. Leon, an astronomer; Alice B. (Rich) Northrop, married to John I. Northrop, a botanist; and Mrs. (Harriet) Sheppard, wife of William Sheppard, one of the founders of the Literary and Historical Society of Quebec.

25. Mrs. Townsend, "A Woman's Experience," *Canadian Bee Journal Weekly and Poultry Weekly* 5,16 (1889–90): 361.

26. Elsie A. Dent, "Women's Work in Astronomy," *Royal Astronomical Society of Canada. Selected Papers and Proceedings* 13 (1902–3): 122–40.

27. Margaret W. Rossiter, "'Women's Work' in Science, 1880–1910," *Isis* 71,258 (1980): 383.

28. Kohlstedt.

29. Arnold; Rossiter, "Women Scientists in America."

30. Ainley's definitions of amateur and professional ornithologists have been adopted and slightly modified for this study. An amateur is "any author publishing . . . but having no institutional affiliation or financial support for research from any official source." A professional is any person occupied with scientific and technological study, having institutional affiliation with universities, museums, federal or state departments, or equivalent, and contributing to science and technology. See Marianne Gosztonyi Ainley, "The Contribution of the Amateur to North American Ornithology: A Historical Perspective," *Living Bird* 18th annual (1979-80): 168.

Gillett • Carrie Derick

ACKNOWLEDGEMENTS

I gratefully acknowledge the assistance of librarians Eleanor MacLean and Karla Kuklis and archivists Phebe Chartrand and Robert Michel.

NOTES

1. Statistics courtesy Dr. Stanley B. Frost, university historian.

2. The lone woman in medicine was Dr. Maude E. Abbott, curator of the Medical Museum, whose biography appears elsewhere in this volume; of the two in agriculture, one was an instructor in home dairying, the other an assistant in manual training; Carrie Derick was the only woman teaching a pure science.

3. Biographical data from Emily P. Weaver, "Pioneer Canadian Women," *The Canadian Magazine* (October 1917): 447–51; Mrs. A.F. Byers, "The Late Miss Carrie Derick," *The McGill News* 23, 3 (April 1942): 13–14; "Carrie M. Derick," *The Montreal Gazette* (November 11, 1941); Jean McKay Bannerman, *Leading Ladies Canada*, pp. 47–49; Maysie S. MacSporran, "McGill Women — Then and Now," *The McGill News* 31, 4 (Summer 1950): 13–17, 87; Blanche Evans Yates, "Through the Years," *The McGill News* 19, 4 (Summer 1938): 18–21, 66; Margaret Gillett, "Derick, Carrie Matilda," *The New Canadian Encyclopedia* (1984). Thanks to Marianne Ainley, Derick's curriculum vitae was discovered in the "Botany" file, MUA, RG 2, Peterson Papers.

4. She was one of an extremely talented group. Her class-mates included Maude Abbott, who became the first woman on staff in the faculty of medicine, and Elizabeth Binmore, one of the first women to earn an M.A. at McGill.

5. Minutes of the meeting of the board of governors, 25 September 1891, *Board of Governors Minute Book, 1891–1897,* p.67.

6. Minutes of the meeting of the board of governors, 25 March 1892, ibid., p.118.

7. Minutes of the meeting of the board of governors, 25 April 1896, *Board of Governors Minute Book, Feb.* 20, 1891–May 19, 1919, MUA Microfilm 2718, Reel #3.

8. Ibid. The Governors resolved "that F.H. Pitcher, B.A.Sc., be hereby appointed one of the Demonstrators in Physics for one year at a salary of seven hundred and fifty ($750)." However, they also appointed two other male demonstrators at $500.

9. Minutes of the meeting of the board of governors, 23 May 1896, item #5, *Minute Book, 1891–1897,* p.445.

10. Ibid.

11. Stephen Leacock, "The Dean's Dinner," verses written for Dean Moyse's dinner for professors, 29 October 1909.

12. Minutes of the meeting of the board of governors, 13 May 1904, *Minute*

Book, 1891–1919, p.287, and letter to Miss Derick from Principal Peterson, dated 16 May 1904, MUA RG 2 Bundle 6, p.364.

13. Minutes of the meeting of the board of governors, 25 January 1896, item #10.

14. Carrie M. Derick, "On the Border," *McGill University Magazine* 5, 1 (December 1905): 125–129.

15. Carrie M. Derick, "The Trees of McGill University," *The McGill News* (December 1929): 28.

16. Recounted to the author ca.1978 by the late Professor Bertha Meyers, Department of German, who knew Derick well.

17. Minutes of the meeting of the board of governors, 27 March 1911, *Minute Book,* 1891–1919, p.89.

18. Letter to Miss Derick, Arts Building from Principal Sir William Peterson, 26 February 1912, MUA RG 2, *Peterson Letter Book* 18, p.215.

19. Cf. Letter to Miss Derick from Principal Peterson, 2 May 1912, MUA RG 2, *Peterson Letter Book* 19, p.22.

20. Letter to Prof. Bradley Moore Davis, University of Pennsylvania, 13 June 1912, MUA RG 2 *Peterson Letter Book* 19, p.244.

21. Letter to Dean Russell, Teachers College, Columbia University, 30 April 1912, MUA RG 2, *Peterson Letter Book* 19, p.5.

22. Letter to Professor Thaxter, Department of Botany, Harvard University, 9 May 1912, MUA RG 2, *Peterson Letter Book* 19, p.75.

23. Ibid.

24. Letter to E.B. Greenshields, Esq. from Principal Peterson, 29 May 1912, MUA RG 2, *Peterson Letter Book* 19.

25. "Francis E. Lloyd," obituary, *Journal of the New York Botanical Garden* 48, 576 (December 1947): 292.

26. "Francis Ernest Lloyd," *Dictionary of British and Irish Botanists and Horticulturalists, including plant collectors and botanical artists,* Ray Desmond, ed. London: Taylor and Francis, 1977.

27. Letter to Dr. F.G. Harrison, Macdonald College, 3 May 1912, MUA RG 2, *Peterson Letter Book* 19.

28. Letter to Dr. C.R. Davenport, Station for Experimental Evolution, Cold Spring Harbour, Long Island, from Principal Peterson, 17 May 1912, MUA RG 2 *Peterson Letter Book* 19, p.127.

29. Letter to Prof. J.P.C. Southall, Auburn, Alabama, from Principal Peterson, 6 May 1912, MUA RG 2, *Peterson Letter Book* 19, p.43.

30. Letter to Mr. Peterson from William Van Horne, 1 June 1912, MUA MG 2013 1066/4.

31. Ibid.

32. Letter to Dr. F.P. Walton from Principal Peterson, 7 June 1912, MUA RG 2 *Peterson Letter Book* 19, p.197.

33. Minutes of the meeting of the board of governors, 12 June 1912, *Minute Book, 1891–1919,* p.131. 34. Letter to Dr. P.F. Walton from Principal Peterson, 4 June 1912, MUA RG 2 *Peterson Letter Book* 19, p.194.

35. Letter to Prof. Francis E. Lloyd from Principal Peterson, 13 June 1912, MUA RG 2 *Peterson Letter Book* 19, p.247.

36. Minutes of the meeting of the board of governors, 12 June 1912, *Minute Book, 1891–1919*, p.131.

37. Letter from W. Vaughan, secretary of the board of governors, to Miss C.M. Derick, 13 June 1912, quoted in a letter from Professor Lloyd to Dean Moyse, 24 December 1912, MUA RG 2, C20.

38. Minutes of the meeting of the board of governors, 9 October 1912.

39. Letter from Carrie M. Derick to Prof. Francis Lloyd, 22 December 1912, quoted in the letter from Profesor Lloyd to Dean Moyse. Peterson had advised Moyse on 17 October that it was only a "courtesy title granted to her by the Board," *Peterson Letter Book* 19, p.338.

40. Letter from Professor Lloyd to Dean Moyse, 24 December 1912.

41. Letter from Professor Derick to Professor Lloyd, 22 December 1912.

42. Letter from Professor Lloyd to Dean Moyse, 24 December 1912.

43. Letter from Francis E. Lloyd to Principal W. Peterson, 26 December 1912, MUA RG 2, C20.

44. Letter from C.M. Derick to Dr. C.F. Martin, acting principal, 29 October 1928, MUA RG 2, C62, 1927–33 — "Botany Department" and "Professor Carrie M. Derick," *McGill News* 10, 4 (September 1929): 17–18.

On her death on November 10th, 1941, the senate of McGill passed a resolution noting that she was the first woman to be appointed to the teaching staff, that she served "with devotion and distinction for thirty eight years and served the public causes she believed in with an equal zeal.

"Eminent in academic circles as a botanist and a geneticist, she was for a wider public an earnest apostle of education and, above all, a brave fighter for recognition of the full contribution women could make to our civilization."
Minutes of Senate, 17 December 1941, p.157.

45. In a letter to Lloyd, 9 January 1928, Derick said, "I have always thought that the title 'Professor of Morphological Botany' does not represent the variety and extent of my work . . . I consider myself justified in asking that I be in future styled 'Professor of Comparative Morphology and Genetics' . . ." She also forwarded the request to Principal Sir Arthur Currie, and it was approved.

Pedersen and Phemister • Women and Photography in Ontario

ACKNOWLEDGEMENTS

This paper has developed out of background research undertaken for a larger project on the use of the historical photograph as a primary document and source for women's history. We gratefully acknowledge the generous financial support of The Canada Council and the Ontario Heritage Foundation. We are indebted to Deborah Gorham and an anonymous reviewer for their careful and helpful readings of an earlier draft of this paper.

NOTES

1. The most important of these studies is Ruth Schwartz Cowan's *More Work for Mother: The Ironies of Household Technology from the Open Hearth to the Microwave* (New York, 1983). Its bibliographic essays are an invaluable introduction to the literature of the field.

2. Ruth Schwartz Cowan, "From Virginia Dare to Virginia Slims: Women and Technology in American Life," in Martha Moore Trescott, ed., *Dynamos and Virgins Revisited: Women and Technological Change in History* (Metuchen, N.J. and London, 1979), pp. 30–44. An earlier version appeared in W.B. Pickett, ed., *Technology at the Turning Point* (San Francisco, 1977).

3. Judith A. McGaw, "Women and the History of American Technology," *Signs* 7,4 (1982): 798–828.

4. Despite a burgeoning international literature on the history of photography, the question of women's response to this new technology is not one which has received any significant attention to date, the first signs of interest being shown by historians in the United States. See, for example, Amy S. Doherty, "Women in Focus: Early American Women Photographers," *Picturescope* 31,2 (1983): 50–56. In Canada, a few early women photographers who left substantial bodies of work have recently attracted some attention, and have even been made the subject of a travelling photograph exhibit. The most substantial study of an early Canadian woman photographer is Claire Weissman Wilks, *The Magic Box: The Eccentric Genius of Hannah Maynard* (Toronto, 1980). For brief biographical accounts and examples of the work of some other Canadian women photographers, see *Canadian Women's Studies/Les cahiers de la femme* 2,3 (1980), a special issue on photography. See also the exhibit catalogue by Laura Jones, *Rediscovery: Canadian Women Photographers, 1841–1941* (London Regional Art Gallery, 1983).

5. Lilly Koltun, "Pre-Confederation Photography in Toronto," *History of Photography* 2,3 (1978): 249. The standard reference work on the history of photography in Canada is Ralph Greenhill and Andrew Birrell, *Canadian Photography 1839-1920* (Toronto, 1979), a revised and expanded version of Greenhill's *Early Photography in Canada* (Toronto, 1965). See, in addition, Lilly

Koltun, ed., *Private Realms of Light: Amateur Photography in Canada* 1839–1940 (Toronto, 1984). Also useful are Andrew Birrell "Private Realms of Light: Canadian Amateur Photography, 1839–1940," *Archivaria* 17 (Winter 1983–4): 106–144; Jim Burant, 'Pre-Confederation Photography in Halifax, Nova Scotia,' *Journal of Canadian Art History* 4,1 (1977): 25–44; Koltun, "Pre-Confederation Photography," and Joan Schwartz, ed., "The Past in Focus: Photography and British Columbia, 1858–1914," a special issue of *BC Studies* 52 (Winter 1981–82).

6. See Beaumont Newhall, *The Daguerreotype in America,* 3rd rev. ed. (New York, 1976), Richard Rudisill, *Mirror Image: The Influence of the Daguerreotype in American Society* (Albuquerque, 1971), and Robert Taft, *Photography and the American Scene: A Social History,* 1839–1889 (New York, 1964).

7. Koltun, "Pre-Confederation Photography," p. 250.

8. 16 January 1850, cited in Lilly Koltun, "Pre-Confederation Photography in Toronto," a checklist compiled for the National Photography Collection, National Archives of Canada, 1976 (Finding Aid 40), hereinafter cited as Koltun, "Checklist."

9. Greenhill and Birrell, pp. 42–43.

10. "Cuthbert Bede" (The Rev Edward Bradley), *Photographic Pleasures* (London, 1855), p. 54, cited in ibid., p. 42.

11. Deborah Jean Warner, "Science Education for Women in Antebellum America," *Isis* 69, 246 (1978): 58. See also Sally Gregory Kohlstedt, "In From the Periphery: American Women in Science, 1830–1880," *Signs* 4, 1 (1978): 81–96, and Lynn Barber, *The Heyday of Natural History* (London, 1980), chapter nine.

12. Brian Coe, *The Birth of Photography: The Story of the Formative Years, 1800–1900* (London, 1976), p. 36.

13. F.J. Erskine, "Photography for Lady Amateurs," *Anthony's Photographic Bulletin* 15 (November 1884), p. 511.

14. Bill Jay, "Death in the Darkroom," *British Journal of Photography* 127:6271 (3 October 1980): 976–979; 127:6272 (10 October 1980): 1002–1007.

15. Ibid., p. 977.

16. Mr. Carleton, photographer, 27 May 1848, cited in Koltun, "Checklist," pp. 82–83.

17. M.A. Root, *The Camera and the Pencil or the Heliographic Art* (1864; reprinted 1971), pp. 72–73.

18. Lois W. Banner, *American Beauty* (New York, 1983), p. 49.

19. Our conclusions about the responses of Ontario women to photography and about patterns in the images which they made and commissioned are derived from an extensive examination of thousands of photographs held in archives, libraries, museums, and private collections across Ontario.

20. See, for example, Julia Hirsch, *Family Photographs: Content, Meaning and Effect* (New York, 1981), and Barbara Norfleet, *Wedding* (New York, 1979).

21. See Alice Echols, "The Demise of Female Intimacy in the Twentieth Century," *Michigan Occasional Paper No. VI* (Ann Arbor, 1978), and Carroll Smith-Rosenberg, "The Female World of Love and Ritual: Relations between Women in Nineteenth-century America," *Signs* 1 ,1 (1975): 1–29.

22. See William C. Darrah, *Stereo Views: A History of Stereographs in America and their Collection* (Gettysburg, PA, 1964), and Edward W. Earle, ed., *Points of View: The Stereograph in America — A Cultural History* (Rochester, NY, 1979).

23. Koltun, "Checklist," p. 118.

24. For an insightful reading of three family albums kept by upper-and middle-class nineteenth-century British women, see Alan Thomas, *The Expanding Eye: Photography and the Nineteenth-Century Mind* (London, 1978), chapter three.

25. Ibid., p. 19.

26. See the views expressed on this question by Lady Eastlake, Charles Baudelaire, Oscar G. Rejlander, John Ruskin, Henry Peach Robinson, and others in Vicki Goldberg, ed., *Photography in Print: Writings from 1816 to the Present* (New York, 1981). See also Ann Thomas, *Canadian Painting and Photography, 1860–1900* (Montreal, 1979).

27. Cited in Goldberg, p. 92.

28. See Helmut Gernsheim, *Julia Margaret Cameron, Her Life and Photographic Work* (1948), and Peter Wollheim, "Julia Margaret Cameron: A Victorian Soul," *Photo Communiqué* (Winter 1982⁄3).

29. Thomas, p. 19.

30. William C. Darrah, *Cartes de Visite in Nineteenth Century Photography* (Gettysburg, Pa., 1981), p. 22.

31. *The Montreal Transcript*, 11 September 1841, cited in Greenhill and Birrell, p. 26.

32. See Mitchell's *Canada Gazetteer and Business Directory 1864–65* (Toronto, 1864), part two, and Mitchell and Co., *Canada's Classified Directory 1865–66* (Toronto, 1866), which together list over twenty women photographers in business in Ontario.

33. Blake and Jennifer McKendry, *Early Photography in Kingston* (Kingston, 1979).

34. J. Anderson, *Kemptville Past and Present* (Kemptville, 1903). It should be noted that there were few photographers, male or female, at this time. Lovell's *Canada Directory* (Montreal, 1850) listed only eleven daguerreotypes in operation for the whole of Quebec and Ontario; there were probably a number of itinerant operators not included in this figure. By 1865, there were 360 listed.

35. For example, the *Dominion of Canada Business Directory 1890–91* (Toronto, 1890), vol. I, mentioned only two professional women in business, 1767–1770. Other potentially useful research tools include census rolls, assessment rolls, local histories, credit ratings such as Bradstreet's, and the Mercantile Agency publications, land registry records, probates of wills, house histories, and newspaper obituaries.

36. Darrah, *Cartes de Visite*, p. 32.

37. Germaine Greer makes a similar point about pre-nineteenth-century women painters. They were invariably related to male artists because women had no other means of access to training. Many male painters, on the other

hand, did not belong to painting dynasties. See *The Obstacle Race: The Fortunes of Women Painters and Their Work* (London, 1981), chapter one. Thanks to Deborah Gorham for this observation.

38. J. Russell Harper, *Early Painters and Engravers in Canada* (Toronto, 1970), p. 199. Some of Lockwood's photographs are held in the Bytown Historical Museum in Ottawa.

39. Greenhill, *Early Photography*, p. 32.

40. Koltun, "Checklist," pp. 90, 101, 128.

41. Koltun, "Pre-Confederation Photography," p. 262.

42. Ibid.

43. Jones, p. 7.

44. For details of the Canadian context, see the essays in Janice Acton et al., eds., *Women at Work: Ontario, 1850–1930* (Toronto, 1974), and Linda Kealey, ed., *A Not Unreasonable Claim: Women and Reform in Canada, 1880s–1920s* (Toronto, 1979).

45. Greenhill and Birrell, p. 114. 46. Coe, p. 43; Greenhill and Birrell, p. 113.

47. H.C. Price, cited in Greenhill, p. 62.

48. Coe, pp. 50–55.

49. Brian Coe and Paul Gates, *The Snapshot Photograph: The Rise of Popular Photography, 1888–1939* (London, 1977), pp. 17–21. On the story of the Kodak enterprise and its profound impact on the structure of the industry, see Reese V. Jenkins' impressive study, *Images and Enterprise: Technology and American Photographic Industry, 1839–1925* (Baltimore, 1975). A brief history of Kodak Canada may be found in *Photographic Canadiana* 1, 7 and 1, 8 (1976).

50. Cited in Coe, p. 53.

51. Eaton S. Lothrop, Jr., "The Brownie Camera," *History of Photography* 2, 1 (1978): 1–10.

52. Carol Wald with Judith Papachristou, *Myth America: Picturing Women, 1865–1945* (New York, 1975), p. 4.

53. A similar marketing strategy was employed by the early aviation industry. See Joseph J. Corn, "Making Flying 'Thinkable': Women Pilots and the Selling of Aviation, 1927–1940." *American Quarterly* 31, 4 (1979): 556–571.

54. Coe and Gates, pp. 34–35.

55. Banner, chapter eight, and Edmund Vincent Gillon, Jr., ed., *The Gibson Girl and Her America: The Best Drawings of Charles Dana Gibson* (New York, 1969).

56. Coe and Gates, p. 38, and George Gilbert, *Collecting Photographica: The Images and Equipment of the First Hundred Years of Photography* (New York, 1976), p. 75.

57. Coe and Gates, p. 34.

58. Beginning in 1898, Eaton's stores featured a new department of photography. In that year, the catalogue advertised cameras at prices ranging from $4.75 to $27.00, including the Pocket Kodak at $4.75, the Klondike at $5.00, and the Folding Kodak at $9.50. In 1920, Eaton's sold the Buster Brown at $3.50, the Vest Pocket Ansco at $14.00 and the Folding Scout at $15.00-$22.00. Thanks to Judith

McErvel at the Eaton's of Canada Ltd. Archives, Toronto, for this information.

59. The album of photographs taken by Helen Little and her friend, Mary Wright, at North-Way Lodge, 1912–1916, was donated to the Ontario Camping Association in 1969 and is held at the Trent University Archives.

60. *Woman's Century* (April 1916), p. 19.

61. See, for example, the album of Ethel Stockwell, a student at Moulton College, ca. 1907–1909, held at the Canadian Baptist Archives, McMaster University.

62. See, for example, the album compiled by Lois Allan during a summer's work at the jam factory at Winona in 1918. National Archives of Canada, Lois Allan Papers, MG 30, C173.

63. Arthur Hope, *The Amateur Photographer's Handbook* (Toronto, 1895), p. 151.

64. Birrell et al., p. 119.

65. Ibid., p. 123. Some of I. May Ballantyne's photographs can be found in the James Ballantyne Collection (1980–232), National Photography Collection, National Archives of Canada.

66. A number of Dixon's glass plate negatives are held at the Hamilton Public Library, Special Collections.

67. National Archives of Canada, Toronto Camera Club Records, MG 18 I 181, vol. 1, "History," Minutes, 1 December 1895.

68. Mrs. H. Coleman Davidson (London, 1894), pp. 235–238.

69. Napoleon Sarony, June 1895, cited in Jones, p. 2.

70. Elizabeth Ketling, *Helpful Talks with Girls* (New York, 1910), p. 82.

71. Although Ontario photographers, male and female, must certainly have numbered in the hundreds by this time, it is very difficult to produce an accurate estimate. Turnover was high and careers in photography were often brief. As itinerants, many photographers would not have advertised in business directories or appeared in census records, while many others who practised photography as a sideline would have been listed under another occupation.

72. Marjory MacMurchy, *The Canadian Girl at Work: A Book of Vocational Guidance* (Toronto, 1920), pp. 90–91.

73. Leslie Horner, *Saturday Night* (19 April 1919): 25.

74. Koltun, "Checklist," p. 155.

75. Photographs of workers at the Toronto factory were provided to us courtesy of Kodak Canada Inc.

76. Ellen M. Knox, *The Girl of the New Day* (Toronto, 1919), p. 241.

77. Reese Jenkins' study, for example, contains many illustrations of women workers, but their presence is not discussed in the text.

78. Interview with Joan Crawford, niece of Elizabeth Archibald, Ottawa, 9 January 1985. Copies of prints from an album of photographs by Archibald are held at the Ottawa City Archives.

79. 39,7 (1 April 1926): 72–74.

¶ This article was awarded the Hilda Neatby Prize by the Canadian Historical Association's Canadian Committee on Women's History in 1986.

De La Cour and Sheinin • The Ontario Medical College for Women

NOTES

1. Carlotta Hacker, *The Indomitable Lady Doctors* (Toronto: James Lorimer, 1984), p. 65; Toronto School of Medicine, Minutes of Faculty Meetings, meeting 7 March 1883, Record Group B-74-007.1, University of Toronto Archives, Toronto.

2. University of Trinity College, Minute Book, 1883–1884, Trinity College Archives, Toronto.

3. Woman's Medical College, Toronto, "Annual Announcement of the Woman's Medical College, Toronto: Fourth Session 1886–1887," Series A7, Container 7, Women's College Hospital Archives, Toronto.

4. Ontario Medical College for Women, *Saturday Globe* (17 August 1895): 1.

5. Dr. Edna Guest, "A Message: On the Laying of the Foundation Stone of the Women's College Hospital," 20 October 1934, File 1, Series A9, Container 9, Women's College Hospital Archives, Toronto.

6. These and subsequent figures for the women's medical college, unless otherwise indicated, are compiled from annual reports for the school located in Series A7, Container 7, Women's College Hospital Archives, Toronto, and Record Groups P78-0121-(02)13M-029.1 / P78-0122-(01-) –029.2 / P78-0122 — (03-)029.2, University of Toronto Archives, Toronto.

7. Dr. J.T. Duncan to Mrs. McEwan, 16 December 1889, File 5, Series C18, Container 21, Women's College Hospital Archives, Toronto.

8. Woman's Medical College, Toronto, "Annual Announcement of the Woman's Medical College, Toronto: 1891–1892," Women's College Hospital Archives, Toronto.

9. Ontario Medical College for Women (Limited), "Annual Announcement of the Ontario Medical College for Women (Limited): 1898," Women's College Hospital Archives, Toronto.

10. Woman's Medical College,Toronto, "Annual Announcement of the Woman's Medical College, Toronto: 1891–1892," Women's College Hospital Archives, Toronto.

11. Ontario Medical College for Women (Limited), "Annual Announcement of the Ontario Medical College for Women (Limited): 1898," Women's College Hospital Archives, Toronto.

12. "The Woman's Medical College, Toronto," *The Canadian Practitioner* (16 October 1891): 479–480.

13. C. Lesley Biggs, "The Case of the Missing Midwives: A History of Midwifery in Ontario from 1795–1900," *Ontario History* 25, 1 (March 1983): 29.

14. Jo Oppenheimer, "Childbirth in Ontario: The Transition from Home to Hospital in the Early Twentieth Century," *Ontario History* 75, 1 (March 1983): 41.

15. Ontario Medical College for Women (Limited), "Annual Announcement

of the Ontario Medical College for Women (Limited): 1899," Record Group P78–0122- (01) –029.2, University of Toronto Archives, Toronto.

16. Ontario Medical College for Women (Limited), "Annual Announcement of the Ontario Medical College for Women (Limited): 1904," Record Group P78–0122- (03) –029.2, University of Toronto Archives, Toronto.

17. Ontario Medical College for Women (Limited), "Annual Calendar for the Ontario Medical College for Women (Limited): 1900," Women's College Hospital Archives, Toronto.

18. Royal Commission on the University of Toronto, *Report of the Royal Commission on the University of Toronto* (Toronto: L.K. Cameron, 1906), p. 146.

19. Ibid., p. 147.

20. Province of Ontario, Letters Patent for the Ontario Medical College for Women (Limited), 29 March 1894, Record Group 55-1-2-B-1, Liber 36, Archives of Ontario, Toronto; Provincial Secretary, Annual Return for the Ontario Medical College for Women (Limited), 31 December 1895, Record Group 8-1-1-G, File 2025, Archives of Ontario, Toronto.

21. Ontario Medical College for Women (Limited), "Annual Announcement of the Ontario Medical College for Women (Limited): 1896," Women's College Hospital Archives, Toronto.

22. Dr. D.J. Gibb Wishart, "Financial Report for the Year Ending October 8th, 1901," 5 December 1901, File 7, Series EZ, Container 26, Women's College Hospital Archives, Toronto.

23. George W. Spragge, "Trinity Medical College," *Ontario History* 48 (June 1966).

24. "Medical Training for Women," [1906], (typewritten), Women's College Hospital Archives, Toronto.

25. Royal Commission on the University of Toronto, *Report*, pp. 143–148.

26. Ontario Medical College for Women (Limited) to The Commissioner upon University Matter, November 1905, File 7, Series C18, Container 21, Women's College Hospital Archives, Toronto.

27. Royal Commission on the University of Toronto, *Report*, p. xxxiv.

28. Augusta Stowe-Gullen, *A Brief History of the Ontario Medical College for Women* (Toronto: n.p., 1906), pp. 7–8.

29. Veronica Strong-Boag, "Canada's Women Doctors: Feminism Constrained," in Linda Kealy, ed., *A Not Unreasonable Claim: Women and Reform in Canada 1880s-1920s*, (Toronto: The Women's Press, 1979), p. 129.

30. Jane Tiel, "Medicine and Woman's Intuition," *The Globe Magazine* (9 August 1958): 4.

Stieb, Coulas, and Ferguson • Women in Ontario Pharmacy

NOTES

1. Charles M. Godfrey, "The Distaff Doctor," in his *Medicine for Ontario* (Belleville, Ont., 1979), pp. 186–190. D.W. Gullett, *A History of Dentistry in Canada* (Toronto, 1971), pp. 87–89, comments mainly on the late entry (1890s) of women into dental practice in Ontario, rather than on any specific opposition from males.

2. It was in 1867 that those practicing pharmacy in what is now Ontario and Quebec first organized, primarily to defend themselves against the attempt by recently-organized medical groups to sweep the control of pharmacy under their aegis. These local pharmaceutical groups coalesced by the late summer and early fall of 1867 to form the Canadian Pharmaceutical "Society," with the hope of obtaining protective federal legislation based on the British model. When these attempts failed, pharmacists in Ontario and Quebec put their energies into promoting provincial legislation, with the result that the OCP came into being officially with the first Ontario Pharmacy Act in February 1871. For a few years between 1867 and 1871, informal arrangements for the instruction of would-be pharmacists had been made by the lineal predecessors of the OCP. Such arrangements were continued by the OCP from 1871 onward primarily to prepare apprentices to write the licensing examinations administered by the OCP. The first formal school was established in 1882, but apprenticeship remained an important part of the training of pharmacists. Registration as an apprentice became compulsory in 1884, with the completion of a three-year term being required. Apprenticeship lengthened to four years in 1889, with completion of the school program becoming a prerequisite for sitting for the licensing examinations. The academic year lengthened from about three months to six-and-a-half months ("one-year program") in 1887–88, and was divided into a junior and senior term; it remained essentially unchanged for the next four decades, until a two-year program was introduced in 1927. With that change in 1927, apprenticeship shrank again to three years, but the Bachelor of Pharmacy (Phm.B.) degree of the University of Toronto became required for practicing pharmacy. Between 1892, when the OCP first affiliated with the university, and 1927, OCP students could take optional examinations to qualify for the Phm.B., but the OCP diploma or its equivalent was really all that was required to practice in Ontario. Furthermore, OCP licensing examinations, initiated in 1871, continued to be a prerequisite for licensure until 1944, quite apart from the academic requirements. While the equivalent of high school entrance (grade eight) was all that was needed for admission in 1884, this was raised in 1887–88 to grade ten, then to grade twelve in 1924, and grade thirteen in 1935. For details, see Ernst W. Stieb, "One Hundred Years of Organized Pharmacy," in *One Hundred Years of Pharmacy in Canada, 1867–1967* (Toronto, 1969), pp. 11–14; and "A Century of Formal Pharmaceutical Education in Ontario," *Canadian Pharmaceutical*

Journal, 116 (1983): 104–107 *passim*.

3. Thomas Radcliff, ed., *Authentic Letters from Upper Canada* (Toronto, 1953), p. 61.

4. Roy W. Hornosty, "Implications of Feminism for the Profession of Pharmacy in Canada," *International Journal of Women Studies* 3 (1980):183–206.

5. Isabel Bassett, *The Labour Rebellion: Profiles in the Struggle for Women's Rights* (Toronto, 1976), p. 16.

6. Wayne Roberts. *Honest Womanhood: Feminism, Femininity, and Class Consciousness among Toronto Working Women, 1893–1914* (Toronto, 1976), pp. 8–9.

7. Bryan D. Palmer, *Working-Class Experience: The Rise and Reconstitution of Canadian Labour, 1800–1980* (Toronto, 1983), p. 196; Veronica Strong-Boag, "The Girl of the New Day: Canadian Working Women in the 1920s," in Michael S. Cross and Gregory S. Kealey, eds., *The Consolidation of Capitalism, 1896–1929* (Toronto, 1983), pp. 169, 181–184; and Leo Johnson, "The Political Economy of Ontario Women in the Nineteenth Century," in Janice Acton, Penny Goldsmith, and Bonnie Shepard, eds., *Women at Work, Ontario, 1850–1930* (Toronto, 1974), pp. 14, 30.

8. "List of Members of the Ontario College of Pharmacy — October 1st, 1871," *Can. Pharm. J.*, 5 (1871–72):134–141. Mrs. Kane and Mrs. Wade had already been in an earlier list that appeared in June; see ibid., p. 4 (1871):69. All those who paid their fees up to May, 1872, were automatically registered under the new act.

9. "List of Members of the Canadian Pharmaceutical Society, prior to its Enrollment as the Ontario College of Pharmacy, July, 1870," *Can. Pharm. J.* 3 (1870):105–107.

10. The printed record, however, does not support the manuscript. Ibid.; OCP Cash Book, 1867–83; and OCP Register, 1867–70, p. 60.

11. "Items of News," *Can. Pharm. J.* 30 (1896–97):137.

12. OCP Register, 1891–1900, p. 78, out of business. May 1896–87.

13. "Election of Council," *Can. Pharm. J.* 13 (1879–80): 21; ibid., 15 (1881–82): 15–16; "Minutes of the Semi-Annual Meeting of the Council [3–5 August 1881]," ibid., p. 35. For the 1881 election, OCP distributed 361 ballots, of which 293 were returned, with twenty-four of these spoiled. The aggregate of votes cast for the thirteen successful candidates was 1,736, for all forty-three candidates, 3,343. The first-place candidate garnered 201 votes; the thirteenth, 100; and the last, 17. Parenthetically, the first woman to be elected to the OCP Council was Maxine Hughes Tenander of Thunder Bay, in 1975; a 1970 graduate of the faculty of pharmacy, University of Toronto, she subsequently also became the first female president of the OCP, 1983–84. Soon afterward, a second woman member was elected, and there are currently three females out of sixteen elected members on council; there are also four females out of six members appointed by the lieutenant-governor in council. Pharmacist members have been elected by geographical districts rather than total votes since 1891.

14. For general comments, see Roberts, *Honest Womanhood* (n. 6), p. 10.

15. Perhaps she viewed it as a challenge to be met by the avowed feminist that

she was. Veronica Strong-Boag, "Canada's Women Doctors: Feminism Constrained," in Linda Kealey, ed., *A Not Unreasonable Claim* (Toronto, 1979), pp. 127, 119.

16. Manuscript list of members of the Canadian Pharmaceutical Society, p. 12; manuscript OCP registration cash book, 1883–89, p. 8, OCP Calendar ("Announcement") 1890, p. 23; "Canadian Pharmaceutical Society," *Can. Pharm. J.* 1 (1868):56; "Additional List of Members [OCP]," ibid., 4 (1871):69; "Report of Board of Examiners, OCP Minutes of Semi Annual Meeting of Council [6–7 February 1884]," ibid., 17 (1883–84):115.

17. OCP advertisement, *Can. Pharm. J.* 16 (1882–83):194.

18. "Officers of 1897 Class," *Canadian Druggists* 9 (1897):52.

19. *Minutes of the Semi-Annual Meeting* [4–7 February 1896), pp. 6, 7.

20. Roberts, *Honest Womanhood*, (n. 6), p. 7; and Ceta Ramkhalanwansingh, "Women during the Great War," in *Women at Work*, (n. 7), p. 296.

21. Glenn Sonnedecker, "Women as Pharmacy Students in 19th-Century America," *Verlfentlichungen der Internationalen Gesellschaft fur Geschichte der Pharmazie e. V* 40 (1973):135–141. See also Robert W. Culp, "The Education of American Women Pharmacists to 1900, Including a Director," *Transactions of the College of Physicians of Philadelphia* 41 (1974):211–227. For details, see Emma Gary Wallace, "Women in Pharmacy," *Pharmaceutical Era* 45 (1912): 17–20, then monthly through the rest of the year with twenty-two chapters in all, well-illustrated, American state by state, notable firsts, many portrait cuts, probably good as an entry wedge, but facts would need to be corroborated.

22. C. Leonard O'Connell, "Report of the Status of Women in Pharmacy," *American Journal of Pharmaceutical Education* 2 (1938):70; and Nellie A. Wakeman, ibid., 1 (1937):146.

23. Eunice R. Bonow, "The History of Professional Pharmaceutical Fraternities for Women," *American Journal of Pharmaceutical Education* 18 (1954): 409–412.

24. George B. Griffenhagen, "Woman Power," *Journal of American Pharmaceutical Association*, NS 13 (1973):609.

25. Sonnedecker, (n. 21), p. 135; Marie-Louise Barcs-Masson, *Les femmes et la pharmacie* (Collection Belisane, Nice, 1977), 149 pp.; Elizabeth Wunsch, "Early Women Pharmacists," *Australasian Journal of Pharmacy* (1962):1290–1292.

26. T.E. Wallis, *History of the School of Pharmacy, University of London* (Pharmaceutical Press, London), pp. 161–162; Hopkin Maddock, "Pharmacy's Past and Future," *Chemist and Druggist*, 222 (1984):468.

27. "Ontario College of Pharmacy Notes," *Canadian Druggist* 13 (1901):2.

28. "OCP Notes," *Can. Pharm. J.* 34 (1900–1901):114.

29. *Can. Pharm. J.* 21 (1887–88):43. The student in question was Mary H. Book of Niagara Falls, who finished in the spring of 1888. Her preceptor was a Dr. E.E. Book.

30. "Pharmaceutical Dinner," *Can. Pharm. J.* 16 (1882–83):252–253.

31. "Editorial: Lady Pharmacists," *Can. Pharm. J.* 6 (1872–73):178–179. The writer's use of the term "avocation" is intriguing, but perplexing. Can we take

it to be merely archaic usage or is the underlying intent to suggest that any occupation other than the domestic one of wife and mother is to be considered merely an avocation rather than a true vocation for a woman?

32. "Editorial: Lady Pharmacists," *Can. Pharm. J.* 13 (1879–1880):22.

33. "The Woman's Journal," *Can. Pharm. J.* 3 (1870):26.

34. "Editorial Summary," *Can. Pharm. J.* 15 (1881–82):261; and "Lady Students," ibid. 9 (1875–76):299–300.

35. "Female Druggists," *The Evening News* Toronto, (Friday, 3 August 1883):,1, col. 5; and (Untitled), *Can. Pharm. J.* 17 (1883–84):10.

36. W.J. Dyas, "Women in Pharmacy," *Can. Drugg.* 13 (1901):1.

37. (G.E. Gibbard, ed.), "Women in Pharmacy," *Can. Pharm. J.* 51 (1917–18): 484.

38. Ibid.

39. Anon., "Pharmacy in Skirts," ibid., p. 188.

40. Ernesto L. Maglalang, "Women in Pharmacy," *Can. Pharm. J.* 57 (1923–24):35.

41. Ibid. The idea that pharmacy was a suitable profession for a woman because her place was obviously in the home, expressed by this writer, was linked to the physical arrangement, popular in former times, which saw the living quarters for the pharmacist at the back of or above the pharmacy.

42. "Report of the Dean" and "Report of the Examiners," OCP *Minutes of Semi-Annual Meeting* [2–6 June 1924], pp. 11, 36–37.

Dodd • Women in Advertising

ACKNOWLEDGEMENTS

The author wishes to thank Dr. Marilyn Barber for her comments and sugges-
tions and gratefully acknowledges the assistance of the Social Science and
Humanities Research Council of Canada and of the Hanna Institute for the
History of Medicine.

NOTES

1. Joan Rothschild, ed., *Machina Ex Dea: Feminist Perspectives on Technology* (New York: Pergamon, 1983); Martha Moore Trescott, ed., *Dynamos and
Virgins Revisited: Women and Technological Change in History* (New Jersey
and London: The Scarecrow Press, 1979).

2. Stuart Ewen, *Captains of Consciousness: Advertising and the Social Roots
of Consumer Culture* (McGraw Hill, 1976); Elaine Fisher, "The Angel and the
Whore: The Growth of Psychological Advertising and its Focus on Women in
Canada," unpublished B.A. thesis, University of Victoria, 1978.

3. Dolores Hayden, *The Grand Domestic Revolution* (Cambridge, MIT Press,
1981): 281–289.

4. Ewen.

5. The circulation of *Maclean's* rose from 71,689 in 1920 to 212,370 in 1934;
Chatelaine's initial circulation (1928) of 57,026 had risen to 217,746 by 1934; and
the *Canadian Home Journal's* circulation increased from 46,945 to 212,116 over
the same period. "Canadian Magazines Top All U.S. Magazines in Canada,"
Marketing (13 April 1935): 3; "Analysis of Circulation Statements," *Marketing*
(15 May 1921): 342; "Analysis of Circulation Statements," *Marketing* (30 March
1929): 200.

6. Ontario Hydro's *Bulletin, Electrical News and Engineering,* the Canadian
advertising journal, *Marketing,* and its American counterpart, *Printers' Ink.*

7. Fisher, p. 49; H.E. Stephenson and Carlton McNaught, *The Story of
Advertising in Canada* (Toronto: Ryerson Press, 1940).

8. Christopher Armstrong and H.V. Nelles, *Monopoly's Moment: The Organization and Regulation of Canadian Utilities, 1830–1930* (Philadelphia: Temple
University Press, 1986), p. 296.

9. H.H. Rimmer and J.S. Keenan, "The Industry's Objective — Selling the
Electric Idea," *Electrical News and Engineering,* (15 July 1939): 19–27.

10. The number of households wired for electricity which owned an appliance, that is, the percentage of the potential market which had been saturated.

11. Dianne Dodd, "Delivering Electrical Technology To The Ontario Housewife, 1920–1939: An Alliance of Professional Women, Advertisers and the
Electrical Industry," unpublished Ph.D. thesis, Carleton University, 1988, p. 163.

12. "Domestic Loads and Rates," *Electrical News and Engineering* (1 April
1934): 19.

13. Home economists suggested such features as rounded corners to facilitate easy cleaning, controls placed out of reach of children, height conducive to back comfort, and moving parts placed out of sight to ensure safety and acceptance by women. Mildred Maddocks, Director, Good Housekeeping Institute, *The Consumer Viewpoint*, 1920.

14. Magazine advice literature and advertisements both assumed that domestic electric technology was the product of male inventive genius. See "Dishwashing Made Easy," *Chatelaine* (April 1939): 75.

15. "Heads Toronto Women's Advertising Club," *Marketing* (29 April 1933): 6; Dorothy Dignam, "Some Women Have Made Good in Advertising But As to Others," *Printers' Ink* (27 April 1939): 15–18.

16. Kathleen Murphy, "What Are You Going To Be?" *Canadian Home Journal* (August 1930): 22, 44.

17. Ibid.

18. Ibid.; Grace Garner, "Advertising as a Career," *Canadian Home Journal* (January 1938): 2, 32, 34; Gertrude E.S. Pringle, "Making Good in the Field of Advertising," *Maclean's* (1 September 1922): 60–63.

19. Mabel Crews Ringland, "Housewifely Wit and Wisdom," *The Canadian Countryman* (6 August 1938): 10.

20. Garner.

21. "Women Held Inconspicuous Place in Advertising Thirty Years Ago," *Marketing* (15 October 1938).

22. Frances Maule, "The 'Woman Appeal'," *Printers' Ink* (31 January 1924): 105–110.

23. "Shows Housewives How Advertising Has Brought Benefits, Lowered Costs," *Marketing* (6 June 1936): 3.

24. Ruth Schwartz Cowan, *More Work for Mother* (New York: Basic, 1983); Susan Strasser, *Never Done* (New York: Pantheon, 1982; Christine Bose, "Technology and Changes in the Division of Labour in the American Home," *Women's Studies International Quarterly* 2 (1979): 295–304; Christine Bose, Philip L. Bereano, and Mary Malloy, "Household Technology and the Social Construction of Housework," *Technology and Culture* 25, 1, (January 1984): 53–82.

25. Strasser; Glenna Matthews, *Just A Housewife: The Rise and Fall of Domesticity in America* (New York: Oxford University Press, 1987).

26. Hayden, pp. 281–289. In Canada, the promotion of consumption for women was accompanied by the promotion of home ownership for working class men. Margaret Hobbes and Ruth Pierson, "When Is a Kitchen Not a Kitchen?" *Canadian Woman's Studies* 7, 4: 71–76.

27. Patricia Saidak, "The Inception of the Home Economics Movement in English Canada, 1890–1910: In Defence of the Cultural Importance of the Home," M.A. thesis, Carleton University, 1987; Saidak, "Home Economics as an Academic Science," *Resources for Feminist Research* 15, 3 (Nov. 1986): 49–51.

28. Diana Pedersen, "The Scientific Training of Mothers: The Campaign for Domestic Science in Ontario Schools, 1890–1913," in (R. Jarrell and A. Roos,

eds.,) *Critical Issues in the History of Canadian Science, Technology and Medicine*, (Ottawa: HSTC Publications, 1983), pp. 178–194.

29. Marilyn Barber, "The Women Ontario Welcomed: Immigrant Domestics for Ontario Homes, 1870–1930," in (Alison Prentice and Susan Mann Trofimenkoff, eds.,) *The Neglected Majority*, Vol. 2 (Toronto: McClelland and Stewart, 1985), pp. 102–121.

30. Mrs. Bertha Landes, "A Woman — on Women," *Printers' Ink* (7 July 1927): 156–160. 31. Mabel Crews Ringland, "To Men Copy Writers," *Printers' Ink* (8 April 1937): 83–86.

32. Alice Edwards, "Why Some Women Distrust All Advertising," *Printers' Ink* (31 May 1934): 44–46.

33. Ewen, p. 19.

34. Howard P. Segal, *Technological Utopianism in American Culture* (Chicago and London: University of Chicago Press, 1985); Armstrong and Nelles, pp. 59–65.

35. "Advertising Makes Good Things Cost Less," *Maclean's* (1 November 1935): 5.

36. "Electricity Brings Prosperity," *Maclean's* (1 October 1930): 29.

37. "Comforts That Kings Would Have Envied," *Maclean's* (1 November 1930): 27.

38. "Vocation," *Maclean's* (15 November 1930): 27.

39. "Born to Rule An Electrical World," *Maclean's* (1 May 1930): 27.

40. S.C. Lambert, "Better Results — The New Appeal in Household Appliance Copy," *Printers' Ink* (14 April 1921): 89–92.

41. Advertisement, *Chatelaine* (September 1936): 3.

42. Advertisement, *Maclean's* (15 July 1920): 67.

43. Advertisement, *Maclean's* (1 October 1920): 5.

44. Advertisement, *Maclean's* (1 April 1920): 75.

45. Advertisement, *Maclean's* (15 January 1936): 3.

46. Advertisement, *Maclean's* (1 April 1926): 53.

47. Advertisement, *Maclean's* (1 September 1920): 7.

48. Advertisement, *Maclean's* (1 July 1920): 54.

49. Suzann Buckley, "Ladies or Midwives? Efforts to Reduce Infant and Maternal Mortality" in Linda Kealey, ed., *A Not Unreasonable Claim: Women and Reform in Canada, 1880–1920* (Toronto: 1979), pp. 131–150.

50. Advertisement, *Maclean's* (15 June 1934): 3; Advertisement, *Maclean's* (15 May 1938): 37; Advertisement, *Maclean's* (1 April 1927): 57.

51. C.M. Frankel, "Advantages of an Advertising Leader," *Marketing* (15 December 1923).

52. Lambert.

53. Advertisement, *Maclean's* (15 May 1923): 74.

54. Advertisement, *Maclean's* (1 April 1920): 75.

55. Advertisement, *Maclean's* (1 May 1920): 75.

56. *Maclean's* (1 October 1920): 69.

57. Advertisement, *Maclean's* (1 October 1920).

58. Advertisement, *Maclean's* (1 April 1936): 29.

59. Veronica Strong-Boag, *The New Day Recalled* (Mississauga: Copp Clark Pitman, 1988), p. 119.

60. Clara Brown Lyman, "Women's Fight for Truth Now Brings Opportunity To The Advertiser," *Printers' Ink* (5 January 1939): 64–67. It is interesting that the American consumer movement, which eventually came to be dominated by male 'experts,' called for many of the same reforms as women's groups, but saw the administration of standards as a scientific enterprise to be conducted solely by experts. Not surprisingly, they tended to downplay women's role in the movement, took the occasional swipe at "lay women, amateur dieticians, self appointed guardians of the public health," and conspicuously referred to the consumer as 'he,' in contrast to advertising and home economics literature. Arthur Kallet and F.J. Schlink, *100,000,000 Guinea Pigs*, (1933; reprint Arno Press, 1976); Stuart Chase and F.J. Schlink, *Your Money's Worth*, (New York: The New Republic Inc., 1927).

61. Christine Foley, "Consumerism, Consumption and Canadian Feminism 1900–1930," unpublished M.A. thesis, University of Toronto, 1979; Joan Sangster, *Dreams of Equality: Women on the Canadian Left, 1920–1950* (Toronto: McClelland and Stewart, 1989).

62. See Mabel Crews Ringland, "Consult the Woman Who Uses One Before Deciding How to Sell Her," *Marketing* (27 November 1937): 2; Ringland, "To Men Copy Writers".

63. Ringland, "On Really Knowing the Consumer," *Printers' Ink* (16 September 1937): 5–8, 100–106.

64. Ibid.

65. Maule.

66. Maule.

67. Maule.

68. Ringland, "Consult the Woman."

69. Ringland, "On Knowing the Consumer."

70. Landes.

71. Ida Bailey Allen, "Helpfulness — The Big Idea in Advertising to Women," *Printers' Ink* (14 June 1923): 138–140.

72. Millicent Yackey Taylor, "To Sell Life's Essentials, Tell Women Facts," *Printers' Ink* (19 July 1934): 65–58.

73. Women Provide Three Fold Market, *Marketing* (4 March 1939): 10.

74. Amos Bradbury, "To The Ladies," *Printers' Ink* (21 February 1935): 7–10, 102–103.

75. Marion Hertha Clarke, "From One Woman to Another —Anent Copy," *Printers' Ink* (1 January 1925): 57, 58.

76. Ringland, "On Knowing the Consumer."

77. "A.C.A. Sees Little Menace in Consumer Movement Here," *Marketing* (22 October 1938): 1.

78. Christine Frederick, *Selling Mrs. Consumer* (New York: Business Bourse, 1929), pp. 320, 321, 331.

79. Frank R. Coutant, "Employed Women," *Advertising and Selling* 31 (June 1938): 21, 23, 68.

80. *Magazine Homes and Branded Merchandise* (Macfadden Publications Inc., 1937), p. 6; "Where People Live is Prime Sales Factor," *Advertising Age* (24 January 1938): 28; "Canadian Family Living Expenses Show Similarity in Main Items," *Marketing* (20 May 1939): 8.

Hoecker-Drysdale • Women Sociologists in Canada

ACKNOWLEDGEMENTS

The author wishes to thank Dr. Aileen Ross, Dr. Jean Burnet, and Elizabeth Hughes Schneewind for their time and cooperation, Dr. Marianne Ainley for use of her interview with Aileen Ross and her valuable suggestions and encouragement, and Nancy Marrelli for her help and patience. Thanks also to Kurt Jonassohn. This article is dedicated to John Drysdale, whose invaluable advice and tenacious support have been so important always.

NOTES

1. Margaret Rossiter has proposed a model, which assumes that sexual discrimination is a function of crowding; that is, in periods of growth, there are higher rates of entrance and employment of women in the scientific disciplines. But once the last hired field is crowded and the growth rate slows, women, especially married women, are first fired. See Margaret W. Rossiter, "Sexual Segregation in the Sciences: Some Data and a Model," *Signs: Journal of Women in Culture and Society*, 4, 1 (1978): 146–151. See also Margaret W. Rossiter, *Women Scientists in America: Struggles and Strategies to* 1940 (Baltimore: Johns Hopkins University Press, 1982). Unfortunately, Rossiter omits sociology from her studies. There is a need for more research on the history of women's participation in Sociology in North America. Also pertinent is *Signs: A Journal of Women in Culture and Society*, 4, 1 (1978) issue on "Women, Science and Society."

2. *The Positive Philosophy of Auguste Comte*, freely translated and condensed by Harriet Martineau, 2 vols. (London: Trubner & Company, 1853).

3. To label these women is difficult; we might call them volunteers. Most nineteenth-century science was done by nonprofessionals, whom we neverthe-

less cannot call amateurs given the word's modern meaning. For a discussion of women's participation in early social science organizations in England, see Kathleen E. McCrone, "The National Association for the Promotion of Social Science and the Advancement of Victorian Women," *Atlantis*, 8, 1 (1982): 44–66. Also relevant are Thomas L. Haskell, *The Emergence of Professional Social Science: The American Social Science Association and the Nineteenth-Century Crisis of Authority* (Urbana: University of Illinois Press, 1977), and Thomas L. Haskell, ed., *The Authority of Experts: Studies in History and Theory* (Bloomington: Indiana University Press, 1984).

4. Books which deal with the careers of women in the early decades of social science in North America include: R. Rosenberg, *Beyond Separate Spheres* (1982); W. Leach, *True Love and Perfect Union* (1980); and Rossiter. For books on women in academe, see for example, Jessie Bernard, *Academic Women* (1964); Alice Rossi and Anne Calderwood, eds., *Academic Women on the Move* (1973); Joan Huber, ed., *Changing Women in a Changing Society* (1973); and Cynthia Fuchs Epstein, *Woman's Place: Options and Limits in Professional Careers* (Berkeley: University of California Press, 1970).

5. S.D. Clark, "Sociology in Canada: an Historical Over-view," *Canadian Journal of Sociology* 53, 2 (Summer 1973): 225–234.

6. Ibid., p. 227. The department of sociology at the University of Toronto was not established until 1963.

7. Ibid., p. 231.

8. One of the best sources for assessing women's status in sociology in the United States, particularly in comparison with other disciplines, is Rossi and Calderwood. For recent reports on women in sociology in Canada, see Neil Guppy, "Rank, Age and Salary in Anthropology and Sociology," *Society/Societe* 13, 2 (May 1989): 14–17, and Katherine Marshall, "Women in Professional Occupations: Progress in the 1980s," *Canadian Social Trends* (Ottawa: Statistics Canada, Spring 1989) 13–16.

9. The Chicago school of sociology is somewhat enigmatic. It represented a variety of theoretical positions, all of which nevertheless "sought to establish the social realm as an independent and autonomous field of study," Martin Bulmer, *The Chicago School of Sociology: Institutionalization, Diversity, and the Rise of Sociological Research* (Chicago: The Univeristy of Chicago Press, 1984), p. 10. Bulmer points out that the department's very diversity was its strength. Perhaps this is best illustrated by the success with which its faculty and students explored through empirical research the richness of social reality and drew from the life experiences of its actors, not only vast amounts of data, but information and insights which were interpreted and integrated into general theories with implications for society in general. The university developed a policy of relieving professors for research to facilitate their 'contributions to the creation of knowledge.' Research committee funds provided a large part of their budgets for research assistants. There was a variety of financial sources available to graduate students for teaching or research activities on a part-time basis, 'making study more feasible for more students'. Ibid., p. 143.

10. Helen MacGill Hughes, "Wasp / Woman / Sociologist," *Society* (July/August 1977): 69–80. This section of the discussion draws heavily on this thorough autobiographical account of Hughes's career.

11. Ibid., p. 72.

12. Winifred Raushenbush was Robert Park's devoted research assistant who wrote much of Park's *Immigrant Press and Its Control* (1946) and later a biography of Park, *Robert E. Park: Biography of a Sociologist* (Durham, N.C.: Duke University Press, 1979).

13. Hughes found Park to be "always patient and encouraging." He and Burgess seemed to be evenhanded in their treatment of students. "That a scholar might be indifferent or even hostile to graduate students who are women, was something I never experienced. Good research was his overriding criterion — this was true of the department as a whole — and with students pursuing that goal he was endlessly patient and helpful." Helen M. Hughes, "On Becoming a Sociologist," *International Journal of the History of Sociology*, 3, (Fall-Winter 1980–81): 27–39.

14. "I used reports of the Lindbergh kidnapping to the American Press 'the greatest human interest story of the decade' as an index of the German newspapers' conception of news. That article was my first published piece." Hughes, "Wasp" p. 76.

15. Helen MacGill Hughes, *News and the Human Interest Story*. Introduction by Robert E. Park. Chicago: University of Chicago Press, 1940. While at McGill Helen published a lengthy article in the *American Journal of Sociology* (AJS) on her doctoral research. See the "Lindbergh Case: A Study of Human Interest and Politics," AJS, 42 32–54.

16. Everett C. Hughes, *French Canada in Transition* (Chicago: The University of Chicago Press, 1943), xi.

17. Helen MacGill Hughes, "Wasp," p. 76.

18. Interview with Elizabeth Hughes Schneewind, 21 June 1989.

19. "This was the beginning of a seventeen-year stint, very rewarding in everything but salary which was one hundred dollars. It was part-time work, the only kind I have ever had ... I worked with the editors ... and the University of Chicago Press, the journal's owners, and my responsibilities included planning special issues and our campaigns for subscribers, writing our publicity, working up the 'News Notes' pages, editing the accepted articles and handling much of the correspondence." Hughes, pp. 76–77. The *American Journal of Sociology* was the principal journal of American sociology until the founding of the *American Sociological Review* in 1936. The *Journal* remained a highly prestigious and perhaps the most intellectual of sociological publications in the United States for several decades.

20. Ibid.

21. Helen MacGill Hughes, "Maid of All Work or Departmental Sister-in-Laws? The Faculty Wife Employed on Campus." AJS 78, 4 (1975): 767–772.

22. Interview with Jean Burnet, 1 June 1989.

23. Hughes, "Wasp," p. 78. Helen MacGill Hughes, *The Fantastic Lodge: The*

Autobiography of a Girl Drug Addict, 1961. Helen knew this young woman, who was very bright with a great deal of potential, but who eventually committed suicide.

24. Hughes, "Wasp," p. 78. Helen's collaborative efforts include: E.C. Hughes, Helen M. Hughes and Irwin Deutscher, *Twenty Thousand Nurses Tell Their Story* (Philadelphia: Lippincott, 1958); Ozzie Simons, *Work and Mental Illness: Eight Case Studies* (New York: John Wiley & Sons, 1965); Everett C. Hughes and Helen MacGill Hughes, *Where Peoples Meet* (Chicago: University of Chicago Press, 1952); Shirley Star and Helen Hughes, "Report on an Educational Campaign: The Cincinnati Plan for the UN," AJS, 55: 389–400.

25. Calendar, Sir George Williams, 1965–66, Concordia University Archives. "There the sociologists were in many cases old friends. I have no idea how my salary compared with that of others. Indeed, one who teaches part-time is likely to know very little of colleagues' circumstances; it is as though precarious appointment made competition between them more personal. On our return to Cambridge, Wellesley College invited me to give a one-term course on public opinion and the mass media. This time I knew the salary suggested was low — I was growing more realistic now — and I asked for and got a higher figure." Hughes, "Wasp," p. 78.

26. Ibid., p. 79.

27. Ibid.

28. "In those months between 1974 and 1976, when I was teaching for one term at a time in three institutions, I learned how hard teaching can be. I also learned to appreciate the realities of part-time employment. There had never been awkward moments when I was part-timing at Wellesley and Sir George Williams. But now I found myself in embarrassing situations which, while exasperating, at this stage of my career were not ego-invading. Yet I kept wondering how I would feel, were I a young sociologist just emerging from student status to a part-time junior faculty position.

"The significant denials and the small slights are probably not sexist behavior, but usages attached to low academic status, to nonladder and part-time positions, regardless of sex. But how can we separate one discrimination from the other?" Ibid.

29. Ibid. "How attribute to the woman's career, with its peculiar domestic interruptions and responsibilities, some value commensurable with the typical 'straight' male course? Not by categorizing into men's and women's work, but by some androgynous rubric . . . In contrast to the male sociologist's well-defined track, the female counterpart, typically in the past and often in the present, has worked any unoccupied portion of the vineyard. There are exceptions, but sociology still awaits its Margaret Mead." Ibid, p. 80. She claims that only two of all the articles she wrote were submitted voluntarily rather than requested. This may be an indication that she found little time to devote to her own projects.

30. "If she had it to do again she would have wanted to teach in a regular full-time position." Interview with Elizabeth Hughes Schneewind, 21 June 1989.

31. See *The Status of Women in Sociology* 1968–1972, Helen MacGill Hughes,

ed. (Washington, D.C.: The American Sociological Association, 1973), and articles already mentioned.

32. Helen MacGill Hughes, "Women in Academic Sociology, 1925–75," NCSA Golden Anniverary Lecture, *Sociological Focus* 8, 3 (August 1975): 217–218.

33. Interview with Aileen D. Ross by Marianne Ainley, 25 November 1988.

34. Interview with Aileen Ross by Susan Hoecker-Drysdale, 6 June 1989. Mannheim was an important sociologist who emigrated from the Frankfurt Institute of Social Research, University of Frankfurt, where he had been dismissed from his post as professor of sociology and economics in 1933. Mannheim, a theorist and sociologist of knowledge, became concerned in this phase of his life with the phenomenon of fascism and antidemocratic movements, and with the problems of the reconstruction of democratic institutions and the strengthening of the moral structure of society. Mannheim was married to Juliska Lang, a psychologist who was his intellectual companion and advisor.

35. These professors, the second generation of Chicago sociologists, had been students of Robert Park and Ernest Burgess.

36. The days of her early employment at McGill were days when Sociology was still having to prove itself. There was considerable resistance to its establishment at McGill in the 1920s where Carl Dawson served as chair, but by 1933 it had gained its autonomy from social work. Dawson hired R.E. Faris and Everett Hughes from Chicago. The sociology faculty in the 1940s included Dawson, Ross, Forrest E. LaViolette, Nathan Keyfitz, and Oswald Hall. In 1948 the department of sociology and anthropology was formed. It was a visit by Margaret Mead which convinced the administration that anthropology was a 'must,' according to Ross. Aileen Ross, "Sociology at McGill in the 1940s," *Society/Société*, 8, 1 (January 1984): 4–5.

37. Aileen D. Ross. "Ethnic Relations and Social Structures: A Study of the Invasion of French-Speaking Canadians into an English Canadian District," Ph.D. thesis, University of Chicago, 1951.

38. Interview with Aileen Ross by Marianne Ainley, 25 November 1988.

39. Ibid.

40. Aileen D. Ross *The Hindu Family in Its Urban Setting* (Toronto: University of Toronto Press, 1961); and Ross, *Becoming a Nurse* (Toronto: Macmillian, 1961).

41. Ibid., p. v.

42. Aileen D. Ross, *Student Unrest in India: A Comparative Approach* (Montreal: McGill-Queen's University Press, 1969).

43. Aileen Ross, Letter from Bangalore, Christmas 1970, unpublished.

44. Aileen D. Ross, *The Lost and the Lonely: Homeless Women in Montreal* McGill University Printing Service, 1982). Doris was a "well-known prostitute and alcoholic who had lived a difficult, troubled life with little help from the community. In November 1974, she was brutally murdered in a shed in a back lane. Her murder was never solved," p. vii.

45. Ross, "Sociology at McGill in the 1940s," p. 5. Ross and her colleagues fought hard for the recognition and acceptance of sociology at McGill, that it

not be viewed as encroaching on other disciplines, or as an inefficacious science. Undoubtedly, the fact of being pioneers of a relatively new discipline created a bond among the sociologists, not only at McGill, but including those at Sir George Williams and the University of Montreal. Sociologists from the three institutions held regular joint meetings.

46. Interview with Aileen Ross by Marianne Ainley, 25 November 1989.

47. Interview with Aileen Ross by S. Hoecker-Drysdale, 13 June 1989.

48. Interview with Jean Burnet by S. Hoecker-Drysdale, 6 June 1989.

49. Jean Burnet, "Minorities I Have Belonged to," *Canadian Ethnic Studies*, 13, 1 (1981). This section of the discussion relies considerably on this article.

50. Ibid., p. 26. The University of Toronto had a connection with Columbia in that Robert M. McIver of Columbia University had taught at Toronto in the 1920s; in fact, Burnet had been awarded fellowships for doctoral studies at Bryn Mawr, Columbia, and Chicago. Ibid., p. 28

51. Ibid., p. 26. The Hughes's made their home a particular haven for Canadians, sharing news from Canada and holiday festivities. They were the centre of a network. Interview with Jean Burnet, S. Hoecker-Drysdale, 6 June 1989.

52. Jean Burnet, *Next-Year Country: A Study of Rural Social Organization in Alberta* (Toronto: University of Toronto Press, 1951). Burnet found this research to be an adventure. She had never been West; both supervisors left her more or less on her own to do the research. At that time, one was expected to go ahead with the dissertation, once it was taken for granted that the student was capable of doing the work.

53. The early years during which Burnet taught at the University of Toronto were years of expansion of sociology at the university and in Canada generally. Still fighting for recognition as a legitimate and distinct science, and still housed within the department of political economy, Burnet and her colleagues experienced solidarity and camaradarie. "We exchanged accounts of triumph and failures in teaching and in writing our doctoral theses over lunch in one restaurant on Bloor Street or afternoon tea in another." Burnet, "Minorities," pp. 26–27.

54. Jean Burnet, *Ethnic Groups in Upper Canada* (Toronto: Ontario Historial Society, 1972).

55. Jean Burnet, ed. *Looking into My Sister's Eyes: An Exploration in Women's History* (Toronto: The Multicultural History Society of Ontario, 1986).

56. Ibid., p. 2. "It is not necessary, however, to be a feminist or a militant 'ethnic' to want to tease out from Ontario history the part played by immigrant and 'ethnic' women. All that is required is a determination to give a new and richer nap to the fabric."

57. "By 1957, there were 50 members; by 1959, there were 71; by 1961, there were 95; and by 1963, there were 101." Burnet, "Minorities," p. 26. And, as Burnet points out, Canadian sociologists even in this period "regarded themselves as a minority in their own country."

58. Burnet and one other woman, Céline Saint-Pierre, served on the executive of the association from 1964–68. In 1968 Burnet left the executive and the editorship.

59. The journal had been started by Malcolm Taylor, principal at the University of Calgary, with twenty thousand dollars from the Calgary Junior League. A western academic wanted to be editor and this was probably a factor in the dispute. John Porter, who was originally asked to take the job, was unable to do so because of illness. As the first editor, Burnet sent out questionnaires soliciting articles. Getting contributions to keep the publication alive was difficult at that time. Burnet selected articles for publication on the basis of three readers' reports and probably had more autonomy as an editor than Helen Hughes, except that Hughes could impose the standards of a prestigious journal. Interview, 6 June 1989.

60. Burnet, "Minorities . . . ," op.cit., 30.

61. Ibid., p. 31.

62. Ibid.

63. Ibid.

64. Ibid.

65. Ibid.

66. Ibid., pp. 31–32.

67. Ibid.

68. Ibid.

69. Ibid., p. 33.

70. Ibid., p. 35.

71. Jean R. Burnet with Howard Palmer. "Coming Canadians": An Introduction to a History of Canada's People. Toronto: McClelland & Stewart, 1988.

72. Helen MacGill Hughes and Everett Hughes had a close relationship and happy family life. They collaborated, read together, learned languages together, and shared a study. They were colleagues. But she took responsibility for childrearing and running the household, and looked up to her husband, whose professional needs came first. While 'she always had some job in the works' and was a woman with great energy, she had to 'work around everyone else,' (that is, to define and structure her work around the needs and activities of her family). Interview with Elizabeth Hughes Schneewind, 21 June 1989. Burnet also remarks that Helen Hughes was a strong woman who "was quite insistent on her identity as a career woman and a professional woman. She couldn't imagine being married to anyone else. It was a very strong marriage . . . They were very devoted." Interview with Jean Burnet, 6 June 1989.

73. Jean Burnet related the story of a professional woman flutist writing in Woodwind World, whose advice was: 'if you marry another flutist, change your instrument'.

74. Hughes, "Wasp," p. 80.

75. Helen Hughes was a collaborator par excellence; she understood that good research can be a cooperative affair. Nevertheless, her career stands in sharp contrast to someone like Dorothy Swain, who in 1935 as a thirty-six-year-

old research associate at the University of Chicago, married her seventy-two year old professor, William I. Thomas, and became an important demographer and the first woman president of the American Sociological Society. Lewis A. Coser, *Masters of Sociological Thought: Ideas in Historical and Social Context,* 2nd ed. (New York: Harcourt Brace Jovanovich, 1977): p. 536.

76. "The position of editorial assistant of *The American Journal of Sociology* would certainly never have been offered to a male Ph.D., or even to a male doctoral student (after 1942, all editorial assistants were women) whose mentor would be watching paternally for an opening in which he could set his disciple's feet on the path to a career like his own. But a female Ph.D., in 1944 and perhaps even in 1972, would find herself in this position, although in 1972 she would probably be better able to negotiate." Hughes, "Maid," p. 772).

77. Helen Hughes reminded us that when women are located outside regular departments of sociology (as happened often because of anti-nepotism rules), or do rather specialized work, they may not be called sociologists. As in the case of "Hazel Kyrk, a Chicago Ph.D. in 1920 in home economics and later in economics, who studied family budgets . . . her subject was not called sociology, though it was called sociology when the French sociologist LePlay studied family budgets one hundred years ago." Hughes, "Women in Academic Sociology," p. 218.

78. Although the articles published by women in the AJS and ASR between 1925–34, for example, amounted to less than ten percent of the total, women probably made up a lower percentage than that of the total number of sociologists. Hughes, Ibid., p. 220. In a more recent analysis, Mackie found that women sociologists' publishing performance exceeds their representation as full-time members of graduate departments. See Marlene Mackie, "Female Sociologists' Productivity, Collegial Relations, and Research Style Examined Through Journal Publications," *Sociology and Social Research* (1985): 69, 189–209.

79. Clark, p. 231.

80. Helen Hughes attended meetings and was active in the profession well into her 80s. Aileen Ross at the current age of 87 is doing research on homeless men. Jean Burnet at 69 is chief executive officer and chair of the board of the Multicultural History Society of Ontario.

Gillett • *Heart of the Matter (Maude E. Abbott)*

ACKNOWLEDGEMENTS

An earlier version of this paper was originally presented at an interdisciplinary seminar in the department of humanities and social studies of medicine, McGill University, 1984. A longer version has been published in G. Clifford, ed., *Lone Voyagers. Academic Women in Coeducational Institutions, 1870–1937*. (New York: Feminist Press, 1989), pp.183–222.

NOTES

1. Stanley B. Frost, "The Abbotts of McGill," *McGill Journal of Education* 13, 3 (Fall 1978): 264.

2. Maude Elizabeth Seymour Abbott, "Diary," MUA, MG 1070.

3. See M. Carey Thomas, "Present Tendencies in Women's College and University Education," in Judith Stacey et al., eds., *And Jill Came Tumbling After: Sexism in American Education* (New York: Laurel, 1974) pp.275–278.

4. See Margaret Gillett, *We Walked Very Warily: A History of Women at McGill* (Montreal: Eden Press, 1981), Ch. 2.

5. "Autobiographical Sketch," 1928, Maude Abbott Papers, MUA, MG 1070.

6. Valedictory Address, 1890, Maude Abbott Papers, MUA, MG 1070.

7. The Montreal *Gazette*, for example, reported on the movement for women's medical education sympathetically, and on March 27, 1889 editorialized: "There are few today who question the wisdom of giving women the opportunity of studying medicine .... The outcome of the movement will be watched with interest and with many hopes for its success."

8. "Women and Medicine — A Meeting in the Interest of Medical Education," Montreal *Gazette*, 4 April 1889.

9. Elizabeth Smith Shortt, *Historical Sketch of Medical Education of Women, Kingston, Canada* (Ottawa: Private Printing, 1916), p.1.

10. Quoted by H.E. MacDermot in *Maude Abbott: A Memoir* (Toronto: Macmillan, 1941), p.50.

11. Dr. Harold Segall, a reknowned cardiac specialist and quondam student of Dr. Abbott, wrote in a private communication to the author, dated 25 July 1984, "When I met her in St. Andrews in 1936 and discussed the illness with Maudie — the diagnosis was manic depressive psychosis."

12. When the paper of Osler's letter threatened to wear out, Dr. Francis, curator of the Osler Library, had it bound for her on condition that she leave it to the library. It is accession #9545.

13. Members of three consecutive classes (1902–04) expressed their appreciation by presenting her with gifts. While this gesture must be applauded, it should not obscure the fact that Dr. Abbott gave very demanding courses for no tangible reward other than a small "purse" or book tokens.

14. See Jessie Boyd Scriver, "Maude E. Abbott," in Mary Quale Innis, ed., *The Clear Spirit: Twenty Canadian Women and Their Times* (Toronto: Canadian Federation of University Women/University of Toronto Press, 1967), p. 142.

15. Letter to Dr. F. Owen Stredder, Bursar, McGill University, 20 December 1935, Osler Library Archives, #606.

16. "Honorary M.D.: Unusual Degree to be Conferred on Lady Doctor," Montreal *Witness*, 13 May 1910, McGill University Scrapbook #2, p. 325. 17. Undated letter to Professor J.G. Adami (chairman of pathology), quoted by H.E. MacDermot, p. 67.

18. Letter to Colonel J.G. Adami, 3 August 1918, Osler Library Archives, #606.

19. Letter to Principal A.E. Morgan, McGill University, 5 November 1935, Osler Library Archives, #606.

20. Another letter to Principal A.E. Morgan, November 1935, Osler Library Archives, #606.

21. Stanley B. Frost, *McGill University: For the Advancement of Learning*, Vol. II, 1895–1971, (Montreal: McGill-Queen's, 1984), p.170.

22. In 1905, when McGill took over Bishop's Faculty of Medicine and Dentistry (the school from which Maude Abbott received her M.D.), there was an agreement that all Bishop's graduates would automatically be accorded McGill degrees. This was honoured in the case of the men, but was not applied to the eligible women. See Frost, *For the Advancement of Learning*, pp. 44–45 and n.28, pp. 57–58.

23. Maude Abbott, "Autobiographical Sketch," last words.

24. H.E. MacDermot, "Dr. Maude Abbott," *McGill News*, 22, 2 (Winter, 1940): 21.

25. Dr. Helen MacMurchy, national corresponding secretary of the Federation of Medical Women of Canada, 17 January 1934, Osler Library Archives, #43884.

26. *Montreal Daily Star*, 3 September 1940.

27. See Mary Walsh, *Doctors Wanted: No Women Need Apply* (New Haven, Conn.: Yale University Press, 1977).

28. Women were excluded from the McGill Faculty Club until 1936. Maude Abbott was the first to break this barrier. In 1984, a room was named in her honour as the first woman member.

29. Maude Abbott diary entry, 7 November 1929, written in the Ross Pavillion, Royal Victoria Hospital, Montreal, MUA, MG 1070.

30. Dr. C.F. Martin, Emeritus Dean of Medicine, McGill University, "Maude Abbott — An Appreciation," *McGill Medical Journal* 10 (1940), pp. 29 and 32.

Canham • Harriet Brooks

ACKNOWLEDGEMENTS

This article is adapted from the paper "Harriet Brooks — Pioneer Nuclear Scientist" which is to appear in the *American Journal of Physics* (AJP) Robert H. Romer, editor of the AJP, is thanked for permission.

We thank Paul Brooks Pitcher and Cicely Grinling (son and niece of Harriet Brooks, respectively) for their help and encouragement. Our thanks must also go to the following: Patricia K. Ballou and Lucinda Manning, Barnard College; Monique Bordry, Curie Institute; L.P. Bykovtseva, Gorky Museum; Phebe Chartrand and Montague Cohen, McGill University; A.E.B. Owen, Cambridge University; Caroline Rittenhouse, Bryn Mawr College; and Elizabeth Behrens, Sir Wilfred Grenfell College.

NOTES

1. Harriet Brooks, "Damping of Electrical Oscillations," *Transactions of Royal Society of Canada*, Sec. III. (1899): 13.

2. Harriet Brooks, "Damping of the Oscillations in the Discharge of a Leyden Jar" M.A. thesis, McGill University (1901).

3. Ernest Rutherford and Harriet T. Brooks, "The New Gas from Radium," *Trans. Roy. Soc. Canada*, Sec. III., (1901): 21; also published in *Chemical News* (25 April 1902): 196.

4. Ernest Rutherford and Harriet T. Brooks, "Comparison of the Radiations from Radioactive Substances," *Philosophical Magazine*, 6th. Ser. (1902): 1.

5. H. Brooks to E. Rutherford, 18 March 1902, Cambridge University Archives (CUA).

6. Ibid.

7. H. Brooks to E. Rutherford, spring 1903 (undated), CUA.

8. A. Stewart Eve, "Some Scientific Centres. VIII, The MacDonald Physics Building, McGill University, Montreal," *Nature* 74 (1906): 272.

9. Harriet Brooks, "A Volatile Product from Radium," *Nature* 70 (1904): 270.

10. Harriet Brooks, "The Decay of the Excited Radioactivity from Thorium, Radium, and Actinium," *Phil. Mag.* 8(1904): 373.

11. L. Gill to H. Brooks, 12 July 1906, Barnard College Archives (BCA).

12. H. Brooks to L. Gill, 18 July 1906, BCA.

13. M. Maltby to L. Gill, 24 July 1906, BCA.

14. L. Gill to M. Maltby, 30 July 1906, BCA.

15. Maxim Gorky, *Letters* (Moscow: Progress Publishers, 1966), p. 49.

16. Alexander Kaun, *Maxim Gorky and His Russia* (New York: Benjamin Blom, 1968), p. 573.

17. Maria F. Andreeva, *Perepiska Vospominaniia* (Moscow: Iskusstvo, 1968), p. 147.

18. H. Brooks to M. Curie, 31 May 1907, Curie Institute, Paris.

19. André Debierne, "Sur le coefficient de diffusion dans l'air de l'émination de l'actinium," *Le Radium* 4 (1907): 213; André Debierne, "Sur le dépôt de la radioactivité induite du radium," *Le Radium* 6 (1909): 97; and L. Blanquies, "Comparaison entre les rayons produits par différentes substances radioactives," *Le Radium* 6 (1909): 230.

20. E. Rutherford to A. Schuster, 25 March 1907, The Royal Society, London.

21. Margaret W. Rossiter, *Women Scientists in America* (Baltimore: John Hopkins University Press, 1982), p. 195.

22. Roberta Frankfort, *Collegiate Women* (New York: New York University Press, 1977), p. 33.

23. M. Rutherford to H. Brooks, 28 November 1907, H. Brooks files of Paul Brooks Pitcher.

24. A fuller account of the life of Harriet Brooks is to be published.

25. H. Brooks, manuscript of presentation, Paul Brooks Pitcher collection.

26. From lists of authors of papers on radioactivity, we have identified the following women nuclear science researchers of the time: Winifred Moller Beilby (Mrs. Soddy), L. Blanquies, Fanny Cook Gates, Ellen Gleditch, May Sybil Leslie, Lise Meitner, Margaret Lindsey Murray (Lady Huggins), Ruth Pirret, Eva Ramstedt, J.M.W. Slater, Jadwiga Szmidt, and E.G. Willcock. Of these, only Lise Meitner subsequently received recognition for her work. A paper on these other women nuclear scientists is in preparation.

27. Lois Arnold, "Marie Curie Was Great, But . . . ," *School Science and Mathematics* 75 (1975): 577.

28. Ernest Rutherford, "Obituary: Harriet Brooks (Mrs. Frank Pitcher)," *Nature* 131 (1933): 865.

29. David Wilson, *Rutherford* (Cambridge, Mass.: MIT Press, 1983); A. Stewart Eve, *Rutherford* (Cambridge: Cambridge University Press, 1939); Daniil S. Danin, *Rezerford* (Moscow: Molodaya gvardiya, 1967).

Meadowcroft • Alice Wilson

ACKNOWLEDGEMENTS

I am grateful to Marianne Ainley for her generosity in making her research available to me. I thank Jocelyne Legault and Anne Montagnes for their help.

NOTES

1. National Archives of Canada (NAC), Records of the Geological Survey of Canada, RG 32, C, 2, Vol. 358, A.E. Wilson to W.H. Collins, 7 November 1924. Hereafter Wilson papers.

2. For information on the Wilson family, see Anne Montagnes, "Alice Wilson," in Mary Quale Innis, Ed., *The Clear Spirit: Twenty Canadian Women and Their Times* (Toronto: University of Toronto Press, 1966), pp. 261–62.

3. Ibid., pp. 263–64.

4. Wilson papers, Wilson to Collins, 19 March 1930.

5. Montagnes, p. 263.

6. Morris Zaslow, *Reading the Rocks: The Story of the Geological Survey of Canada, 1842–1972* (Ottawa: Macmillan, 1975), p. 4.

7. Ibid., p. 286.

8. NAC, RG 32, C, 2, Vol. 256, File 6193.

9. G.W. Sinclair, "Alice Evelyn Wilson, 1881–1964," *Proceedings and Transactions of the Royal Society of Canada*, 4th Series, Vol. 4 (1966): 118.

10. Wilson, "A New Ordovician Pelecypod from the Ottawa District," *Ottawa Naturalist* 29 (November 1915): 85–86.

11. NAC, records of the CFUW MG 28, I, 196, Wilson to Thom, 4 July 1926, p. 4. Hereafter CFUW papers.

12. Zaslow, pp. 285–87.

13. CFUW papers, Wilson to Thom, 23 January 1926, p. 2.

14. Taped interview with Madeleine Fritz, 1973, University of Toronto Archives, B74–0022, side 1.

15. Wilson papers, Wilson to Collins, 7 November 1924.

16. CFUW papers, Wilson to Thom, 23 January 1926, p. 3.

17. CFUW papers, Thom to Wilson, 1 March 1926.

18. CFUW papers, letter from the office of the president of the University of Toronto to the president of the CFUW, 26 April 1926.

19. Wilson papers, review of Wilson's application for permission to undertake post-graduate studies, 28 April 1926, p. 5.

20. Wilson papers, Bolton to Collins, 12 May 1926.

21. CFUW papers, Wilson to Vaughan, 15 June 1926.

22. Wilson papers, Camsell to Wilson, 15 June 1926.

23. CFUW papers, Wilson to Thom, 4 July 1926.

24. Wilson papers, Collins to Camsell, 4 November 1926.

25. The palaeontological section of Wilson's thesis appeared in the *Proceedings and Transactions of the Royal Society of Canada* (1932).

26. Alice spent four terms at the University of Chicago: October 1 to Christmas, 1926; April 1 to June 30, 1927; October 1 to Christmas, 1928; January 1 to March 23, 1929.

27. Montagnes, p. 261.

28. Wilson papers, Memorandum re Proposed Reappraisal of the Duties of Dr. Alice E. Wilson, MI-G-157, 8 July 1931.

29. Wilson papers, Camsell to Collins, 15 September 1931.

30. Zaslow, pp.378–80.

31. NAC, RG 32, C, 2, Vol. 256, File 6193.

32. Alice's annual pension was $2,461.29. Ibid.

33. Wilson papers, Wilson to Burpee, 18 August 1953.

34. Quoted by Montagnes, p. 276.

35. *A Guide to the Geology of the Ottawa District*, monograph issue of *The Canadian Field-Naturalist*, Vol. 70 (1956) p. 6.

36. *Globe and Mail* (25 February 1960): 18.

Von Baeyer • Isabella Preston

NOTES

1. Margaret Burtner, interview, 29 October 1985. Readers wishing to know more of Preston's originations, awards, and writings can consult the extended version of this biography in *Canadian Horticultural History* 1, 3, (1987): 125–175. My special thanks to Ina Vrugtman of the Royal Botanical Gardens, who not only made the library's Isabella Preston Collection accessible to me, but also provided encouragement and information all along the way.

2. Isabella Preston, letter to Toronto Horticultural Society, 1939. This material is in the custody of Records Services, Corporate Management Branch, Agriculture Canada, to be transferred to RG 17 — Records of Agriculture Canada, at the National Archives of Canada.

3. Ibid.

4. Royal Botanical Gardens Library, Hamilton, Ontario, Isabella Preston Collection [Hereafter RGB I. Preston Coll.], handwritten autobiographical fragment, n.d.

5. RGB I. Preston Coll., handwritten draft of an article for *Iris Bulletin*, 1954, p. 2.

6. Bob Collins, "Canada's Lady of the Lilies," *Canadian Homes and Gardens*, [hereafter *Can. Homes and Gard.*] 30 (July 1953): 47.

7. In 1903, the Macdonald Institute was founded, which granted degrees in home economics to women. However, women were not admitted to the degree course in agriculture until 1918. See Alexander M. Ross, *The College on the Hill: A History of the Ontario Agricultural College 1874–1974* (Toronto: Copp Clark, 1974).

8. D.W. MacDonald, "The Preston Touch," *Family Herald and Weekly Star* (15 November 1951): 5.

9. Collins, p. 47.

10. RGB I. Preston Coll., handwritten autobiographical fragment.

11. RGB I. Preston Coll., handwritten autobiographical fragment.

12. Edwinna von Baeyer, *Rhetoric and Roses: A History of Canadian Gardening, 1900–1930.* (Toronto: Fitzhenry & Whiteside, 1984), p. 163.

13. Isabella Preston, "Hybridization of Lilies," Royal Horticultural Society Lily Year-Book, Conference Number, London, 1933, p. 173.

14. Ibid., pp. 173–174.

15. E.S. Archibald to J.H. Grisdale, 10 November 1920. This material is in the custody of Records Services, Corporate Management Branch, Agriculture Canada, to be transferred to RG 17 — Records of Agriculture Canada — National Archives Canada.

16. RBG I., Preston Coll., typewritten draft of autobiography, p. 2.

17. Kathleen Archibald, *Sex and the Public Service: A Report to the Public Service Commission of Canada* (Ottawa: Queen's Printer for Canada, 1970), pp. 14–16.

18. E.S. Archibald to J.H. Grisdale, 10 November 1920.

19. Ibid.

20. In spring, 1938, she received her only promotion: from specialist in ornamental horticulture to assistant horticulturist. She never went higher, as the next level was dominion horticulturist.

21. W.T. Macoun, "Some New Lilac Hybrids," *The National Horticultural Magazine* 10 (July 1931): 187.

22. Isabella Preston, "Rose Breeding at the Horticulture Division, Central Experimental Farm, Ottawa," *Yearbook of the Rose Society of Ontario* (Toronto, 1922), p. 41.

23. Isabella Preston, "Roses for the Home Garden," *Can. Hort. and Home Mag.*, Floral Edition (April 1931): 117.

24. Preston, "Rose Breeding," p. 43.

25. Isabella Preston, "Progress in Breeding Hardy Roses," *American Rose Annual* (Harrisburg, Pa.: The American Rose Society, 1946), p. 51.

26. L.F. Randolph, ed., *Garden Irises*, (St. Louis, Missouri: American Iris Society, 1959), p. 426.

27. Ibid., p. 89.

28. RBG I., Preston Coll., Percy Wright to I. Preston, 17 March 1950.

29. Margaret Burtner, interview.

30. Isabella Preston, "Books for the Gardener's Library," *Can. Hort. and Home Mag.*, Floral Edition 61 (April 1938): 11.

31. Dorothy Burt, interview, January 1986.

32. "Presentation of the Carter Medal," *Annual Report of the Horticultural Societies of Ontario for 1937* (Toronto, 1938), p. 37.

33. RBG I., Preston Coll., work diary, 20 July 1939.

34. RBG I., Preston Coll., work diary, 5 August 1942.

35. D.R. Sampson, interview, Fall 1985.

36. A.R. Buckley, interview, 25 October 1982.

37. National Archives of Canada, William Lyon Mackenzie King Papers, MG 26 J 10, Vol. 26, File 3, W.L. Mackenzie King to W.T. Macoun, 30 September 1922.

38. Preston, "Hybridization of Lilies," pp. 186–190.

39. Charles H. Curtis, "Miss Isabella Preston," *The Lily Yearbook* (London: Royal Horticultural Society, 1956), p. 10.

40. Isabella Preston, "Stenographer Lilies and Some of Their Descendants," *Can. Hort. and Home Mag.*, Floral Edition 69 (Nov.–Dec. 1946): 225.

41. Vita Sackville-West, *A Joy of Gardening, A Selection for Americans*, Hermine I. Popper, ed. (Harper & Brothers, New York, 1958), p. 120.

42. Margaret Burtner, interview.

43. D.F. Cameron, interview, 12 October 1982.

44. Manitoba Archives, MG 14 C 45, I. Preston to Frank Skinner, 12 October 1922.

45. Marjorie Nazer, interview, 19 November 1981.

46. RBG I., Preston Coll., "Lilacs," n.d., p. 1.

47. D.F. Cameron, interview, 12 October 1982.

48. Collins, p. 27.

49. Ibid.

Estey • Margaret Newton

ACKNOWLEDGEMENTS

The author is indebted to Dr. Dorothy Swales, sister of Margaret Newton, for many helpful suggestions, and for making available to him some unpublished memoirs of her brother, the late Dr. Robert Newton. The assistance of Mr. M. Malyk, librarian, Winnipeg Research Station, and of archivists at the Universities of Manitoba, Saskatchewan, and Victoria is gratefully acknowledged.

NOTES

1. Most of the non-referenced information in this paper was provided by Dr. Dorothy (Newton) Swales, sister of Margaret Newton, or comes from the unpublished memoirs of her brother, the late Dr. Robert Newton.

2. The class photograph, and the comments of the class historian, are from the publication *Old McGill*, 1915, unpaginated. The names of the students who registered in agriculture in 1913–14 are listed in *McGill University Annual Calendar for 1914–15*, p. 445. 3. The Governor General's bronze medal for highest standing at the end of the second year was the only medal given to agriculture students. There were no gold or silver medals given between 1910 and at least 1920.

4. That "ten-o'clock rule" remained in the *Macdonald College Announcement* until at least 1943–44. See p. 901.

5. Anon., "Members of the Quebec Society for the Protection of Plants," *Annual Report Quebec Society for the Protection of Plants* (1917): 5–7.

6. An account of this accomplishment, with a photograph of "the first ladies to receive a degree in Agriculture in Canada," appeared in the Montreal *Herald*, 17 May 1918.

7. J.H. Grisdale, "Report of the Acting Dominion Botanist for the year 1919," (Ottawa, 1919) p. 60.

8. J.H. Craigie, "Epidemiology of Stem Rust in Western Canada," *Scientific Agriculture* 25 (1945): 391.

9. W.P. Fraser, "Report of the Saskatoon Laboratory of Plant Pathology — for 1920–21," In *Report of the Director, Dominion Experimental Farms for 1921* (Ottawa, 1922), pp. 93–107.

10. Ibid.

11. This information was gleaned from the *Calendars of the University of Saskatchewan* for the years 1922–25.

12. W.P. Thompson, "Report of the Department of Biology for 1921–21, to the President of the University of Saskatchewan," April 20, 1922, University Archives.

13. For a complete list of Dr. Newton's publications, see R.H. Estey, "Margaret Newton: Distinguished Canadian Scientist and First Woman Member of the

Quebec Society for the Protection of Plants," *Phytoprotection* 68 (1987): 84–85.

14. E.M. Rive, "Pioneer of the Rust Lab," *Free Press Weekly* (13 September 1969): 22.

15. E. Cora Hind, *Seeing for Myself: Agricultural Conditions Around the World* (Toronto, 1937). p. 83.

16. Dr. Newton wrote an account of her voyage to Russia that was published as a letter to "Dear Aurora" in the newsletter for staff and students of the University of Minnesota's Department of Plant Pathology, *Aurora Sporealis*, 10 (1934): 1–2. Her letter did not mention the duration of her stay in Russia, nor of any work or lecturing that she may have done while there. The comment about her refusing payment is from her brother's unpublished memoir.

17. H.T. Gussow, "Report of the Official Representative Committee of the Society. Sixth International Botanical Congress and International Union of the Biological Sciences. September 1935, Amsterdam." *Phytopathology* 26 (1936): 301–303.

18. T. Johnson, Unpublished memoirs, in the Library of the Agriculture Canada Research Station, Winnipeg, Manitoba.

19. Ibid.

20. That quotation is from an unsigned, non-paginated, typescript titled, "Dr. Margaret Newton at Saskatchewan University 1919–1925," in the Archives of the University of Saskatchewan.

21. Anon. "Flavelle Medal: Margaret Newton." *Proceedings of the Royal Society of Canada*, Series 3, 42 (1948): 47–48.

22. Thorvaldur Johnson, "Margaret Newton 1887–1971." *Proceedings of the Royal Society of Canada*, Series 4, 9 (1971): 84–86.

23. Anon. "Round and About." *Alumni News* (University of Minnesota) 59 (1966): 31.

Anand • Cypra Krieger

ACKNOWLEDGEMENTS

I am indebted to my colleagues all across Canada and the United States who gave me important leads and valuable information about Cecelia Krieger. I would like to thank, in particular, Cathleen Morawetz, Alex and Edith Rosenberg, my daughter, Anita Anand, and Sharon Larade, of Archives, University of Toronto, for their help and encouragement.

NOTES

1. C. Morawetz, personal communication, August 1987.

2. Gilbert de B. Robinson, *The Mathematics Department in the University of Toronto 1827–1978*, p. 32.

3. K. Anand, "Canadian Women Mathematicians from Early Nineteenth Century to 1960, a More Comprehensive Study," *Canadian Mathematical Society Notes*, forthcoming.

4. Nancy Bush, University of Toronto Communications Office. Basic information about Cecilia Krieger from Archives, University of Toronto, conveyed July 1988.

5. Edith E. Rosenberg, personal communication, February 1989.

6. (a) Jacques Chapleon gave the course on modern elliptic function; (b) John L. Synge gave the course on minimum principles of mechanics; (c) S. Beatty gave the course on theory of sets; (d) I. C. Fields, after whom Fields Medal is named, taught theory of numbers.

7. G. de B. Robinson, *The Mathematics Department in the University of Toronto, 1827–1978*, p. 30.

8. *Comprehensive Dissertation Index 1861–1972*.

9. Edith E. Rosenberg, personal communication, 7 February 1989.

10. *Toronto Telegraph*, 19 January 1934.

11. Cecilia Krieger, "On the Summability of Trigonometric Series with Localised Properties," *Royal Society of Canada Transactions* 22, 3 (1928): 139–147.

12. Cecilia Krieger, "On Fourier Series in Two Variables and On Questions in the Theory of Sets," *Royal Society of Canada Proceeding and Transactions*.

13. Cecilia Krieger, "On Fourier Constants and Convergence Factors of Double Fourier Series," *Royal Society of Canada Transactions*, Series 3, Vol. 24, Sec. 3 (May 1930): 161–196.

14. G. de B. Robinson, *The Mathematics Department*, p. 72. Also personal communication, January 1989.

15. *Telegraph*, 18 January 1934, and 19 January 1934, and *University of Toronto Monthly*, March 1934.

16. Alex and Edith Rosenberg, personal communications.

17. Nancy Bush.

18. *Toronto Telegraph*, 19 January 1934.
19. Morawetz.
20. J.L. Synge, personal communication, February 1988.
21. *Toronto Star*, 25 January 1934.

Beaveridge • Getting a Job Done (Blossom Wigdor)

NOTES

1. Alfred Holden, "Ahead of Her Time," *Toronto Star,* 31 January 1989.
2. Marilyn Froggatt and Lorraine Hunter, *Pricetag: Canadian Women and the Stress of Success* (Nelson Canada), p. 83.
3. Judith Sheinin, *The Development and Social Adjustment of the Jewish Community in Montreal,* unpublished M.A. thesis, 1939, McGill University Library, Rare Books Department, Introduction.
4. Marlene Shore, *The Science of Social Redemption: McGill, the Chicago School and the Origins of Social Research in Canada* (University of Toronto Press, 1987) pp. 244–245, quoting Stanley Brice Frost, *McGill University: For the Advancement of Learning,* Vol. II.
5. Froggatt and Hunter, p. 81.
6. Oral History Interview, Concordia University, Montreal, April 1989.
7. Lykke de la Cour, "The 'Other' Side of Psychology: Women Psychologists in Toronto from 1920 to 1945," *Canadian Woman Studies* (8, 4): 44.
8. Ibid.
9. Ibid., p. 45.
10. George A. Ferguson, "Psychology at McGill," in Mary J. White and C. Roger Myers, *History of Academic Psychology in Canada,* (C.J. Hogrefe, Inc., Toronto, 1982), p. 59.
11. Oral History.
12. Margaret Gillett, *We Walked Very Warily,* (Montreal: Eden Press Women's Publications 1981), p. 400.
13. Gillett, p. 409.
14. Oral History.
15. Gillett, p. 412.
16. Ibid., p. 393.
17. Ibid.

18. McGill University Archives, Science, Botany, R62–62.

19. Stanley Brice Frost, *McGill University: For the Advancement of Learning*, Vol. II (Montreal: McGill-Queen's University Press, 1984), p. 137, n19. 20. Frost., p. 128.

21. Ibid.

22. Gordon W. Allport, *The Nature of Prejudice* (Reading Mass.: Addison Wesley Publishing Co., 1976), p. 469.

23. For the reaction of American universities, such as Columbia and Harvard, to similar pressures concerning enrolment of Jewish students, Frost refers his readers to Harold Wechsler, *The Qualified Student* (New York, 1977), pp. 131–85; Frost, p. 137 n. 19. Further, the University of Toronto was not immune during the 1940s to eminent people freely expressing personal prejudices about faculty membership. Harold Innes, chairman of the department of political economy, claimed that there were already too many women and Jews in the social sciences, (Jean Burnet, "Minorities I Have Belonged To," *Canadian Ethnic Studies*, 13 (1981).

24. Edward C. Webster, *The Development of Professional Psychology in One University*, unpublished, McGill University Archives, PSY 991 1983, p. 3.

25. Ibid.

26. Ibid.

27. Ferguson, p. 63

28. Ibid.

29. Webster.

30. Ibid., p. 7.

31. Ibid., p. 6.

32. Gillett.

33. Pnina G. Abir-Am and Dorinda Outram, eds., *Uneasy Careers and Intimate Lives: Women in Science 1789–1979* (New Brunswick: Rutgers University Press, 1987) p. 15.

34. Ibid.

35. Gillett., p. 400.

36. Gillett, p. 18.

37. Oral History.

Collis • *Adolescent Females And Computers*

NOTES

1. British Columbia Ministry of Education, *Computers in Canadian Education*, Research Report, (Victoria, B.C., 1985).
2. L.R. Smith, "The Ontario Initiatives Introducing Microtechnology to Schools," paper presented at the Fifth Canadian Symposium on Instructional Technology, Ottawa, May 1986. 3. E. Gonzalez, "Manitoba Strategy to Stimulate the Implementation of Educational Technologies," Ibid.
4. G. Romaniuk, ed. *Computers in Schools. A Strategic Planning Symposium*, (Edmonton, Alberta: Alberta Education, 1986).
5. D. Yocam, "Computers in Education," Fifth Annual Conference of the Alberta Teachers' Association Computer Council, Edmonton, March 1987.
6. H.J. Becker, "Using Computers for Instruction," *Byte* (February 1987): 149–162; M.E. Lockheed, "Women, Girls and Computers. A First Look at the Evidence," *Sex Roles* 13, 3/4 (1985):115–122; R.A. Smith, "Women, Education, and Computers," *The Monitor* 24, 5/6 (1985):10, 27.
7. R.E. Anderson, W.W. Welch, and L.J. Harris, "Inequities in Opportunities for Computer Literacy," *The Computing Teacher* 11, 8 (1984):10–12.
8. R.E. Anderson, D.L. Klassen, K.R. Krohn, and P. Smith-Cunnien, *Assessing Computer Literacy* (St. Paul, Minn.: MECC, 1982), Publication 503; J. Lipkin and L.M. McCormick, "Sex Bias at the Computer Terminal:How Schools Program Girls," *The Monitor* 24 (1985):14–17; Newsnotes, "Problems of Equity in High School Programming Courses," *Phi Delta Kappa* 66, 7 (1985):515–516.
9. R.D. Hess and I. Miura, "Gender Differences in Enrollment in Computer Camps and Classes. The Extracurricular Acquisition of Computer Training," *Sex Roles* 13, 3/4 (1985):193–203; G. Revelle *et al*, "Sex Differences in the Use of Computers," paper presented at the Annual Meeting of the American Educational Research Association, New Orleans, La., April 1984.
10. M. Fetler, "Computer Literacy in California Schools," *Sex Roles* 13 3/4 (1985):181–192; J. S. Sanders, "The Computer, Male, Female or Androgynous?" *The Computing Teacher* 11, 8 (1984):31–34.
11. Becker.
12. Lockheed.
13. G. McKelvey, cited in *Education Daily* 17, 17 (25 January 1984):6.
14. Becker.
15. I. Miura and R. D. Hess, "Sex Differences in Computer Access, Interest, and Usage," paper presented at the Annual Meeting of the American Psychological Association, Anaheim, Calif., 1983.
16. S. Kiesler, L. Sproull, and J. Eccles, "Second-class Citizens?" *Psychology Today* (March 1983):19–26.
17. B. A. Collis, "The Development of an Instrument to Measure Attitudes of Secondary School Males and Females Toward Computers," unpublished Ph. D.

thesis, University of Victoria, 1984; Revelle *et al.*

18. Collis; Lockheed; L. E. Temple *Gender Differences in Attitudes Towards Computers*, unpublished M. A. thesis, University of Winnipeg, 1986; G. Wilder, D. Mackie, and J. Cooper, "Gender and Computers:Two Surveys of Computer Related Attitudes," *Sex Roles* 13, 3/4 (1985):215–228.

19. B. A. Collis, "Sex Differences in Secondary School Students' Attitudes Toward Computers," *The Computing Teacher* 12, 7 (1985):33–36.

20. H. M. Levin and R. W. Rumberger, *Education and Training Needs for Using Computers in Small Businesses*, (Stanford, Calif.:Stanford Education Policy Institute, 1986), Report 86-SEPI–7.

21. B. A. Collis, "Reflections on Inequities in Computer Education:Do the Rich Get Richer?" *Education and Computing* 1 (1985):180–181.

22. M. Sadker, "Sexism in Schools," *Journal of Teacher Education* 26, 4 (1975):317–322.

23. J. M. Armstrong and R. A. Price, "Correlates and Predictors of Women's Mathematics Participation," *Journal for Research in Mathematics Associations*, 13 (1982):99–107; E. Fennema, "Sex-related Differences in Mathematics Achievement:Where and Why?" in L. H. Fox, L. Brody and D. Tobin, eds., *Women and the Mathematical Mystique* (Baltimore:Johns Hopkins University Press, 1980), pp. 76–93; H. W. Marsh, I. D. Smith, and J. Barnes, "Multidimensional Self-concepts:Relations with Sex and Academic Achievement," *Journal of Educational Psychology* 77, 5 (1985):581–596.

24. S. J. Dasho and L. C. Beckum, "Microcomputers and Educational Equity:The Promise and the Peril," paper presented at the Annual Meeting of the American Educational Research Association, Montreal, April, 1983; M. E. Lockheed *et al*, *Sex and Ethnic Differences in Middle School Mathematics, Science and Computer Science:What Do We Know?* (Princeton, N. J.: Educational Testing Service, 1985); Sanders; J. G. Schubert, "Gender Equity in Computer Learning," *Theory Into Practice* 25, 4 (1986):267–275.

25. Dasho and Beckum.

26. Schubert.

27. Lockheed *et al.*, p.24.

28. H. J. Becker, *School Use of Computer.Reports from a National Survey*, Issue 2, (Baltimore:Johns Hopkins University, Center for Social Organization of Schools, 1983); Becker, 1987.

29. M. Lockheed and S. Frakt, "Sex Equity:Increasing Girls' Use of Computers," *The Computing Teacher* 11, 8 (1984):16–18; Sanders.

30. Becker, *School Uses.*

31. Becker, "Using Computers."

32. N. Flodin, *British Columbia Public Schools Microcomputer Inservice Survey*, (Victoria, B. C.: British Columbia Teachers' Federation, 1984).

33. Fennema.

34. C. Daiute, *Writing and Computers* (Reading, Mass.:Addison-Wesley, 1985).

35. M. B. Gredler, "A Taxonomy of Computer Simulations," *Educational*

Technology 26, 4 (1986):7–12; T. Lam, "Probing Microcomputer-based Laboratories," *Hands On!* 8, 1 (1984–85):1, 4–5.

36. J. Parker, "Tools for Thought," *The Computing Teacher* 14, 2 (1986):21–23.

37. M. Lamb, "An Interactive Graphical Modeling Game for Teaching Musical Concepts," *Journal of Computer-Based Instruction* 9, 2 (1982):59–63.

38. J. S. Sanders, "Making the Computer Neutral," *The Computing Teacher* 12, 7 (1985):23–32.

39. B. A. Collis and L. Ollila, "An Examination of Sex Differences in Secondary School Students' Attitudes Toward Writing and Toward Computers," *The Alberta Journal of Educational Research* 32, 4 (1986):297–306; Lockheed and Frakt.

40. H. J. Becker, *Instructional Uses of School Computers* (Baltimore:Johns Hopkins University, Center for Organization of Schools, 1986), Issue 1; J. R. Lehman, "Survey of Microcomputer Use in the Science Classroom," *School Science and Mathematics* 85, 7 (1985):578–583; Newsnotes, "School Use of Micros Spreading Out of Math Classes," *Phi Delta Kappa* 67, 2 (1985):165–166.

41. Becker, *School Uses*; *Instructional Uses*.

42. B. A. Collis, "Psychosocial Implications of Sex Differences in Attitudes Towards Computers," *International Journal of Women's Studies* 8, 3 (1985):207–213; Lockheed and Frakt.

43. Lockheed and Frakt; R. A. Smith.

44. Becker, *Instructional Uses*.

45. M. Matson, "Networks? Maybe. Computer Rooms? No." *Micro-scope* 16 (1985):8–10.

46. R. T. Johnson, D. W. Johnson, and M. B. Stanne, "Comparison of Computer-assisted Cooperative, Competitive, and Individualistic Learning," *American Educational Research Journal* 23, 3 (1986):382–392; P. L. Peterson and E. Fennema, "Effective Teaching, Student Engagement in Classroom Activities, and Sex-related Differences in Learning Mathematics," *American Educational Research Journal*, 22, 3 (1985):309–335.

47. Johnson, Johnson, and Stanne, p. 390.

48. C. A. Dwyer, "Influence of Student's Sex Role Standards on Reading and Arithmetic Achievement," *Journal of Educational Psychology* 66 (1973):811–816.

49. A. H. Stein, S. R. Pohly, and E. Mueller, "The Influence of Masculine, Feminine, and Neutral Tasks on Children's Achievement Behavior, Expectancies of Success, and Attainment Values," *Child Development* 42 (1971):195–207.

50. B. A. Collis and L. Ollila, "Gender Stereotypes About Reading, Writing, and Computer Use in Preschool, Kindergarten, and Grade 1 Boys and Girls," paper presented at the Annual Meeting of the Canadian Society for Studies in Education, Winnipeg, June 1986.

51. Wilder, Mackie, and Cooper.

52. K. Swoope and C. S. Johnson, "Students' Perceptions of Interest in Using Computers:Boys, Girls, or Both?" paper presented at the Annual Meeting of the American Educational Research Association, Chicago, April 1985.

53. Sanders, "Making the Computer."

54. M. C. Ware and M. F. Stuck, "Sex-role Messages vis-a-vis Microcomputer Use: A Look at the Pictures," paper presented at the Annual Meeting of the American Educational Research Association, New Orleans. 1984.

55. C. Bodger, "Sixth Annual Salary Survey: Who Does What and for How Much?" *Working Women* (January 1985): 65–72; P. Stanton, *Women in the Labour Market*:1983 (Victoria: British Columbia Ministry of Labour, 1983).

56. Collis, Ph. D. thesis; Sanders, "Making the Computer."

57. Sanders, Ibid., p. 23.

58. Collis, "Psychosocial Implications,"; J. Hawkins, "Computers and Girls: Rethinking the Issues," *Sex Roles* 13, 3/4 (1985):163–180.

59. Lockheed and Frakt.

60. "High Test Scores Don't Bring Confidence, Automatic Success," *The Stanford Observer* (November 1984):3.

61. Marsh, Smith and Barnes.

62. Collis, "Sex Differences."

63. Ibid.

64. D. Ellis and L. Sayer, *When I Grow Up: Career Expectations and Aspirations of Canadian Schoolchildren* (Ottawa: Government of Canada, Minister of Labour, 1986).

65. Ibid., p. 55.

66. Lockheed and Frakt.

67. D. Tobin and l.H. Fox, "Career Interests and Career Education: A Key to Change," in *Women and the Mathematical Mystique*, pp. 179–192.

68. S.E. Cooper and D.A.G. Robinson, "Students in Highly Technical Careers: Sex Differences in Interpersonal Characteristics and Vocational Identity," *Journal of College Student Personnel* 26 (1985):215–219. 69. Ellis and Sayer, p. 56.

70. Ibid.

71. C. Dowling, *The Cinderella Complex; Women's Hidden Fear of Independence* (New York: Simon and Schuster, 1981).

72. Schubert.

73. R.B. Ekstrom, "Intervention Strategies to Reduce Sex-role Stereotyping in Education," in O. Hartnett, G. Boder, and M. Fuller, eds. *Sex-role Stereotyping* (London: Tavistock, 1979).

74. Collis and Ollila, "An Examination of Sex Differences."

75. G. Salomon, "Computers in Education: Add-ons or Levers?" paper presented to the meeting of the International Committee of the International Council for Computers in Education, Tel Aviv, February 1987.

76. Sanders, "Making the Computer."

Nevitte, Giddings, and Codding • Career Goals of Science Students

ACKNOWLEDGEMENTS

We would like to thank Janet Harvie for her assistance with the data analysis. An earlier version of this paper was presented at the Annual Meetings of the Chemical Institute of Canada, Laval University, Quebec City, June 1987.

NOTES

1. M.S. Devereaux and E. Rechnitzer, *Higher Education — Hired? Sex Differences in Employment Characteristics of 1976 Post-Secondary Graduates*, (Ottawa: Women's Bureau, Statistics Canada and Labour Canada, Supply and Services Canada, 1980), p. 37, Table 3.

2. T.H.B. Symmons and T.E. Page, "Some Questions of Balance: Human Resources, Higher Education and Canadian Studies," in *To Know Ourselves. Report of the Royal Commission on Canadian Studies.* Vol. 3. (Ottawa: Association of Universities and Colleges of Canada, 1984).

3. A recent Statistics Canada report, *Who are the Professional Women* (Ottawa, 1987), indicates that the number of female civil engineers has increased threefold in the last ten years — from 1.1 percent to 3.3 percent, and that this constitutes the highest representation of women in any of the eight categories of the engineering profession. Of all the forty-six professional groups considered, thirty-four are "male dominated," and five are "female dominated" — and all those five are related to teaching.

4. *Who Turns the Wheel? Proceedings of the Workshop on the Science Education of Women* (Ottawa:Science Council of Canada, 1982), pp. 7–8.

5. J. Scott, "Is There a Problem?" in *Who Turns the Wheel?*, pp. 21–44.

6. M.W. Steinkamp and M.L. Maehr, "Gender Differences in Motivational Orientations Toward Achievement in School Science: A Quantitative Synthesis," *American Educational Research Journal* 21, 1 (1986):39–59.

7. Ibid., pp. 49–50.

8. J. Hyde, "How Large are Cognitive Gender Differences?" *American Psychologist* 38, 8 (1981):892–901; A. Kelly, "Why Girls Don't Do Science?" *New Scientist* 94 (1306):497–500; E. Maccoby and C. Jacklin, *The Psychology of Sex Differences* (Stanford, Calif.: Stanford University Press, 1974); R.R. Struik and R.J. Flexer, "Sex Differences in Mathematical Achievement: Adding Data to the Debate," *International Journal of Women's Studies* 7, 714 (1984):336–342.

9. M.M. Kimball, "Sex Differences in Intellectual Ability," in *Who Turns the Wheel?*, pp. 45–59.

10. A.M. Decore, "Vive la Difference: A Comparison of Male Female Academic Performance," *Canadian Journal of Higher Education* 14, 3 (1981):35–57; Steinkamp and Maehr, p. 45.

11. Kelly, p. 497.

12. Ibid., pp. 497–500; G. Ferry and J. Moore, "True Confessions of Women in Science," *New Scientist* 95, 1312 (1982):27–30.

13. L. Fischer, "Science and the Environment of Young Girls," in *Who Turns the Wheel?*, pp. 61–74.

14. D. Ellis. "Rite Models, Career Expectations and Counseling," in *Who Turns the Wheel?*, pp. 75–85.

15. Steinkamp and Maehr report that girls are both more negative about the relationship between themselves and science, and less likely to express interest in science through active involvement with science-related extra-curricular activities (p. 45).

16. Symmons and Page, pp. 193, 206.

17. D. Ellis, "A Study of a Cohort of Ontario Engineering Students from 1955 to 1976," *Canadian Journal of Education* 2, 4, (1977):11–22.

18. S.G. Brush, "Women in Physical Science," *The Physics Teacher* 23, 1 (1985):11–19; Ferry and Moore, pp. 27–30.

19. Ferry and Moore, p. 27.

20. These data were collected by Roger Gibbins and Neil Nevitte; they constitute the Canadian segment of the Cross-National Equality Project, a seven-country study of the values of selected elites in western industrialized societies. The original project was designed under the direction of Sidney Veba, Department of Government, Harvard University.

21. These include: Memorial, Dalhousie, Montreal, Laval, Toronto, Queen's, Wilfrid Laurier, Calgary, and British Columbia. Students at the Université de Montréal and Laval were sent a French-language questionnaire. The usual precautions relating to translation and back-translation were taken, and both the English and French versions of the questionnaire were field tested.

22. Standard reliability tests indicate no systematic biases within the respondent pool.

23. Respondents were asked: "Do you rate your academic performance as, Above Average? _____ Average? _____ or Below Average? _____". Self-reported performance evaluation are far from ideal. But we have no grounds for suspecting that women are more likely than men to misrepresent their performance. The nominal practice is to assume that any sources of error will be random rather than systematic. If error is systematic then the sociological evidence regarding gender and such issues as self-esteem would lead us to believe that males are more likely than females to overestimate their performance. Further, if that is the case with our data, then by assuming random error in self-reported academic performance we are adopting a conservative strategy. We assume random error.

Beauchamp and McDaniel • Women Inventors

ACKNOWLEDGEMENTS

Many individuals have contributed to the research and the intervention program described here. We would particularly like to acknowledge the large contribution of Helene Cummins, University of Waterloo, who carried out much of the research described here as part of her master's thesis. Lisa Avedon, Ontario Ministry of Labour, is the Co-Director of the Women Inventors Project and was instrumental in designing the Project and obtaining funding for it. Dr Carol Brooks, Quinta Consulting, carried out follow-up interviews with the women participating in the Project, and Marie Le Lievre was the administrator involved. Finally, we wish to thank all the women inventors, nameless here, who generously shared with us their time and expertise.

The Women Inventors Project (Suite 500, 22 King Street South, Waterloo, Ontario, 519–746–3443) is funded by the Innovations Program of Employment and Immigration Canada, Science Culture Canada, and the Ontario Women's Directorate.

NOTES

1. See Marilyn A. Brown and Sherri A. Snell, *The Energy-Related Inventions Program: An Assessment of Recent Commercial Progress* (Oak Ridge, Tennessee: Oak Ridge National Laboratory, 1988); David Abbott, *Engineers and Inventors* (London: Blond Educational, 1985); J.J. Brown, *Ideas in Exile* (Toronto: McClelland and Stewart, 1967); John Jewkes, David Sawers, and Richard Stillerman, *The Sources of Invention* (London: Macmillan, 1958).

2. Autumn Stanley, "From Africa to America: Black Women Inventors," in Jan Zimmerman, ed., *The Technological Woman: Interfacing with Tomorrow* (New York: Praeger, 1983).

3. Nancy M. Tanner and Adrienne Zihlman, "Women in Evolution. Part 1: Innovation and Selection in Human Origins," *Signs* 1, 3 (1976): 585–608.

4. Elise Boulding, *The Understanding of History* (Boulder, Colorado: Westview, 1976).

5. Fred M. Amram, "The Innovative Woman," *New Scientist* 24 (May 1984): 10–12.

6. Ibid.

7. Judit Brody, "Pattern of Patents: Early British Inventions by Women," in E. Vamos, ed., *Women in Science: Options and Access* (Budapest: National Museum of Science and Technology, 1985).

8. Autumn Stanley, "The Patent Office Clerk as Conjurer," in Barbara Drygulsky: Wright *et al* eds., *Women, Work and Technology Transformations* (Ann Arbor: University of Michigan Press, 1987).

9. Margaret Alic, *Hypatia's Heritage* (Boston: Beacon Press, 1986).

10. Autumn Stanley, "Women Hold Up Two-Thirds of The Sky," in Joan

Rothschild, ed., *Machinea Ex Dea: Feminist Perspectives on Technology* (New York: Pergamon Press, 1983).

11. Isabel Romero, Canadian Patent Office, personal communication.

12. Amram.

13. Andrew Robertson, "Characteristics of the Successful Inventor: Some Notes on the Nature of Creativity and the Creative Mind," *Technovation* 2 (1984): 141–45. 14. Dorothy E. Smith, "A Peculiar Eclipsing," *Women's Studies Int. Quart.* 1 (1978): 282–96.

15. Dale Spender, *Women of Ideas and What Men Have Done to Them: From Aphea Behn to Adrienne Rich* (London: Routledge and Kegan Paul, 1982).

16. Evelyn Fox Keller, *Reflections on Gender and Science* (New Haven: Yale University Press, 1985).

17. Anne Sayre, *Rosalind Franklin and DNA* (New York: Norton, 1975).

18. Evelyn Fox Keller, *A Feeling for the Organism: The Life and Work of Barbara McClintock* (New York: Freeman, 1983).

19. Susan A. McDaniel, "Just Gender," lecture given in the Arts Lecture Series, University of Waterloo, 1986, p. 6.

20. B.L. Florisha, "Creativity and Images in Men and Women," *Perceptual and Motor Skills* 47 (1978): 1262.

21. For a detailed description of the methodology used, see Susan A. McDaniel, Helene Cummins, and Rachelle S. Beauchamp, "Mothers of Invention? Meshing the Roles of Inventor, Mother and Worker," *Women's Studies International Forum* 11, 1 (1988): 1–12; Cummins, McDaniel, and Beauchamp, "Women Inventors in Canada in the 1980s," *Canada Review of Sociology and Anthropology* 25, 3 (1988): 389–405.

22. Dina Lavoie, *Women Entrepreneurs: Building A Stronger Canadian Economy* (Ottawa: Canadian Advisory Council on the Status of Women, 1988).

23. Heather-Jane Robertson, The IDEA Book: A Resource for Improving the Participation and Success of Female Students in Math, Science and Technology (Ottawa: Canadian Teachers' Federation, 1988).

24. Carol Brooks, *Instructor's Handbook: Working with Female Relational Learners in Technology and Trades Training* (Toronto: Ontario Ministry of Skills Development, 1986); Mary F. Belenky, Blythe M. Clinchy, Nancy R. Goldberger, and Jill M. Tarule, *Women's Ways of Knowing* (New York: Basic Books, 1986).

25. Carol Brooks and Rachelle S. Beauchamp, "The Woman Inventors Project," *Women's Education des Femmes* 6, 4 (1988): 22–24.

26. Rachelle S. Beauchamp, "Entrepreneurial Inventors: Support Programs and the Role of Women Inventors," *The Entrepreneurship Development Review* 4 (1988): 33–34; Karen Koziara, "To Market, To Market: Women Inventors as Entrepreneurs," unpublished, 1988.

27. Ursula Franklin, "Will Women Change Technology or Will Technology Change Women?" *The* CRIAW Papers 9 (1985).

28. Heather Menzies, "Back to Grandma's Place: Democratizing Science and Technology," *Canadian Woman Studies* 5, 4 (1984).

Scott • *Disadvantagement of Women*

NOTES

1. Dorothy E. Smith, "The Renaissance of Women," *Knowledge Reconsidered: A Feminist Overview*, (Ottawa, Canadian Research Institute for the Advancement of Women, CRIAW/ICREF, 1984), p. 7.

2. Sandra Harding, in *The Science Question in Feminism* (Ithaca and London: Cornell University Press, 1986), p. 21 describes five different projects in the feminist critique of science. One of these is the equality project which documents the massive historical resistance to women getting into science employment in comparison with similarly talented men. The others are: outlining the way science serves anti-emancipatory projects, such as identifying supposed innate inferiorities for use by biological determinists; challenging the existence of value-free science; exploring hidden symbolic agendas; and developing feminist epistemologies.

3. An earlier version of this article was presented at the Third International Interdisciplinary Congress on Women, *Women's world: Visions and Revisions*, July 6–10, 1987, Trinity College, University of Dublin.

4. I am grateful to Ms Bernadine Conran, a librarian at Memorial University of Newfoundland who suggested *The Commonwealth Universities Yearbook*, 1985, as a source of the names of faculty members which distinguishes between women and men. As its name suggests this annual directory covers all of the "Commonwealth" countries and so could be useful in many other studies.

Some interpret the great difference in numbers of women and men as evidence that women are not as scientifically talented as men, while to others the difference in numbers demonstrates the resistance of science to females. It is true that once there were lower numbers of qualified women than men in the pool from which job candidates could be drawn. In the late 1960s only 10% of Canadian Ph.D.s in biology were awarded to women. This situation however has been much improved so that by 1983–84, according to Statistics Canada, *Universities: Enrollment and Degrees* (Catalogue 81–204 Annual: 1983), the proportion of women enrolled in biology doctorates Canada-wide was 28.5%, which is four times the proportion of female faculty in bioscience departments two years later.

5. Dorothy E. Smith, "A Peculiar Eclipsing: Woman's Exclusion from Man's Culture," *The Everyday World as Problematic: A Feminist Sociology* by Smith (Toronto: University of Toronto Press, 1987), p. 26.

"Gatekeepers" is a term used by Dorothy Smith to identify the men who have the power to decide what will be published as legitimated knowledge. Smith says, "Equality of opportunity is only one aspect of the problem. I want rather to draw attention to the significance of the inequalities which we find for how women are located in the processes of setting standards, producing social knowledge, acting as "gatekeepers" over what is admitted into the system of distribution, innovating in thought or knowledge or values, and in other ways participating as authorities in the ideological work done in the educational process."

6. Most of the people in the sample were hired between 1959 and 1974, during the period of university expansion. The data suggests that the hiring of women accelerated more than that of men during expansion. It would be interesting to explore this further.

7. Margaret W. Rossiter, *Women Scientists in America: Struggles and Strategies to* 1940 (Baltimore and London: Johns Hopkins UP, 1982), p. 17.

8. Alison Prentice. "Towards a Feminist History of Women and Education," *Approaches to Educational History*, Monographs in Education, eds. D.G. Jones *et al*, (Winnipeg: University of Manitoba, 1980).

Prentice articulated the concept of women teachers being accepted into the profession of teaching but not into the male system of ladders of advancement. Women were admitted only to a truncated career ladder.

9. Rossiter, p. 196.

Armour • Careers in Chemistry

NOTES

1. D.R. Carson, F. Press, R.M. White, and S.O. Thier, "Opportunities in Chemistry," National Academy of Sciences —National Research Council, 1986, Appendix 2.

2. G.H.M. Adams, J.R. Bolton, H.C. Clark, P. Deslongchamps, J. Halpern, K.U. Ingold, R.U. Lemieux, J.A. Morison, J. Rokach, and I.C.P. Smith, "Towards Excellence in Chemistry," *Canadian Chemical News* 38, 8 (1986).

3. Statistics Canada, Science and Technology Indicators, 1985, Ministry of Supply and Services, Ottawa, 1986.

4. *Chemical and Engineering News*, 64, 20 (1986): 8.

5. Statistics Canada, Science and Technology Indicators, 1985, Ministry of Supply and Services, Ottawa, 1986.

6. H.B. Symons and J.E. Page in "Some Questions of Balance: Human Resources, Higher Education and Canadian Studies," Association of Universities and Colleges of Canada, 1984, p. 193.

7. D.E. Rivington, *Canadian Chemical News*, 36, 8 (1984): 28; 37, 6 (1985): 21; 38, 7 (1986): 12; 39, 7 (1987): 17; 40, 7 (1988): 17.

8. N.M. Roscher and M.A. Cavanaugh, *Journal of Chemical Education*, 64, 10 (1987): 823.

9. A.M. Decore, Canadian Journal of Higher Education, 14, 3 (1984): 35.

10. See for example "Who Turns the Wheel?" *Proceedings of a Workshop on the Science Education of Women in Canada* (Science Council of Canada, 1982); "Science for Every Student: Educating Canadians for Tomorrow's World," Science Council of Canada, 1984; Alison Kelly, ed., "The Missing Half: Girls and Science Education," (Manchester University Press, 1981).

11. A.E. Alper, Symposium on Women and Careers in Chemistry, CIC Annual Conference, Quebec City, June 1987; see *Canadian Chemical News*, 39, 9 (1987): 19.

12. See for example Alison Kelly, Judith Whyte, and Barbara Smail, "Girls Into Science and Technology," Final Report, University of Manchester 1984.

13. Strategies: Intervention Techniques to Retain Women in Mathematics and Science Studies, WISH, York University, 1988.

14. Rose Sheinin, "Women in Science: Issues and Actions," *Canadian Women Studies* 5, 4 (1984): 70. 15. See F. Geis, M. Carter, and D. Butler, "Seeing and Evaluating People," University of Delaware, 1986.

16. See for example "Employment Equity for Women: A University Handbook," The Committee on the Status of Women, Council of Ontario Universities, 1988.

17. R. Leger, text of address, Third World Academy of Sciences Conference, Trieste, Italy, 1988.

Dagg • Are Conditions Improving?

NOTES

1. Anne Innis Dagg, "The Status of Some Canadian Women Ph.D. Scientists," *Atlantis* 11, 1 (1985): 66–78.

2. See Statistics Canada Catalogue 81–204, Tables 10 and 22.

3. Anne Burger, *Report on Sexual Harassment and Sexual Assault at Simon Fraser University* (Vancouver: British Columbia Public Interest Research Group, December 1986).

4. Anne Innis Dagg and Patricia J. Thompson, *MisEducation: Women and Canadian Universities* (Toronto: Ontario Institute for Studies in Education, 1988).

5. The twelve universities were Brock, Carleton, Guelph, Lakehead, Laurentian, Ottawa, Queen's, Toronto, Waterloo, Western Ontario, Wilfrid Laurier, and Windsor.

6. Dagg and Thompson, p. 74.

Messing • Genetic Hazards in the Workplace

ACKNOWLEDGEMENTS

This essay was previously published in *Alternatives* (1987).

NOTES

1. Protocole d'entente UQAM-CSN-FTQ sur la formation syndicale. Université du Québec à Montréal, 1976; see also D. Mergler, "Worker Participation In Occupational Health Research: Theory and Practice," *International Journal of Health Services* 17,1 (1987): 151–167.

2. See K. Messing, "Do Men and Women have Different Jobs Because of Their Biological Differences?" *International Journal of Health Services* 12,1 (1982): 43–52; J.D. Erickson, J. Mulinare, P.Q. McClain, T. Fitch, L.M. James, A.B. McClearn, and M.J. Adams, "Vietnam Veterans' Risks for Fathering Babies with Birth Defects," *Journal of the American Medical Association* 252,7 (1984): 903–912; J.R. Goldsmith, G. Potashnik, and R. Israeli, "Reproductive Outcomes in Families of DBCP-exposed Men," *Archives on Environmental Health* 39,2 (1984): 85–89; and J.R. Wilkins and T.H. Sinks, "Occupational Exposure Among Fathers of Children with Wilms' Tumor," *Journal of Occupational Medicine* 26,6 (1984): 427–435.

3. See R. St-Amand, "Taking Action: An Interview with Saskia Post," *Healthsharing* (Summer 1985): 18–20.

4. Se G.B. Kolata, "Love Canal: False Alarm Caused by Botched Study," *Science* 208 (1980): 1239–1240, and L. Gibbs, *Love Canal: My Story* (New York: Grove Press, 1982).

5. K. Messing, and W.E.C. Bradley, "*In Vivo* Mutant Frequency Rises Among Breast Cancer Patients after Exposure to High Doses of Gamma Radiation," *Mutation Research* 152 (1985): 107–112.

6. K. Messing, A.M. Seifert, and W.E.C. Bradley, "*In Vivo* Mutant Frequency of Radiotherapy Technicians Appears to Reflect Recent Exposure to Ionizing Radiation," *Health Physics* October 1989.

7. See Mergler (note 1); K. Messing and J-P. Reveret, "Are Women in Female Jobs for their Health? A Study of Working Conditions and Health Effects in the Fish-processing Industry in Québec," *International Journal of Health Services* 13,4 (1983): 635–642.

8. This work is in progress.

9. D. Mergler, N. Vézina, and A. Beauvais, "Warts among Workers in Poultry Slaughterhouses," *Scandinavian Journal of Workplace Environment and Health* 8: supp. 1 (1982): 180–184; D. Mergler and N. Vézina, "Dysmennorrhea and Cold Exposure," *Journal of Reproductive Medicine* 30, 2 (1985): 106–111; and S. de Grosbois and D. Mergler, "La Santé Mentale et L'exposition aux Solvants Organiques en Milieu de Travail," *Santé mentale au Québec* 10, 2 (1982): 99–113.

10. See National Science and Engineering Council of Canada (NSERC), "Industry and University: Partners in R & D," brochure describing grant programme (Ottawa: NSERC, 1985), 1 page.

11. H.F. Stich, and M.P. Rosin, "Towards a More Comprehensive Evaluation of a Genotoxic Hazard in Man," *Mutation Research* 150 (1985): 43–50. 12. See A. Garg, D. Sharma, D.B. Chaffin, and J.M. Schmidler, "Biomechanical Stresses as Related to Motion Trajectory of Lifting," *Human Factors* 25,5 (1983): 527–539; and E.J. Celentano, J.W. Nottrodt, and P.L. Saunders, "The Relationship Between Size, Strength and Task Demands," *Ergonomics* 27,5 (1984): 481–488.

13. D. Mergler (note 1).

14. See J. Deverell, "Job Threatened over Studies of Cancer Links," *Toronto Star* (22 October 1986).

15. VDT News, "NIOSH Cuts Back Reproductive Hazards Study," *VDT News* (January/February 1985): 4–7.

16. See D. Mergler and N. Vézina (note 9).

17. See K. Messing (note 2); K. Messing and J.P. Reveret (note 7); and D. Mergler, C. Brabant, N. Vézina, and K. Messing, "The Weaker Sex? Men in Women's Working Conditions Report Similar Health Symptoms," *Journal of Occupational Medicine* 29,5 (1987): 417–421.

Kranias • *Changing Faces of Science*

NOTES

1. Sue V. Rosser, "The Relationship Between Women's Studies and Women in Science," in Ruth Bleier, ed., *Feminist Approaches to Science*, (New York: Pergamon Press, 1986), p. 178.

2. Elizabeth Fee, "Is Feminism a Threat to Scientific Objectivity?" *International Journal of Women's Studies* 4, 4, (Sept./Oct. 1981): 388.

3. Karen Messing, "The Scientific Mystique: Can a White Lab Coat Guarantee Purity in the Search for Knowledge about the Nature of Women?" in (Marian Lowe and Ruth Hubbard, eds.,) *Women's Nature: Rationalizations of Inequality*, (New York: Pergamon Press, 1983), p. 78.

4. Karen Messing, interview. 7 April 1988.

5. Yanick Villedieu, "Karen Messing: Faire de la Science pour changer des choses," *Interface* (Jan./Feb. 1988): 9. For details see: K. Messing and D. Mergler,

"Determinants of Success in Obtaining Grants for Action-Oriented Research in Occupational Health," Las Vegas, Nevada: American Public Health Association, October 1986.

6. Bernard La Mothe, "La sante des travailleurs vue d'un angle different," L'IRSST, 4, 1 (Spring 1987): 18.

7. Ruth Bleier, "Introduction," in *Feminist Approaches to Science*, p. 16.

8. Karen Messing, interview.

9. Karen Messing, "The Scientific Mystique," p. 77.

10. Karen Messing, interview.

11. Marion Namenwirth, "Science Seen Through a Feminist Prism," in *Feminist Approaches to Science*, p.37.

12. Ibid., p. 32.

13. Hilary Rose, "Beyond Masculinist Realities: A Feminist Epistemology for the Sciences," in *Feminist Approaches to Science*; Evelyn Fox Keller, *Reflections on Gender and Science* (New Haven: Yale University Press, 1985); Hilde Hein, "Women and Science: Fitting Men to Think About Nature," *International Journal of Women's Studies* 4. 4 (Sept./Oct. 1981); and Karen Messing, "Putting Our Two Heads Together: A Mainly Women's Research Group Looks At Women's Occupational Health." (forthcoming).

14. Hilde Hein, "Women and Science," p. 375.

15. Karen Messing, "What Would a Feminist Approach to Science Be?" RFR/DRF *Resources for Feminist Research* 15, 3 (Nov. 1986): 66.

16. Karen Messing, "Do Men and Women Have Different Jobs Because of Their Biological Differences?" in Greta Nemiroff, ed., *Women and Men: Interdisciplinary Reading on Gender* (Toronto: Fitzhenry & Whiteside, 1987).

17. Karen Messing and Jean-Pierre Reveret, "Are Women in Female Jobs for their Health? A Study of Working Conditions and Health Effects in the Fish-Processing Industry in Quebec," *International Journal of Health Services* 13, 4 (1983): 644.

18. Karen Messing, "What Would a Feminist Approach to Science Be?" p. 66.

19. Karen Messing, "L'importance d'écouter les travailleuses et travailleurs quand on fait de la formation en santé au travail," *Travail et Santé*, March 1989.

20. Karen Messing, interview.

21. Marion Namenwirth, "Science Seen Through a Feminist Prism," p. 35.

22. Karen Messing, interview.

23. Ibid.

24. Ibid.

25. Sue V. Rosser, "The Relationship Between Women's Studies and Women in Science," p. 177.

26. Karen Messing, interview; also: "Putting Our Two Heads Together."

27. Karen Messing, "What Would a Feminist Approach to Science Be?" p. 65.

28. Evelyn Fox Keller, *Reflections on Gender and Science*, p. 166.

29. Bernard La Mothe, "La santé des travailleurs vue d'un angle différent," p. 15.

30. Elizabeth Fee, "Is Feminism a Threat to Scientific Objectivity?" p. 388.

Index

Botanical Society of Canada 28
Botany 27, 28, 29, 30, 36–44, 60,
   74–87, 317
Bower, M.E. 35
Boyle, Susanna 115
Broad, Katie 237
Brooks, Harriet 195–203
Brown, M.C. 33
Buckley, A.R. 230
Buller, Henrietta F. 68
Buller, Reginald 39
Burenin, Nikolai 199
Burnet, Jean Robertson 154, 158,
   168–76

Cameron, Julia Margaret 96
Cameron, T.W.M. 56
Canada Department of Agriculture
   36, 41–42, 54, 225
Canadian Entomologist, The 54
Canadian Federation of University
   Women (CFUW) 39, 62, 211–13, 215
Canadian Institute of Mining and
   Metallurgy 34
Canadian Journal on Aging 262
Canadian Public Health Association
   79
*Canadian Review of Sociology and
   Anthropology* 171, 174
Canadian Sociology and Anthro-
   pology Association (CSAA) 171
Career: advancement 31–35, 38, 42, 43,
   50–55, 60, 62, 74–87, 110, 118, 138,
   157, 170, 172–73, 179, 188–90,
   215–16, 224, 226, 248–49, 257–61,
   269–70, 318, 321–28, 334, 344;
   choice 289; goals of female science
   students 284–303; paths 31, 296,
   300, 302
Career-marriage conflict 21, 30, 34,
   35, 40, 42, 44, 55, 61, 70, 157, 159, 161,
   175, 198–99, 201 , 224, 250, 256–57,
   310–11, 324–28
Cassels, Elsie 29, 58
Chemistry 285, 329–36, 338

Chez Doris 167
Child care 332
Child development 256
Clark, S. Del 169, 176
Clemens, Lucy Smith 56
Clemens, W.A. 52
Collaboration: between laboratories
   318–28; feminist 367; husband-
   wife 55–58, 123, 156; in laboratories
   318–19
Collins, W.H. 211, 212–13, 215–16
Computers and adolescent females
   272–83
Confédération des syndicats
   nationaux (CSN) 350, 361
Consumer advocacy 139
Consumerism 134–51
Consumers: women as 89, 102–06
Convent of Sainte Croix, Montreal
   29
Coombs, Mrs. William H. 97
Cox, Philip 51
Crewe, Elizabeth 101
Crow, J.W. 221–22, 224
Cummins, George B. 244
Curie, Marie 200–03
Currie, Sir Arthur 56, 157

Dalhousie, Lady 27, 66
Dalhousie University 44
Darlington, William 27
Dart, J.D. 33
Davidson, Viola M. 52
Davis, Bergen 198
de Bandeville, Madame 26
Depression, the 38–39, 50, 52–53, 157
Debierne, André 200
Defries, Kyra (Emo) 35
Dent, Elsie A. 68
Derick, Carrie 36, 74–87, 191
Discrimination. *See* Anti-Semitism;
   Career advancement; Pay equity;
   Faculty Club membership
Dixon, Jessie 107
DNA 356; research 308